# THE NEW INTERNATIONAL DICTIONARY OF QUOTATIONS

# THE NEW INTERNATIONAL DICTIONARY OF QUOTATIONS

Selected by

## Hugh Rawson
and
## Margaret Miner

E. P. DUTTON
New York

Published in the United States by E. P. Dutton, a division of
New American Library, 2 Park Avenue, New York, N.Y. 10016

**Library of Congress Cataloging-in-Publication Data**

Rawson, Hugh.
    The new international dictionary of quotations.

    Includes index.
    1. Quotations, English.    I. Miner, Margaret.
II. Title.
PN6081.R38    1986        082        85-31132
ISBN 0-525-24436-0

W

Published simultaneously in Canada by Fitzhenry & Whiteside Limited, Toronto

Designed by Julian Hamer

10 9 8 7 6 5 4 3 2 1

FIRST EDITION

*For*
*Nathaniel and Catherine*

# ACKNOWLEDGMENTS

WE'D LIKE TO THANK first our superb copy editor, Henry Price, who is not only completely conscientious, but also reads five languages and is witty as well. Our friends Bob Nadder, Ken Silverman, Pat Barrett, and Bob Creamer all helped in verifying quotes and sources. Tim Beard, Susie Juram, and Betty Synnestuedt of the Hodge Memorial Library graciously coped with numerous odd questions. Helen Stark at *The New Yorker* saved us a lot of time on an E. B. White quote, for she had already spent hours herself tracking it down and generously passed on the information. Victor K. McElheny was present at the occasion when Edwin Herbert Land said, "The bottom line is in heaven"; he was able not only to describe the context but to suggest several other excellent quotes. These, and many others offered at the last moment by friends, must wait for the second edition (which is already incubating in a shoe box). Finally, we thank Arnold Dolin for suggesting to us that we undertake this project.

*Hugh Rawson and Margaret Miner*

# INTRODUCTION

THE AIM OF *The New International Dictionary of Quotations* is to distill the most memorable words of the past with a view to the concerns of the present. The most memorable words are not necessarily the "best" words in a literary sense. Rather, they are the words that best encapsule the ideas, hopes, fears, loves, hates, that have been common to men and women throughout history. Thus, this dictionary is international in scope and it covers all periods, from ancient times to the present. Its bias, however, is toward the tried and the true—the familiar quotations that are on, or almost on, the tip of everyone's tongue, but whose exact wording, authorship, or source may have been forgotten.

To this end, *The New International Dictionary of Quotations* includes ample selections from *The Bible*, Shakespeare, Aesop, Burke, Carlyle, Churchill, Disraeli, Emerson, Euripides, Johnson, Pope, Shaw, Tennyson, and the works of other famous writers whose words have shaped the thoughts of everyone who has lived after them. At the same time, the dictionary also includes the observations of such luminaries as P. T. Barnum, Ambrose Bierce, Leo Durocher, W. C. Fields, Don Marquis, Satchel Paige, Dorothy Parker, and Mae West, who in their own highly quotable ways have contributed to the residual wisdom of the human race.

In sum, this dictionary of quotations differs from others that have been compiled by including in it relatively more quotes from well-known writers; relatively more prose compared to poetry; relatively more quotes from doers—politicians, entertainers, generals, athletes, and so on—as opposed to strictly literary figures; relatively more American material; and relatively more quotes from women, minority leaders, scientists, and others who have addressed topics of special importance to our times. Meanwhile, an attempt has been made to weed out platitudes and other trite expressions that do not bear repetition; nursery rhymes; lyrics from popular songs whose currency depends largely on knowing the accompanying music; quotations that are so closely linked to particular historic occasions that they are rarely used in

I

other contexts; and contemporary quotes and catch phrases that have not yet been ratified by the test of time. Some exceptions have been allowed to these rules, and any readers who feel that their own favorite quotations have been unfairly excluded for whatever reason are invited to submit them to the editors, in care of the publisher, and they will be considered for inclusion when this dictionary is revised.

Although not an encyclopedic work (several excellent examples of which already exist, including *Bartlett's Familiar Quotations*, 15th edition, 1980; *The Oxford Dictionary of Quotations*, 3rd edition, 1979; *The International Thesaurus of Quotations*, Rhoda Thomas Tripp, 1970; and H. L. Mencken's *A New Dictionary of Quotations on Historical Principles*, 1942), *The New International Dictionary of Quotations* should be a useful addition to most bookshelves. It brings together in compact, easily accessible form the basic stock of quotations that will satisfy most needs of most contemporary users of English. It should be of especial value to students and others seeking to track down references to quotations they have read; to writers and speakers who wish to enhance their own words by drawing upon the best of the rhetoric of the past; and, finally, to all lovers of language, who will relish the riches here.

*The New International Dictionary of Quotations* is arranged to give readers at least two chances to find the quotes they want—through the main text, which is organized by subject, and through the author index. In the main text, subjects are listed alphabetically, with the principal topics printed in boldface capital letters along the left-hand margin of the page. Thus:

**ACCOMPLISHMENT**

**ADVERTISING**

**ADVICE**

and so on, through to

**UNIVERSE**

**WORLD, END OF**

## YOUTH

Most subject categories also include references to related topics. These are printed in upper and lower case letters and cap letters along the right-hand margin of the text. For example:

**ACCOMPLISHMENT**                    See also DOING; GREATNESS;

                                        SUCCESS & FAME; WORK

Within the subject categories, quotations are arranged alphabetically by author, frequently beginning with that wise and prolific writer, ANONYMOUS. In cases of well-known works by unknown authors, or by groups of authors, such as The Bible, The Book of Common Prayer, and the Talmud, the titles are treated as though they are authors' names and quotations from them are alphabetized accordingly.

All foreign quotations have been translated into English. Those from *The Bible* are from the Authorized, or King James, Version unless noted specifically otherwise. Quotations are given in a foreign language as well as in English in instances where they are encountered frequently in their original form.

Following each quotation is the name of the author and the title of its source. In addition, many quotes are followed by notes from the editors. These are printed in brackets, i.e., [brackets]. The notes provide additional information on a variety of topics: earlier examples of a particular turn of phrase; use of similar expressions by later writers; the circumstances in which something was first said or written; the way a particular quote has been commonly mistranslated, misquoted, or "improved," and so on. The notes often cite additional sources for attributions and refer the reader to other subject categories.

Where the name of the author is known, the user of this dictionary may find the sought-for quotation even more quickly by consulting the index, beginning on page 353. Here, names of authors (and titles of some works) are listed alphabetically in the same way as in the subject categories, along with key words, phrases, and page numbers for each of their quotations. Birth and death dates of authors also are given in the index.

Whether approaching the text via the subject categories or the author index, the user of this dictionary is likely to make many happy discoveries, including the fact that it is possible to drive home any point one wishes to make through the artful use of quotation. As Winston

Churchill noted, "It is a good thing for an uneducated man to read books of quotations" (*Roving Commission* in *My Early Life*). Or as Ralph Waldo Emerson wrote in his *Journal* (1849): "I hate quotations. Tell me what you know." The same authority may even support both sides of the question: "Next to the originator of a good sentence is the first quoter of it" (Emerson, *Quotation and Originality*, 1876).

## ACCOMPLISHMENT

See also DOING; GREATNESS; SUCCESS & FAME; WORK

Better is the end of a thing than the beginning thereof.
—BIBLE, *Ecclesiastes* 7:8

I have fought a good fight, I have finished my course, I have kept the faith.
—BIBLE, *II Timothy* 4:7

Let's meet, and either do or die.
—JOHN FLETCHER, *The Island Princess*

There are no gains without pains.
—ADLAI STEVENSON, presidential nomination acceptance speech, 1952

Death closes all: but something ere the end,
Some work of noble note, may yet be done,
Not unbecoming men that strove with gods.
—ALFRED, LORD TENNYSON, *Ulysses*

## ACTORS & ACTING

See ARTS: DRAMA & ACTING

## ACTS

See DOING

## ADVERSITY

See TROUBLE

## ADVERTISING

You can tell the ideals of a nation by its advertisements.
—NORMAN DOUGLAS, *South Wind*

We grew up founding our dreams on the infinite promise of American advertising.
—ZELDA FITZGERALD, *Save Me the Waltz*

The trade of advertising is now so near perfection that it is not easy to propose any improvement.
—SAMUEL JOHNSON, in the *Idler* papers, 1758

Ads push the principle of noise all the way to the plateau of persuasion. The are quite in accord with the procedures of brain-washing.
—MARSHALL MCLUHAN, *Understanding Media*

5

Half the money I spend on advertising is wasted, and the trouble is, I don't know which half.
—JOHN WANAMAKER, quoted in David Ogilvy,
*Confessions of an Advertising Man*

## ADVICE

Good but rarely came from good advice.
—LORD BYRON, *Don Juan*

Advice is seldom welcome; and those who want it the most always like it the least.
—EARL OF CHESTERFIELD,
letter to his son, Jan. 29, 1748

When we ask advice, we are usually looking for an accomplice.
—MARQUIS DE LAGRANGE, *Pensées*

One gives nothing so freely as advice.
—LA ROCHEFOUCAULD, *Maxims*

People ask you for criticism, but they only want praise.
—W. SOMERSET MAUGHAM, *Of Human Bondage*

## AESTHETICS
See ARTS: AESTHETICS

## AFRICA
See NATIONS

## AFTERNOON
See NATURE: TIMES OF DAY

## AGE & AGING
See also MIDDLE AGE & MID-LIFE CRISIS;
OLD THINGS, OLD FRIENDS

Old men are always young enough to learn, with profit.
—AESCHYLUS, *Agamemnon*

To me, old age is always fifteen years older than I am.
—BERNARD BARUCH, news reports on his
85th birthday, Aug. 20, 1955

When everything else physical and mental seems to diminish, the appreciation of beauty is on the increase.
—BERNARD BERENSON, *Sunset and Twilight*

With the ancient is wisdom; and in length of days understanding.
—BIBLE, *Job* 12:12

Grow old along with me!
The best is yet to be,
The last of life, for which the first was made.
—ROBERT BROWNING, *Rabbi Ben Ezra*

So, we'll go no more a roving
So late into the night,
Though the heart be still as loving,
And the moon be still as bright.
—LORD BYRON, *So, We'll Go No More a Roving*

"You are old, Father William," the young man said,
"And your hair has become very white;
And yet you incessantly stand on your head—
Do you think, at your age, it is right?"
—LEWIS CARROLL, *Alice's Adventures in Wonderland*
[This is a parody of Robert Southey's pious *The Old Man's Comforts and How He Gained Them*, which also begins, " 'You are old, Father William . . ." The young man then asks why William is so hale. The answer:
In the days of my youth, I remember my God,
And he hath not forgotten my age.]

When a man fell into his anecdotage it was a sign for him to retire from the world.      —BENJAMIN DISRAELI, *Lothair*

I grow old . . . I grow old . . .
I shall wear the bottoms of my trousers rolled.
—T. S. ELIOT, *The Love Song of J. Alfred Prufrock*

One aged man—one man—can't fill a house.
—ROBERT FROST, *An Old Man's Winter Night*

To be seventy years young is sometimes far more cheerful and hopeful than to be forty years old.
—OLIVER WENDELL HOLMES, letter to
Julia Ward Howe on her 70th birthday

Oh, to be seventy again! [At age 92, upon seeing a pretty, young woman]      —OLIVER WENDELL HOLMES, JR., attributed
[Also attributed to Georges Clemenceau]

My only fear is that I may live too long. This would be a subject of dread to me. —THOMAS JEFFERSON,
letter to Philip Mazzei, March 1801

Where are the songs of spring? Ay, where are they?
Think not of them, thou hast thy music too . . .
—JOHN KEATS, *To Autumn*

All, all are gone, the old familiar faces.
—CHARLES LAMB, *The Old Familiar Faces*

*La vieillesse est l'enfer des femmes.*
Old age is woman's hell.        —NINON DE LENCLOS, attributed

dance mehitabel dance
caper and shake a leg
what little blood is left will fizz like wine in a keg.
—DON MARQUIS, *archy and mehitabel*

Old age has its pleasures, which, though different, are not less than the pleasures of youth.        —W. SOMERSET MAUGHAM,
*The Summing Up*

Being seventy is not a sin. —GOLDA MEIR, quoted by David Reed,
*Reader's Digest*, July 1971

The older I grow, the more I distrust the familiar doctrine that age brings wisdom.        —H. L. MENCKEN, *Prejudices: Third Series*

How old would you be if you didn't know how old you was?
—SATCHEL PAIGE, attributed

Old age has a great sense of calm and freedom. When the passions have relaxed their hold, you have escaped not from one master but from many.        —PLATO, *The Republic*

Darling, I am growing old,
Silver threads among the gold.
—EBEN EUGENE REXFORD, *Silver Threads among the Gold*

For you and I are past our dancing days.
—SHAKESPEARE, *Romeo and Juliet*, I, v

Nobody loves life like him who is growing old.
—SOPHOCLES, *Acrisius*

Being over seventy is like being engaged in a war. All our friends are going or gone and we survive amongst the dead and dying as on a battlefield. —MURIEL SPARK, *Memento Mori*

There are so few who can grow old with a good grace. —RICHARD STEELE, *The Spectator*, no. 263, 1711

Every man desires to live long, but no man would be old. —JONATHAN SWIFT, *Thoughts on Various Subjects*

Old age is the most unexpected of all the things that can happen to a man. —LEON TROTSKY, *Diary in Exile*

The tragedy of old age is not that one is old, but that one is young. —OSCAR WILDE, *The Picture of Dorian Gray*

**AGES** See FUTURE, THE; GENERATIONS; MODERN TIMES; PAST, THE; PRESENT, THE; TURBULENT TIMES

**ALCOHOL & DRINKING** See also FOOD, WINE, & EATING

*In vino veritas.*
With wine comes truth. —ANONYMOUS (PROVERB)
[Can be traced to Greek sources, including Alcaeus and Plato; the closest Latin source is Pliny the Elder.]

Let's get out of these wet clothes and into a dry martini. —ROBERT BENCHLEY, quoted by Howard Teichmann, *George S. Kaufman*
[Can also be credited to Billy Wilder, who with Charles Brackett wrote the movie *The Major and the Minor*, in which Benchley appeared. One of his lines was, "Why don't you slip out of those wet clothes and into a dry martini?" The quip has also been ascribed to Alexander Woollcott. But if the joke was not original with Benchley, he made it his own.]

Drink no longer water, but use a little wine for thy stomach's sake and thine often infirmities. —BIBLE, *II Thessalonians* 5:23

I have taken more good from alcohol than alcohol has taken from me. —WINSTON CHURCHILL, quoted by Quentin Reynolds, *By Quentin Reynolds*

Malt does more than Milton can
To justify God's ways to man.
                              —A. E. HOUSEMAN, *A Shropshire Lad*
[The reference is to Milton's stated purpose in writing *Paradise Lost*; see Milton at PRAYERS.]

Better sleep with a sober cannibal than a drunken Christian.
                              —HERMAN MELVILLE, *Moby-Dick*

Candy
Is dandy
But liquor
Is quicker.          —OGDEN NASH, *Reflections On Ice-Breaking*

Three highballs, and I think I'm St. Francis of Assisi.
                              —DOROTHY PARKER, *Just a Little One*
[See also Parker at SIN, VICE, & NAUGHTINESS.]

Water is best.          —PINDAR, *Olympian Odes*

It's a long time between drinks.
                              —ROBERT LOUIS STEVENSON, *The Wrong Box*
[Quoting a governor of South Carolina, probably John M. Morehead.]

Father, dear father, come home with me now;
The clock in the steeple strikes one;
You promised, dear father, that you would come home
As soon as your day's work was done.
                              —HENRY CLAY WORK, *Father,*
                              *Dear Father, Come Home with Me Now*

Though in silence, with blighted affection, I pine,
Yet the lips that touch liquor must never touch mine!
                              —GEORGE W. YOUNG, *The Lips That Touch Liquor*

## ALIENATION

I have been a stranger in a strange land.     —BIBLE, *Exodus* 2:22
[The same phrase was used by Sophocles in *Oedipus at Colonus*.]

I, a stranger and afraid
In a world I never made.          —A. E. HOUSEMAN, *Last Poems*

**AMBITION**  See also BOLDNESS & INITIATIVE;
ELITE; GREATNESS; PRIDE & VANITY

*Aut Caesar, aut nihil.*
Either Caesar or nothing.  —CESARE BORGIA, motto

Ah, but a man's reach should exceed his grasp,
Or what's a heaven for?  —ROBERT BROWNING, *Andrea del Sarto*

Hitch your wagon to a star.  —RALPH WALDO EMERSON,
*Civilization*

First say to yourself what you would be; and then do what you
have to do.  —EPICTETUS, *Discourses*

All or nothing.  —HENRIK IBSEN, *Brand*

I would sooner fail than not be among the greatest.
—JOHN KEATS, letter to J. A. Hessey, Oct. 9, 1818

Ambition . . .
The glorious fault of angels and of gods.
—ALEXANDER POPE, *Elegy to the Memory
of an Unfortunate Lady*

The ripest peach is highest on the tree.
—JAMES WHITCOMB RILEY, *The Ripest Peach*

Ambition, old as mankind, the immemorial weakness of the strong.
—VITA SACKVILLE-WEST, *No Signposts in the Sea*

Ambition should be made of sterner stuff.
—SHAKESPEARE, *Julius Caesar*, III, ii

**AMERICA & AMERICANS**  See also AMERICAN HISTORY:
MEMORABLE MOMENTS

Don't sell America short.  —ANONYMOUS, slogan ca. 1925–1929

Westward the course of empire takes its way;
The four first acts already past,
A fifth shall close the drama with the day:
Time's noblest offspring is the last.
—BISHOP GEORGE BERKELEY, *On the Prospect of
Planting Arts and Learning in America*

The chief business of the American people is business.
—CALVIN COOLIDGE, speech, Jan. 17, 1925

America is a country of young men.
—RALPH WALDO EMERSON, *Old Age*

There are no second acts in American lives.
—F. SCOTT FITZGERALD, *The Last Tycoon*, Notes

The American system of rugged individualism.
—HERBERT HOOVER, speech, Oct. 22, 1928

Indeed, I tremble for my country when I reflect that God is just.
—THOMAS JEFFERSON, *Notes on the State of Virginia*

I am willing to love all mankind, *except an American.*
—SAMUEL JOHNSON, Boswell's *Life of Johnson*,
April 15, 1778

The essential American soul is hard, isolate, stoic, a killer.
—D. H. LAWRENCE, *Cooper's Leatherstocking Novels*
in *Studies in Classic American Literature*

This country, with its institutions, belongs to the people who
inhabit it. Whenever they shall grow weary of the existing government, they can exercise their constitutional right of amending it, or
their revolutionary right to dismember or overthrow it.
—ABRAHAM LINCOLN, *First Inaugural Address*, 1861

Thou, too, sail on O Ship of State!
Sail on, O Union, strong and great!
Humanity with all its fears,
With all the hopes of future years,
Is hanging breathless on thy fate!
—HENRY WADSWORTH LONGFELLOW,
*The Building of the Ship*

The men the American people admire most extravagantly are the
most daring liars; the men they detest most violently are those who
try to tell the truth.     —H. L. MENCKEN, quoted in Alistair Cooke,
ed., *The Vintage Mencken*

No man ever went broke underestimating the intelligence of the
American voter.     —H. L. MENCKEN, attributed

[Another variation is: "No man ever went broke underestimating
the taste of the American people."]

Of nothing [in the U.S.] are you allowed to get the real odor or savor. Everything is sterilized and wrapped in cellophane.
—HENRY MILLER, *The Air-Conditioned Nightmare*, title essay

If when the chips are down the United States acts like a pitiful helpless giant, the forces of totalitarianism and anarchy will threaten free nations and free institutions throughout the world.
—RICHARD NIXON, speech, April 30, 1970

Our manifest destiny is to overspread the continent allotted by Providence for the free development of our yearly multiplying millions.    —JOHN L. O'SULLIVAN,
*United States Magazine*, July–Aug., 1845

In America, public opinion is the leader.
—FRANCES PERKINS, *People at Work*

You cannot conquer America.
—WILLIAM PITT, EARL OF CHATHAM, speech, Nov. 18, 1777

We must be the great arsenal of democracy.
—FRANKLIN D. ROOSEVELT, radio speech, Dec. 29, 1940

There can be no fifty-fifty Americanism in this country. There is room here for only hundred percent Americanism.
—THEODORE ROOSEVELT, speech, July 19, 1918

Americans are suckers for good news.
—ADLAI STEVENSON, speech, June 8, 1958

I know of no country, indeed, where the love of money has taken a stronger hold on the affections of men.
—ALEXIS DE TOCQUEVILLE, *Democracy in America*

America is a land of wonders, in which everything is in constant motion and every change seems an improvement. . . . No natural boundary seems to be set to the efforts of man; and in his eyes, what is not yet done is only what he has not yet attempted to do.
—*Ibid.*

The next Augustan age will dawn on the other side of the Atlantic.
—HORACE WALPOLE, letter to Horace Mann, Nov. 24, 1774

The Constitution does not provide for first and second class citizens.          —WENDELL WILLKIE, *An American Programme*

For we must consider that we shall be a city upon a hill. The eyes of all people are upon us.   —JOHN WINTHROP, speech founding the
Massachusetts Bay Colony, 1630
[The allusion is to the Sermon on the Mount, Matthew 5:14: "Ye are the light of the world. A city that is set on an hill cannot be hid."]

America is God's crucible, the great melting pot.
—ISRAEL ZANGWILL, *The Melting Pot*
[The image was not original to Zangwill. Michel Guillaume Jean de Crèvecoeur reported in *Letters from an American Farmer* (1782) that "Here individuals of all nations are melted into a new race of men."]

**AMERICAN HISTORY:**          See also AMERICA & AMERICANS;
**MEMORABLE MOMENTS**          MILITARY BATTLES; PATRIOTISM

What a glorious morning for America!
—SAMUEL ADAMS, upon hearing the sound of guns
at Lexington, 1775 [a traditional attribution]

Declare the United States the winner and begin de-escalation.
—SEN. GEORGE AIKEN, advice to Lyndon B. Johnson
on the Vietnam War, 1966

Let us not be deceived—we are today in the midst of a cold war.
—BERNARD BARUCH, speech, April 16, 1947

Bury my heart at Wounded Knee.
—STEPHEN VINCENT BENÉT, *American Names*

You shall not press down upon the brow of labor this crown of thorns. You shall not crucify mankind upon a cross of gold.
—WILLIAM JENNINGS BRYAN, speech,
Democratic National Convention, 1896
[Bryan had already developed the metaphor some years before. *Bartlett* cites a similar passage from a speech he gave in Congress in 1894.]

Well, I think we ought to let him hang there. Let him twist slowly, slowly in the wind.
—JOHN EHRLICHMAN, speaking to John Dean about
Patrick Gray, March 6, 1973

In the councils of government, we must guard against the acquisition of unwarranted influence, whether sought or unsought, by the military–industrial complex.
          —DWIGHT D. EISENHOWER, farewell speech, Jan. 17, 1961
[See also Eisenhower at MILITARY, THE.]

Here once the embattled farmers stood,
And fired the shot heard round the world.
          —RALPH WALDO EMERSON, *Hymn Sung at the*
               *Completion of the Battle Monument, Concord*

Damn the torpedoes! Full speed ahead.
          —DAVID FARRAGUT, Battle of Mobile Bay, Aug. 5, 1864

Praise the Lord and pass the ammunition.
          —HOWELL M. FORGY, chaplain on the cruiser *New Orleans*,
               during the attack on Pearl Harbor, December 7, 1941

We must, indeed, all hang together or, most assuredly, we shall all hang separately.   —BENJAMIN FRANKLIN, at the signing of the
               Declaration of Independence, July 4, 1776

I would remind you that extremism in the defense of liberty is no vice. And let me remind you also that moderation in the pursuit of justice is no virtue!   —BARRY GOLDWATER, presidential nomination
               acceptance speech, 1964

I propose to fight it out on this line if it takes all summer.
          —ULYSSES S. GRANT, dispatch to Washington, May 11, 1864

I only regret that I have but one life to lose for my country.
          —NATHAN HALE, before being hanged as a spy, Sept. 22, 1776
[The thought comes from Joseph Addison's play, *Cato* (1713):
What a pity is it
That we can die but once to serve our country.]

As for me, give me liberty or give me death!
          —PATRICK HENRY, speech, March 23, 1775

We hold these truths to be self-evident; that all men are created equal; that they are endowed by their creator with certain unalienable rights; that among these are life, liberty, and the pursuit of happiness.   —THOMAS JEFFERSON, *Declaration of Independence*

Peace, commerce, and honest friendship with all nations—entangling alliances with none.   —THOMAS JEFFERSON,
               *First Inaugural Address*, 1801

The spirit of this country is totally adverse to a large military force.          —THOMAS JEFFERSON, letter to Chandler Price, 1807

I have not yet begun to fight.
                    —JOHN PAUL JONES, on the *Bonhomme Richard*,
                    Sept. 23, 1779

*Ich bin ein Berliner.*
                              —JOHN F. KENNEDY, speech, June 26, 1963

Don't give up the ship.
                    —JAMES LAWRENCE, said repeatedly while dying
                    aboard the *Chesapeake*, June 1, 1813

Give me your tired, your poor,
Your huddled masses yearning to breathe free.
                    —EMMA LAZARUS, *The New Colossus:*
                    *Inscription for the Statue of Liberty*

First in war, first in peace, first in the hearts of his countrymen.
                    —HENRY LEE, memorial address to Congress after
                    the death of George Washington, 1799

A house divided against itself cannot stand. I believe this government cannot endure permanently half slave and half free.
                    —ABRAHAM LINCOLN, speech, June 16, 1858
[For the Biblical allusion, see UNITY & LOYALTY.]

Fourscore and seven years ago our fathers brought forth on this continent, a new nation conceived in Liberty, and dedicated to the proposition that all men are created equal.
                    —ABRAHAM LINCOLN, Address at Gettysburg, Nov. 19, 1863

With malice toward none, with charity for all, with firmness in the right, as God gives us to see the right, let us strive on to finish the work we are in, to bind up the nation's wounds.
                    —ABRAHAM LINCOLN, *Second Inaugural Address*, 1865

I shall return.
                    —DOUGLAS MACARTHUR, after leaving the Philippines,
                    March 1942

Old soldiers never die; they just fade away. And like the old soldier in that ballad, I now close my military career and just fade

away, an old soldier who tried to do his duty as God gave him the sight to see that duty.
>—DOUGLAS MACARTHUR, speech to Congress after having been relieved of duty by President Truman, April 19, 1951

Nuts!
>—ANTHONY MCAULIFFE, in refusing to surrender at Bastogne in the Battle of the Bulge, Dec. 22, 1944

[This is the reply publicized, evidently a euphemism for a stronger term.]

All quiet along the Potomac.
>—GEORGE B. MCCLELLAN, in dispatches to Washington, 1861

You won't have Nixon to kick around anymore, because, gentlemen, this is my last press conference.
>—RICHARD M. NIXON, after losing the California gubernatorial race, 1962

I'm not a crook.
>—RICHARD M. NIXON, press conference, Nov. 11, 1973

These are the times that try men's souls. The summer soldier and the sunshine patriot will, in this crisis, shrink from the service of their country.    —THOMAS PAINE, *The American Crisis*

We have met the enemy, and they are ours.
>—OLIVER PERRY, dispatch, Battle of Lake Erie, Sept. 10, 1813

[For Walt Kelly's version, see HUMANS & HUMAN NATURE.]

Don't fire until you see the whites of their eyes.
>—ISRAEL PUTNAM, Battle of Bunker Hill, June 17, 1775

[Also attributed to William Prescott, but we accept the word of militiaman Israel Potter, cited in Richard Wheeler's *The Voices of 1776.*]

I pledge you, I pledge myself, to a new deal for the American people.    —FRANKLIN D. ROOSEVELT, presidential nomination acceptance speech, 1932

The only thing we have to fear is fear itself.
>—FRANKLIN D. ROOSEVELT, *First Inaugural Address*, 1933

[Cf. Wellington's similar comment, under FEAR.]

To some generations much is given. Of others much is expected. This generation of Americans has a rendezvous with destiny.
> —FRANKLIN D. ROOSEVELT, second presidential nomination acceptance speech, 1936

Yesterday, December 7, 1941—a date which will live in infamy— the United States of America was suddenly and deliberately attacked by naval and air forces of the Empire of Japan.
> —FRANKLIN D. ROOSEVELT, speech to Congress

A man who is good enough to shed his blood for his country is good enough to be given a square deal afterward.
> —THEODORE ROOSEVELT, speech, July 4, 1903

Hold the fort! I am coming.
> —WILLIAM SHERMAN, message to Gen. John M. Corse, Oct. 5, 1864

I will not accept if nominated, and will not serve if elected.
> —WILLIAM SHERMAN, telegram to Republican National Convention, 1884

Go west young man, go west.
> —JOHN B. L. SOULE, editorial, *Terre Haute Express*, 1851; popularized by Horace Greeley

I'm going to fight hard. I'm going to give them hell.
> —HARRY S. TRUMAN, to Alben Barkley, Sept. 17, 1948

[William Safire cites this as Truman's recollection of the remark.]

It is our true policy to steer clear of permanent alliances with any portion of the foreign world.
> —GEORGE WASHINGTON, *Farewell Address*, published Sept. 19, 1796

The world must be made safe for democracy.
> —WOODROW WILSON, speech, April 2, 1917, asking Congress for a declaration of war

## AMERICAN INDIANS                See RACES & PEOPLES

## ANGER                See also HATE; VIOLENCE & FORCE

Whosoever shall say, Thou fool, shall be in danger of hell fire.
> —BIBLE, *Matthew* 5:22

Be ye angry, and sin not: let not the sun go down upon your
wrath. —BIBLE, *Ephesians* 4:26

Envy and wrath shorten the life. —BIBLE, *Ecclesiasticus* 30:24

Speak when you are angry and you will make the best speech you
will ever regret. —AMBROSE BIERCE, *The Devil's Dictionary*

I was angry with my friend:
I told my wrath, my wrath did end.
I was angry with my foe:
I told it not, my wrath did grow.
—WILLIAM BLAKE, *A Poison Tree*

The tigers of wrath are wiser than the horses of instruction.
—WILLIAM BLAKE, *The Marriage of Heaven and Hell*

Anger makes dull men witty, but it keeps them poor.
—ELIZABETH I, quoted in Francis Bacon, *Apophthegms*

Anger is a brief madness. —HORACE, *Epistles*

When angry, count four; when very angry, swear.
—MARK TWAIN, *Pudd'nhead Wilson*

Anger supplies the arms. —VIRGIL, *Aeneid*

**ANIMALS** See NATURE: ANIMALS

**ANNUNCIATION** See JESUS CHRIST

**APPEARANCES** See also FASHION & CLOTHES; STYLE

Appearances are often deceiving.
—AESOP, *The Wolf in Sheep's Clothing*

To establish oneself in the world, one has to do all one can to
appear established. —LA ROCHEFOUCAULD, *Maxims*

Common-looking people are the best in the world: that is the
reason the Lord makes so many of them.
—ABRAHAM LINCOLN, quoted by John Hay,
*Letters of John Hay and Extracts from
His Diary*, C. L. Hay, ed.

Men should not care too much for good looks; neglect is becoming.                              —Ovid, *Ars Amatoria*

All that glisters is not gold.
                    —Shakespeare, *The Merchant of Venice*, II, vii
[Shakespeare observed that this was a popular proverb.]

It is only shallow people who do not judge by appearances. The true mystery of the world is the visible, not the invisible.
                    —Oscar Wilde, *The Picture of Dorian Gray*

## APPEASEMENT VS. RESISTANCE

See also OBEDIENCE; PACIFISM; PEACE; RESIGNATION; SURVIVAL

Better Red than dead.
    —Anonymous, slogan of the British ban-the-bomb movement,
        based on comments by Bertrand Russell
[Equally well known was the response, "Better dead than Red," which William Safire in his *Political Dictionary* notes was also the title of a book by an Englishman, Stanley Reynolds.]

I believe it is peace for our time.
                    —Neville Chamberlain, speech, Sept. 30, 1938,
                        after the Munich Conference

The name of peace is sweet and the thing itself is good, but between peace and slavery there is the greatest difference.
                    —Cicero, *Philippics*

'Tis better to have fought and lost,
Than never to have fought at all.
                    —Arthur Hugh Clough, *Peschiera*

If once you have paid him the Dane-geld
You never get rid of the Dane.      —Rudyard Kipling, *Dane-geld*

Better that we should die fighting than be outraged and dishonored. . . . Better to die than to live in slavery.
                    —Emmeline Pankhurst, speech in Petrograd, Aug. 1917

There is a price which is too great to pay for peace, and that price can be put in one word. One cannot pay the price of self-respect.                    —Woodrow Wilson, speech, Feb. 1, 1916

**APRIL**  See NATURE: SEASONS

**ARCHITECTURE**  See ARTS: ARCHITECTURE

**ARMIES**  See MILITARY, THE;
MILITARY BATTLES; WAR

**ARTS**  See also LANGUAGE; STYLE

*Ars longa, vita brevis.*
Art is long, life is short.
—ANONYMOUS
[This has been the most common rendering of the concept expressed by Hippocrates—see under LIFE—and others. Longfellow put it thus: "Art is long, and Time is fleeting," *A Psalm of Life.*]

The object of art is to give life shape.
—JEAN ANOUILH, *The Rehearsal*

*Il faut épater le bourgeois.*
One must shock the bourgeois.  —CHARLES BAUDELAIRE,
attributed

In everything that can be called art there is a quality of redemption.  —RAYMOND CHANDLER, *The Simple Art of Murder*

An artist will betray himself by some sort of sincerity.
—G. K. CHESTERTON, *The Dagger with Wings,*
in *The Incredulity of Father Brown*

Art is a jealous mistress.  —RALPH WALDO EMERSON, *Wealth*

Art without life is a poor affair.  —HENRY JAMES,
*The Art of Fiction*

Is not a patron, my Lord, one who looks with unconcern on a man struggling for life in the water, and, when he has reached ground, encumbers him with help?
—SAMUEL JOHNSON, letter to Lord Chesterfield, Feb. 7, 1755

Whenever I hear the word "culture," . . . I release the safety catch on my Browning!  —HANNS JOHST, *Schlageter*
[Usually attributed to Hermann Goering thus: "When I hear anyone talk of culture, I reach for my revolver."]

Welcome O Life! I go to encounter for the millionth time the reality of experience and to forge in the smithy of my soul the uncreated conscience of my race.
—JAMES JOYCE, *A Portrait of the Artist as a Young Man*

Music is the universal language of mankind—poetry their universal pastime and delight.
—HENRY WADSWORTH LONGFELLOW, *Outre-Mer*

Great artists have no country.
—ALFRED DE MUSSET, *Lorenzaccio*

Only through art can we emerge from ourselves and know what another person sees.
—MARCEL PROUST, *Maxims*

All art is but imitation of nature.
—SENECA, *Epistles*

O! for a Muse of fire, that would ascend
The brightest heaven of invention!
—SHAKESPEARE, *Henry V*, Prologue to the play

The true artist will let his wife starve, his children go barefoot, his mother drudge for his living at seventy, sooner than work at anything but his art.    —GEORGE BERNARD SHAW, *Man and Superman*

Mrs. Ballinger is one of the ladies who pursue Culture in bands, as though it were dangerous to meet it alone.
—EDITH WHARTON, *Xingu*

All art is quite useless.
—OSCAR WILDE, *The Picture of Dorian Gray*

## ARTS: AESTHETICS    See also BEAUTY; SIMPLICITY; STYLE

Tragedy is an imitation of an action that is serious, complete, and of a certain magnitude, effecting through pity and fear the proper purgation [*katharsis*] of these emotions.    —ARISTOTLE, *Poetics*

That willing suspension of disbelief for the moment, which constitutes poetic faith.    —SAMUEL TAYLOR COLERIDGE, *Biographia Literaria*

The only way of expressing emotion in the form of art is by finding an "objective correlative"; in other words, a set of objects, a situation, a chain of events which shall be the formula of that *particular* emotion.    —T. S. ELIOT, *Hamlet*

Less is more. —LUDWIG MIES VAN DE ROHE, motto
[Borrowed from Robert Brownings—see Browning at SIMPLICITY]

A falseness in all our impressions of external things, which I would
generally characterize as the "pathetic fallacy."
                                   —JOHN RUSKIN, *Modern Painters*

Form ever follows function.
            —LOUIS HENRI SULLIVAN, *The Tall Office Building
            Artistically Considered*, in *Lippincott's Magazine*,
            March 1896

## ARTS: ARCHITECTURE

Architecture is inhabited sculpture.
                  —BRANCUSI, quoted by Igor Stravinsky and
                  Robert Craft, *Themes and Episodes*

*Une maison est une machine à habiter.*
A house is a machine for living in.
                  —LE CORBUSIER, *Vers une architecture*

I call architecture frozen music.
                  —GOETHE, letter to Eckermann, Feb. 4, 1829
[Goethe made the phrase famous; Friedrich von Schelling, how-
ver, used the "frozen music" metaphor earlier, in *Philosophie der
Kunst*, 1809.]

One might regard architecture as history arrested in stone.
                  —A. L. ROWSE, *The Use of History*

When we build, let us think that we build forever.
                  —JOHN RUSKIN, *The Seven Lamps of Architecture*

## ARTS:                                 See also INSULTS & PUT-DOWNS
## CRITICISM & CRITICS

Pleasure is by no means an infallible guide, but it is the least
fallible.                  —W. H. AUDEN, *The Dyer's Hand*

Reviewers are usually people who would have been poets, historians, biographers, if they could; they have tried their talents at
one or the other, and have failed; therefore they turn critics.
                  —SAMUEL TAYLOR COLERIDGE,
                  *Lectures on Shakespeare and Milton*

[Reviewing] is no easy matter. To begin with, you must be sure that writing is your vocation, next you must be convinced that reviewing is not writing, hence the conclusion that your vocation is not reviewing. Well, once you feel that, you can start.
—CYRIL CONNOLLY, journal, quoted in
*The New Yorker*, Sept. 3, 1984

A man is a critic when he cannot be an artist, in the same way that a man becomes an informer when he cannot be a soldier.
—GUSTAVE FLAUBERT, letter to Louise Colet, Oct. 1846

A good critic is one who describes his adventures among masterpieces.                    —ANATOLE FRANCE, *La Vie littéraire*

You *may* abuse a tragedy, though you cannot write one. You may scold a carpenter who has made you a bad table, though you cannot make a table. It is not your trade to make tables.
—SAMUEL JOHNSON, quoted in James Boswell,
*Life of Johnson*, May 24, 1763

I would rather be attacked than unnoticed. For the worst thing you can do to an author is to be silent as to his works.
—SAMUEL JOHNSON, quoted in James Boswell,
*Life of Johnson*, March 26, 1779

Our American professors like their literature clear and cold and pure and very dead.
—SINCLAIR LEWIS, Nobel Prize acceptance speech, 1930

I cried all the way to the bank [response to negative reviews].
—LIBERACE, *Liberace: An Autobiography*

Nor in the critic let the man be lost.
—ALEXANDER POPE, *An Essay on Criticism*

Interpretation is the revenge of the intellect upon art.
—SUSAN SONTAG, *Against Interpretation*, title essay

## ARTS: DRAMA & ACTING

Never meddle with play actors, for they're a favored race.
—CERVANTES, *Don Quixote*

If a gun is hanging on the wall in the first act, it must fire in the last.              —ANTON CHEKHOV, advice to a novice playwright,
quoted in John Gassner and Edward Quinn, eds.,
*The Reader's Encyclopedia of World Drama*

Satire is what closes on Saturday night.
—GEORGE S. KAUFMAN, attributed, Howard Teichmann,
*George S. Kaufman*

Drama is action, sir, action and not confounded philosophy.
—LUIGI PIRANDELLO,
*Six Characters in Search of an Author*

The play's the thing
Wherein I'll catch the conscience of the king.
—SHAKESPEARE, *Hamlet*, II, ii

Speak the speech, I pray you, as I pronounced it to you, trip-
pingly on the tongue. —*Ibid.*, III, ii

Suit the action to the word, the word to the action, with this
special observance, that you o'erstep not the modesty of nature.
—*Ibid.*

Hold as 'twere the mirror up to nature. —*Ibid.*

*Exit, pursued by a bear.*
—SHAKESPEARE, *The Winter's Tale*, stage direction, III, iii

## ARTS: MUSIC & DANCE

Music, the greatest good that mortals know,
And all of heaven we have here below.
—JOSEPH ADDISON, *A Song for St. Cecilia's Day*

Whether angels play only Bach in praising God, I am not sure. I
am sure, however, that *en famille* they play Mozart.
—KARL BARTH, quoted in *The New York Times*
obituary, Dec. 11, 1968

A symphony is no joke.
—JOHANNES BRAHMS, cited by Donal Henahan,
*The New York Times*, March 17, 1985

The heart of the melody can never be put down on paper.
—PABLO CASALS, *Conversations*

Where there's music, there can be no evil.
—CERVANTES, *Don Quixote*

Opera . . . is one of the strangest inventions of Western man. It could not have been foreseen by any logical process.
—Sir Kenneth Clark, *Civilization*

Extraordinary how potent cheap music is.
—Noël Coward, *Private Lives*

What passion cannot music raise and quell?
—John Dryden, *A Song for St. Cecilia's Day*

Dance is the loftiest, the most moving, the most beautiful of the arts, because it is no mere translation or abstraction from life; it is life itself.   —Havelock Ellis, *The Dance of Life*

Dancing is just discovery, discovery, discovery.
—Martha Graham, interview,
*The New York Times*, March 31, 1985

Dance is the hidden language of the soul.   —*Ibid.*

If the king loves music, there is little wrong in the land.
—Mencius, *Discourses*

All art constantly aspires towards the condition of music.
—Walter Pater, *Giorgione*, in
*Studies in the History of the Renaissance*

If music be the food of love, play on.
—Shakespeare, *Twelfth Night*, I, i

I am never merry when I hear sweet music.
—Shakespeare, *The Merchant of Venice*, V, i

Hell is full of musical amateurs.
—George Bernard Shaw, *Man and Superman*

My soul is an enchanted boat,
Which, like a sleeping swan, doth float
Upon the silver waves of thy sweet singing.
—Percy Bysshe Shelley, *Prometheus Unbound*

Our sweetest songs are those that tell of saddest thoughts.
—Percy Bysshe Shelley, *To a Skylark*

If, as is nearly always the case, music appears to express something, this is only an illusion and not a reality.
—Igor Stravinsky, *An Autobiography*

Lady, if you got to ask, you ain't got it [on being asked to explain rhythm].   —THOMAS "FATS" WALLER, quoted in Eddie Condon and Thomas Sugrue, *We Called It Music*

[Sign over a piano] Please do not shoot the pianist. He is doing his best.   —OSCAR WILDE, *Leadville*, in *Impressions of America*

## ARTS: PAINTING

One is never tired of painting, because you have to set down, not what you knew already, but what you have just discovered. There is a continual creation out of nothing going on.
   —WILLIAM HAZLITT, *The Pleasure of Painting*

All art worthy of the name is religious. Be it a creation of lines and colors, if it is not religious, it does not exist. If it is not religious, it is only a matter of documentary art, anecdotal art, which is no longer art.   —HENRI MATISSE, quoted in Pierre Schneider, *Matisse*

With color one obtains an energy that seems to stem from witch-craft.   —HENRI MATISSE, quoted by Michael Brenson, *The New York Times*, May 26, 1985

I try to apply colors like words that shape poems, like notes that shape music.   —JOAN MIRÓ, quoted in John Gruen, *Close-Up*

The painter who draws by practice and judgment of the eye without the use of reason is like the mirror which reproduces within itself all the objects which are set opposite to it without knowledge of the same.   —LEONARDO DA VINCI, *Notebooks*

A picture is a model of reality.
   —LUDWIG WITTGENSTEIN, *Tractatus logico-philosophicus*

## ARTS: POETRY & POETS

All poets are mad.   —ROBERT BURTON, *The Anatomy of Melancholy*

Poetry does not necessarily have to be beautiful to stick in the depths of our memory.   —COLETTE, *Under the Blue Lantern*, in *Earthly Paradise*

Genuine poetry can communicate before it is understood.
   —T. S. ELIOT, *Dante*

The only thing that can save the world is the reclaiming of the awareness of the world. That's what poetry does.
—ALLEN GINSBERG, quoted in Helen Weaver's review of Ginsberg's *Collected Poems*, in *The Litchfield County Times*, May 31, 1985

The poetical language of an age should be the current language heightened.          —GERARD MANLEY HOPKINS, letter to Robert Bridges, Aug. 14, 1879

To be a mediocre poet, neither gods, nor men, nor booksellers have allowed.                      —HORACE, *Art of Poetry*

To a poet nothing can be useless.      —SAMUEL JOHNSON, *Rasselas*

Poetry should surprise by a fine excess and not by singularity—it should strike the reader as a wording of his own highest thoughts, and appear almost a remembrance.
—JOHN KEATS, letter to John Taylor, Feb. 27, 1818

If poetry comes not as naturally as the leaves to a tree, it had better not come at all.                                  —*Ibid.*

When power narrows the areas of man's concern, poetry reminds him of the richness and diversity of his existence. When power corrupts, poetry cleanses.      —JOHN F. KENNEDY, speech, Oct. 26, 1963

Publishing a volume of poetry is like dropping a rose petal down the Grand Canyon and waiting for the echo.
—DON MARQUIS, *The Sun Dial*

Chameleons feed on light and air:
Poets' food is love and fame.
—PERCY BYSSHE SHELLEY, *An Exhortation*

Poetry is the record of the best and happiest moments of the happiest and best minds.
—PERCY BYSSHE SHELLEY, *A Defence of Poetry*

Poets tell many lies.                        —SOLON, fragment
[For another less than flattering view of poets see the note at Swift in the category NATURE: ANIMALS.]

The poet is the priest of the invisible.
—WALLACE STEVENS, *Adagia*

To have great poets, there must be great audiences, too.
>—WALT WHITMAN, *Ventures on an Old Theme*
>in *Notes Left Over*

Poetry is the spontaneous overflow of powerful feelings: it takes its origin from emotion recollected in tranquillity.
>—WILLIAM WORDSWORTH, *Lyrical Ballads*,
>Preface to 2nd ed.

We poets in our youth begin in gladness;
But thereof come in the end despondency and madness.
>—WILLIAM WORDSWORTH, *Resolution and Independence*

## ARTS: STYLE IN WRITING & EXPRESSION

See also LANGUAGE; SIMPLICITY; STYLE

The greatest thing in style is to have a command of metaphor.
>—ARISTOTLE, *Poetics*

A good style must, first of all, be clear. It must . . . be appropriate.
>—ARISTOTLE, *Rhetoric*

A good style must have an air of novelty, at the same time concealing its art.
>—*Ibid*.

This is the sort of English up with which I will not put.
>—WINSTON CHURCHILL

[Comment in margin of a document—it refers to a proofreader's excessive nicety in avoiding placing a preposition at the end of a sentence], attributed, quoted by Sir Ernest Gowers, *Plain Words*.

Read over your compositions, and wherever you meet with a passage which you think is particularly fine, strike it out.
>—SAMUEL JOHNSON, quoting a college tutor,
>in James Boswell's *Life of Johnson*, April 30, 1773

For a man to write well, there are required three necessaries: to read the best authors, observe the best speakers, and much exercise of his own style.
>—BEN JONSON, *Discoveries*

Whatever is clearly expressed is well wrote.
>—LADY MARY WORTLEY MONTAGU, letter to
>James Steuart, July 19, 1759

Verbal felicity is the fruit of art and diligence and refusing to be false.                              —MARIANNE MOORE, quoted by
Louise Bogan, *College English*, Feb. 1953

I have made this letter longer than usual, because I lack the time to make it short.                              —PASCAL, *Letters Provinciales*

True wit is nature to advantage dressed,
What oft was thought, but ne'er so well expressed.
—ALEXANDER POPE, *Essay on Criticism*

Brevity is the soul of wit.        —SHAKESPEARE, *Hamlet*, II, ii

Vigorous writing is concise.                              —WILLIAM STRUNK,
*Elements of Style*

Proper words in proper places make the true definition of style.
—JONATHAN SWIFT, letter to a young clergyman,
Jan. 9, 1720

The difference between the almost right word and the right word is really a large matter—'tis the difference between the lightning bug and the lightning.        —MARK TWAIN, *The Art of Authorship*

As to the Adjective: when in doubt, strike it out.
—MARK TWAIN, *Pudd'nhead Wilson*

Take eloquence and wring its neck.
—PAUL VERLAINE, *L'art poétique* in *Jadis et Naguère*

Style is the dress of thought.        —SAMUEL WESLEY, *An Epistle
to a Friend Concerning Poetry*
[Later, in 1746, the Earl of Chesterfield wrote to his son, "Style is the dress of thoughts." See also Johnson at LANGUAGE.]

## ARTS: WRITING        See also ARTS: POETRY; ARTS: STYLE
IN WRITING & EXPRESSION;
BOOKS & READING; LANGUAGE

Of making many books, there is no end.        —BIBLE,
*Ecclesiastes* 12:12
[Also translated as, "Writing books involves endless hard work," The Jerusalem Bible, 1966.]

Writing is nothing more than a guided dream.
—JORGE LUIS BORGES, *Dr. Brodie's Report*, preface

A well-written life is almost as rare as a well-spent one.
—THOMAS CARLYLE, *Richter*

A good novel tells us the truth about its hero; but a bad novel tells us the truth about its author. —G. K. CHESTERTON, *Heretics*

A work that aspires, however humbly, to the condition of art should carry its justification in every line.
—JOSEPH CONRAD, *Nigger of the Narcissus*, preface

All writing comes by the grace of God.
—RALPH WALDO EMERSON, *Experience*

If a writer has to rob his mother, he will not hesitate; the "Ode on a Grecian Urn" is worth any number of old ladies.
—WILLIAM FAULKNER, quoted in
*The Paris Review Interviews*, 1959

It is with noble sentiments that bad literature gets written.
—ANDRÉ GIDE, *Journal*, Sept. 2, 1940

Often you must turn your stylus to erase, if you hope to write anything worth a second reading. —HORACE, *Satires*

A man may write at any time, if he will set himself doggedly to it.
—SAMUEL JOHNSON, quoted in Boswell's
*Life of Johnson*, March 1750

No man but a blockhead ever wrote, except for money.
—SAMUEL JOHNSON, *ibid.*, April 5, 1776

*Lexicographer, n.* A writer of dictionaries, a harmless drudge.
—SAMUEL JOHNSON, *Dictionary*

An inveterate and incurable itch for writing besets many and grows old with their sick hearts. —JUVENAL, *Satires*

He writes nothing whose writings are not read.
—MARTIAL, *Epigrams*

If you steal from one author it's plagiarism; if you steal from many it's research. —WILSON MIZNER, quoted in
John Burke, *Rogue's Progress*

Satire should, like a polished razor keen,
Wound with a touch that's scarcely felt or seen.
—LADY MARY WORTLEY MONTAGU,
*To the Imitator of the First Satire of Horace*

If there's a book you really want to read but it hasn't been written yet, then you must write it.                    —TONI MORRISON

[This has been attributed to Ms. Morrison in *The New York Times* and elsewhere; she does not remember precisely the occasion on which she said it—just that it was in a speech.]

True ease in writing comes from art, not chance.
                    —ALEXANDER POPE, *An Essay on Criticism*

Our passions shape our books, repose writes them in the intervals.
                    —MARCEL PROUST, *Remembrance of Things Past:
                    The Past Recaptured*

An honest tale speeds best being plainly told.
                    —SHAKESPEARE, *Richard III*, IV, iv

Of all those arts in which the wise excel,
Nature's chief masterpiece is writing well.
                    —JOHN SHEFFIELD, *Essay on Poetry*

There's nothing to writing. All you do is sit down at a typewriter and open a vein.                    —WALTER "RED" SMITH,
                    in *Reader's Digest*, July 1982

A great writer is, so to speak, a second government in his country. And for that reason no regime has ever loved great writers, only minor ones.          —ALEXANDER SOLZHENITSYN, *The First Circle*

Writing, when properly managed (as you may be sure I think mine is), is but a different name for conversation.
                    —LAURENCE STERNE, *Tristram Shandy*

Three hours a day will produce as much as a man ought to write.
                    —ANTHONY TROLLOPE, *An Autobiography*

Being a great writer is not the same as writing great.
                    —JOHN UPDIKE, *The New Yorker*, May 20, 1985

**ASTRONOMY**                              See SCIENCE: PHYSICS
                                           & COSMOLOGY

**ATHEISM**                                See also SKEPTICISM

The fool hath said in his heart, There is no God.
                    —BIBLE, *Psalms* 14:1 & 53:1

I am an atheist still, thank God.
  —Luis Buñuel, quoted in
  Ado Kyrou, *Luis Buñuel*

There are no atheists in the foxholes.
  —William Thomas Cummings, field sermon,
  Bataan, 1942

In spite of all the yearnings of men, no one can produce a single fact or reason to support the belief in God and in personal immortality.  —Clarence Darrow, *Sign* magazine, May 1938

I believe that when I die I shall rot, and nothing of my ego will survive. . . . But I should scorn to shiver with terror at the thought of annihilation. Happiness is nonetheless true happiness because it must come to an end, nor do thought and love lose their value because they are not everlasting.  —Bertrand Russell, *What I Believe*

My atheism . . . is true piety towards the universe and denies only gods fashioned by men in their own image, to be servants of their human interests.  —George Santayana, *On My Friendly Critics*

An atheist is a man who has no invisible means of support.
  —Fulton J. Sheen, *Look* magazine, Dec. 14, 1955

**AUTOMOBILES**                           See TECHNOLOGY

**AUTUMN**                                 See NATURE: SEASONS

**BABIES**                                 See CHILDREN & CHILDHOOD

**BATTLES**                                See MILITARY BATTLES

**BEAUTY**                                 See also ART: AESTHETICS;
                                           GRACE; WOMEN,
                                           BEAUTIFUL & HOMELY

Beauty is the gift of God.
  —Aristotle, quoted in Diogenes Laërtius,
  *Lives of Eminent Philosophers*

For beauty being the best of all we know
Sums up the unsearchable and secret aims
Of nature.  —Robert Bridges, *The Growth of Love*

Think of all the beauty still left around you and be happy.
—ANNE FRANK, *Diary of a Young Girl*

Beauty is in the eye of the beholder.
—MARGARET HUNGERFORD, *Molly Bawn*
[David Hume, in *Of Tragedy*, put it: "Beauty in things exists in the mind which contemplates them."]

A thing of beauty is a joy for ever:
Its loveliness increases; it will never
Pass into nothingness.
—JOHN KEATS, *Endymion*

"Beauty is truth, truth beauty,"—that is all
Ye know on earth, and all ye need to know.
—JOHN KEATS, *Ode on a Grecian Urn*

I'm tired of all this business about beauty being only skin-deep. That's deep enough. What do you want—an adorable pancreas?
—JEAN KERR, *Mirror, Mirror on the Wall*, in
*The Snake Has All the Lines*

Beauty is everlasting
And dust is for a time.   —MARIANNE MOORE, *In Distrust of Merits*

Remember that the most beautiful things in the world are the most useless: peacocks and lilies, for instance.
—JOHN RUSKIN, *The Stones of Venice*

It is amazing how complete is the delusion that beauty is goodness.
—LEO TOLSTOY, *The Kreutzer Sonata*

The superior gratification derived from the use and contemplation of costly and supposedly beautiful products is, commonly, in great measure, a gratification of our sense of costliness masquerading under the name of beauty.   —THORSTEIN VEBLEN, *The Theory of the Leisure Class*

The beauty of the world which is soon to perish, has two edges, one of laughter, one of anguish, cutting the heart asunder.
—VIRGINIA WOOLF, *A Room of One's Own*

## BEGINNINGS                                                    See also FATE

A good beginning makes a good ending.
—ANONYMOUS (ENGLISH PROVERB)

A hard beginning maketh a good ending.
—JOHN HEYWOOD, *Proverbs*

Who has begun has half done. Have the courage to be wise.
—HORACE, *Epistles*

A journey of a thousand miles must begin with a single step.
—LAO-TZU, *Tao Te Ching*

Things are always at their best in their beginning.
—PASCAL, *Lettres provinciales*

The beginning is the most important part of the work.
—PLATO, *The Republic*

**B E L I E F**                                    See FAITH; RELIGION

**B E T R A Y A L**

This night, before the cock crow, thou shalt deny me thrice.
—BIBLE, *Matthew* 26:34

Judas, betrayest thou the Son of man with a kiss?
—BIBLE, *Luke* 23:48

Et tu, Brute!          —SHAKESPEARE, *Julius Caesar*, III, i

This was the most unkindest cut of all.          —SHAKESPEARE,
*ibid.*, III, ii

Each man kills the thing he loves.
—OSCAR WILDE, *The Ballad of Reading Gaol*
[For more of this and other malfeasance, see CRIME.]

**B I B L E**                                    See RELIGION

**B I R D S**                                    See NATURE: ANIMALS

**B L A C K S**                                    See RACES & PEOPLES

**B O A T I N G**                                    See SEAS & SHIPS,
SAILING & BOATING

BODY, HUMAN                          See also HEALTH;
                                       ILLNESS & REMEDIES

The spirit indeed is willing, but the flesh is weak.
                              —BIBLE, *Matthew* 26:41
[See also TEMPTATION.]

Your body is the temple of the Holy Ghost, which is in you,
which ye have of God, and ye are not your own.
                              —BIBLE, *I Corinthians* 6:19

Alas, after a certain age, every man is responsible for his own face.
                              —ALBERT CAMUS, *The Fall*

The strongest, surest way to the soul is through the flesh.
                              —MABEL DODGE, *Lorenzo in Taos*

Love's mysteries in souls do grow,
But yet the body is his book.       —JOHN DONNE, *The Ecstasy*

I see no objection to stoutness, in moderation.
                              —W. S. GILBERT, *Iolanthe*

The body says what words cannot.
                              —MARTHA GRAHAM, interview,
                              *The New York Times*, March 31, 1985

I'm fat, but I'm thin inside. Has it ever struck you that there's a
thin man inside every fat man?       —GEORGE ORWELL,
                                       *Coming Up for Air*

From a man's face, I can read his character; if I can see him walk, I
know his thoughts.                   —PETRONIUS, *Satyricon*

O! that this too too solid flesh would melt,
Thaw and resolve itself into a dew.   —SHAKESPEARE, *Hamlet*, I, ii

I have more flesh than another man, and therefore more fraility.
                              —SHAKESPEARE, *Henry IV, Part I*, III, iii

If anything is sacred the human body is sacred.
                              —WALT WHITMAN, *I Sing the Body Electric*

**BOLDNESS & INITIATIVE**  See also AMBITION; COURAGE;
GREATNESS; SELF-CONFIDENCE;
SELF-RELIANCE

Ask, and it shall be given you; seek, and ye shall find; knock, and
it shall be opened unto you.  —BIBLE, *Matthew* 7:7

The die is cast.  —JULIUS CAESAR, quoted in Plutarch,
*Parallel Lives*

Faint heart never won fair lady.  —CERVANTES, *Don Quixote*
[Identified as "an old saying."]

He who seizes the right moment,
Is the right man.  —GOETHE, *Faust*

The first blow is half the battle.
—OLIVER GOLDSMITH, *She Stoops to Conquer*

Cruelties should be committed all at once.
—MACHIAVELLI, *The Prince*

Take calculated risks. That is quite different from being rash.
—GEORGE S. PATTON, letter to his son, June 6, 1944

If it were done when 'tis done, then 'twere well
It were done quickly.  —SHAKESPEARE, *Macbeth*, I, vii

There is a tide in the affairs of men
Which, taken at the flood, leads on to fortune;
Omitted, all the voyage of their life
Is bound in shallows and in miseries.
—SHAKESPEARE, *Julius Caesar*, IV, iii

Fortune sides with him who dares.  —VIRGIL, *Aeneid*

**BOOKS & READING**  See also ARTS: POETRY; ARTS:
WRITING; CENSORSHIP

Reading all the good books is like a conversation with the finest
men of past centuries.  —RENÉ DESCARTES, *Discourse on Method*

Books are for nothing but to inspire.
—RALPH WALDO EMERSON, *The American Scholar*

Read in order to live.                    —GUSTAVE FLAUBERT, letter to
                                          Mlle de Chantpie, June 1857

All good books are alike in that they are truer than if they really
happened and after you are finished reading one you will feel that it
all happened to you, and afterwards it all belongs to you.
                —ERNEST HEMINGWAY, *An Old Newsman Writes*

I cannot live without books.              —THOMAS JEFFERSON, letter to
                                          John Adams, June 10, 1815

Literature is my utopia.   —HELEN KELLER, *The Story of My Life*

We shouldn't teach great books; we should teach a love of reading.
                        —B. F. SKINNER, quoted in Richard I. Evans,
                        *B. F. Skinner: The Man and His Ideas*

✗ People say that life is the thing, but I prefer reading.
                        —LOGAN PEARSALL SMITH, *Afterthoughts*

Literature . . . becomes the living memory of a nation.
                        —ALEXANDER SOLZHENITSYN, Nobel Prize
                        acceptance speech, 1972

Reading is to the mind what exercise is to the body.
                        —RICHARD STEELE, *The Tatler*, no. 147

Books are good enough in their own way, but they are a mighty
bloodless substitute for life.
                —ROBERT LOUIS STEVENSON,
                    *An Apology for Idlers*, in *Virginibus Puerisque*

Books are the treasured wealth of the world and the fit inheritance
of generations and nations.              —THOREAU, *Walden*

How many a man has dated a new era in his life from the reading
of a book.                                            —*Ibid.*

A good book is the best of friends, the same today and forever.
                        —MARTIN F. TUPPER, *Of Reading*, in
                        *Proverbial Philosophy*

There is no such thing as a moral or an immoral book. Books are
well written, or badly written.
                —OSCAR WILDE, *The Picture of Dorian Gray*

**BOSTON**                                        See CITIES

**BRAVERY**                                       See COURAGE

**BROTHERHOOD**              See EQUALITY; HUMANS & HUMAN
                                                  NATURE; RACES & PEOPLES

**BUSINESS**                    See also AMERICA & AMERICANS;
                                            CAPITALISM; ECONOMICS;
                                                      MONEY; WORK

Buying and selling is essentially antisocial.
—EDWARD BELLAMY, *Looking Backward*

What is robbing a bank compared with founding a bank?
—BERTOLT BRECHT, *The Threepenny Opera*

It is better to lose opportunity than capital.
—SUSAN M. BYRNE, *Wall St. Week in Review*
[TV show], Feb. 15, 1985

Few people do business well who do nothing else.
—EARL OF CHESTERFIELD, letter to his son,
Aug. 7, 1749

They [corporations] cannot commit treason, nor be outlawed, nor excommunicate, for they have no souls.
—EDWARD COKE, *Sutton's Hospital Case*

No nation was ever ruined by trade.
—BENJAMIN FRANKLIN, *Thoughts on
Commercial Subjects*

When a person with experience meets a person with money, the person with experience will get the money. And the person with the money will get some experience.
—LEONARD LAUDER, on the early years of the Estée
Lauder company, speech, Woman's Economic
Development Corporation, Feb. 1985

Trade is a social act.        —JOHN STUART MILL, *On Liberty*

The customer is always right.      —H. GORDON SELFRIDGE,
slogan of his store in London

Corporations have neither bodies to be punished, nor souls to be condemned, they therefore do as they like.
—EDWARD, FIRST BARON THURLOW, attributed by Poynder, *Literary Extracts*

The public be damned! I'm working for my stockholders.
—WILLIAM HENRY VANDERBILT, news reports, Oct. 2, 1882

What is good for the country is good for General Motors, and what is good for General Motors is good for the country.
—CHARLES E. WILSON, testimony, Senate Armed Forces Committee, 1952

There was a time when corporations played a minor part in our business affairs, but now they play the chief part, and most men are the servants of corporations.
—WOODROW WILSON, *The New Freedom*

**C A N A D A**                                    See NATIONS

**C A P I T A L I S M**            See also BUSINESS; ECONOMICS; MONEY; WORK

A market is a place set apart for men to deceive and get the better of one another.        —ANACHARSIS, quoted in Diogenes Laërtius, *Lives of Eminent Philosophers*

*Laissez faire.*
Let business go forward. No interference.
—MARQUIS D'ARGENSON, *Mémoires*, 1736, Vol. 5
[The phrase is difficult to translate and has complicated origins: *The Concise Oxford Dictionary of Quotations* notes that in 1751, when Jean Baptiste Colbert, minister of finance, asked a group of commerce deputies what he could do to help business, one of them replied, "*Laissez-nous faire,*" which might be translated: "Let us get on with it." In 1758, in a speech, the economist Vincent de Gournay urged "*Laissez faire, laissez passer,*" calling for free passage of goods and people; the phrase was a favorite with him. François Quesnay also used "*laissez passer . . . laissez faire*" with reference to buyers, sellers, and sound commerce.]

The forces of a capitalist society, if left unchecked, tend to make the rich richer and the poor poorer.   —JAWAHARLAL NEHRU, *Credo*

*La propriété c'est le vol.*
Property is theft.
—Pierre-Joseph Proudhon, *Qu'est-ce que la Propriété?*

The revolution eats its own. Capitalism recreates itself.
—Mordecai Richler, *Cocksure*

Property is organized robbery.
—George Bernard Shaw, *Major Barbara*, Preface

Every individual . . . intends only his own gain, and he is in this, as in many other cases, led by an invisible hand to promote an end which was no part of his intention. . . . By pursuing his own interest he frequently promotes that of the society more effectively than when he really intends to promote it. I have never known much good done by those who affected to trade for the public good.
—Adam Smith, *Wealth of Nations*

It is not from the benevolence of the butcher, the brewer, or the baker that we expect our dinner, but from their regard to their own self-interest.
—*Ibid.*

Conspicuous consumption of valuable goods is a means of reputability to the gentleman of leisure.
—Thorstein Veblen, *The Theory of the Leisure Class*

The trouble with the profit system has always been that it was highly unprofitable to most people.
—E. B. White,
*One Man's Meat*

**CARDS**                                                    See GAMES

**CARS**                                              See TECHNOLOGY

**CATS**                                        See NATURE: ANIMALS

**CAUTION**                                          See PRUDENCE &
PRACTICAL WISDOM

**CENSORSHIP**                                   See also FREE SPEECH;
PRESS, THE

Every suppressed or expunged word reverberates through the earth from side to side.    —Ralph Waldo Emerson, *Compensation*

Wherever they burn books, they will also, in the end, burn people.
—Heinrich Heine, *Almansor*

As good almost kill a man as kill a good book: who kills a man kills a reasonable creature, God's image; but he who destroys a good book kills reason itself.        —John Milton, *Aeropagitica*

Scenes of passion should not be introduced when not essential to the plot. In general, passion should be so treated that these scenes do not stimulate the lower and baser element.
—The Motion Picture Producers and Distributors of America, Inc., Code for the Industry, 1931

Sex perversion or any inference of it is forbidden. White slavery shall not be treated. Miscegenation is forbidden. . . . Scenes of actual childbirth, in fact or in silhouette, are never to be represented.
—*Ibid.*

Assassination is the extreme form of censorship.
—George Bernard Shaw, *The Rejected Statement*

We write frankly and freely but then we "modify" before we print.        —Mark Twain, *Life on the Mississippi*
[Self-censorship—a hot contemporary issue, an old problem.]

CHANGE                                See also NEW THINGS;
                                         PROGRESS; VARIETY

Nature's mighty law is change.
—Robert Burns, *Let Not Women E'er Complain*

Change is inevitable in a progressive society. Change is constant.
—Benjamin Disraeli, speech, Oct. 20, 1867

Unless one says goodbye to what one loves, and unless one travels to completely new territories, one can expect merely a long wearing away of oneself and an eventual extinction.
—Jean Dubuffet, quoted in *The New York Times*, obituary, May 15, 1985

You can't step twice into the same river.
—Heraclitus, *On the Universe*

Everything flows, nothing stays still.
—Heraclitus, quoted in Plato, *Cratylus*

Nothing is permanent but change.
> —HERACLITUS, quoted in Diogenes Laërtius,
> *Lives of Eminent Philosophers*

*Plus ça change, plus c'est la même chose.*
The more things change, the more they remain the same.
> —ALPHONSE KARR, *Les Guêpes*

The wind of change is blowing through this Continent.
> —HAROLD MACMILLAN, speech, Cape Town,
> Feb. 3, 1960

[More of this is given at NATIONS.]

The basic fact of today is the tremendous pace of change in human life.
> —JAWAHARLAL NEHRU, *Credo*

The old order changeth, yielding place to new,
And God fulfills Himself in many ways,
Lest one good custom should corrupt the world.
> —ALFRED, LORD TENNYSON, *Morte D'Arthur*

[Later added to *Idylls of the King*.]

**CHARITY**                     See CHARITY: PHILANTHROPY;
                                          LOVE & CHARITY:
                                          BIBLICAL REFERENCES

## CHARITY: PHILANTHROPY

The living need charity more than the dead.
> —GEORGE ARNOLD, *The Jolly Old Pedagogue*

Cast thy bread upon the waters.         —BIBLE, *Ecclesiastes* 11:1

Take heed that ye do not your alms before men, to be seen of them: otherwise you have no reward of your Father which is in heaven.
Therefore when thou doest thine alms, do not sound a trumpet before thee, as the hypocrites do in the synagogues and in the streets, that they may have glory of men. Verily, I say unto you, They have their reward.
But when thou doest alms, let not thy left hand know what thy right hand doeth.         —BIBLE, *Matthew* 6:1–3

Jesus said unto him, If thou would be perfect, go and sell that thou hast, and give to the poor, and thou shalt have treasure in heaven.
> —BIBLE, *Matthew* 19:21

I was an hungred, and ye gave me meat: I was thirsty, and ye gave me drink: I was a stranger, and ye took me in:

Naked, and ye clothed me: I was sick, and ye visited me: I was in prison, and ye came unto me.                    —*Ibid.*, 25:35, 36

It is more blessed to give than to receive.        —BIBLE, *Acts* 20:35

God loveth a cheerful giver.        —BIBLE, *II Corinthians* 9:7

He is rich who hath enough to be charitable.
                    —SIR THOMAS BROWNE, *Religio Medici*

Philanthropy is commendable, but it must not cause the philanthropist to overlook the circumstances of economic injustice which make philanthropy necessary.        —MARTIN LUTHER KING, JR.,
                    *Strength of Love*

He gives twice who gives promptly.
                    —PUBLILIUS SYRUS, *Moral Sayings*
[Also, Cervantes in *Don Quixote*: "He that gives quickly gives twice."]

## CHARM                                              See also GRACE

It's a sort of bloom on a woman. If you have it, you don't need to have anything else; and if you don't have it, it doesn't much matter what else you have.    —J. M. BARRIE, *What Every Woman Knows*

Charm is a way of getting the answer yes without ever having asked a clear question.        —ALBERT CAMUS, *The Fall*

All charming people have something to conceal, usually their total dependence on the appreciation of others.
                    —CYRIL CONNOLLY, *Enemies of Promise*

All charming people, I fancy, are spoiled. It is the secret of their attraction.        —OSCAR WILDE, *The Portrait of Mr. W. H.*

## CHICAGO                                            See CITIES

## CHILDREN & CHILDHOOD        See also INNOCENCE; FAMILY;
                    PARENTS & PARENTHOOD

Out of the mouth of babes and sucklings hast thou ordained strength.        —BIBLE, *Psalms* 8:2

A little child shall lead them.
[The entire verse is given under PEACE.]     —BIBLE, *Isaiah* 11:6

But whoso shall offend one of these little ones which believe in me, it were better for him that a millstone were hanged about his neck, and that he were drowned in the depth of the sea.
    —BIBLE, *Matthew* 18:6

Suffer the little children to come unto me, and forbid them not: for of such is the kingdom of God.     —BIBLE, *Mark* 10:14

When I was a child, I spake as a child, I understood as a child, I thought as a child: but when I became a man, I put away childish things.     —BIBLE, *I Corinthians* 9:11

Every baby born into the world is a finer one than the last.
    —CHARLES DICKENS, *Nicholas Nickleby*

There is always one moment in childhood when the door opens and lets the future in.     —GRAHAM GREENE,
    *The Power and the Glory*

Between the dark and the daylight,
When the night is beginning to lower,
Comes a pause in the day's occupations,
That is known as the Children's Hour.
    —HENRY WADSWORTH LONGFELLOW,
    *The Children's Hour*

There was a little girl
Who had a little curl
Right in the middle of her forehead;
And when she was good
She was very, very good,
But when she was bad she was horrid.
    —HENRY WADSWORTH LONGFELLOW,
    *There Was a Little Girl*

Childhood is the kingdom where no one dies.
    —EDNA ST. VINCENT MILLAY, title of poem in
    *Wine from these Grapes*

Of all the animals, the boy is the most unmanageable.
    —PLATO, *Theaetetus*

But soon a milder age will follow. An age of truer wisdom. Then the careful state will spare her children.
> —JOHANN FRIEDRICH VON SCHILLER, *Don Carlos*

A child should always say what's true
And speak when he is spoken to,
And behave mannerly at table:
At least as far as he is able.
> —ROBERT LOUIS STEVENSON, *A Child's Garden of Verses*

A baby is an inestimable blessing and bother.
> —MARK TWAIN, letter to Annie Webster,
> Sept. 1, 1876

Our birth is but a sleep and a forgetting:
The soul that rises with us, our life's Star,
Hath had elsewhere its setting,
And cometh from afar:
Not in entire forgetfulness,
And not in utter nakedness,
But trailing clouds of glory do we come
From God, who is our home:
Heaven lies about us in our infancy!
> —WILLIAM WORDSWORTH, *Intimations of Immortality*

The child is father of the man.
> —WILLIAM WORDSWORTH, *My Heart Leaps Up*

**CHINA**                                    See NATIONS; ORIENT, THE

**CHRIST**                                    See CHRISTMAS; JESUS CHRIST

**CHRISTMAS**                                    See also JESUS CHRIST

And she brought forth her first-born son, and wrapped him in swaddling clothes, and laid him in a manger; because there was no room for them in the inn.                          —BIBLE, *Luke* 2:7

Glory to God in the highest, and on earth peace, good will toward men.                          —*Ibid.*, 2:14

"Bah," said Scrooge. "Humbug!"                          —CHARLES DICKENS,
                                                        *A Christmas Carol*

"God bless us every one!" said Tiny Tim, the last of all.   —*Ibid.*

A cold coming we had of it,
Just the worst time of the year.            —T. S. ELIOT,
                                              *Journey of the Magi*


It was the winter wild
While the Heaven-born child
All meanly wrapt in the rude manger lies.
            —JOHN MILTON, *On the Morning of Christ's Nativity*


'Twas the night before Christmas, when all through the house
Not a creature was stirring, not even a mouse;
The stockings were hung by the chimney with care,
In hopes that St. Nicholas soon would be there.
The children were nestled all snug in their beds,
While visions of sugar-plums danced in their heads.
            —CLEMENT C. MOORE, *The Night Before Christmas*


Now, *Dasher!* now, *Dancer!* now, *Prancer* and *Vixen!* On, *Comet!*
on, *Cupid!* on, *Donner* and *Blitzen!*                        —*Ibid.*


He had a broad face and a little round belly,
That shook when he laughed, like a bowlful of jelly.      —*Ibid.*


But I heard him exclaim, ere he drove out of sight,
"Happy Christmas to all and to all a good night!"        —*Ibid.*


Heap on more wood! the wind is chill,
But let it whistle as it will,
We'll keep our Christmas merry still.        —SIR WALTER SCOTT,
                                              *Marmion*


The time draws near the birth of Christ;
The moon is hid; the night is still;
The Christmas bells from hill to hill
Answer each other in the mist.
            —ALFRED, LORD TENNYSON, *In Memoriam*


## CHURCH                                      See RELIGION


## CITIES

Ten measures of beauty came into the world; Jerusalem received
nine measures, and the rest of the world one.
            —ANONYMOUS (HEBREW PROVERB)

See Naples and die.                    —Anonymous (Italian Proverb)

And this is good old Boston,
The home of the bean and the cod,
Where the Lowells talk to the Cabots
And the Cabots talk only to God.
                              —John Collins Bossidy, toast at
                              Holy Cross alumni dinner, 1910

Everyone soon or late comes round by Rome.
                    —Robert Browning, *The Ring and the Book*

Match me such a marvel save in Eastern clime,
A rose-red city "half as old as time."
                              —John William Burgon, *Petra*

*Carthago delenda est.*
Carthage must be destroyed.            —Cato, in speeches after the
                                       Second Punic War

Chicago is the product of modern capitalism, and, like other great
commercial centers is unfit for human habitation.
              —Eugene Debs, 1908, quoted in Kevin Tierney, *Darrow*

The first requisite to happiness is to be born in a famous city.
                              —Euripides, *On Alcibiades*

On the whole I'd rather be in Philadelphia.
                              —W. C. Fields, epitaph
[See also Fields in INSULTS & PUT-DOWNS.]

If you are lucky enough to have lived in Paris as a young man,
then wherever you go for the rest of your life, it stays with you, for
Paris is a moveable feast.
              —Ernest Hemingway, *A Moveable Feast*, epigraph

Paris is well worth a mass.            —Henry IV, attributed

It couldn't have happened anywhere but in little old New York.
                              —O. Henry, *A Little Local Color*

O sweep of stars over Harlem streets,
O little breath of oblivion that is night.
A city building to a mother's song,
A city dreaming to a lullaby.
              —Langston Hughes, *Stars* in *From My People*

By seeing London, I have seen as much of life as the world can show. —SAMUEL JOHNSON, quoted by James Boswell, *Tour to the Hebrides*

Washington is a city of southern efficiency and northern charm. —JOHN F. KENNEDY, quoted in Arthur M. Schlesinger, Jr., *A Thousand Days*

Today's city is the most vulnerable social structure ever conceived by man. —MARTIN OPPENHEIMER, *Urban Guerilla*

Cities are the abyss of the human species. —JEAN JACQUES ROUSSEAU, *Émile*

Hog butcher for the world,
Tool maker, stacker of wheat,
Player with railroads and the nation's freight handler;
Stormy, husky, brawling,
City of the big shoulders. —CARL SANDBURG, *Chicago*

What is the city but the people? —SHAKESPEARE, *Coriolanus*, III, i

Hell is a city much like London—
A populous amd smoky city. —PERCY BYSSHE SHELLEY, *Peter Bell the Third*

The City is of night; perchance of death,
But certainly of night. —JAMES THOMSON, *The City of Dreadful Night*

## CIVIL SERVANTS                         See GOVERNMENT

## CIVILIZATION                      See also PROGRESS

The three great elements of modern civilization, Gunpowder, Printing, and the Protestant Religion. —THOMAS CARLYLE, *The State of German Literature*

Civilized men arrive in the Pacific, armed with alcohol, syphilis, trousers, and the Bible. —HAVELOCK ELLIS, *The Dance of Life*

We think our civilization near its meridian, but we are yet only at the cock-crowing and the morning star.
—RALPH WALDO EMERSON, *Politics*

What men call civilization
always results in deserts.    —DON MARQUIS, *archy and mehitabel*

Civilization is the progress toward a society of privacy.
—AYN RAND, *The Fountainhead*

You can't say civilization don't advance . . . in every war they kill you in a new way.
—WILL ROGERS, *The Autobiography of Will Rogers*

Civilization advances by extending the number of important operations which we can perform without thinking about them.
—ALFRED NORTH WHITEHEAD,
*An Introduction to Mathematics*

## CLEANLINESS

[Re not doing housework] After the first four years, the dirt doesn't get any worse.    —QUENTIN CRISP, *The Naked Civil Servant*

Cleanliness is indeed next to godliness.
—JOHN WESLEY, sermon 93

**CLERGY**                                        See GOD; RELIGION

**CLOTHES**                                  See FASHION & CLOTHES

**COLOR**                                       See ARTS: PAINTING

**COMEDY**                                             See HUMOR

**COMMUNICATION**                        See LANGUAGE; MEDIA

**COMMUNISM**                                  See also ECONOMICS;
REVOLUTION; SOCIALISM

That which is common to the greatest number has the least care bestowed upon it.                              —ARISTOTLE, *Politics*

From Stettin in the Baltic to Trieste in the Adriatic, an iron curtain has descended across the Continent.
—Winston Churchill, speech, March 5, 1946
[Churchill made the phrase famous. *Bartlett's*, however, notes several earlier uses, including one by Queen Elizabeth of Belgium in 1914, referring to Germany. *The Penguin Dictionary of Quotations* cites an article by St. Vincent Troubridge in 1945, stating, "There is an iron curtain across Europe." William Safire, in his dictionary of political terms, points out that the phrase has a theatrical origin, an iron curtain having been used in theaters since the 18th century to retard fires. He believes the metaphor was used in the political sense as early as 1819, and notes that Goebbels, in 1945, employed it with specific reference to Russia.]

What is a communist? One who hath yearnings
For equal division of unequal earnings.
—Ebenezer Elliott, *Epigram*

[Communism] has never come to power in a country that was not disrupted by war or internal corruption or both.
—John F. Kennedy, speech, July 3, 1963

We Communists are like seeds and the people are the soil. Wherever we go, we must unite with the people, take root and blossom among them. —Mao Tse-tung, *Quotations from Chairman Mao Tse-tung*, 1966

A specter is haunting Europe—the specter of Communism.
—Karl Marx, *Manifesto of the Communist Party*

From each according to his abilities, and to each according to his needs. —Karl Marx, *Critique of the Gotha Program*

Its [Communism's] unfortunate association with violence encourages a certain evil tendency in human beings.
—Jawaharlal Nehru, *Credo*

The economy of Communism is an economy which grows in an atmosphere of misery and want. —Eleanor Roosevelt, *My Day*, syndicated column, Feb. 12, 1947

Communism is the corruption of a dream of justice.
—Adlai Stevenson, speech, Urbana, Ill., 1951

## COMPARISONS

Comparisons are odious.
—John Fortescue, *De Laudibus Legum Angliae*
[*Bartlett* gives this as the earliest use, noting that the phrase was common in the 14th century; and it appears often hereafter. Shakespeare wrote "Comparisons are *odorous*"—italics added—*Much Ado About Nothing*, III, v.]

## CONFIDENCE
See BOLDNESS & INITIATIVE;
SELF-CONFIDENCE

## CONSCIENCE
See also ETHICS & MORALITY

Conscience is the perfect interpreter of life.
—Karl Barth, *The Word of God and the Word of Man*

I cannot and will not cut my conscience to suit this year's fashions.
—Lillian Hellman, letter to the chairman of the House Committee on Un-American Activities, May 19, 1952

Conscience is the inner voice that warns us somebody may be looking.     —H. L. Mencken, *A Mencken Chrestomathy*, 1949

## CONSISTENCY

Consistency requires you to be as ignorant today as you were a year ago.     —Bernard Berenson, *Notebook*, 1892

A foolish consistency is the hobgoblin of little minds, adored by little statesmen and philosophers and divines.
—Ralph Waldo Emerson, *Self-Reliance*

Do I contradict myself?
Very well then I contradict myself,
(I am large, I contain multitudes.)
—Walt Whitman, *Song of Myself* in *Leaves of Grass*

## CONVERSATION

"The time has come," the Walrus said,
"To talk of many things:
Of shoes—and ships—and sealing wax—
Of cabbages—and kings—
And why the sea is boiling hot—
And whether pigs have wings."
—LEWIS CARROLL, *Through the Looking-Glass*

In the room the women come and go
Talking of Michelangelo.
—T. S. ELIOT, *The Love Song of J. Alfred Prufrock*

If you can't say anything good about someone, sit right here by me.
—ALICE ROOSEVELT LONGWORTH, saying, quoted in
*The New York Times*, obituary

We do not talk—we bludgeon one another with facts and theories
gleaned from cursory readings of newspapers, magazines, and digests.
—HENRY MILLER, *The Shadows* in
*The Air-Condtiioned Nightmare*

The more the pleasures of the body fade away, the greater to me
is the pleasure and charm of conversation.   —PLATO, *The Republic*

Teas,
Where small talk dies in agonies.
—PERCY BYSSHE SHELLEY, *Peter Bell the Third*

I cannot hold with those who wish to put down the insignificant
chatter of the world.   —ANTHONY TROLLOPE, *Framley Parsonage*

## COUNTRY, ONE'S OWN                              See PATRIOTISM

## COUNTRY, THE                              See also NATURE

It is my belief Watson, founded upon my experience, that the
lowest and vilest alleys in London do not present a more dreadful
record of sin than does the smiling and beautiful countryside.
—A. CONAN DOYLE, *Adventure of the Copper Beeches*

When I am in the country I wish to vegetate like the country.
—WILLIAM HAZLITT, *On Going a Journey*

I have no relish for the country; it is a kind of healthy grave.
—SYDNEY SMITH, letter to Miss G. Harcourt, 1838

Anybody can be good in the country.
—OSCAR WILDE, *The Picture of Dorian Gray*

## COURAGE

See also BOLDNESS & INITIATIVE;
FEAR; HEROES

Often the test of courage is not to die but to live.
—VITTORIO ALFIERI, *Oreste*

Until the day of his death, no man can be sure of his courage.
—JEAN ANOUILH, *Becket*

Courage is almost a contradiction in terms. It means a strong desire
to live taking the form of a readiness to die.
—G. K. CHESTERTON, *Orthodoxy*

Tender-handed stroke a nettle,
And it stings you for your pains;
Grasp it like a man of mettle,
And it soft as silk remains.      —AARON HILL, *Verses Written on a
Window in Scotland*

Cowards die many times before their deaths;
The valiant never taste of death but once.
—SHAKESPEARE, *Julius Caesar*, II, ii

But screw your courage to the sticking place
And we'll not fail.      —SHAKESPEARE, *Macbeth*, I, vii

Courage is resistance to fear, mastery of fear—not absence of fear.
—MARK TWAIN, *Pudd'nhead Wilson*

## CRAFTINESS

See also DISHONESTY

To make a living, craftiness is better than learnedness.
—P. A. C. DE BEAUMARCHAIS, *The Marriage of Figaro*

Let not thy left hand know what thy right hand doeth.
—BIBLE, *Matthew* 6:3
[For the context, see CHARITY: PHILANTHROPY.]

Make to yourselves friends of the mammon of unrighteousness.
—BIBLE, *Luke* 16:9

Open not thine heart to every man, lest he requite thee with a shrewd turn.                    —BIBLE, *Ecclesiasticus* 8:19

Never fight fair with a stranger, boy. You'll never get out of the jungle that way.         —ARTHUR MILLER, *Death of a Salesman*

The fox knows many tricks, but the hedgehog's trick is the best of all.                         —PIGRES, attributed by Zenobius
[A different version of this, attributed to Archilochus, is given under WISDOM.]

I know a trick worth two of that.
—SHAKESPEARE, *Henry IV, Part I*, II, i

Friends, Romans, countrymen, lend me your ears;
I come to bury Caesar, not to praise him.
—SHAKESPEARE, *Julius Caesar*, III, ii

## CREATION, DIVINE                    See also NATURE; UNIVERSE

All things bright and beautiful,
All creatures great and small,
All things wise and wonderful,
The Lord God made them all.
—CECIL FRANCES ALEXANDER, hymn,
*All Things Bright and Beautiful*

In the beginning God created the heaven and the earth.
And the earth was without form, and void; and darkness was upon the face of the deep. And the spirit of God moved upon the face of the waters.
And God said, Let there be light: and there was light.
—BIBLE, *Genesis* 1:1–4

We made from water every living thing.                    —KORAN

Nothing can be created out of nothing.         —LUCRETIUS,
*De Rerum Natura*

**CRIME**                                          See also EVIDENCE; EVIL; GUILT;
                                                   PUNISHMENT; VIOLENCE & FORCE

Murder will out.                                   —ANONYMOUS (PROVERB)
[The idea has been expressed by many writers, including Chaucer
and Cervantes; and see Emerson, below.]

*Le mauvais goût mène au crime.*
Poor taste leads to crime.
                        —ANONYMOUS (FRENCH PROVERB), quoted by
                           A. Conan Doyle in *The Sign of Four*

And the Lord set a mark upon Cain.       —BIBLE, *Genesis* 4:15

These, having not the law, are a law unto themselves.
                                         —BIBLE, *Romans* 2:14

The soul of a murderer is blind.   —ALBERT CAMUS, *The Plague*

It's a wicked world, and when a clever man turns his brains to
crime, it is the worst of all.
            —A. CONAN DOYLE, *Adventure of the Speckled Band*

Any man might do a girl in
Any man has to, needs to wants to
Once in a lifetime, do a girl in.
                           —T. S. ELIOT, *Sweeney Agonistes*
[Dickens, in *Our Mutual Friend*, similarly commented on the uni-
versality of homicidal feelings: "If a murder, anybody might have
done it. Burglary or pocket-picking wanted 'prenticeship. Not so
murder. We were all of us up to that."]

Character is always known. Thefts never enrich; alms never im-
poverish; murder will speak out of stone walls.
                        —RALPH WALDO EMERSON, commencement
                           address, Harvard Divinity School, 1838

*Cherchez la femme.*
Find the woman.                    —JOSEPH FOUCHÉ, attributed
[Also used by Alexandre Dumas, in *The Mohicans of Paris*, one of
the first collections of detective stories: "There is a woman in every
case; as soon as they bring me a report, I say, 'Look for the
woman.'" Fouché, by the way, was Napoleon's feared minister of
justice.]

I've got a little list—I've got a little list.
Of society offenders who might well be underground,
And who never would be missed—who never would be missed.
—W. S. GILBERT, *The Mikado*

The policeman's lot is not a happy one.
—W. S. GILBERT, *Pirates of Penzance*

It was beautiful and simple, as all truly great swindles are.
—O. HENRY, *The Octopus Marooned*, in
*The Gentle Grafter*

Crime, like virtue, has its degrees. —RACINE, *Phèdre*

Successful and fortunate crime is called virtue.
—SENECA, *Hercules Furens*

Murder most foul, as in the best it is,
But this most foul, strange, and unnatural.
—SHAKESPEARE, *Hamlet*, I, v

Yet who would have thought the old man to have had so much
blood in him? —SHAKESPEARE, *Macbeth*, V, i

The robbed that smiles steals something from the thief.
—SHAKESPEARE, *Othello*, I, iii

He who bears the brand of Cain shall rule the earth.
—GEORGE BERNARD SHAW, *Back to Methuselah*

People of the same trade seldom meet together, even for merri-
ment and diversion, but the conversation ends in a conspiracy against
the public, or in some contrivance to raise prices.
—ADAM SMITH, *Wealth of Nations*

The rich rob the poor and the poor rob one another.
—SOJOURNER TRUTH, saying

Yet each man kills the thing he loves
.... The coward does it with a kiss,
The brave man with a sword.
—OSCAR WILDE, *The Ballad of Reading Gaol*

**CRISIS**

See MIDDLE AGE & MID-LIFE
CRISIS; RUIN; TROUBLE;
TURBULENT TIMES

**CRITICISM**                    See ADVICE; ARTS: CRITICISM & CRITICS

**CULTURE**                        See ARTS entries; CIVILIZATION

**CUSTOM**                                  See also HABIT

Custom reconciles us to everything.
            —EDMUND BURKE, *On the Sublime and Beautiful*

Custom, then, is the great guide of human life.
            —DAVID HUME, *An Enquiry Concerning
            Human Understanding*

Custom is king over all.                    —PINDAR, fragment

It is a custom
More honored in the breach than the observance
            —SHAKESPEARE, *Hamlet*, I, iv

**DANCE**                          See ARTS: MUSIC & DANCE

**DANGER**                        See also RUIN; TROUBLE;
                                  TURBULENT TIMES

Dangers by being despised grow great.
            —EDMUND BURKE, speech on the Petition
            of the Unitarians, 1792

'Twas brillig, and the slithy toves
Did gyre and gimble in the wabe;
All mimsy were the borogoves,
And the mome raths outgrabe.
Beware the Jabberwock, my son!
The jaws that bite, the claws that catch!
Beware the Jubjub bird, and shun
The frumious Bandersnatch!   —LEWIS CARROLL, *Jabberwocky* in
                              *Through the Looking-Glass*

Nothing in life is so exhilarating as to be shot at without result.
            —WINSTON CHURCHILL,
                *The Story of the Malakand Field Force*
[Often misquoted as: ". . . shot at and missed." Ronald Reagan, in
1981, after being wounded in an assassination attempt, offered a close

variant on Churchill's observation: "There is no more exhilarating feeling than being shot at without result."]

To vanquish without danger is to triumph without glory.
—PIERRE CORNEILLE, *Le Cid*

Wisdom consists in being able to distinguish among dangers and make a choice of the least harmful.  —MACHIAVELLI, *The Prince*

Beware the ides of March  —SHAKESPEARE, *Julius Caesar*, I, ii

Yond Cassius has a lean and hungry look;
He thinks too much: such men are dangerous.  —*Ibid.*

A snake lurks in the grass.  —VIRGIL, *Eclogues*

**DAY**  See NATURE: TIMES OF DAY

**DEATH**  See also SUICIDE

O death, where is thy sting? O grave, where is thy victory?
—BIBLE, *I Corinthians* 15:55

And I looked, and behold a pale horse: and his name that sat on him was Death.  —BIBLE, *Revelation* 6:8

Because I could not stop for Death—
He kindly stopped for me—
The Carriage held but just Ourselves—
And Immortality.
—EMILY DICKINSON, *Because I could not stop for Death*

Death be not proud, though some have called thee
Mighty and dreadful, for, thou art not so,
For, those, whom thou think'st thou dost overthrow,
Die not, poor death, nor yet can'st thou kill me.
—JOHN DONNE, *Death be not proud*

It hath often been said that it is not death but dying that is terrible.
—HENRY FIELDING, *Amelia*

Let us pass over the river and rest under the shade of the trees.
—STONEWALL JACKSON, dying words, May 10, 1863
[He had been inadvertently shot by his own men.]

Depend upon it, Sir, when a man knows he is to be hanged in a fortnight, it concentrates his mind wonderfully.
—SAMUEL JOHNSON, Boswell's *Life of Johnson*,
            Sept. 19, 1777

The only religious way to think of death is as part and parcel of life.                      —THOMAS MANN, *The Magic Mountain*

Whom the gods love dies young.
                      —MENANDER, *The Double Deceiver*
[Expressed by many other writers, including Wordsworth, see below.]

It costs me never a stab not squirm
To tread by chance upon a worm.
"Aha, my little dear," I say,
"Your clan will pay me back one day."
            —DOROTHY PARKER, *Thoughts for a Sunshiny Morning*

He hath joined the great majority.        —PETRONIUS, *Satyricon*

Dying
Is an art, like everything else.        —SYLVIA PLATH, *Lady Lazarus*

*Je vais quérir un grand peut-être. . . . Tirez le rideau, la farce est jouée.* I am going to seek a great perhaps. . . . Pull down the curtain, the farce is ended.        —RABELAIS, by tradition, his last words
[Note similar last words in Leoncavallo, *I Pagliacci*, "*La commedia è finita*"—"The comedy is ended."]

So little done, so much to do.    —CECIL RHODES, dying words, 1902

When I am dead, my dearest,
Sing no sad songs for me.        —CHRISTINA G. ROSSETTI, *Song*

Death is an evil; the gods have so judged; had it been good, they would die.                      —SAPPHO, fragment

There is no death. Only a change of worlds.
            —SEATTLE, quoted in Joseph Epes Brown,
                *The Spiritual Legacy of the American Indian*

I have a rendezvous with Death
At some disputed barricade.
            —ALAN SEEGER, *I Have a Rendezvous with Death*

All that live must die,
Passing through nature to eternity.   —SHAKESPEARE, *Hamlet*, I, ii

Alas! poor Yorick. I knew him, Horatio.               —*Ibid.*, V, i

A man can die but once. We owe God a death.
                              —SHAKESPEARE, *Henry IV*, *Part II*, III, ii

Men must endure
Their going hence even as their coming hither.
                                        —SHAKESPEARE, *King Lear*, V, ii

Nothing in his life
Became him like the leaving it.   —SHAKESPEARE, *Macbeth*, I, iv

How oft when men are at the point of death
Have they been merry!   —SHAKESPEARE, *Romeo and Juliet*, V, iii

Death is the veil which those who live call life:
They sleep, and it is lifted.
                      —PERCY BYSSHE SHELLEY, *Prometheus Unbound*

A single death is a tragedy, a million deaths is a statistic.
                                        —JOSEPH STALIN, attributed
[George Seldes in *The Great Quotations* is the only collector we
know to offer a citation for this—Anne Fremantle, *The New York
Times Book Review*, Sept. 28, 1958.]

Here he lies where he longs to be;
Home is the sailor, home from the sea,
And the hunter home from the hill.
                —ROBERT LOUIS STEVENSON, *Requiem*, in *Underwoods*

Sunset and evening star,
And one clear call for me!
And may there be no moaning of the bar,
When I put out to sea.
                      —ALFRED, LORD TENNYSON, *Crossing the Bar*

He seems so near and yet so far.
                      —ALFRED, LORD TENNYSON, *In Memoriam*

And a day less or more
At sea or shore,
We die—does it matter when?
                      —ALFRED, LORD TENNYSON, *The Revenge*

Man comes and tills the field and lies beneath,
And after many a summer dies the swan.
                    —ALFRED, LORD TENNYSON, *Tithonus*

Do not go gentle into that good night,
Old age should burn and rave at close of day;
Rage, rage against the dying of the light.
                    —DYLAN THOMAS,
                        *Do Not Go Gentle into That Good Night*

Death is not an event in life; we do not experience death.
        —LUDWIG WITTGENSTEIN, *Tractatus logico-philosophicus*
[Diderot, in *Le Neveu de Rameau*, said it thus: "The dead do not
hear the bells tolling."]

The good die first,
And they whose hearts are dry as summer dust
Burn to the socket     —WILLIAM WORDSWORTH, *The Excursion*

**DECEPTION**                    See CRAFTINESS; DISHONESTY

**DEEDS**                        See DOING

**DEFEAT**              See WINNING & LOSING, VICTORY & DEFEAT

**DELAY**                        See PROCRASTINATION

**DEMOCRACY**                    See also AMERICA & AMERICANS;
                    AMERICAN HISTORY: MEMORABLE MOMENTS;
                    EQUALITY; FREEDOM; PEOPLE, THE; RIGHTS

Democracy is the worst form of government except all those other
forms that have been tried from time to time.
                    —WINSTON CHURCHILL, speech,
                    House of Commons, Nov. 1947

The ballot is stronger than the bullet.
                    —ABRAHAM LINCOLN, speech, May 19, 1856

Under democracy, one party always devotes its chief efforts to
trying to prove that the other is unfit to rule—and both commonly
succeed and are right.
                    —H. L. MENCKEN, *Minority Report: Mencken's Notebooks*

The blind lead the blind. It's the democratic way.
—HENRY MILLER, *With Edgard Varèse in the Gobi Desert,*
in *The Air-Conditioned Nightmare*

Democracy and socialism are means to an end, not the end itself.
—JAWAHARLAL NEHRU, *Credo*

Democracy passes into despotism.      —PLATO, *The Republic*

Democracy substitutes election by the incompetent many for ap-
pointment by the corrupt few.
—GEORGE BERNARD SHAW, *Man and Superman*

**DEPRESSION**                         See DESPAIR, DEPRESSION, MISERY

**DEPRESSION, ECONOMIC**                          See ECONOMICS

**DESPAIR, DEPRESSION, MISERY**      See also SUICIDE;
                                                    TROUBLE

My days are swifter than a weaver's shuttle, and are spent without
hope.                                        —BIBLE, *Job* 5:7

My God, my God, why hast thou forsaken me?
—BIBLE, *Psalms* 22:1; *Matthew* 27:46; *Mark* 15:34

Vanity of vanities, saith the preacher, vanity of vanities: all is
vanity.                                 —BIBLE, *Ecclesiastes* 1:2

In the real dark night of the soul it is always three o'clock in the
morning.
—F. SCOTT FITZGERALD, *The Hours,* in *The Crack-Up*
[The allusion is to St. John of the Cross; see under MYSTICISM.]

Here lies one whose name was writ in water.
—JOHN KEATS, epitaph for himself

*La chair est triste, hélas! et j'ai lu tous les livres.*
The flesh is sad, alas, and I've read all the books.
—STÉPHANE MALLARMÉ, *Brise Marine*

O! what a rogue and peasant slave am I.
—SHAKESPEARE, *Hamlet*, II, ii

Tomorrow, and tomorrow, and tomorrow,
Creeps in this petty pace from day to day,
To the last syllable of recorded time.
—SHAKESPEARE, *Macbeth*, V, v

I was much further out than you thought
And not waving but drowning.
—STEVIE SMITH, *Not Waving But Drowning*

**DESPOTS**                              See TYRANNY & TOTALITARIANISM

**DESTINY**                                              See FATE

**DETAILS & OTHER SMALL THINGS**

He that contemneth small things shall fall by little and little.
—BIBLE, *Ecclesiasticus* 19:1

Little drops of water,
Little grains of sand,
Make the mighty ocean
And the pleasant land.

So the little minutes,
Humble though they be,
Make the mighty ages
Of eternity.

. . .
Little deeds of kindness,
Little words of love,
Help to make earth happy
Like the heaven above.          —JULIA CARNEY, *Little Things*

Little things affect little minds.          —BENJAMIN DISRAELI, *Sybil*

I neglect God and his Angels for the noise of a fly, for the rattling
of a coach, for the whining of a door.
—JOHN DONNE, sermon, Dec. 12, 1626

It has long been an axiom of mine that the little things are infinitely
the most important.          —A. CONAN DOYLE, *A Case of Identity*

Large streams from little fountains flow,
Tall oaks from little acorns grow.
        —DAVID EVERETT, *Lines written for a school declamation*
[Drawn from proverbial comment on acorns and oaks.]

A little neglect may breed great mischief . . . for the want of a
nail the shoe was lost; for the want of a shoe the horse was lost; and
for the want of a horse the rider was lost.
        —BENJAMIN FRANKLIN, *Poor Richard's Almanac*

Men who love wisdom should acquaint themselves with a great
many particulars.        —HERACLITUS, fragment

Small is beautiful.        —E. F. SCHUMACHER, book title

Our life is frittered away by detail. . . . Simplify, simplify.
        —THOREAU, *Walden*

# DEVIL

How art thou fallen from heaven, O Lucifer, son of the morning!
        —BIBLE, *Isaiah* 14:12

An apology for the Devil: It must be remembered that we have
only heard one side of the case. God has written all the books.
        —SAMUEL BUTLER, *Higgledy-Piggledy*, in *Notebooks*

Wherever God erects a house of prayer,
The Devil always builds a chapel there,
And 'twill be found upon examination,
The latter has the largest congregation.
        —DANIEL DEFOE, *The True-Born Englishman*

The prince of darkness is a gentleman.
        —SHAKESPEARE, *King Lear*, III, iv
[Also, Shelley, "Sometimes/The Devil is a gentleman,"
        —*Peter Bell the Third*.]

# DICTATORS         See TYRANNY & TOTALITARIANISM

## DIPLOMACY

All diplomacy is a continuation of war by other means.
—CHOU EN-LAI, quoted by Edgar Snow,
*Saturday Evening Post*, March 27, 1954
[The unstated reference is to von Clausewitz's famous observation on war and diplomacy; see under WAR.]

Diplomacy is to do and say
The nastiest thing in the nicest way.                    —ISAAC GOLDBERG,
*The Reflex*

Let us never negotiate out of fear, but let us never fear to negotiate.                    —JOHN F. KENNEDY, Inaugural Address, 1961

An ambassador is an honest man sent to lie abroad for the good of
his country.         —SIR HENRY WOTTON, *Reliquiae Wottonianae*

## DISCOVERY                                        See SCIENCE: DISCOVERY

## DISHONESTY                         See also CRAFTINESS; CRIME; HYPOCRISY

Unless a man feels he has a good enough memory, he should never
venture to lie.                                    —MONTAIGNE, *Essays*

White lies always introduce others of a darker complexion.
—WILLIAM PALEY, *The Principles of Moral
and Political Philosophy*

O, what a tangled web we weave,
When first we practise to deceive!                    —SIR WALTER SCOTT,
*Marmion*

A lie is an abomination unto the Lord and a very present help in
trouble.       —ADLAI STEVENSON, speech, Springfield, Ill., Jan. 1951;
probably not original with him

Don't lie if you don't have to.                    —LEO SZILARD, *Science*,
no. 176, 1972

## DOCTORS & THE PRACTICE                    See also ILLNESS &
## OF MEDICINE                                    REMEDIES; SCIENCE:
PSYCHOLOGY & PSYCHOANALYSIS

Physician, heal thyself.
[Identified as a proverb.]                    —BIBLE, *Luke* 4:23

Honour a physician with the honour due unto him for the uses which you may have of him: for the Lord hath created him.
—BIBLE, *Ecclesiasticus* 38:1

The most high hath created medicines out of the earth, and a wise man will not abhor them. —*Ibid.*, 38:4

Every physician almost hath his favorite disease
—HENRY FIELDING, *Tom Jones*

God heals and the doctor takes the fees.
—BENJAMIN FRANKLIN, *Poor Richard's Almanac*

Wherever the art of medicine is loved, there also is love of humanity. —HIPPOCRATES, *Aphorisms*

I often say a great doctor kills more people than a great general.
—G. W. LEIBNIZ, attributed

I hate doctors! They'll do anything—anything to keep you coming to them. They'll sell their souls! What's worse, they'll sell yours, and you never know it till one day you find yourself in hell!
—EUGENE O'NEILL, *Long Day's Journey Into Night*

Who shall decide when doctors disagree?
—ALEXANDER POPE, *Of the Use of Riches*

Cured yesterday of my disease,
I died last night of the physician.
—MATTHEW PRIOR, *The Remedy Worse than the Disease*

**DOGS**                                                    See NATURE: ANIMALS

**DOING**                                                    See also ACCOMPLISHMENT;
PERSEVERANCE & ENDURANCE;
VIRTUE; WORK

We become just by performing just actions, temperate by performing temperate actions, brave by performing brave actions.
—ARISTOTLE, *Nicomachean Ethics*

Whatsoever thy hand findeth to do, do it with thy might; for there is no work, nor device, nor knowledge, nor wisdom, in the grave, whither thou goest. —BIBLE, *Ecclesiastes* 9:10

It is better to light one candle than to curse the darkness.
—CHRISTOPHER SOCIETY, motto
[At VIRTUE, see Adlai Stevenson for his use of this idea with reference to Eleanor Roosevelt.]

Our deeds determine us, as much as we determine our deeds.
—GEORGE ELIOT, *Adam Bede*

Do noble things, do not dream them all day long.
—CHARLES KINGSLEY, *A Farewell*
[More of this at VIRTUE.]

Men are all alike in their promises. It is only in their deeds that they differ.   —MOLIÈRE, *The Miser*

Saying is one thing and doing is another.   —MONTAIGNE, *Essays*

Our nature lies in movement; complete rest is death.
—PASCAL, *Pensées*

No one knows what he can do till he tries.
—PUBLILIUS SYRUS, *Moral Sayings*

One must learn by doing the thing; though you think you know it, you have no certainty until you try.   —SOPHOCLES, *Trachiniae*
[Aristotle expressed the same idea in the *Nicomachean Ethics*, and the phrase became proverbial in the form "learn by doing."]

**DOUBT**                                    See SKEPTICISM

**DRAMA**                          See ARTS: DRAMA & ACTING

**DREAMERS & DREAMS**                    See AMBITION;
SCIENCE: PSYCHOLOGY &
PSYCHOANALYSIS; SLEEP & DREAMS;
VISION & VISIONARIES

**DRINKING**                        See ALCOHOL & DRINKING;
FOOD, WINE, & EATING

**EARTH**                   See CREATION, DIVINE; ENVIRONMENT;
NATURE; SCIENCE

**EAST, THE**                              See ORIENT, THE

**EATING**                    See FOOD, WINE, & EATING

**ECONOMICS**                 See also BUSINESS; CAPITALISM;
                              COMMUNISM; MONEY;
                              SOCIALISM; TAXES

There's no such thing as a free lunch.
[Most often associated with Milton Friedman.]    —ANONYMOUS

Recession is when your neighbor loses his job; depression is when
you lose yours.
[Sometimes attributed to Harry S. Truman.]       —ANONYMOUS

What we might call, by way of eminence, the Dismal Science.
                    —THOMAS CARLYLE, *On the Negro Question*

Political institutions are a superstructure resting on an economic
foundation.            —V. I. LENIN, *The Three Sources and*
                              *Three Constituent Parts of Marxism*

We have heard it said that five percent is the natural interest of
money.                    —THOMAS BABINGTON MACAULAY,
                              *Southey's Colloquies on Society*

He is well paid that is well satisfied.
                    —SHAKESPEARE, *The Merchant of Venice*

The truth is we are all caught in a great economic system which is
heartless.            —WOODROW WILSON, *The New Freedom*

**EDUCATION & LEARNING**

They know enough who know how to learn.
                    —HENRY BROOKS ADAMS,
                              *The Education of Henry Adams*

Learn by doing.                    —ANONYMOUS (PROVERB)
[Associated with the educational views of John Dewey; see also
Sophocles at DOING.]

Knowledge itself is power.        —FRANCIS BACON, *Of Heresies*

What I want is Facts. Teach these boys and girls nothing but
Facts. Facts alone are wanted in life. Plant nothing else, and root
out everything else.        —CHARLES DICKENS, *Hard Times*

The foundation of every state is the education of its youth.
—Diogenes ("the cynic"), quoted in
Diogenes Laërtius, *Lives of Eminent Philosophers*

Only the educated are free.                —Epictetus, *Discourses*

*Education, c'est délivrance.*
Education is freedom.                —André Gide, *Journal*

I find that the three major administrative problems on a campus are sex for the students, athletics for the alumni, and parking for the faculty.    —Clark Kerr, speech as the University of Washington, reported in *Time*, Nov. 17, 1958

If by being overstudious, we impair our health and spoil our good humor, let us give it up.                —Montaigne, *Essays*

The direction in which education starts a man will determine his future life.                —Plato, *The Republic*

A little learning is a dangerous thing.
—Alexander Pope, *An Essay on Criticism*

'Tis education forms the common mind,
Just as the twig is bent, the tree's inclined.
—Alexander Pope, *Moral Essays*, Epistle I

In an examination those who do not wish to know ask questions of those who cannot tell.
—Sir Walter A. Raleigh, *Some Thoughts on Examinations*

He who can, does. He who cannot, teaches.
—George Bernard Shaw, *Man and Superman*

Education is what survives when what has been learnt has been forgotten.                —B. F. Skinner, *Education in 1984*

Education has for its object the formation of character.
—Herbert Spencer, *Social Statics*

Education . . . has produced a vast population able to read but unable to distinguish what is worth reading.
—G. M. Trevelyan, *English Social History*

Training is everything. The peach was once a bitter almond; cauliflower is nothing but a cabbage with a college education.
—MARK TWAIN, *Pudd'nhead Wilson*

Soap and education are not as sudden as a massacre, but they are more deadly in the long run.
—MARK TWAIN, *The Facts Concerning the Recent Resignation* in *Sketches New and Old*

The founding fathers in their wisdom decided that children were an unnatural strain on parents. So they provided jails called schools, equipped with torture called education. School is where you go between when your parents can't take you and industry can't take you.
—JOHN UPDIKE, *The Centaur*

**EFFORT**                    See PERSEVERANCE & ENDURANCE

**ELITE**                           See also GENIUS; GREATNESS;
                          HIGH POSITION: RULERS & LEADERS

The difficult we do immediately. The impossible takes a little longer.
—U. S. ARMY CORPS OF ENGINEERS, slogan

For many are called, but few are chosen.  —BIBLE, *Matthew* 22:14

What is aristocracy? A corporation of the best, of the bravest.
—THOMAS CARLYLE, *Chartism*
[The similar phrase, "the best and the brightest," used as a book title by David Halberstam in 1969, comes from a hymn by Bishop Reginald Heber:
Brightest and best of the sons of the morning,
Dawn on our darkness, and lend us Thine aid!]

The minority is always right.        —HENRIK IBSEN,
                                *An Enemy of the People*

I don't want to belong to any club that would accept me as a member.                    —GROUCHO MARX, attributed

We few, we happy few, we band of brothers.
—SHAKESPEARE, *Henry V*, IV, iii

To consider oneself different from ordinary men is wrong, but it is right to hope that one will not remain like ordinary men.
—YOSHIDA SHOIN, *Yoshida Shoin Zenshu*

**EMOTIONS**                    See ANGER; GUILT; HAPPINESS;
                                 HATE; HEART; LOVE

**ENDINGS**                     See ACCOMPLISHMENT;
                                 BEGINNINGS

**ENDURANCE**                   See PERSEVERANCE; SURVIVAL

**ENEMIES**

Love your enemies.                         —BIBLE, *Matthew* 5:44

You shall judge of a man by his foes as well as by friends.
                          —JOSEPH CONRAD, *Lord Jim*

The art of leadership . . . consists in consolidating the attention of
the people against a single adversary and taking care that nothing
will split up that attention.      —ADOLF HITLER, *Mein Kampf*

He makes no friend who never made a foe.
              —ALFRED, LORD TENNYSON, *Lancelot and Elaine*, in
                  *Idylls of the King*

A man cannot be too careful in the choice of his enemies.
                  —OSCAR WILDE, *The Picture of Dorian Gray*

**ENERGY**                      See ENTHUSIASM, ENERGY, ZEAL

**ENGLAND**                     See also CITIES; NATIONS

If I should die, think only this of me:
That there's some corner of a foreign field
That is forever England.
                          —RUPERT BROOKE, *The Soldier*

Oh, to be in England now that April's there.
              —ROBERT BROWNING, *Home Thoughts, from Abroad*

I have nothing to offer but blood, toil, tears, and sweat.
              —WINSTON CHURCHILL, speech, May 13, 1940

We shall go on to the end . . . we shall defend our island, whatever the cost may be, we shall fight on the beaches, we shall fight on the landing grounds, we shall fight in the fields and in the streets, we shall fight in the hills; we shall never surrender.
—WINSTON CHURCHILL, speech, June 4, 1940
[See also Churchill on victory at WINNING & LOSING, VICTORY & DEFEAT.]

This was their finest hour.
—WINSTON CHURCHILL, speech, June 18, 1940

Never in the field of human conflict was so much owed by so many to so few.   —WINSTON CHURCHILL, speech, Aug. 20, 1940
[He was speaking of the Royal Air Force.]

England is the paradise of women, the purgatory of men, and the hell of horses.   —JOHN FLORIO, *Second Frutes*

The stately homes of England!
How beautiful they stand.
—FELICIA HEMANS, *The Homes of England*
[For a different perspective, see Virginia Woolf below.]

England is a nation of shopkeepers.
—NAPOLEON BONAPARTE, attributed, B. E. O'Meara,
*Napoleon at St. Helena*
[This is the usual attribution, but the phrase had been around for a while; *Bartlett* quotes a tract by Josiah Tucker dated 1763.]

There'll always be an England.
—ROSS PARKER & HUGHIE CHARLES, poem title

Once more into the breach, dear friends, once more,
Or close the wall up with our English dead!
—SHAKESPEARE, *Henry V*, III, i

The game's afoot.
Follow your spirit, and upon this charge
Cry "God for Harry, England, and Saint George!"   —*Ibid.*

This England never did, nor never shall,
Lie at the proud foot of a conqueror.
—SHAKESPEARE, *King John*, V, vii

This royal throne of kings, this sceptered isle,

. . .

This happy breed of men, this little world
This precious stone set in the silver sea,

. . .

This blessed plot, this earth, this realm, this England.
—SHAKESPEARE, *Richard II*, II, i


An Englishman thinks he is moral when he is only uncomfortable.
—GEORGE BERNARD SHAW, *Man and Superman*


The English take their pleasures sadly after the fashion of their country.
—DUC DE SULLY, *Memoirs*


Those comfortably padded lunatic asylums which are known, euphemistically, as the stately homes of England.
—VIRGINIA WOOLF, *Lady Dorothy Nevill*, in
*The Common Reader*


## ENTHUSIASM, ENERGY, ZEAL

Energy is eternal delight.
—WILLIAM BLAKE, *The Marriage of Heaven and Hell*


Only passions, great passions, can elevate the soul to great things.
—DENIS DIDEROT, *Discours sur la poésie dramatique*


Nothing great was ever achieved without enthusiasm.
—RALPH WALDO EMERSON, *Circles*


Nothing great in the world has been accomplished without passion.
—HEGEL, *Philosophy of History*


Fanaticism consists in redoubling your efforts when you have forgotten your aim.
—GEORGE SANTAYANA, *The Life of Reason*


*Pas trop de zèle.*
Not too much enthusiasm.
—CHARLES-MAURICE DE TALLEYRAND, attributed by
several writers, including C. A. Saint-Beuve,
*Portrait des Femmes*

# ENVIRONMENT                        See also NATURE

We are the children of our landscape.
> —LAWRENCE DURRELL, *Justine*

I am a passenger on the spaceship Earth.
> —R. BUCKMINSTER FULLER, *Operating Manual
> for Spaceship Earth*

What would the world be once bereft
Of wet and wildness? Let them be left,
O let them be left, wildness and wet;
Long live the weeds and the wilderness yet.
> —GERARD MANLEY HOPKINS, *Inversnaid*

The earth is given as common stock for man to labor and live on.
> —THOMAS JEFFERSON, letter to James Madison, 1785

The supreme reality of our time is . . . the vulnerability of our planet.
> —JOHN F. KENNEDY, speech, June 28, 1963

Conservation is a state of harmony between men and land.
> —ALDO LEOPOLD, *A Sand County Almanac*

Pity the Meek, for they shall inherit the earth.
> —DON MARQUIS, quoted in Frederick B. Wilcox,
> *A Little Book of Aphorisms*

The nation that destroys its soil destroys itself.
> —FRANKLIN D. ROOSEVELT, letter to
> state governors, Feb. 26, 1937

We have forgotten how to be good guests, how to walk lightly on the earth as its other creatures do.
> —STOCKHOLM CONFERENCE, *Only One Earth*, 1972

In wildness is the preservation of the world.        —THOREAU,
> *Walking*

# EQUALITY

When Adam delved and Eve span,
Who was then a gentleman?
> —JOHN BALL, sermon at Blackheath in
> Wat Tyler's Rebellion, 1381

[From an earlier poem—by Richard Rolle, according to *The Penguin Dictionary of Quotations.*]

Have we not all one father? hath not one God created us?
　　　　　　　　　　　　　　　　　—BIBLE, *Malachi* 2:10

A man's a man for a'that!　　　　　—ROBERT BURNS, poem title

There is no king who has not had a slave among his ancestors, and no slave who has not had a king among his.
　　　　　　　　　—HELEN KELLER, *The Story of My Life*

The boundaries of democracy have to be widened so as to include economic equality also. This is the great revolution through which we are all passing.　　　　　　　—JAWAHARLAL NEHRU,
　　　　　　　　　　　　　　　*Glimpses of World History*

All animals are equal, but some animals are more equal than others.
　　　　　　　　　　　　　—GEORGE ORWELL, *Animal Farm*

**ERAS**　　　　　　　　　　　See FUTURE; GENERATIONS;
　　　　　　　　　　　　　MODERN TIMES; PAST; PRESENT;
　　　　　　　　　　　　　　　　TURBULENT TIMES

**ERROR**　　　　　　　　　See FAILINGS; MISTAKES

**ESCAPE**　　　　　　　　　　See also TRAVEL

Oh that I had wings like a dove! for then I would fly away, and be at rest.　　　　　　　　　　—BIBLE, *Psalms* 55:6

listen: there's a hell
of a good universe next door: let's go.
　　　　　　　　　　　—E. E. CUMMINGS, *Times One*

O! for a horse with wings!　　—SHAKESPEARE, *Cymbeline*, III, iii

Let us rise up and part; she will not know.
Let us go seaward as the great winds go,
Full of blown sand and foam.
　　　　　　—ALGERNON CHARLES SWINBURNE, *A Leave-taking*

I will arise and go now, and go to Innisfree,
And a small cabin build there, of clay and wattles made:
Nine bean-rows will I have there, a hive for the honeybee,
And live alone in the bee-loud glade.
—WILLIAM BUTLER YEATS, *The Lake Isle of Innisfree*

**ESTHETICS** See ARTS: AESTHETICS

**ETHICS & MORALITY** See also CONSCIENCE;
EVIL; VIRTUE

It is easier to fight for one's principles than to live up to them.
—ALFRED ADLER, quoted in P. Bottome, *Alfred Adler*

No morality can be founded on authority, even if the authority
were divine. —A. J. AYER, *Essay on Humanism*

Expedients are for the hour, but principles are for the ages.
—HENRY WARD BEECHER, *Proverbs from Plymouth Pulpit*

The greatest happiness of the greatest number is the foundation of
morals and legislation. —JEREMY BENTHAM,
*The Commonplace Book*

No actions are bad in themselves—even murder can be justified.
—DIETRICH BONHOEFFER, *No Rusty Swords*

The world has achieved brilliance without conscience. Ours is a
world of nuclear giants and ethical infants.
—OMAR BRADLEY, speech, Armistice Day, 1948

It doesn't matter what you do, as long as you don't do it in public
and frighten the horses.
—MRS. PATRICK CAMPBELL, traditional attribution

"Do the duty which lies nearest thee," which thou knowest to be a
duty! Thy second duty will already have become clearer.
—THOMAS CARLYLE, *Sartor Resartus*

The number of people in possession of any criteria for discriminating between good and evil is very small.
—T. S. ELIOT, Virginia lectures, 1933

Rise above principle and do what's right.
> —WALTER HELLER,
> speech to Congress, May 7, 1985

I know only that what is moral is what you feel good after and what is immoral is what you feel bad after.
> —ERNEST HEMINGWAY, *Death in the Afternoon*

If he does really think that there is no distinction between virtue and vice, why, Sir, when he leaves our houses, let us count our spoons. —SAMUEL JOHNSON, James Boswell's *Life of Johnson*, July 14, 1763
[The quote refers to James Macpherson, the Scotsman who wrote *The Poems of Ossian* and tried to pass it off as a translation of ancient Gaelic poetry. For another occasion on which to count spoons, see Emerson under SELF-RIGHTEOUSNESS.]

Morality is not properly the doctrine of how we may make ourselves happy, but how we may make ourselves worthy of happiness.
> —IMMANUEL KANT, *Critique of Practical Reason*

Act only on that maxim which you can at the same time wish that it should become a universal law [definition of the categorical imperative]. —IMMANUEL KANT, *Foundations of the Metaphysics of Morals*

Morality is the herd instinct in the individual.
> —FRIEDRICH NIETZSCHE, *Die fröhliche Wissenschaft*

My country is the world, and my religion is to do good.
> —THOMAS PAINE, *The Rights of Man*

The end must justify the means.   —MATTHEW PRIOR, *Hans Carvel*

As soon as one is unhappy, one becomes moral.
> —PROUST, *Remembrance of Things Past: Within a Budding Grove*

Ethical metaphysics is fundamentally an attempt, however disguised, to give legislative force to our own wishes.
> —BERTRAND RUSSELL, *On Scientific Method in Philosophy* in *Mysticism and Logic*

No one can be perfectly free till all are free; no one can be perfectly moral till all are moral; no one can be perfectly happy till all are happy.   —HERBERT SPENCER, *Social Statics*

One impulse from a vernal wood
May teach you more of man,
Of moral evil and of good,
Than all the sages can.
—WILLIAM WORDSWORTH, *The Tables Turned*

**EVENING**                          See NATURE: TIMES OF DAY

**EVIDENCE**                          See also GUILT

You should not decide until you have heard what both have to say.
—ARISTOPHANES, *The Wasps*

Hear the other side.      —ST. AUGUSTINE, *De Duabus Animabus*

By their fruits you shall know them.      —BIBLE, *Matthew* 7:20

Out of thine own mouth will I judge thee.      —BIBLE, *Luke* 19:22

"Is there any point to which you would wish to draw my attention?"
"To the curious incident of the dog in the night-time."
"The dog did nothing in the night-time."
"That was the curious incident," remarked Sherlock Holmes.
—A. CONAN DOYLE, *Silver Blaze*

If it walks like a duck, and quacks like a duck, then it just may be
a duck.      —WALTER REUTHER, attributed, William Safire,
*Political Dictionary*

The most savage controversies are about those matters as to which
there is no good evidence either way.
—BERTRAND RUSSELL, *An Outline of*
*Intellectual Rubbish* in *Unpopular Essays*

Things seen are mightier than things heard.
—ALFRED, LORD TENNYSON, *Enoch Arden*
[The notion can be traced as far back as Herodotus: "We are less
convinced by what we hear than by what we see."]

Some circumstantial evidence is very strong, as when you find a
trout in the milk.      —THOREAU, *Miscellanies*

**EVIL**
See also CRIME; ETHICS & MORALITY;
HELL; SIN, VICE & NAUGHTINESS;
TEMPTATION; TROUBLE;
VIOLENCE & FORCE

Evil is unspectacular and always human
And shares our bed and eats at our own table.
—W. H. AUDEN, *Herman Melville*

I had rather be a doorkeeper in the house of my God, than to dwell in the tents of wickedness.          —BIBLE, *Psalms* 84:10

For wide is the gate, and broad is the way, that leadeth to destruction.          —BIBLE, *Matthew* 7:13

Men loved darkness rather than light, because their deeds were evil.          —BIBLE, *John* 3:19

For the wages of sin is death.          —BIBLE, *Romans* 6:23

Be not overcome of evil, but overcome evil of good.
—BIBLE, *Romans* 12:21

He that toucheth pitch shall be defiled therewith.
—BIBLE, *Ecclesiasticus* 13:1

The only thing necessary for the triumph of evil is for good men to do nothing.          —EDMUND BURKE, traditional attribution
but no known source
[For a similar concept in Burke, see UNITY & LOYALTY.]

The evil that is in the world almost always comes of ignorance, and good intentions may do as much harm as malevolence if they lack understanding.          —ALBERT CAMUS, *The Plague*

There is a capacity of virtue in us, and there is a capacity of vice to make your blood creep.          —RALPH WALDO EMERSON, *Journals*

Sin is whatever obscures the soul.
—ANDRÉ GIDE, *La Symphonie pastorale*

Wickedness is always easier than virtue; for it takes the short cut to everything.          —SAMUEL JOHNSON, quoted by James Boswell,
*Tour to the Hebrides*, Sept. 17, 1773

No one becomes depraved all at once. —JUVENAL, *Satires*

He who accepts evil without protesting against it is really co-operating with it. —MARTIN LUTHER KING, JR.,
*Stride Towards Freedom*

Surely God wrongs not men, but themselves men wrong. —KORAN

A man does not sin by commission only, but often by omission.
—MARCUS AURELIUS, *Meditations*

So farewell hope, and with hope farewell fear,
Farewell remorse: all good to me is lost;
Evil be thou my good. —JOHN MILTON, *Paradise Lost*

Whoever fights monsters should see to it that in the process he does not become a monster. And when you look long into an abyss, the abyss also looks into you.
—FRIEDRICH NIETZSCHE, *Beyond Good and Evil*

All human evil comes from this: a man's being unable to sit still in a room. —PASCAL, *Pensées*

No man is justified in doing evil on the ground of expediency.
—THEODORE ROOSEVELT, *The Strenuous Life*, title essay

The evil that men do lives after them,
The good is oft interred with their bones.
—SHAKESPEARE, *Julius Caesar*, III, ii

If one good deed in all my life I did,
I do repent it from my very soul.
—SHAKESPEARE, *Titus Andronicus*, V, iii

All spirits are enslaved that serve things evil.
—PERCY BYSSHE SHELLEY, *Prometheus Unbound*

Between two evils, I always like to take the one I've never tried before. —MAE WEST, *Klondike Annie*

**EVOLUTION** See SCIENCE: BIOLOGY

**EXCELLENCE** See AMBITION; ELITE;
GRACE; GREATNESS

**EXCESS** See also HEDONISM

Drinking when we are not thirsty and making love at any time, madame: that is all there is to distinguish us from the other animals.
—PIERRE-AUGUSTIN DE BEAUMARCHAIS, *The Marriage of Figaro*

The road of excess leads to the palace of wisdom.
—WILLIAM BLAKE, *The Marriage of Heaven and Hell*

Those who have great passions find themselves all their lives both happy and unhappy at being cured of them.
—LA ROCHEFOUCAULD, *Maxims*

Excess on occasion is exhilarating. It prevents moderation from acquiring the deadening effect of habit.
—W. SOMERSET MAUGHAM, *The Summing Up*

My candle burns at both ends;
It will not last the night;
But ah, my foes, and oh my friends—
It gives a lovely light!   —EDNA ST. VINCENT MILLAY,
*First Fig* in *A Few Figs from Thistles*

Can one desire too much of a good thing?
—SHAKESPEARE, *As You Like It*, IV, i

These violent delights have violent ends.
—SHAKESPEARE, *Romeo and Juliet*, II, vi

Nothing to excess.   —SOLON, quoted in Diogenes Laërtius,
*Lives of Eminent Philosophers*

Too much of a good thing can be wonderful.
—MAE WEST, quoted in Joseph Weintraub, ed.,
*The Wit and Wisdom of Mae West*

Nothing succeeds like excess.
—OSCAR WILDE, *A Woman of No Importance*
[See Dumas at SUCCESS.]

**EXCUSES**

*Qui s'excuse, s'accuse.*
Who excuses himself, accuses himself.   —ANONYMOUS (PROVERB)

Several excuses are always less convincing than one.
—ALDOUS HUXLEY, *Point Counter Point*

[On being observed by his wife kissing a chorus girl] I wasn't kissing her, I was whispering into her mouth.
—CHICO MARX, attributed

And oftentimes excusing of a fault
Doth make the fault the worse by the excuse.
—SHAKESPEARE, *King John*, IV, ii

I am a man
More sinned against than sinning. —SHAKESPEARE, *King Lear*, III, ii

Two wrongs don't make a right, but they make a good excuse.
—THOMAS SZASZ, *Social Relations* in *The Second Sin*

**EXPERIENCE**                    See also DOING; LIFE

A man should have the fine point of his soul taken off to become fit for this world.          —JOHN KEATS, letter to J. H. Reynolds, Nov. 22, 1817

No man's knowledge here can go beyond his experience.
—JOHN LOCKE, *Essay Concerning Human Understanding*

Experience is the name everyone gives to their mistakes.
—OSCAR WILDE, *Lady Windermere's Fan*

**EXPERTS**                    See also DOCTORS & THE PRACTICE OF MEDICINE; LAW & LAWYERS

Professionals built the *Titanic*—amateurs the ark.
—ANONYMOUS, cited by Frank S. Pepper, *Handbook of 20th Century Quotes*, source: BBC radio, The News Quiz, Oct. 27, 1979

An expert is one who knows more and more about less and less.
—NICHOLAS MURRAY BUTLER, attributed, commencement speech, Columbia University

An expert is someone who knows some of the worst mistakes that can be made in his subject and how to avoid them.
—WERNER HEISENBERG, *Physics and Beyond*

**EXPLORATION**                          See SCIENCE: DISCOVERY; TRAVEL

**FACE**                                              See BODY, HUMAN

**FACTS**

In this life we want nothing but facts, sir; nothing but facts.
—CHARLES DICKENS, Hard Times

[For more of Gradgrind's philosophy, see under EDUCATION.]

A little fact is worth a whole limbo of dreams.
—RALPH WALDO EMERSON, The Superlative

Her taste exact
For faultless fact
Amounts to a disease.                    —W. S. GILBERT, *The Mikado*

The smallest fact is a window through which the infinite may be
seen.            —ALDOUS HUXLEY, cited in Richard Norton Smith,
*Thomas E. Dewey*

Learn, compare, collect the facts!
—IVAN PETROVICH PAVLOV, Bequest to the<br>Academic Youth of Soviet Russia

The facts are to blame my friend. We are all imprisoned by facts.
—LUIGI PIRANDELLO, The Rules of the Game

Let us not underrate the value of a fact; it will one day flower
into a truth.                            —THOREAU, *Excursions*

Get your facts first, and then you can distort them as much as
you please.                    —MARK TWAIN, quoted in Rudyard Kipling,
*From Sea to Sea*

**FAILINGS**                                        See also MISTAKES

Thou art weighed in the balances, and art found wanting.
—BIBLE, Daniel 5:27

No rose without a thorn.          —ANONYMOUS (FRENCH PROVERB)

She had
A heart—how shall I say?—too soon made glad,
Too easily impressed.          —ROBERT BROWNING, *My Last Duchess*

Sometimes even excellent Homer nods.     —HORACE, *Ars Poetica*

Ignorance, pure ignorance.
>   —SAMUEL JOHNSON, explaining why in his *Dictionary* he had
>   defined *pastern* as the knee of a horse, quoted in
>   James Boswell, *Life of Johnson*, 1762

All men are liable to error; and most men are, in many points, by
passion or interest, under temptation to it.
>   —JOHN LOCKE, *Essay Concerning Human Understanding*

He's liked, but he's not well liked.
>   —ARTHUR MILLER, *Death of a Salesman*

But men are men, the best sometimes forget.
>   —SHAKESPEARE, *Othello*, II, iii

**FAILURE**                                 See HAVES & HAVE-NOTS; RUIN;
WINNING & LOSING, VICTORY & DEFEAT

**FAIRNESS**                                 See EVIDENCE; JUSTICE

**FAITH**                             See also GOD; RELIGION; SKEPTICISM

O thou of little faith, wherefore didst thou doubt?
>   —BIBLE, *Matthew* 14:31

For by grace are ye saved through faith; and that not of yourselves; it is the gift of God.     —BIBLE, *Ephesians* 2:8

Faith without works is dead.          —BIBLE, *James* 2:20

You can do very little with faith, but you can do nothing without
it.     —SAMUEL BUTLER, *Rebelliousness*, in *Notebooks*

"Well, now that we *have* seen each other," said the Unicorn, "if
you believe in me, I'll believe in you. Is that a bargain?"
>   —LEWIS CARROLL, *Through the Looking-Glass*

Faith in a holy cause is to a considerable extent a substitute for the
lost faith in ourselves.     —ERIC HOFFER, *The True Believer*

The constant assertion of belief is an indication of fear.
—KRISHNAMURTI, *The Second Penguin Krishnamurti Reader*

Faith may be defined briefly as an illogical belief in the occurrence of the improbable. —H. L. Mencken, *Prejudices*

Faith has need of the whole truth.
—Pierre Teilhard de Chardin, *The Appearance of Man*

*Certum est quia impossible.*
It is certain because it is impossible. —Tertullian,
*De Carne Cristi*
[Traditionally given as: *Credo quia impossible*, "I believe because it is impossible."]

To believe in God is to yearn for His existence, and furthermore, it is to act as if He did exist.
—Miguel de Unamuno, *The Tragic Sense of Life*

**FALL** See NATURE: SEASONS

**FAME** See SUCCESS & FAME

**FAMILIARITY** See INTIMACY & FAMILIARITY

**FAMILY** See also CHILDREN & CHILDHOOD;
HOME; MARRIAGE;
PARENTS & PARENTHOOD

He that hath a wife and children hath given hostages to fortune; for they are impediments to great enterprises.
—Francis Bacon, *Of Marriage*

It is a melancholy truth that even great men have their poor relations. —Charles Dickens, *Bleak House*

Accidents will occur in the best regulated families.
—Charles Dickens, *David Copperfield*

Good families are generally worse than any others.
—Anthony Hope, *The Prisoner of Zenda*

Home life ceases to be free and beautiful as soon as it is founded on borrowing and debt. —Henrik Ibsen, *A Doll's House*

One would be in less danger
From the wiles of the stranger
If one's own kin and kith
Were more fun to be with.        —OGDEN NASH, *Family Court*

Crabbèd age and youth cannot live together:
Youth is full of pleasance, age is full of care.
                        —SHAKESPEARE, *Passionate Pilgrim*

Happy families are all alike; every unhappy family is unhappy in
its own way.                —LEO TOLSTOY, *Anna Karenina*

Birds in their little nest agree;
And 'tis a shameful sight,
When children of one family
Fall out, and chide, and fight.
            —ISAAC WATTS, *Love Between Brothers and Sisters*

**FANATICISM**            See ENTHUSIASM, ENERGY, ZEAL

**FASHION & CLOTHES**            See also APPEARANCES

A little of what you call frippery is very necessary towards looking like the rest of the world.
            —ABIGAIL ADAMS, letter to John Adams, May 1, 1780

It is not only fine feathers that make fine birds.
            —AESOP, *The Jay and the Peacock*

Clothes make the man.        —ANONYMOUS (LATIN PROVERB)

The fashion of this world passeth away.        —BIBLE,
                        *I Corinthians* 7:31

The sense of being well-dressed gives a feeling of inward tranquillity which religion is powerless to bestow.
            —RALPH WALDO EMERSON, *Social Aims*
[He was reporting a comment by Miss C. F. Forbes.]

Good clothes open all doors.        —THOMAS FULLER, *Gnomologia*

A sweet disorder in the dress
Kindles in clothes a wantonness.
            —ROBERT HERRICK, *Delight in Disorder*

A good exterior is a silent recommendation.
                                —Publilius Syrus, *Sententiae*

The apparel oft proclaims the man.   —Shakespeare, *Hamlet*, I, iii

Beware of all enterprises that require new clothes.
                                —Henry David Thoreau, *Walden*

All dressed up, with nowhere to go.
                                —William Allen White, attributed
[He was referring to the Progressive Party after Theodore Roosevelt
left the presidential campaign.]

**FATE**                              See also LUCK; RESPONSIBILITY;
                                             SELF-RELIANCE

I want to seize fate by the throat.
                                —Ludwig van Beethoven, letter to
                                Dr. Franz Wegeler, Nov. 16, 1801

In my beginning is my end.          —T. S. Eliot, *East Coker*

A man's character is his fate.
                                —Heraclitus, quoted by Diogenes Laërtius,
                                *Lives of Eminent Philosophers*

I claim not to have controlled events, but confess plainly that
events have controlled me.
                                —Abraham Lincoln, letter to A. G. Hodges, April 4, 1864

O! I am Fortune's fool.   —Shakespeare, *Romeo and Juliet*, III, i

For man is man and master of his fate.
                                —Alfred, Lord Tennyson, *Lancelot and Elaine*, in
                                *Idylls of the King*

**FATHERS**                           See PARENTS & PARENTHOOD

**FATNESS**                           See BODY, HUMAN

**FEAR**                              See also COURAGE

A fool without fear is sometimes wiser than an angel with fear.
                                —Nancy Astor, *My Two Countries*

Fear has many eyes and can see things underground.
—CERVANTES, *Don Quixote*

The thing I fear most is fear.
—MONTAIGNE, *Essays: To the Reader*
[See also Wellington, below; for Roosevelt's version, see AMERICAN
HISTORY: MEMORABLE MOMENTS.]

Fear is the main source of superstition, and one of the main sources
of cruelty. To conquer fear is the beginning of wisdom.
—BERTRAND RUSSELL, *An Outline of Intellectual Rubbish*

If we let things terrify us, life will not be worth living.
—SENECA, *Epistles*

The only thing I am afraid of is fear.
—DUKE OF WELLINGTON, quoted in Philip Henry, Earl of
Stanhope, *Notes of Conservations with . . . Wellington*
[In addition to Montaigne, quoted above, and Roosevelt, cited at
AMERICAN HISTORY: MEMORABLE MOMENTS, Francis Bacon, Thoreau,
and others made similar comments. Thoreau put it: "Nothing is so
much to be feared as fear."]

**FEMINISM**                          See WOMEN; WOMEN & MEN

**FIGHTING BACK**          See APPEASEMENT VS. RESISTANCE;
STRENGTH

**FLATTERY**

Every woman is infallibly to be gained by every sort of flattery,
and every man by one sort or other.
—EARL OF CHESTERFIELD, letter to his son, March 16, 1752

Imitation is the sincerest of flattery.
—CHARLES CALEB COLTON, *The Lacon*

But when I tell him he hates flatterers,
He says he does, being then most flattered.
—SHAKESPEARE, *Julius Caesar*, II, i

None are more taken in by flattery than the proud who wish to
be first and are not.                          —SPINOZA, *Ethics*

'Tis an old maxim in the schools,
That flattery's the food of fools;
Yet now and then your men of wit
Will condescend to take a bit.
—JONATHAN SWIFT, *Cadenus and Vanessa*

**FLESH**                                        See BODY, HUMAN

**FLOWERS**                              See NATURE: GARDENS,
FLOWERS & TREES

**FOOD, WINE, & EATING**    See also ALCOHOL & DRINKING

A man hath no better thing under the sun than to eat, and to drink, and to be merry.                    —BIBLE, *Ecclesiastes* 8:15

A feast is made for laughter, and wine maketh merry.
—*Ibid.*, 10:19
[The quote is cited at greater length at MONEY.]

Bring hither the fatted calf and kill it; and let us eat, and be merry.
—BIBLE, *Luke* 15:23

The destiny of countries depends on the way they feed themselves.       —ANTHELME BRILLAT-SAVARIN, *Physiologie du Goût*

Tell me what you eat, and I will tell you what you are.      —*Ibid.*

Hunger is the best sauce in the world.            —CERVANTES,
*Don Quixote*

Life is too short to stuff a mushroom.
—SHIRLEY CONRAN, *Superwoman*, epigraph

It's a very odd thing—
As odd as can be—
That whatever Miss T. eats
Turns into Miss T.              —WALTER DE LA MARE, *Miss T.*

Gluttony is an emotional escape, a sign something is eating us.
—PETER DE VRIES, *Comfort Me With Apples*

*Der Mensch ist, was er isst.*
Man is what he eats.
—LUDWIG FEUERBACH, *Lehre der Nahrungsmittel:*
*Für das Volk*

Eat to live, and not live to eat.
>—BENJAMIN FRANKLIN, *Poor Richard's Almanac*

More die in the United States of too much food than of too little.
>—JOHN KENNETH GALBRAITH, *The Affluent Society*

I want there to be no peasant in my kingdom so poor that he cannot have a chicken in his pot every Sunday.
>—HENRY IV, attributed

[The modern political slogan "A chicken in every pot" was not, according to William Safire, uttered by Herbert Hoover. Rather it was the title of a Republican campaign flyer of 1928.]

He was a bold man who first swallowed an oyster.
>—JAMES I, attributed by Thomas Fuller,
>Jonathan Swift, and others

*Oats, n.* A grain, which in England is generally given to horses, but in Scotland supports the people.
>—SAMUEL JOHNSON, *Dictionary*

[Lord Elibank responded, "Very true, and where will you find such horses, and such men?"]

Some people have a foolish way of not minding, or pretending not to mind, what they eat. For my part, I mind my belly very studiously, and very carefully; for I look upon it, that he who does not mind his belly will hardly mind anything else.
>—SAMUEL JOHNSON, James Boswell, *Life of Johnson*,
>Aug. 5, 1763

*Qu'ils mangent de la brioche.*
Let them eat cake.
>—MARIE ANTOINETTE, traditional but wrong attribution

[The remark, perhaps apocryphal, was attributed to others much earlier.]

By and by
God caught his eye.      —DAVID McCORD, *Epitaphs: The Waiter*

Lunch kills half of Paris, supper the other half.
>—MONTESQUIEU, *Variétés*

A good cook is like a sorceress who dispenses happiness.
>—ELSA SCHIAPARELLI, *Shocking Life*

He hath eaten me out of house and home.
>—SHAKESPEARE, *Henry IV*, *Part II*, II, i

I am a great eater of beef and I believe that does harm to my wit.
—SHAKESPEARE, *Twelfth Night*, I, iii

Digestion is the great secret of life.
—REV. SYDNEY SMITH, letter to Arthur Kinglake, Sept. 30, 1837

In eating, a third of the stomach should be filled with food, a third with drink, and the rest left empty.   —TALMUD

It's a Naïve Domestic Burgundy, Without Any Breeding, But I Think You'll be Amused by its Presumption.
—JAMES THURBER, *Men, Women, & Dogs*, cartoon caption

It's broccoli dear.
I say it's spinach, and I say the hell with it.
—E. B. WHITE, cartoon caption, *The New Yorker*, Dec. 12, 1928

One cannot think well, love well, sleep well, if one has not dined well.   —VIRGINIA WOOLF, *A Room of One's Own*

## FOOLS & STUPIDITY

There's a sucker born every minute.   —P. T. BARNUM, attributed

A fool uttereth all his mind.   —BIBLE, *Proverbs* 29:11

For ye suffer fools gladly, seeing ye yourselves are wise.
—BIBLE, *II Corinthians* 11:19

We are the hollow men
We are the stuffed men
Leaning together
Headpiece filled with straw. Alas!
—T. S. ELIOT, *The Hollow Men*

Nothing is more humiliating than to see idiots succeed in enterprises we have failed in.   —FLAUBERT, *Sentimental Education*

There are some who speak one moment before they think.
—LA BRUYÈRE, *Les caractères*

Small things amuse small minds.
—DORIS LESSING, *A Woman on a Roof* in *A Man and Two Women*

For fools rush in where angels fear to tread.
>—ALEXANDER POPE, *An Essay on Criticism*

They never taste who always drink:
They always talk who never think.
>—MATTHEW PRIOR, *Upon this Passage in the Scaligeriana*

Against stupidity, the gods themselves struggle in vain.
>—FRIEDRICH VON SCHILLER, *The Maid of Orleans*

Lord, what fools these mortals be!
>—SHAKESPEARE, *A Midsummer Night's Dream*

[Seneca said the same thing, though in Latin, in his *Epistles*: "*Tanta stultitia mortalium est.*"]

Let us be thankful for the fools. But for them the rest of us could not succeed.
>—MARK TWAIN, "Pudd'nhead Wilson's New Calendar," in *Following the Equator*

There is no sin except stupidity.
>—OSCAR WILDE, *The Critic as Artist*

**FORCE**                                            See VIOLENCE & FORCE

**FORGIVENESS & MERCY**                 See also TOLERANCE & UNDERSTANDING

Blessed are the merciful: for they shall obtain mercy.
>—BIBLE, *Matthew* 5:7

[For other verses from the Sermon on the Mount, see VIRTUE.]

Forgive, and ye shall be forgiven.
>—BIBLE, *Luke* 6:37

[More of this verse is cited under TOLERANCE & UNDERSTANDING.]

Rejoice with me; for I have found my sheep which was lost.
. . . joy shall be in heaven over one that repenteth, more than over ninety and nine just persons, which need no repentance.
>—BIBLE, *Luke* 15:6,7

Father forgive them; for they know not what they do.
>—*Ibid.*, 23:34

To err is human, to forgive, divine.
>—ALEXANDER POPE, *An Essay on Criticism*

The quality of mercy is not strained,
It droppeth as the gentle rain from heaven.
—SHAKESPEARE, *Merchant of Venice*, IV, i

No beast so fierce but knows some touch of pity.
—SHAKESPEARE, *Richard III*, I, ii

Sweet mercy is nobility's true badge.
—SHAKESPEARE, *Titus Andronicus*, I, i

It is by forgiving that one is forgiven.
—MOTHER TERESA, *For the Brotherhood of Man*

Love truth, but pardon error.
—VOLTAIRE, *Sept discours en vers sur l'homme*

**FORM**                    See ARTS: AESTHETICS

**FORTUNE**                    See FATE; HAPPINESS; LUCK

**FRANCE**                    See CITIES; NATIONS

**FREEDOM**                    See also DEMOCRACY;
FREE SPEECH; RIGHTS

The condition upon which God has given liberty to man is
eternal vigilance.    —JOHN PHILPOT CURRAN, speech, July 10, 1790

You can only protect your liberties in this world by protecting
the other man's freedom. You can only be free if I am free.
—CLARENCE DARROW, *People v. Lloyd*, 1920

I only ask to be free. The butterflies are free.
—CHARLES DICKENS, *Bleak House*

There can be no real freedom without the freedom to fail.
—ERIC HOFFER, *The Ordeal of Change*

What stands if freedom fall?
—RUDYARD KIPLING, *For All We Have and Are*

Those who deny freedom to others deserve it not for themselves.
—ABRAHAM LINCOLN, letter to H. L. Pierce *et al.*, April 6, 1859

Like bone to the human body, and the axle to the wheel, and the song to a bird, and air to the wing, thus is liberty the essence of life. Whatever is done without it is imperfect.
—José Martí, quoted by William Pfaff,
*The New Yorker*, May 27, 1985

License they mean when they cry liberty.
—John Milton, *On the Same*
["The same" refers to his sonnet *On the Detraction . . .*]

A nation may lose its liberties in a day, and not miss them for a century.
—Montesquieu, *De l'Esprit des lois*

Liberty is the right to do everything which the laws allow.
—*Ibid.*

Those men and women are fortunate who are born at a time when a great struggle for human freedom is in progress.
—Emmeline Pankhurst, *My Own Story*

O liberty, o liberty, what crimes are committed in your name.
—Madame Roland, being taken to the guillotine,
attributed in Lamartine, *Histoire des Girondins*

We look forward to a world founded upon four essential freedoms [freedom of speech, freedom of worship, freedom from want, freedom from fear].
—Franklin Delano Roosevelt, speech, Jan. 6, 1941

Man is condemned to be free.
—Jean-Paul Sartre, *Existentialism Is a Humanism*

Carelessness about our security is dangerous; carelessness about our freedom is also dangerous.
—Adlai Stevenson,
speech, Oct. 7, 1952

I had reasoned this out in my mind: There was two things I had a right to, liberty and death. If I could not have one, I would have the other, for no man should take me alive.
—Harriet Tubman, quoted in Marcy Galen,
*Lost Women: Harriet Tubman . . .*

Caged birds accept each other but flight is what they long for.
—Tennessee Williams, *Camino Real*

**FREE SPEECH**  See also CENSORSHIP; FREEDOM; PRESS, THE

Some people's idea of [free speech] is that they are free to say what they like, but if anyone says anything back, that is an outrage.
—WINSTON CHURCHILL, speech, Oct. 13, 1943

In a free state there must be free speech.
—DOMITIAN, attributed

Let reason be opposed to reason, and argument to argument, and every good government will be safe.
—THOMAS ERSKINE, *In Defense of Thomas Paine*

The most stringent protection of free speech would not protect a man from falsely shouting fire in a theater and causing a panic.
—OLIVER WENDELL HOLMES, JR., *Schenck* v. *U.S.*, 1919

I disapprove of what you say, but I will defend to the death your right to say it.
—VOLTAIRE, attributed
[The source for the attribution is E. Beatrice Hall's *The Friends of Voltaire*. But the author later said that the statement was meant as a paraphrase, not an exact quote. *Bartlett* credits Norbert Guterman's *A Book of French Quotations* with finding the closest verifiable quotation, in a letter from Voltaire to M. le Riche, Feb. 6, 1770: "I detest what you write, but I would give my life to make it possible for you to continue to write."]

**FRIENDS & FRIENDSHIP**  See also OLD THINGS, OLD FRIENDS

One friend in a life is much, two are many, three are hardly possible.  —HENRY BROOKS ADAMS, *The Education of Henry Adams*

Greater love has no man than this, that a man lay down his life for his friends.  —BIBLE, *John* 15:13

Forsake not an old friend; for the new is not comparable to him; a new friend is as new wine.  —BIBLE, *Ecclesiasticus* 9:10

Have no friends not equal to yourself.  —CONFUCIUS, *Analects*

A friend may well be reckoned the masterpiece of nature.
—RALPH WALDO EMERSON, *Friendship*

A friend is a person with whom I may be sincere. Before him, I may think aloud. —*Ibid.*

If I had to choose between betraying my country and betraying my friend, I hope I should have the guts to betray my country.
—E. M. FORSTER, *What I Believe*, in
*Two Cheers for Democracy*

Friendship needs no words—it is solitude delivered from the anguish of loneliness. —DAG HAMMARSKJÖLD, *Markings*

If a man does not make new acquaintances as he advances through life, he will soon find himself left alone.
—SAMUEL JOHNSON, quoted in Boswell's
*Life of Johnson*, April 1755

A true friend is the most precious of all possessions and the one we take the least thought about acquiring.
—LA ROCHEFOUCAULD, *Maxims*

Those friends thou hast, and their adoption tried,
Grapple them to thy soul with hoops of steel.
—SHAKESPEARE, *Hamlet*, I, iii

To me fair friend, you never can be old.
—SHAKESPEARE, sonnet 104

The holy passion of friendship is so sweet and steady and loyal and enduring in nature that it will last through a whole lifetime, if not asked to lend money. —MARK TWAIN, *Pudd'nhead Wilson*

May God defend me from my friends, I can defend myself from my enemies. —DUC DE VILLARS, attributed
[Sometimes attributed to Voltaire.]

It is not often that someone comes along who is a true friend and a good writer. —E. B. WHITE, *Charlotte's Web*

**FUTURE**                                    See also PROGRESS

The future struggles against being mastered.
—ANONYMOUS (LATIN PROVERB)

I hold that man is in the right who is most closely in league with the future. —HENRIK IBSEN, letter to George Brandes, Jan. 3, 1882

You ain't heard nothin' yet, folks.   —AL JOLSON, *The Jazz Singer*

I like the dreams of the future better than the history of the past.
—THOMAS JEFFERSON, letter to John Adams, 1816

In the long run . . . we are all dead.
—JOHN MAYNARD KEYNES, attributed, in Claude Cockburn,
*Aspects of English History*

Population, when unchecked, increases in a geometric ratio. Subsistence increases only in an arithmetical ratio.
—THOMAS MALTHUS, *An Essay on the Principle of Population*

I'll think of it all tomorrow at Tara. . . . After all, tomorrow is another day.   —MARGARET MITCHELL, *Gone with the Wind*

If you want a picture of the future, imagine a boot stamping on a human face—forever.   —GEORGE ORWELL, *1984*

There's a gude time coming.   —SIR WALTER SCOTT, *Rob Roy*

I have seen the future and it works.   —LINCOLN STEFFENS, saying,
after visiting Russia in 1919

Time and space—time to be alone, space to move about—these may well be the greatest scarcities of tomorrow.
—EDWIN WAY TEALE, *Autumn Across America*

GAMBLING   See GAMES

GAMES   See also SPORTS; WINNING & LOSING,
VICTORY & DEFEAT

To play billiards is a sign of misspent youth.   —ANONYMOUS
[Often attributed to Herbert Spencer, because he recorded this remark in a letter. It had been said to him by a Mr. Charles Roupell, but it's not clear if it was original.]

There are two great pleasures in gambling: winning and losing.
—ANONYMOUS (FRENCH PROVERB)

Life's too short for chess.   —HENRY J. BYRON, *Our Boys*

Poets do not go mad, but chess players do.
—G. K. CHESTERTON, *Orthodoxy*

When in doubt, win the trick.
> —EDMOND HOYLE, *Hoyle's Games*, rule 12 for whist

I am sorry I have not learnt to play at cards. It is very useful in life: it generates kindness and consolidates society.
> —SAMUEL JOHNSON, quoted by James Boswell,
> *Tour to the Hebrides*, Nov. 21, 1773

Cards are war in disguise of a sport.
> —CHARLES LAMB, *Mrs. Battle's Opinions on Whist*

The roulette table pays nobody except him who keeps it. Nevertheless, a passion for gaming is common, though a passion for keeping roulette wheels is unknown.
> —GEORGE BERNARD SHAW, *Man and Superman*,
> "Maxims for Revolutionists"

**GARDENS**                                   See NATURE: GARDENS,
                                              FLOWERS, & TREES

**GENERATIONS**                               See also LIFE

One generation passeth away, and another generation cometh: but the earth abideth forever.
The sun also ariseth.                         —BIBLE, *Ecclesiastes* 1:4,5

Let us now praise famous men, and our fathers that begat us.
> —*Ibid.*, 44:1

The gods
Visit the sins of the fathers upon the children.
> —EURIPIDES, *Phrixus*
[Similar lines are found in *Exodus, The Merchant of Venice*, and elsewhere.]

As is the generations of leaves, so is that of humanity.
The wind scatters the leaves on the ground, but the live timber
Burgeons with leaves again in the season of spring returning.
So one generation of men will grow while another
Dies.                                         —HOMER, *Iliad*

The generations of living things pass in a short time, and like runners hand on the torch of life.   —LUCRETIUS, *De Rerum Natura*

each generation wastes a little more
of the future with greed and lust for riches.
—Don Marquis, *archy and mehitabel*

What has posterity ever done for me?
—Groucho Marx, attributed

Every generation revolts against its fathers and makes friends with
its grandfathers.        —Lewis Mumford, *The Brown Decades*

Every moment dies a man,
Every moment one is born.
—Alfred, Lord Tennyson, *The Vision of Sin*
[Charles Babbage, inventor of the analytical engine, similar to a
modern computer, put matters this way in a letter to Tennyson:
"Every moment dies a man. Every moment one and one sixteenth is
born."]

## GENEROSITY        See CHARITY: PHILANTHROPY;
HOSPITALITY

## GENIUS        See also GREATNESS; MIND, THOUGHT, &
UNDERSTANDING; VISION & VISIONARIES

A genius is a man who has *two* great ideas.
—Jacob Bronowski, *The Ascent of Man*

*Genius* . . . means transcendent capacity of taking trouble.
—Thomas Carlyle, *Life of Frederick the Great*

Genius is one per cent inspiration and ninety-nine per cent
perspiration.        —Thomas Alva Edison, *Life*

Towering genius disdains a beaten path. It seeks regions hitherto
unexplored.        —Abraham Lincoln, speech, Jan. 27, 1838

Genius is an African who dreams up snow.
—Vladimir Nabokov, *The Gift*

There is no great genius without some touch of madness.
—Seneca, *On Tranquillity of the Mind*

Everybody is born with genius, but most people only keep it a
few minutes.        —Edgard Varèse, quoted by Martha Graham,
*New York Times* interview, March 31, 1985

**GERMANY** See NATIONS

**GETTING AWAY FROM IT ALL** See ESCAPE; TRAVEL

**GIVING** See CHARITY: PHILANTHROPY

**GLORY** See SUCCESS & FAME; WAR

**GOD** See also CREATION, DIVINE; FAITH;
JESUS CHRIST; PRAYERS;
PROVIDENCE, DIVINE; RELIGION

God is not dead but alive and well and working on a much less ambitious project. —ANONYMOUS (GRAFFITO)
[This has been so widely quoted that it may be aprocryphal; however, some sources trace it to London; *The Penguin Dictionary of Modern Quotations* says that it was noted in the *Guardian*, Nov. 27, 1975.]

I am all that has been, and that is, and that shall remain, and no one unworthy has ever unraveled, loosened, or even touched the surface of my woven veil.
—ANONYMOUS, carving on an ancient statue of
Pallas Athena, cited in Plutarch's *Lives*

God is that, the greater than which cannot be conceived.
—ST. ANSELM, *Proslogion*

And God said unto Moses, I AM THAT I AM.
—BIBLE, *Exodus* 3:14

The Lord is my shepherd; I shall not want. —BIBLE, *Psalms* 23:1
[The entire psalm is given at PROVIDENCE, DIVINE.]

God is our refuge and strength, a very present help in trouble.
—*Ibid.*, 46:1

Thy word is lamp unto my feet, and a light unto my path.
—*Ibid.*, 119:105

His mercy endureth forever. —*Ibid.*, 136:1

With God all things are possible. —BIBLE, *Matthew* 19:26

Thou shalt love the Lord thy God with all thy heart, and with all thy soul, and with all thy mind.                    —*Ibid.*, 22:37

I am the resurrection, and the life.          —BIBLE, *John* 11:25

In my Father's house are many mansions.          —*Ibid.*, 14:2

I am the way, the truth, and the life: no man cometh unto the Father, but by me.                    —*Ibid.*, 14:6

God is no respecter of persons.          —BIBLE, *Acts* 10:34

All things work together for good to them that love God.
                              —BIBLE, *Romans* 8:28

If God be for us, who can be against us?          —*Ibid.*, 8:31

He that loveth not knoweth not God, for God is love.
                              —BIBLE, *I John* 4:8

I am the Alpha and the Omega, the beginning and the end, the first and the last.          —BIBLE, *Revelation* 22:13

Do not take liberties with the gods, or weary them.
                              —CONFUCIUS, *The Book of Rites*

It is the final proof of God's omnipotence that he need not exist in order to save us.          —PETER DE VRIES, *The Mackerel Plaza*

*Raffiniert ist der Herr Gott, aber boshaft ist er nicht.*
God is subtle, but he is not malicious.
                    —ALBERT EINSTEIN, inscription in Fine Hall,
                              Princeton University.
[Alan L. Mackay, in *The Harvest of a Quiet Eye*, gives Einstein's own translation as "God is slick, but he ain't mean." For Einstein's dictum on God playing dice, see under SCIENCE.]

God is a circle whose center is everywhere and whose circumference is nowhere.          —EMPEDOCLES, fragment

At bottom God is nothing more than an exalted father.
                              —FREUD, *Totem and Taboo*

God, to me, it seems
is a verb.                              —R. BUCKMINSTER FULLER,
                              *No More Secondhand God*

Toward what should we aim if not toward God?
—ANDRÉ GIDE, *Thésée*

God lies ahead. . . . He depends on us. It is through us that God is achieved.
—ANDRÉ GIDE, *Journals*

God will forgive me, it is his business.
—HEINRICH HEINE, last words, attributed in many sources, including the Goncourt *Journals*

The world is charged with the grandeur of God.
—GERARD MANLEY HOPKINS, *God's Grandeur*

An honest God's the noblest work of man.
—ROBERT G. INGERSOLL, *The Gods*
[Also in Samuel Butler, *Notebooks*.]

My dear child, you must believe in God despite what the clergy tell you.
—BENJAMIN JOWETT, quoted by Margot Asquith, *Autobiography*

*Nam homo proponit, sed Deus disponit.*
For man proposes, but God disposes.
—THOMAS À KEMPIS, *Of the Imitation of Christ*

He is the first and the last, the manifest and the hidden: and He knoweth all things.
—KORAN

Though the mills of God grind slowly, yet they grind exceedingly small.
—FRIEDRICH VON LOGAU, *Retribution*, translated by Henry Wadsworth Longfellow
[Cf. Zenobius, below.]

A mighty fortress is our God
A bulwark never failing.
—MARTIN LUTHER, *A Mighty Fortress*

A safe stronghold our God is still,
A trusty shield and weapon.
—*Ibid.*

It takes a long while for a naturally trustful person to reconcile himself to the idea that after all God will not help him.
—H. L. MENCKEN, *Minority Report*

There is a very good saying that if triangles invented a god, they would make him three-sided.
—MONTESQUIEU, *Lettres persanes*

God is dead: but considering the state the species Man is in, there will perhaps be caves, for ages yet, in which his shadow will be shown.          —FRIEDRICH NIETZSCHE, *Die fröhliche Wissenschaft*

It is convenient that there be gods, and, as it is convenient, let us believe there are.                          —OVID, *Ars amatoria*

Be comforted. You would not be seeking Me if you had not found Me.                                    —PASCAL, *Pensées*

Lo, the poor Indian! whose untutored mind
Sees God in clouds, or hears him in the wind;
His soul proud science never taught to stray
Far as the solar walk, or milky way.
                          —ALEXANDER POPE, *Essay on Man*

As flies to wanton boys are we to the gods
They kill us for their sport.          —SHAKESPEARE, *King Lear*, IV, i

A god does not change his ways.
                    —TERTULLIAN, *The Christian's Defense*

I fled Him, down the nights and down the days;
I fled Him, down the arches of the years;
I fled Him, down the labyrinthine ways
Of my own mind.
                    —FRANCIS J. THOMPSON, *The Hound of Heaven*

If God did not exist, it would be necessary to invent him.
          —VOLTAIRE, *A l'auteur du livre des trois imposteurs*

If God made us in His image, we have certainly returned the compliment.                          —VOLTAIRE, *Le sottisier*

Jupiter is slow looking into his notebook, but he always looks.
                          —ZENOBIUS, *Sententiae*

**GOODNESS**                                    See VIRTUE

**GOVERNMENT**                    See also DIPLOMACY; HIGH POSITION:
                                        RULERS & LEADERS; POLITICS;
                                        TAXES; TYRANNY & TOTALITARIANISM

*Divide et impera.*
Divide and rule

                          —ANONYMOUS (LATIN PROVERB)
[Also appears as *Divide ut regnes*—"Divide in order to rule."]

Government is a contrivance of human wisdom to provide for human wants. Men have a right that these wants should be provided for by this wisdom.
    —EDMUND BURKE, *Reflections on the Revolution in France*
[For Burke on government and compromise, see under Bismarck at POLITICS, the second quote.]

No man should be in public office who can't make more money in private life.    —THOMAS E. DEWEY, maxim, cited in
                    Richard Norton Smith, *Thomas E. Dewey*

The less government we have, the better.
                    —RALPH WALDO EMERSON, *Politics*

In every society some men are born to rule, and some to advise.
            —RALPH WALDO EMERSON, *The Young American*

A government that is big enough to give you all you want is big enough to take it all away.
            —BARRY GOLDWATER, speech, Oct. 21, 1964

A civil servant doesn't make jokes.        —EUGÈNE IONESCO,
                                            *The Killer*

The natural progress of things is for liberty to yield and government to gain ground.
                —THOMAS JEFFERSON, letter to
                Colonel Edward Carrington, 1788

The whole art of government consists in being honest.
                —THOMAS JEFFERSON, *Works*, VI, 186

It is perfectly true that the government is best which governs least. It is equally true that the government is best which provides most.        —WALTER LIPPMANN, *A Preface to Politics*
[The reference is to John O'Sullivan's maxim, see below.]

Every nation has the government that it deserves.
                —JOSEPH DE MAISTRE, letter to X, Aug. 1811

The worst government is the most moral. One composed of cynics is often very tolerant and humane. But when fanatics are on top there is no limit to oppression.        —H. L. MENCKEN, *Notebooks*

All government is evil. . . . The best government is that which governs least.
—JOHN L. O'SULLIVAN, Introduction, *The United States Magazine and Democratic Review*, 1837
[For a response, see Walter Lippmann, above.]

Society in every state is a blessing, but government even in its best state, is but a necessary evil; in its worst state, an intolerable one.
—THOMAS PAINE, *Common Sense*

For forms of government let fools contest,
Whate'er is best administered is best.
—ALEXANDER POPE, *Essay on Man*

Government can easily exist without law, but law cannot exist without government.    —BERTRAND RUSSELL, *Unpopular Essays*

GRACE                                        See also BEAUTY; CHARM;
                                                  STYLE; VIRTUE

A soft answer turneth away wrath.        —BIBLE, *Proverbs* 15:1

There be three things which are too wonderful for me, yea, four which I know not.
The way of an eagle in the air; the way of a serpent upon a rock; the way of a ship in the midst of the sea; and the way of a man with a maid.        —*Ibid.*, 30:18,19

Whatever is worth doing at all, is worth doing well.
—EARL OF CHESTERFIELD, letter to his son, March 10, 1746

Grace is the absence of everything that indicates pain or difficulty, hesitation or incongruity.        —WILLIAM HAZLITT, *On Beauty*

Grace under pressure.
—ERNEST HEMINGWAY, definition of *guts*, quoted in John F. Kennedy, *Profiles in Courage*
[The citation was probably based on Hemingway's *Life* magazine articles on bullfighting, which are now part of the book *The Dangerous Summer*. Hemingway wrote of Antonio Ordoñez, "He had the three great requisites for a matador: courage, skill in his profession, and grace in the presence of the danger of death."]

Do every act of your life as if it were your last.
—MARCUS AURELIUS, *Meditations*

To know how to live is my trade and my art.
—MONTAIGNE, *Essays*

**GRACE, DIVINE**　　　　　　See FAITH; PROVIDENCE, DIVINE

**GREATNESS**　　　　　　See also AMBITION; GENIUS; HEROES;
HIGH POSITION: RULERS & LEADERS;
SUCCESS & FAME

A great man is always willing to be little.
—RALPH WALDO EMERSON, *Compensation*

To be great is to be misunderstood.
—RALPH WALDO EMERSON, *Self-reliance*

Great deeds are usually wrought at great risks.
—HERODOTUS, *Histories*

Four things greater than all things are,—
Women and Horses and Power and War.
—RUDYARD KIPLING, *The Ballad of the King's Jest*

The great man is he who does not lose his child's heart.
—MENCIUS, *Works*

Great men can't be ruled.　　　—AYN RAND, *The Fountainhead*

Be not afraid of greatness. Some are born great, some achieve greatness, and some have greatness thrust upon them.
—SHAKESPEARE, *Twelfth Night*, II, v

In order to carry out great enterprises, one must live as if one will never have to die.
—MARQUIS DE VAUVENARGUES, *Réflexions et maximes*

*Le mieux est l'ennemie du bien.*
The best is the enemy of the good.
—VOLTAIRE, *Dictionnaire philosophique*, "Art dramatique"

**GREECE**　　　　　　See NATIONS

**GUILT**　　　　　　See also CRIME; EVIDENCE;
EVIL; INNOCENCE

The guilty think all talk is of themselves.
—CHAUCER, *The Canterbury Tales*

Where guilt is, rage and courage doth abound.
—BEN JONSON, *Sejanus*

Alas! how difficult it is not to betray guilt by our countenance.
—OVID, *Metamorphoses*

Nobody becomes guilty by fate.         —SENECA, *Oedipus*

The lady doth protest too much, methinks.
—SHAKESPEARE, *Hamlet*, III, ii

Here's the smell of the blood still. All the perfumes of Arabia will not sweeten this little hand.         —SHAKESPEARE, *Macbeth*, V, i

## HABIT                                                    See also CUSTOM

The nature of men is always the same; it is their habits that separate them.         —CONFUCIUS, *Analects*

Nothing is more powerful than habit.         —OVID, *Ars amatoria*

Habit is a second nature that prevents us from knowing the first, of which it has neither the cruelties nor the enchantments.
—PROUST, *Remembrance of Things Past: The Guermantes Way*

To fall into a habit is to begin to cease to be.
—MIGUEL DE UNAMUNO, *The Tragic Sense of Life*

Rigid, the skeleton of habit alone upholds the human frame.
—VIRGINIA WOOLF, *Mrs. Dalloway*

## HAPPINESS                    See also ETHICS & MORALITY; HAPPINESS, EXPRESSIONS OF; LOVE, EXPRESSIONS OF

A joy that's shared is a joy made double.
—ANONYMOUS (ENGLISH PROVERB), recorded by John Ray, *English Proverbs*

Weeping may endure for a night, but joy cometh in the morning.
—BIBLE, *Psalms* 30:5

Judge none blessed before his death.
—BIBLE, *Ecclesiasticus* 11:28

[This concept was expressed by other ancient writers, including Solon; see below.]

The joyfulness of a man prolongeth his days.      *—Ibid.*, 30:22

The secret of happiness is to admire without desiring. And that is not happiness.                  —F. H. BRADLEY, *Aphorisms*

Make us happy and you make us good.
                  —ROBERT BROWNING, *The Ring and the Book*

The latter end of joy is woe.
                  —GEOFFREY CHAUCER, *The Canterbury Tales*

All seek joy, but it is not found on earth
                  —ST. JOHN CHRYSOSTOM, *Homilies*

It is neither wealth nor splendor, but tranquillity and occupation, which give happiness.
                  —THOMAS JEFFERSON, letter to Mrs. A. S. Marks, 1788

One is never as fortunate or as unfortunate as one imagines.
                  —LA ROCHEFOUCAULD, *Maxims*

To live happily is an inward power of the soul.
                  —MARCUS AURELIUS, *Meditations*

toujours gai, archy, toujours gai.
                  —DON MARQUIS, *archy's life of mehitabel*

Ask yourself whether you are happy, and you will cease to be so.
                  —JOHN STUART MILL, *Autobiography*

The secret of happiness is to face the fact that the world is horrible, horrible, *horrible*.
                  —BERTRAND RUSSELL, quoted in Alan Wood,
                  *Bertrand Russell: The Passionate Skeptic*

Happiness is the only sanction in life; where happiness fails, existence remains a mad and lamentable experiment.
                  —GEORGE SANTAYANA, *The Life of Reason*

We have no more right to consume happiness without producing it than to consume wealth without producing it.
                  —GEORGE BERNARD SHAW, *Candida*

A lifetime of happiness! No man alive could bear it: it would be hell on earth.   —GEORGE BERNARD SHAW, *Man and Superman*

There are two things to aim at in life: first, to get what you want; and, after that, to enjoy it. Only the wisest of mankind achieve the second.   —LOGAN PEARSALL SMITH, *Afterthoughts*

Call no man happy until he dies; he is at best but fortunate.
   —SOLON, quoted in Herodotus, *Histories*

Our happiness depends on wisdom all the way.
   —SOPHOCLES, *Antigone*

The world is so full of a number of things,
I'm sure we should all be as happy as kings.
   —ROBERT LOUIS STEVENSON, *Happy Thought*, in
   *A Child's Garden of Verses*

Happiness is an imaginary condition formerly often attributed by the living to the dead, now usually attributed by adults to children, and by children to adults.   —THOMAS SZASZ, *Emotions*, in
   *The Second Sin*

## HAPPINESS, EXPRESSIONS OF   See also HAPPINESS;
LOVE, EXPRESSIONS OF

"And hast thou slain the Jabberwock?
Come to my arms, my beamish boy!
O frabjous day! Callooh! Callay!"
He chortled in his joy.
   —LEWIS CARROLL, *Jabberwocky* in *Through the Looking-Glass*

Everyone suddenly burst out singing.
   —SIEGFRIED SASSOON, *Everyone Sang*

O wonderful, wonderful, and most wonderful! and yet again wonderful, and after that, out of all whooping!
   —SHAKESPEARE, *As You Like It*, III, ii

## HARLEM   See CITIES

## HASTE

*Festina lente.*
Hasten slowly.   —ANONYMOUS (PROVERB)

What is done well is done quickly enough.
                    —AUGUSTUS CAESAR, favorite proverbial saying,
                        quoted in Suetonius, *Lives of the Caesars*

No man who is in a hurry is quite civilized.
                    —WILL DURANT, *What Is Civilization?*

Nothing is more vulgar than haste.
                    —RALPH WALDO EMERSON, *The Conduct of Life*

Haste in every business brings failures.   —HERODOTUS, *Histories*

We haven't the time to take our time.
                    —EUGÈNE IONESCO, *Exit the King*

Wisely and slowly; they stumble that run fast.
                    —SHAKESPEARE, *Romeo and Juliet*, II, iii

More haste, less speed.                    —THEOGNIS, fragment

Never hurry and never worry!    —E. B. WHITE, *Charlotte's Web*
[Charlotte's brilliant advice to Wilbur.]

HATE                                    See also ANGER; REVENGE

Hatred watches while friendship sleeps.
                    —ANONYMOUS (FRENCH PROVERB)

Thou shalt not hate thy brother in thy heart.
                    —BIBLE, *Leviticus* 19:17

The bloodthirsty hate the upright.    —BIBLE, *Proverbs* 29:10

Now hatred is by far the longest pleasure;
Men love in haste, but they detest at leisure.
                    —LORD BYRON, *Don Juan*

I tell you there is such a thing as creative hate.
                    —WILLA CATHER, *The Song of the Lark*

Heaven has no rage like love to hatred turned,
Nor hell a fury like a woman scorned.
                    —WILLIAM CONGREVE, *The Mourning Bride*

Violent antipathies are always suspicious, and betray a secret
affinity.                    —WILLIAM HAZLITT, *Table-Talk*

We can scarcely hate anyone that we know.
—WILLIAM HAZLITT, *On Criticism*

Hate is the coward's revenge for being humiliated.
—GEORGE BERNARD SHAW, *Major Barbara*

It is human to hate those whom we have injured.
—TACITUS, *Life of Agricola*

**HAVES & HAVE-NOTS**    See also MONEY; POVERTY & HUNGER;
POWER; RUIN; WINNING & LOSING,
VICTORY & DEFEAT

Never give a sucker an even break.

—ANONYMOUS
[Popularized by Texas Guinan about 1925, according to H. L.
Mencken.]

The rich would have to eat money, but luckily the poor provide
food.    —ANONYMOUS (RUSSIAN PROVERB)

The poor is hated even of his own neighbor, but the rich have
many friends.    —BIBLE, *Proverbs* 14:20

For unto everyone that hath shall be given, and he shall have
abundance: but from him that hath not shall be taken even that
which he hath.    —BIBLE, *Matthew* 25:29

There are only two families in the world, my old grandmother
used to say, the *Haves* and the *Have-nots*.
—CERVANTES, *Don Quixote*

The meek shall inherit the earth but not the mineral rights.
—J. PAUL GETTY, attributed

If you are poor today, you will always be poor. Only the rich
acquire riches.    —MARTIAL, *Epigrams*

Half the world does not know how the other half lives.
—RABELAIS, *Pantagruel*

Really, if the lower orders don't set us a good example, what on
earth is the use of them?
—OSCAR WILDE, *The Importance of Being Earnest*

## HEALTH

See also DOCTORS & THE PRACTICE OF
MEDICINE; ILLNESS & REMEDIES; MADNESS

There is a limit to the best of health: disease is always a near neighbor. —AESCHYLUS, *Agamemnon*

Health and good estate of body are above all good.
—BIBLE, *Ecclesiasticus* 30: 15

Early to bed and early to rise, makes a man healthy, wealthy, and wise. —BENJAMIN FRANKLIN, *Poor Richard's Almanac*

*Orandum est ut sit mens sana in corpore sano.*
We should pray for a sound mind in a sound body.
—JUVENAL, *Satires*

A sound mind in a sound body is a short but full description of a happy state in this world.
—JOHN LOCKE, *Some Thoughts Concerning Education*

*Non est vivere, sed valera vita est.*
Life is not merely living but living in health.
—MARTIAL, *Epigrams*

Too much attention to health is a hindrance to learning, to invention, and to studies of any kind, for we are always feeling suspicious shootings and swimmings in our heads, and we are prone to blame our studies for them. —PLATO, *The Republic*

People who feel well are sick people neglecting themselves.
—JULES ROMAINS, *Knock, où le triomphe de la mèdecine*

Use your health, even to the point of wearing it out. That is what it is for. Spend all you have before you die; and do not outlive yourself. —GEORGE BERNARD SHAW, *The Doctor's Dilemma*

Keep breathing [key to longevity].
—SOPHIE TUCKER, newspaper reports, Jan. 13, 1964

## HEART

See also LOVE

When I was one-and-twenty
I heard a wise man say,
Give crowns and pounds and guineas
But not your heart away. —A. E. HOUSEMAN, *A Shropshire Lad*

The intellect is always fooled by the heart.
—LA ROCHEFOUCAULD, *Maxims*

In the human heart, there is a ceaseless birth of passions, so that the destruction of one is almost always the establishment of another.
—*Ibid.*

The human heart is like a ship on a stormy sea driven about by winds blowing from all four corners of heaven.
—MARTIN LUTHER, preface to his translation of the *Psalms*

My heart is a lonely hunter that hunts on a lonely hill.
—FIONA MACLEOD, *The Lonely Hunter*

*La coeur a ses raisons que la raison ne connaît point.*
The heart has its reasons which reason does not know at all.
—PASCAL, *Pensées*

I follow my heart for I can trust it.
—J. C. FRIEDRICH VON SCHILLER, *Wallensteins Tod*

Great thoughts always come from the heart.
—MARQUIS DE VAUVENARGUES, *Réflexions et maximes*

Now that my ladder's gone,
I must lie down where all the ladders start,
In the foul rag-and-bone shop of the heart.
—WILLIAM BUTLER YEATS, *The Circus Animals' Desertion*
[These famous lines were written in the poet's old age; the missing "ladder" is the power of "pure mind" to create masterful themes out of the refuse of experience.]

**HEAVEN**                    See LAST JUDGMENT & THE HEREAFTER

**HEAVENS, THE**             See NATURE: THE HEAVENS, THE SKY

**HEDONISM**                 See also EXCESS; SEX & SENSUALITY

Who loves not wine, women, and song
Remains a fool his whole life long.          —ANONYMOUS
[Traditionally but probably wrongly attributed to Martin Luther.]

Let us eat and drink; for tomorrow we shall die.
—BIBLE, *Isaiah* 22:13
[The same is found at I Corinthians 15:32, "Let us eat and drink; for tomorrow we die."]

Gather ye rosebuds while ye may,
Old Time is still a-flying;
And this same flower that smiles today,
Tomorrow will be dying.
  —ROBERT HERRICK, *To the Virgins, To Make Much of Time*

Had we but world enough, and time,
This coyness, Lady, were no crime.
    —ANDREW MARVELL, *To His Coy Mistress*

But at my back I always hear
Times wingèd chariot hurrying near;
And yonder all before us lie
Deserts of vast eternity.      *—Ibid.*

The grave's a fine and private place,
But none, I think, do there embrace.   *—Ibid.*

I seek the utmost pleasure and the least pain.
    —PLAUTUS, *Captivi*

*Fait ce que voudras.*
Do what you will.   —RABELAIS, *Gargantua and Pantagruel*

Pleasure is the only thing to live for. Nothing ages like happiness.
  —OSCAR WILDE, *An Ideal Husband*

Give me the luxuries of life and I will willingly do without the
necessities.   —FRANK LLOYD WRIGHT, quoted in
    *The New York Times*, obituary, April 9, 1959

H E L L         See also DEVIL; EVIL;
        LAST JUDGMENT & THE HEREAFTER

Hell, madame, is to love no longer.
  —GEORGES BERNANOS, *The Diary of a Country Priest*

All hope abandon, ye who enter here!
  —DANTE, *Inferno*, in *The Divine Comedy*

Hell is oneself.     —T. S. ELIOT, *Cocktail Party*

When all the world dissolves,
And every creature shall be purified,
All place shall be hell that is not heaven.
  —CHRISTOPHER MARLOWE, *Dr. Faustus*

The road to Hell is paved with good intentions.
—KARL MARX, *Capital*
[Essentially proverbial. Also attributed to St. Bernard—"Hell is full
of good intentions and desires"—and others.]

Long is the way
And hard, that out of hell leads up to light.
—JOHN MILTON, *Paradise Lost*

Which way I fly is hell; myself am hell;
And in the lowest deep a lower deep
Still threatening to devour me opens wide,
To which the hell I suffer seems a heaven.          —*Ibid.*

Hell has no terrors for pagans.          —ARTHUR RIMBAUD,
*Mauvais Sang*

To work hard, to live hard, to die hard, and then to go to hell
after all would be too damned hard.
—CARL SANDBURG, *The People, Yes*

Hell is other people.          —JEAN-PAUL SARTRE, *No Exit*

The way down to hell [Hades] is easy.
The gates of black Dis stand open night and day.
But to retrace one's steps and escape to the upper air
That is toil, that is labor.          —VIRGIL, *Aeneid*

**HEROES**          See also COURAGE; GREATNESS;
HIGH POSITION: RULERS & LEADERS

No hero is mortal till he dies.
—W. H. AUDEN, *A Short Ode to a Philologist*

Unhappy the land that needs heroes.   —BERTOLT BRECHT, *Galileo*

Down these mean streets a man must go who is not himself mean;
who is neither tarnished nor afraid.
—RAYMOND CHANDLER, *The Simple Art of Murder*

Every hero becomes a bore at last.
—RALPH WALDO EMERSON, *Representative Men*

Show me a hero and I will write you a tragedy.
—F. SCOTT FITZGERALD, *Notebooks*

The boy stood on the burning deck
Whence all but he had fled.        —FELICIA HEMANS, *Casabianca*
[The boy was Giacomo Casabianca, who died during the Battle of
the Nile on the French flagship *L'Orient*. His father, Louis, the
ship's commander, was also killed.]


Listen, my children, and you shall hear,
Of the midnight ride of Paul Revere,
On the eighteenth of April, in Seventy-five;
Hardly a man is now alive
Who remembers that famous day and year.
              —HENRY WADSWORTH LONGFELLOW,
                 *Paul Revere's Ride* in *Tales of a Wayside Inn*


One if by land, and two if by sea;
And I on the opposite shore will be,
Ready to ride and spread the alarm
Through every Middlesex village and farm.        —*Ibid.*


Then out spake brave Horatius,
The Captain of the Gate:
"To every man upon this earth
Death cometh soon or late.
And how can man die better
Than facing fearful odds,
For the ashes of his fathers,
And the temples of his Gods?"
              —THOMAS BABINGTON MACAULAY, *Horatius* in
                 *Lays of Ancient Rome*


See, the conquering hero comes!
Sound the trumpets, beat the drums!
                        —THOMAS MORRELL, *Joshua*


We seek him here, we seek him there,
Those Frenchies seek him everywhere.
Is he in heaven?
Is he in hell?
That demmed, elusive Pimpernel.
              —BARONESS ORCZY, *The Scarlet Pimpernel*
[The Masterpiece Theater series on the Pankhurst family reported
that this bit of doggerel was applied to Christabel Pankhurst when
she was in hiding to avoid arrest:
   Is she in heaven? Is she in hell?
   That damned, elusive Christabel!]

The hero is strangely akin to those who die young.
                    —RAINER MARIA RILKE, *Duineser Elegien*

He was born with the gift of laughter and a sense that the world
was mad.                    —RAFAEL SABATINI, *Scaramouche*

Hail to the chief who in triumph advances!
                    —SIR WALTER SCOTT, *The Lady of the Lake*

O, young Lochinvar is come out of the west.
                    —SIR WALTER SCOTT, *Marmion*

He was a man, take him for all in all.
I shall not look upon his like again.    —SHAKESPEARE, *Hamlet*, I, ii

This was the noblest Roman of them all.
                    —SHAKESPEARE, *Julius Caesar*, V, v
[The reference is to Brutus.]

His life was gentle, and the elements
So mixed in him that Nature might stand up
And say to all the world, "This was a man."            —*Ibid.*

Arms and the man I sing, the first who came,
Compelled by fate, an exile out of Troy,
To Italy and the Lavinian coast.        —VIRGIL, *The Aeneid*

## HIGHLANDS OF SCOTLAND                    See NATIONS

## HIGH POSITION:                    See also GOVERNMENT;
## RULERS & LEADERS                    POWER; SUCCESS & FAME

Princes are like to heavenly bodies, which cause good or evil
times, and which have much veneration but no rest.
                    —FRANCIS BACON, *Of Empire*

Caesar's wife must be above suspicion.
                    —JULIUS CAESAR, attributed, based on Plutarch's
                    biography of Caesar

I had rather be right than be President.
                    —HENRY CLAY, Senate speech, 1850

To be a leader of men one must turn one's back on men.
—HAVELOCK ELLIS, Introduction to *A Rebours*
by J. K. Huysmans

A president's hardest task is not to do what is right but to know what is right. —LYNDON B. JOHNSON, State of the Union speech, 1965

*Noblesse oblige.*
Nobility [or, rank] has its obligations.
—DUC DE LÉVIS, *Maxims and Reflections*

*L'état c'est moi.*
I am the state.

—LOUIS XIV
[Reputedly said in a speech on April 13, 1665, but very possibly apocryphal—see also Napoleon Bonaparte at TYRANNY & TOTALITARIANISM.]

A prince who desires to maintain his position must learn to be not always good, but to be so or not, as needs require.
—MACHIAVELLI, *The Prince*

A prince who is a man of courage and is able to command, who knows how to preserve order in his state, need never regret having founded his security on the affection of the people.        —*Ibid.*

A leader is a dealer in hope.        —NAPOLEON BONAPARTE, *Maxims*

Uneasy lies the head that wears a crown.
—SHAKESPEARE, *Henry IV*, *Part II*, III, i

And what have kings that privates have not too,
Save ceremony, save general ceremony.
—SHAKESPEARE, *Henry V*, IV, i

Nice customs curtsey to great kings.        —*Ibid.*, V, ii

I would not be a queen
For all the world.        —SHAKESPEARE, *Henry VIII*, II, iii

Now is the winter of our discontent
Made glorious summer by this sun of York.
—SHAKESPEARE, *King Richard III*, I, i

I met a traveler from an antique land
Who said: "Two vast and trunkless legs of stone
Stand in the desert. . . . Near them, on the sand,
Half sunk, a shattered visage lies, whose frown,
And wrinkled lip, and sneer of cold command,
Tell that its sculptor well those passions read."
        —PERCY BYSSHE SHELLEY, *Ozymandias*

"My name is Ozymandias, king of kings:
Look on my works, yet Mighty, and despair!"
Nothing beside remains. Round the decay
Of that colossal wreck, boundless and bare,
The lone and level sands stretch far away.        —*Ibid.*

To know nor faith, nor love nor law; to be
Omnipotent but friendless is to reign.
        —PERCY BYSSHE SHELLEY, *Prometheus Unbound*

The only emperor is the emperor of ice-cream.
        —WALLACE STEVENS, *The Emperor of Ice-Cream*

All kings is mostly rapscallions.
        —MARK TWAIN, *The Adventures of Huckleberry Finn*

**HISTORY**                              See also PAST, THE

Man is a history-making creature who can neither repeat his past
nor leave it behind.        —W. H. AUDEN, *The Dyer's Hand*

*History, n.* an account mostly false, of events mostly unimportant,
which are brought about by rulers, mostly knaves, and soldiers,
mostly fools.        —AMBROSE BIERCE, *The Devil's Dictionary*

Happy the people whose annals are blank in history books!
        —THOMAS CARLYLE, *Frederick the Great*

The history of the world is but the biography of great men.
        —THOMAS CARLYLE, *Heroes and Hero Worship*

History has many cunning passages, contrived corridors and
issues.        —T. S. ELIOT, *Gerontion*

History is more or less bunk.
        —HENRY FORD, quoted in *Chicago Tribune*, May 25, 1916

History . . . is little more than the register of the crimes, follies, and misfortunes of mankind.
—EDWARD GIBBON, *The Decline and Fall of the Roman Empire*

People and governments have never learned anything from history.
—HEGEL, *Philosophy of History*, Introduction

History is the autobiography of a madman.
—ALEXANDER HERZEN, *Dr. Krupov*

It is not the neutrals or the lukewarms who make history.
—ADOLF HITLER, speech, April 23, 1933

History, Stephen said, is a nightmare from which I am trying to awake.
JAMES JOYCE, *Ulysses*

The history of all hitherto existing society is the history of class struggle.
—KARL MARX, *The Communist Manifesto*

World history is the world's verdict.
—J. C. FRIEDRICH VON SCHILLER, *Resignation*

A historian is a prophet in reverse.
—FRIEDRICH VON SCHLEGEL, *Athenaeum*

History is no more than the portrayal of crimes and misfortunes.
—VOLTAIRE, *L'Ingénu*

History can be well written only in a free country.
—VOLTAIRE, letter to Frederick the Great, May 27, 1773

Human history becomes more and more a race between education and catastrophe.
—H. G. WELLS, *The Outline of History*

Nothing has really happened until it has been recorded.
—VIRGINIA WOOLF, quoted in Harold Nicolson, *Diaries*

**HOLIDAYS**
See CHRISTMAS; NEW YEAR

**HOME**
See also FAMILY; MARRIAGE; PRIVACY

To make a happy fireside clime
To wean & wife,
That's the true pathos and sublime
Of human life.
—ROBERT BURNS, *To Dr. Blacklock*

Home is where one starts from.            —T. S. ELIOT, *East Coker*

Home is the place where when you have to go there
They have to take you in.
                                    —ROBERT FROST, *The Death of the Hired Man*

I remember, I remember,
The house where I was born,
The little window where the sun
Came peeping in at morn.              —THOMAS HOOD, *I Remember*

A man travels the world over in search of what he needs and returns home to find it.           —GEORGE MOORE, *The Brook Kerith*

Happy the man whose wish and care
A few paternal acres bound,
Content to breathe his native air
In his own ground.            —ALEXANDER POPE, *Ode on Solitude*

Home is the girl's prison and the woman's workhouse.
                            —GEORGE BERNARD SHAW, *Man and Superman*,
                            "Maxims for Revolutionists"

You Can't Go Home Again.           —THOMAS WOLFE, book title

## HONESTY & SINCERITY                              See also TRUTH

An honest man's word is as good as his bond.
                                    —CERVANTES, *Don Quixote*

A few honest men are better than numbers.
                —OLIVER CROMWELL, letter to Sir W. Spring, Sept. 1643

Being entirely honest with oneself is a good exercise.
                —FREUD, letter to Wilhelm Fliess, Oct. 15, 1897

He that resolves to deal with none but honest men must leave off
dealing.                         —THOMAS FULLER, *Gnomologia*

The secret of success is sincerity. Once you can fake that, you've
got it made.              —JEAN GIRADOUX, quoted by A. Bloch,
                            *Murphy's Law Book Two*

Honesty is praised and starves.                —JUVENAL, *Satires*

We only confess our little faults to persuade people that we have no large ones. —La Rochefoucauld, *Maxims*

Children and fools speak true. —John Lyly, *Endymion*

Some persons are likeable in spite of their unswerving integrity.
—Don Marquis, quoted by Edward Anthony,
*O Rare Don Marquis*

Honesty is for the most part less profitable than dishonesty.
—Plato, *The Republic*

An honest man's the noblest work of God.
—Alexander Pope, *An Essay on Man*

God looks at the clean hands, not the full ones.
—Publilius Syrus, *Moral Sayings*

Men should be what they seem. —Shakespeare, *Othello*, III, iii

Take note, take note, O world!
To be direct and honest is not safe. —*Ibid.*

Every man has his fault, and honesty is his.
—Shakespeare, *Timon of Athens*, III, i

I hold the maxim no less applicable to public than to private affairs, that honesty is the best policy.
—George Washington, *Farewell Address*, 1796
[The maxim was already time-honored; Cervantes also used it in *Don Quixote*.]

A little sincerity is a dangerous thing, and a great deal of it is absolutely fatal. —Oscar Wilde, *The Picture of Dorian Gray*

If you do not tell the truth about yourself you cannot tell it about other people. —Virginia Woolf, *The Moment and Other Essays*

## HONOR
See VIRTUE

## HOPE
See also OPTIMISM & PESSIMISM

Hope is a waking dream.
—Aristotle, quoted in Diogenes Laërtius,
*Lives of Eminent Philosphers*
[Cf. Matthew Prior, below.]

Hope is a good breakfast, but it is a bad supper.
—Francis Bacon, *Apophthegms*

He that lives upon hope will die fasting.
—Benjamin Franklin, *Poor Richard's Almanac*, Preface

If it were not for hopes, the heart would break.
—Thomas Fuller, *Gnomologia*

Hope, like the gleaming taper's light,
Adorns and cheers our way;
And still, as darker grows the night,
Emits a lighter ray.       —Oliver Goldsmith, *The Captivity*

Hope springs eternal in the human breast:
Man never is, but always to be blest.
—Alexander Pope, *An Essay on Man*

For hope is but the dream of those that wake.
—Matthew Prior, *Solomon*
[Cf. Aristotle, above.]

Extreme hopes are born of extreme misery.
—Bertrand Russell, *The Future of Mankind* in
*Unpopular Essays*

True hope is swift and flies with swallow's wings;
Kings it makes Gods, and meaner creatures kings.
—Shakespeare, *Richard III*, V, ii

Hope deceives more men than cunning can.
—Marquis Vauvenargues, *Réflections et maximes*

## HORSES                                        See NATURE: ANIMALS

## HOSPITALITY

What is there more kindly than the feelings between host and
guest?                    —Aeschylus, *The Libation Bearers*

One cannot have too large a party.       —Jane Austen, *Emma*

Go out into the highways and hedges and compel them to come
in, that my house may be filled.        —Bible, *Luke* 14:23

Use hospitality one to another without grudging.
—BIBLE, *I Peter* 4:9

Hospitality consists in a little fire, a little food, and an immense quiet. —RALPH WALDO EMERSON, *Journal*, 1856

Why don't you come up sometime, 'n see me?
—MAE WEST, *She Done Him Wrong*

**HUMAN BODY** See BODY, HUMAN

**HUMANS & HUMAN NATURE** See also LIFE; MEN; MIND; MISANTHROPY; WOMEN

For Mercy has a human heart,
Pity a human face,
And Love, the human form divine,
And Secrecy, the human dress.
—WILLIAM BLAKE, *The Divine Image* in *Songs of Innocence*

Cruelty has a human heart,
And Jealousy a human face;
Terror, the human form divine,
And secrecy, the human dress.
—WILLIAM BLAKE, *A Divine Image* in *Songs of Experience*

Man's inhumanity to man makes countless thousands mourn.
—ROBERT BURNS, *Man Was Made To Mourn*

Man is a tool-using animal. . . . Without tools he is nothing, with tools, he is all.
—THOMAS CARLYLE, *Sartor Resartus*
[Earlier, James Boswell ascribed the definition of man as "a tool-making animal," to Benjamin Franklin (*The Life of Johnson*, April 17, 1778). Johnson retorted: "But many a man never made a tool; and suppose a man without arms, he could not make a tool."]

Human nature is the same all over the world.
—EARL OF CHESTERFIELD, letter to his son, Oct. 2, 1747

No man is an island entire of itself; every man is a part of the continent, a part of the main. —JOHN DONNE, *Devotions XVII*

Any man's death diminishes me, because I am involved in mankind. And therefore never send to know for whom the bell tolls. It tolls for thee. —*Ibid.*

Man is slightly nearer to the atom than the star. . . . From his central position man can survey the grandest works of nature with the astronomer, or the minutest works with the physicist.
—SIR ARTHUR EDDINGTON, *Stars and Atoms*

In spite of everything I still believe that people are really good at heart. —ANNE FRANK, *The Diary of a Young Girl*

Wild animals never kill for sport. Man is the only one to whom the torture and death of his fellow creatures is amusing in itself.
—JAMES A. FROUDE, *Oceana*

When God at first made man,
Having a glass of blessings standing by,
Let us, said he, pour on him all we can.
Let the world's riches, which dispersèd lie,
Contract into a span.
—GEORGE HERBERT, *The Pulley* in *The Temple*
[God withholds only one gift: rest.]

At last,
If goodness lead him not, yet weariness
May toss him to My breast. —*Ibid.*

We has met the enemy, and it is us. —WALT KELLY, *Pogo*
[For Oliver Hazard Perry's version, see under AMERICAN HISTORY: MEMORABLE MOMENTS.]

I teach you the superman. Man is something to be surpassed.
—FRIEDRICH NIETZSCHE, *Thus Spake Zarathustra*

Man is the measure of all things, of things that are, that they are, of things that are not, that they are not.
—PROTAGORAS, quoted in Diogenes Laërtius,
*Lives of Eminent Philosophers*

Everything is good when it leaves the Creator's hands; everything degenerates in the hands of man. —JEAN JACQUES ROUSSEAU, *Émile*

Brief and powerless is man's life; on him and all his race the slow, sure doom falls pitiless and dark.
—BERTRAND RUSSELL, *The Free Man's Worship*

We are such stuff
As dreams are made on, and our little life
Is rounded with a sleep.     —SHAKESPEARE, *The Tempest*, IV, i

How beauteous mankind is! O brave new world,
That has such people in it.     —*Ibid.*, V, i

Wonders are many, and none is more wonderful than man.
—SOPHOCLES, *Antigone*

Man is a social animal.     —BENEDICT SPINOZA, *Ethics*

We feel and know that we are eternal.     —*Ibid.*

I am a man; nothing human is alien to me.
—TERENCE, *Heuton Timoroumenos*
(*The Self-Tormentor*)

If you pick up a starving dog and make him prosperous, he will
not bite you. This is the principal difference between a dog and a
man.     —MARK TWAIN, *Pudd'nhead Wilson*

**HUMOR**     See also LAUGHTER

A man who could make so vile a pun would not scruple to pick a
pocket.     —JOHN DENNIS, *The Gentleman's Magazine*, 1781

There is no better role to play among the great than that of
jester.     —DENIS DIDEROT, *Le Neveu de Rameau*

A difference of taste in jokes is a great strain on the affections.
—GEORGE ELIOT, *Daniel Deronda*

Wit makes its own welcome and levels all distinctions.
—RALPH WALDO EMERSON, *The Comic*

Humor is an affirmation of dignity, a declaration of man's superiority to all that befalls him.     —ROMAIN GARY, *Promise at Dawn*

You can pretend to be serious; but you can't pretend to be witty.
—SACHA GUITRY, quoted in *Workshop on
World Humor*, Nov. 1984
[Cited by Donal Henahan in *The New York Times*, March 17, 1985.]

Leave jesting while it pleaseth, lest it turn to earnest.
—GEORGE HERBERT, *Jacula Prudentum*

Impropriety is the soul of wit.
>—SOMERSET MAUGHAM, *The Moon and Sixpence*

[For Shakespeare on the soul of wit, see ARTS: STYLE IN WRITING & EXPRESSION.]

Everybody likes a kidder, but nobody lends him money.
>—ARTHUR MILLER, *Death of a Salesman*

Wit is the epitaph of an emotion.
>—FRIEDRICH NIETZSCHE, *Miscellaneous Maxims
>and Opinions*

Everything is funny as long as it happens to somebody else.
>—WILL ROGERS, *Warning to Jokers: Lay Off the
>Prince* in *The Illiterate Digest*

The quality of wit inspires more admiration than confidence.
>—GEORGE SANTAYANA, *Wit* in *The Sense of Beauty*

My way of joking is to tell the truth.
>—GEORGE BERNARD SHAW, *John Bull's
>Other Island*

Humor is emotional chaos remembered in tranquillity.
>—JAMES THURBER, *New York Post*, Feb. 29, 1960

The secret source of humor is not joy but sorrow. There is no humor in heaven.    —MARK TWAIN, *Pudd'nhead Wilson*

We are not amused.
>—QUEEN VICTORIA, after seeing an imitation of
>herself by a groom-in-waiting, in
>*Notebooks of a Spinster*, Jan. 2, 1900

It's hard to be funny when you have to be clean.
>—MAE WEST, quoted in Joseph Weintraub, ed.,
>*The Wit and Wisdom of Mae West*

**HUNGER**                    See FOOD, WINE & EATING;
>POVERTY & HUNGER

**HURRYING**                                    See HASTE

# HYPOCRISY

See also CRAFTINESS; DISHONESTY

Only the hypocrite is really rotten to the core.
—HANNAH ARENDT, *On Revolution*

And when thou prayest, thou shalt not be as the hypocrites are: for they love to pray standing in the synagogues and in the corners of the streets, that they may be seen of men.   —BIBLE, *Matthew* 6:6

Beware of false prophets, which come to you in sheep's clothing, but inwardly they are ravening wolves.   —*Ibid.*, 7:15

Woe unto you, scribes and Pharisees, hypocrites! for ye are like unto whitened sepulchres, which indeed appear beautiful outward, but are within full of dead men's bones, and of all uncleanness.
—*Ibid.*, 23:27

Be a hypocrite if you like; but don't talk like one!
—DENIS DIDEROT, *Le Neveu de Rameau*

I detest that man who hides one thing in the depth of his heart and speaks forth another.   —HOMER, *Iliad*

No man is a hypocrite in his pleasures.
—SAMUEL JOHNSON, quoted in James Boswell, *Life of Johnson*, June 19, 1784

Hypocrisy is the homage which vice pays to virtue.
—LA ROCHEFOUCAULD, *Maxims*

A hypocrite is a person who . . . but who isn't?
—DON MARQUIS, quoted by Frederick B. Wilcox, *A Little Book of Aphorisms*

For neither man nor angel can discern
Hypocrisy, the only evil that walks
Invisible, except to God alone.   —JOHN MILTON, *Paradise Lost*

Being a hypocrite has marvelous advantages!   —MOLIÈRE, *Don Juan*

With devotion's usage
And pious action we do sugar o'er
The devil himself.   —SHAKESPEARE, *Hamlet*, III, i

A nice man is man of nasty ideas.
——JONATHAN SWIFT, *Thoughts on Various Subjects*

As for conforming outwardly, and living your own life inwardly,
I don't think much of that.        ——THOREAU, *Excursions* (letter to
Harrison Blake, Aug. 9, 1850)

**IDEAS  &  IDEALS**                    See also ETHICS & MORALITY;
MIND, THOUGHT &
UNDERSTANDING; VISION
& VISIONARIES

If you believe in an ideal, you don't own you, it owns you.
——RAYMOND CHANDLER, quoted by F. MacShane,
*The Life of Raymond Chandler*

You can't shoot an idea.
——THOMAS E. DEWEY, debate with Harold Stassen on
whether to outlaw the Communist party, 1948

An invasion of armies can be resisted, but not an idea whose time
has come.              ——VICTOR HUGO, *Histôire d'un Crime*
[This famous line is a free translation of the original, which does not
contain the phrase "whose time has come."]

An idea isn't responsible for the people who believe in it.
——DON MARQUIS, *The Sun Dial*

To die for an idea: it is unquestionably noble. But how much
nobler would it be if men died for ideas that were true.
——H. L. MENCKEN, *Prejudices: Fifth Series*

As there are misanthropists, or haters of mankind, so there are mis-
logists, or haters of ideas.              ——PLATO, *Phaedo*

Loyalty to petrified opinion never yet broke a chain or freed a
human soul.        ——MARK TWAIN, attributed, inscribed beneath his
bust in the Hall of Fame

Serious people have few ideas. People with ideas are never serious.
——PAUL VALÉRY, *Mauvaises Pensées*

The true God, the mighty God, is the God of ideas.
——ALFRED DE VIGNY, *La Bouteille à la mer*

All great ideas are dangerous.        ——OSCAR WILDE, *De Profundis*

**IDLENESS**                                        See LAZINESS

**ILLNESS & REMEDIES**          See also DOCTORS & THE
                                          PRACTICE OF MEDICINE;
                                          HEALTH; MADNESS

Illness tells us what we are.     —ANONYMOUS (ITALIAN PROVERB)

The greatest evil is physical pain.     —ST. AUGUSTINE, *Soliloquies*

Look into the depths of your own soul and learn first to know
yourself, then you will understand why this illness was bound to
come upon you and perhaps you will thenceforth avoid falling ill.
          —FREUD, *One of the Difficulties of Psychoanalysis*

Natural forces within us are the true healers of disease.
                    —HIPPOCRATES, *Aphorisms*

The patient must combat the disease along with the physician.
                                        —*Ibid.*

To live by medicine is to live horribly.
          —LINNAEUS, *Diaeta Naturalis*, introduction

Illness is not something a person *has*. It's another way of being.
          —JONATHAN MILLER, *The Body in Question*

Nearly all men die of their medicines, and not of their illnesses.
          —MOLIÈRE, *La Malade imaginaire*

Everything great that we know has come to us from neurotics.
They alone have founded our religions and created our masterpieces.
Never will the world be aware of how much it owes to them, nor
above all what they have suffered in order to bestow their gifts on it.
          —MARCEL PROUST, *Remembrance of Things Past:
          The Guermantes Way*

There are maladies we must not seek to cure because they alone
protect us from others that are more serious.          —*Ibid.*

There are some remedies worse than the disease.
                    —PUBLILIUS SYRUS, *Moral Sayings*
[Also, Francis Bacon in *Of Seditions and Troubles*: "The remedy is
worse than the disease."]

There never was yet philosopher
That could endure the toothache patiently.
—SHAKESPEARE, *Much Ado About Nothing*, V, i

**ILLUSIONS**                   See REALITY & ILLUSIONS

**IMAGINATION**                 See MIND, THOUGHT &
                                UNDERSTANDING; VISION &
                                VISIONARIES

**INACTION**                    See LAZINESS; PROCRASTINATION

**INDIANS**                     See RACES & PEOPLES

**INITIATIVE**                  See BOLDNESS & INITIATIVE;
                                SELF-RELIANCE

**INNOCENCE**        See also CHILDREN & CHILDHOOD; VIRTUE

Where, my God, where, Oh Lord, where or when was I, Your
servant, innocent?              —ST. AUGUSTINE, *Confessions*

Blessed are the pure in heart: for they shall see God.
                                —BIBLE, *Matthew* 5:8
[For other verses from the Sermon on the Mount see VIRTUE.]

Except ye be converted and become as little children, ye shall not
enter into the kingdom of heaven.          —*Ibid.*, 18:3

Innocence dwells with wisdom, but never with ignorance.
                                —WILLIAM BLAKE, *The Four Zoas*

The innocent are God's elect.
                                —ST. CLEMENT, *First Epistle to the Corinthians*

Teach us delight in simple things,
And mirth that has no bitter springs.
                                —RUDYARD KIPLING, *The Children's Song*

Innocence is ashamed of nothing.
                                —JEAN JACQUES ROUSSEAU, *Émile*

If you carry with you your childhood, you never become older.
> —ABRAHAM SUTZKEVER, interview,
> *The New York Times*, March 17, 1985

[The slightly eccentric syntax results from Sutzkever's linguist orientation—he is probably the foremost living Yiddish poet.]

I used to be Snow White—but I drifted.
> —MAE WEST, quoted in Joseph Weintraub, ed.,
> *The Wit and Wisdom of Mae West*

**INNOVATION**                                      See NEW THINGS;
                                              SCIENCE: DISCOVERY

**INSANITY**                                      See MADNESS

**INSIGHT**                                  See MIND, THOUGHT &
                              UNDERSTANDING; SCIENCE: DISCOVERY;
                                            VISION & VISIONARIES

**INSULTS & PUT-DOWNS**              See also MANNERS

California is a great place to live—if you happen to be an orange.
> —FRED ALLEN, attributed

There is less in this than meets the eye.        —TALLULAH BANKHEAD
[*Bartlett* says that she made this remark to Alexander Woollcott at Maurice Maeterlinck's play *Aglavaine and Selysette*.]

There goes the famous good time that was had by all.
> —BETTE DAVIS, speaking of a starlet,
> quoted in Leslie Halliwell,
> *The Filmgoer's Book of Quotes*

I went to Philadelphia one Sunday. The place was closed.
> —W. C. FIELDS, attributed

[One of many cracks at Philadelphia by Fields; see also under CITIES.]

Another damned, thick square book! Always scribble, scribble, scribble! Eh! Mr. Gibbon?
> —WILLIAM HENRY, DUKE OF GLOUCESTER,
> upon receiving from Edward Gibbon Vol. II of
> *Decline and Fall of the Roman Empire*,
> quoted in note to James Boswell's *Life of Johnson*

They teach the morals of a whore, and the manners of a dancing master.    —SAMUEL JOHNSON, speaking of the Earl of Chesterfield's letters, in a letter to the same, Feb. 7, 1754

The noblest prospect that a Scotchman ever sees is the high road that leads to London. —SAMUEL JOHNSON, quoted by James Boswell, *Tour to the Hebrides*, Nov. 10, 1773

Sir, a woman's preaching is like a dog's walking on his hinder legs. It is not done well; but you are surprised to find it done at all.
                                                —*Ibid.*, July 31, 1763

Mad, bad, and dangerous to know.
            —LADY CAROLINE LAMB, speaking of Lord Byron, *Journal*

She looked as though butter wouldn't melt in her mouth—or anywhere else.          —ELSA LANCHESTER, cited in Leslie Halliwell, *The Filmgoer's Book of Quotes*

My dear, I don't give a damn.
                  —MARGARET MITCHELL, *Gone with the Wind*

She ran the whole gamut of emotions from A to B.
                  —DOROTHY PARKER, re Katherine Hepburn in *The Lake*

It is not a novel to be thrown aside lightly. It should be thrown aside with great force.
                  —DOROTHY PARKER, book review, quoted by A. Johnston, *Legend of a Sport, The New Yorker*

*House Beautiful* is the play lousy.
                  —DOROTHY PARKER, theater review

He never said a foolish thing
Nor never did a wise one.
                  —EARL OF ROCHESTER, *The King's Epitaph*, for Charles II

You blocks, you stones, you worse than senseless things!
                  —SHAKESPEARE, *Julius Caesar*, I, i

He wants the natural touch.
                  —SHAKESPEARE, *Macbeth*, IV, ii

Dear Sir, Your profession has, as usual, destroyed your brain.
—GEORGE BERNARD SHAW, letter to a journalist,
*Collected Letters*, Dan H. Laurence, ed.

No matter how thin you slice it, it's still baloney.
—ALFRED E. SMITH, campaign speeches, 1936

I am just going to pray for you at St. Paul's, but with no very lively hope of success.
—REV. SYDNEY SMITH, quoted by H. Pearson,
*The Smith of Smiths*

I regard you with an indifference closely bordering on aversion.
—ROBERT LOUIS STEVENSON, *Story of the Bandbox* in
*New Arabian Nights*

## INTEGRITY

See HONESTY & SINCERITY;
SELF; VIRTUE

## INTELLIGENCE

See GENIUS; MIND,
THOUGHT & UNDERSTANDING

## INTIMACY & FAMILIARITY

Familiarity breeds contempt.   —AESOP, *The Fox and the Lion*
[See Mark Twain's amendment, below.]

No man is a hero to his valet.
—ANNE BIGOT DU CORNUEL, quoted in
*Lettres de Mme. Aissé*, Aug. 13, 1728

Many a man has been a wonder to the world, whose wife and valet have seen nothing in him that was even remarkable. Few men have been admired by their servants.   —MONTAIGNE, *Essays*

Familiarity breeds contempt—and children.
—MARK TWAIN, *Notebooks*

## INVENTION

See NEW THINGS; SCIENCE:
DISCOVERY; TECHNOLOGY

## IRELAND & THE IRISH

See NATIONS

**IRON CURTAIN**                              See COMMUNISM

**ITALY**                                      See NATIONS

**JAPAN**                                       See NATIONS

**JEALOUSY**

Jealousy is nothing but the foolish child of pride.
—PIERRE-AUGUSTIN DE BEAUMARCHAIS,
*The Marriage of Figaro*

Love is as strong as death; jealousy is as cruel as the grave.
—BIBLE, *Song of Solomon* 8:6

It is not love that is blind, but jealousy.
—LAWRENCE DURRELL, *Justine*

Jealousy is always born with love, but does not always die with it.
—LA ROCHEFOUCAULD, *Maxims*

O! beware, my lord, of jealousy.
It is the green-eyed monster which doth mock the meat it feeds on.
—SHAKESPEARE, *Othello*, III, iii

There is no greater glory than love, nor any greater punishment
than jealousy.        —LOPE DE VEGA, *Cantorcillo de la Virgen*

**JERUSALEM**                                 See CITIES

**JESUS CHRIST**        See also ANNUNCIATION; CHRISTMAS;
PROVIDENCE, DIVINE

And the angel came in unto her, and said, Hail, thou that art highly
favored, the Lord is with thee: blessed art thou among women.
—BIBLE, *Luke* 1:28

Thou shalt conceive in thy womb, and bring forth a son, and shalt
call his name *Jesus*.        —*Ibid.*, 1:31

In the beginning was the Word, and the Word was with God, and
the Word was God.        —BIBLE, *John* 1:1

In him was life; and the life was the light of men.

And the light shineth in darkness; and the darkness comprehended it not. —*Ibid.*, 1.4,5

And the Word was made flesh, and dwelt among us (and we beheld his glory, the glory as of the only begotten of the Father), full of grace and truth. —*Ibid.*, 1:14

For God so loveth the world, that he gave his only begotten son, that whosoever believeth in him should not perish, but have everlasting life. —*Ibid.*, 3:16

I am the good shepherd. The good shepherd giveth his life for the sheep. —*Ibid.*, 10:11

Thou hast conquered, Galilean!
—JULIAN THE APOSTATE, attributed death-bed words

Jesus died too soon. He would have repudiated his doctrine if he had lived to my age.
—FRIEDRICH NIETZSCHE, *Thus Spake Zarathustra*

Thou hast conquered, O pale Galilean; the world has grown gray from thy breath;
We have drunken of things Lethean, and fed on the fullness of death. —ALGERNON C. SWINBURNE, *Hymn to Prosperine*

Christ is God clothed with human nature.
—BENJAMIN WHICHCOTE,
*Moral and Religious Aphorisms*

**JEWS**　　　　　　　　　　See RACES & PEOPLES

**JOY**　　　　　　　　　　See HAPPINESS; HAPPINESS, EXPRESSIONS OF

**JUDGING OTHERS**　　　　　See EVIDENCE; FORGIVENESS & MERCY; JUSTICE; TOLERANCE & UNDERSTANDING

**JUNE**　　　　　　　　　　See NATURE: SEASONS

# JUSTICE

See also EVIDENCE; FORGIVENESS
& MERCY; LAW & LAWYERS;
PUNISHMENT; REVENGE

All virtue is summed up in dealing justly.
—ARISTOTLE, *Nicomachean Ethics*

With what measure ye mete, it shall be meted to you.
—BIBLE, *Mark* 4:24

God is not mocked: for whatsoever a man soweth, that shall he also reap. —BIBLE, *Galatians* 6:7

Justice is the crowning glory of the virtues.   —CICERO, *De officiis*

There is no such thing as justice—in or out of court.
—CLARENCE DARROW, interview,
*The New York Times*, April 19, 1936

Justice is truth in action.
—BENJAMIN DISRAELI, speech, Feb. 11, 1851

Justice . . . is a kind of compact not to harm or be harmed.
—EPICURUS, *Principal Doctrines*

Only the just man enjoys peace of mind.     —EPICURUS, fragment

A fox should not be of the jury at a goose's trial.
—THOMAS FULLER, *Gnomologia*

Justice consists in taking from no man what is his.
—THOMAS HOBBES, *Leviathan*

Injustice anywhere is a threat to justice everywhere.
—MARTIN LUTHER KING, JR., letter from
the Birmingham, Ala., jail, 1963

Love of justice in most men is no more than the fear of suffering injustice.      —LA ROCHEFOUCAULD, *Maxims*

Your justice would freeze beer!  —ARTHUR MILLER, *The Crucible*

I shall temper . . . justice with mercy.
—JOHN MILTON, *Paradise Lost*

Justice without force is impotent; force without justice is tyranny.
—PASCAL, *Pensées*

Everywhere there is one principle of justice, which is the interest of the stronger. —PLATO, *The Republic*

All justice comes from God—he alone is its source.
—JEAN JACQUES ROUSSEAU, *Social contract*

There are times when even justice brings harm with it.
—SOPHOCLES, *Electra*

If they are just, they are better than clever.
—SOPHOCLES, *Philoctetes*

There is one universal law. . . . That law is justice. Justice forms the cornerstone of each nation's law.
—ALEXIS DE TOCQUEVILLE, *Democracy in America*

The laws of changeless justice bind
Oppressor and oppressed;
And close as sin and suffering joined,
We march to fate abreast.
—JOHN GREENLEAF WHITTIER, *At Port Royal*

The good ended happily, and the bad unhappily. That is what Fiction means. —OSCAR WILDE, *The Importance of Being Earnest*

**KINDNESS** See VIRTUE

**KINGS** See HIGH POSITION:
RULERS & LEADERS

**KNOWLEDGE** See EDUCATION & LEARNING;
SCIENCE

**LAISSEZ FAIRE** See CAPITALISM

**LANGUAGE & WORDS** See also ARTS: STYLE IN
WRITING & EXPRESSION;
ARTS: WRITING

By thy words thou shalt be justified, and by the words thou shalt be condemned. —BIBLE, *Matthew* 12:37

What so wild as words are?
—ROBERT BROWNING, *A Woman's Last Word*

A blow with a word strikes deeper than a blow with a sword.
—ROBERT BURTON, *The Anatomy of Melancholy*

"When I use a word," Humpty Dumpty said, in a rather scornful tone, "it means just what I choose it to mean—neither more nor less."
"The question is," said Alice, "whether you can make words mean so many different things."
"The question is," said Humpty Dumpty, "which is to be master —that's all."    —LEWIS CARROLL, *Through the Looking-Glass*

I speak Spanish to God, Italian to women, French to men, and German to my horse.    —EMPEROR CHARLES V, attributed

A word is dead
When it is said,
Some say.
I say it just
Begins to live
That day.    —EMILY DICKINSON, poem, 1872

Language is the archives of history.
—RALPH WALDO EMERSON, *The Poet*

The chief merit of language is clarity, and we know that nothing detracts so much from this as do unfamiliar terms.
—GALEN, *On the Natural Faculties*

Fair words cost nothing.    —JOHN GAY, *The Mohocks*

Words are mere sound and smoke, dimming the heavenly light.
—GOETHE, *Faust*

In two words: im–possible.    —SAMUEL GOLDWYN, attributed

The tongue of man is a twisty thing.    —HOMER, *Iliad*

Once a word has been allowed to escape, it can never be recalled.
—HORACE, *Epistles*, I, 18

Language is the dress of thought.
—SAMUEL JOHNSON, *Lives of the English Poets*
[See also Wesley at ARTS: STYLE IN WRITING & EXPRESSION.]

My heavens! I've been talking prose for the last forty years without knowing it. —MOLIÈRE, *Le Bourgeois Gentilhomme*

Every word is a preconceived judgment.
—FRIEDRICH NIETZSCHE, *Human All-too-Human*

Speech is a mirror of the soul: as a man speaks, so he is.
—PUBLILIUS SYRUS, *Moral Sayings*

Slang is a language that rolls up its sleeves, spits on its hands, and goes to work. —CARL SANDBURG, *The New York Times*,
Feb. 13, 1959

Words are weapons, and it is dangerous . . . to borrow them from the arsenal of the enemy. —GEORGE SANTAYANA, *Obiter Scripta*

What's in a name? That which we call a rose
By any other name would smell as sweet.
—SHAKESPEARE, *Romeo and Juliet*, II, ii

Words pay no debts. —SHAKESPEARE, *Troilus and Cressida*, III, ii

An idea does not pass from one language to another without change. —MIGUEL DE UNAMUNO, *Tragic Sense of Life*

## LAST JUDGMENT & THE HEREAFTER

See also HELL; WORLD, END OF

But many that are first shall be last; and the last shall be first.
—BIBLE, *Matthew* 19:30

And whosoever shall exalt himself shall be abased; and he that shall humble himself shall be exalted. —*Ibid.*, 23:12

He shall separate them one from another, as a shepherd divideth his sheep from his goats. —*Ibid.*, 25:32

Don't wait for the Last Judgment. It takes place every day.
—ALBERT CAMUS, *The Fall*

Abou Ben Adhem (may his tribe increase!)
Awoke one night from a deep dream of peace,
And saw, within the moonlight of the room,
Making it rich, and like a lily in bloom,
An angel writing in a book of gold.
—LEIGH HUNT, *Abou Ben Adhem and the Angel*

Write me as one that loves his fellow men.                     —*Ibid.*

The angel wrote, and vanished. The next night
It came again with a great wakening light,
And showed the names whom love of God had blessed
And lo! Ben Adhem's name led all the rest.                     —*Ibid.*

The bottom line is in heaven.
> —EDWIN HERBERT LAND, 1977, Shareholders'
> Meeting, Polaroid Corp., April 26, 1977

Now hast thou but one bare hour to live
And then thou must be damned perpetually!
Stand still you ever-moving spheres of heaven,
That time may cease and midnight never come.
> —CHRISTOPHER MARLOWE, *Doctor Faustus*

**LAUGHTER**                                    See also HUMOR

Meaningless laughter is a sign of ill-breeding.
> —ANONYMOUS (ARAB PROVERB)

A maid that laughs is half taken.
> —ANONYMOUS (ENGLISH PROVERB), quoted in
> John Ray, *English Proverbs*

[St. John Chrysostom may have had this in mind when he related laughter to sin; see below.]

He laughs best who laughs last.
> —ANONYMOUS (ENGLISH PROVERB)

[H. L. Mencken noted that this appears to be proverbial in all European languages.]

Man thinks. God laughs.        —ANONYMOUS (JEWISH PROVERB)

I force myself to laugh at everything for fear of being obliged to weep.        —PIERRE-AUGUSTIN DE BEAUMARCHAIS, *The Barber of Seville*

Laughter has no greater enemy than emotion.
> —HENRI BERGSON, *Laughter*

[Bergson went on to say that laughter requires "a momentary anesthesia of the heart."]

No man who has once heartily and wholly laughed can be altogether irreclaimably bad.        —THOMAS CARLYLE, *Sartor Resartus*

Nothing is sillier than silly laughter.     —CATULLUS, *Carmina*

The most wasted of all days is that in which we have not laughed.
    —SÉBASTIEN R. N. CHAMFORT, *Maximes et pensées*

In my mind, there is nothing so illiberal and so ill-bred as audible laughter.     —EARL OF CHESTERFIELD, letter to his son,
March 9, 1748

Laughter does not seem to be a sin, but it leads to sin.
    —ST. JOHN CHRYSOSTOM, *Homilies*

One must laugh before one is happy or one may die without ever having laughed at all.     —LA BRUYÈRE, *Les Caractères*

Laugh, and the world laughs with you;
Weep, and you weep alone.     —ELLA WHEELER WILCOX, *Solitude*

## LAW & LAWYERS     See also EVIDENCE; JUSTICE

Go to law for a sheep and lose your cow.
    —ANONYMOUS (GERMAN PROVERB)

Law is a bottomless pit.     —JOHN ARBUTHNOT, pamphlet title

Law means good order.     —ARISTOTLE, *Politics*

All law has for its object to confirm and exalt into a system the exploitation of the workers by a ruling class.
    —MIKHAIL A. BAKUNIN, *Dieu et l'état*

It is better that ten guilty persons escape than one innocent suffer.
    —WILLIAM BLACKSTONE, *Commentaries on
the Laws of England*
[See also Voltaire, below.]

One law for the lion and ox is oppression.
    —WILLIAM BLAKE, *The Marriage of Heaven and Hell*

If we would guide by the light of reason, we must let our minds be bold.     —LOUIS D. BRANDEIS, *N.Y. State Ice Co.* vs.
*Liebmann,* 1932

The people's good is the highest law.     —CICERO, *De Legibus*

One with the law is a majority.
　　　　　—CALVIN COOLIDGE, speech, July 27, 1920

Law [is] a horrible business.
　　　　　—CLARENCE DARROW, interview, *The New
　　　　　York Times*, April 19, 1936

The law is bigger than money—but only if the law works hard
enough.　　　　　—THOMAS E. DEWEY, quoted in
　　　　　Richard Norton Smith, *Thomas E. Dewey*

"If the law supposes that," said Mr. Bumble . . . "the law is a ass
—a idiot."　　　　　—CHARLES DICKENS, *Oliver Twist*

Good men must not obey the laws too well.
　　　　　—RALPH WALDO EMERSON, *Politics*

Public opinion is always in advance of the law.
　　　　　—JOHN GALSWORTHY, *Windows*

There is no better way of exercising the imagination than the study
of law. No poet ever interpreted nature as freely as a lawyer inter-
prets the truth.　　　　　—JEAN GIRADOUX, *Tiger at the Gates*

Laws grind the poor, and rich men rule the law.
　　　　　—OLIVER GOLDSMITH, *The Traveller*

A verbal contract isn't worth the paper its printed on.
　　　　　—SAMUEL GOLDWYN, attributed

The law is not the same at morning and at night.
　　　　　—GEORGE HERBERT, *Jacula Prudentum*

The life of the law has not been logic; it has been experience.
　　　　　—OLIVER WENDELL HOLMES, JR., *The Common Law*

Great cases like hard cases make bad law.
　　　　　—OLIVER WENDELL HOLMES, JR.,
　　　　　*Northern Securities Co.* v. *U.S.*, 1904
[Holmes is alluding to the legal byword: "Hard cases make bad
law."]

The execution of the laws is more important than the making
them.　　　　　—THOMAS JEFFERSON, letter to the Abbé Arnond, 1789

Morality cannot be legislated but behavior can be regulated. Judicial decrees may not change the heart, but they can restrain the heartless.　　　　—MARTIN LUTHER KING, JR., *Strength to Love*

Wherever law ends, tyranny begins.
　　　　　　　　—JOHN LOCKE, *Two Treatises on Government*
[The almost identical observation was made, or borrowed, by William Pitt, see below.]

Useless laws weaken the necessary laws.
　　　　　　　　—MONTESQUIEU, *De l'esprit des lois*

They have no lawyers among them [in Utopia] for they consider them as the sort of people whose profession it is to disguise matters.
　　　　　　　　—THOMAS MORE, *Utopia*

Laws were made to be broken.
　　　　　　　　—CHRISTOPHER NORTH, *Noctes Ambrosianae*

A judge is not supposed to know anything about the facts of life until they have been presented into evidence and explained to him at least three times.　　　—LORD CHIEF JUSTICE PARKER, quoted in the
*Observer*, March 12, 1961

Where laws end, tyranny begins.
　　　　　　　　—WILLIAM PITT, EARL OF CHATHAM, speech,
Jan. 9, 1770, on the Wilkes case
[Note similarity to John Locke's comment, above.]

The law must be stable, but it must not stand still.
　　　　　　　　—ROSCOE POUND, *Introduction to the Philosophy of Law*

The law does not generate justice. The law is nothing but a declaration and application of what is just.
　　　　　　　　—PIERRE-JOSEPH PROUDHON, *De la justice
dans la révolution*

Necessity knows no law.
　　　　　　　　—PUBLILIUS SYRUS, *Moral Sayings*
[Also said by St. Augustine and Oliver Cromwell.]

No man is above the law and no man is below it; nor do we ask any man's permission when we require him to obey it.
　　　　　　　　—THEODORE ROOSEVELT, speech, Jan. 1904

Laws are always useful to persons of property and hurtful to those who have none.    —JEAN JACQUES ROUSSEAU, *Social Contract*

Ignorance of the law excuses no man: not that all men know the law, but because 'tis an excuse every man will plead, and no man can tell how to refute him.    —JOHN SELDEN,
*Judgments* in *Table Talk*

The first thing we do, let's kill all the lawyers.
—SHAKESPEARE, *Henry VI, Part II*, III, i

Laws are like spiders' webs: If some poor weak creature come up against them, it is caught; but a big one can break through and get away.    —SOLON, quoted in Diogenes Laërtius,
*Lives of the Eminent Philosophers*

Extreme law is often extreme injustice.
—TERENCE, *Heauton Timoroumenos*

It is better to risk saving a guilty man than to condemn an innocent one.    —VOLTAIRE, *Zadig*
[The idea is probably better known in Blackstone's formulation, see above.]

**LAZINESS**    See also PROCRASTINATION;
PRUDENCE & PRACTICAL
WISDOM

Laziness is often mistaken for patience.
—ANONYMOUS (FRENCH PROVERB)

Laziness travels so slowly that poverty soon overtakes him.
—BENJAMIN FRANKLIN, *Poor Richard's Almanac*

Idle men are dead all their life long.
—THOMAS FULLER, *Gnomologia*

I have all my life long been lying [in bed] till noon; yet I tell all young men, and tell them with great sincerity, that nobody who does not rise early will ever do any good.
—SAMUEL JOHNSON, quoted by James Boswell,
*Tour to the Hebrides*, Sept. 14, 1773

Lazy people are always looking for something to do.
—MARQUIS DE VAUVENARGUES, *Maximes et pensées*

Iron rusts from disuse, stagnant water loses its purity and in cold weather becomes frozen; even so does inaction sap the vigors of the mind. —Leonardo da Vinci, *Notebooks*

For Satan finds some mischief still
For idle hand to do.
—Isaac Watts, *Against Idleness and Mischief*

**L E A D E R S**
See high position:
rulers & leaders

**L E A R N I N G**
See education & learning

**L I B E R T Y**
See freedom

**L I E S**
See dishonesty

**L I F E**
See also experience;
generations

And here we are as on a darkling plain
Swept with confused alarms of struggle and flight,
Where ignorant armies clash by night.
—Matthew Arnold, *Dover Beach*

To every thing there is a season, and a time to every purpose under the heaven:
A time to be born and a time to die; a time to plant, and a time to pluck up that which is planted;
A time to kill, and a time to heal; a time to break down, and a time to build up;
A time to weep, and a time to laugh; a time to mourn, and a time to dance;
A time to cast away stones, and a time to gather stones together; a time to embrace, and a time to refrain from embracing;
A time to get, and a time to lose; a time to keep, and a time to cast away;
A time to rend, and a time to sew; a time to keep silence, and a time to speak;
A time to love, and a time to hate; a time of war, and a time of peace. —Bible, *Ecclesiastes* 3:1

Oh, the wild joys of living! —Robert Browning, *Saul*

How good is man's life, the mere living! how fit to employ
All the heart and the soul and the sense for ever in joy!     —*Ibid*.

We are involved in a life that passes understanding and our highest
business is our daily life.     —JOHN CAGE, *Where Are We Going and
What Are We Doing?* in *Silence*

There are only two or three human stories, and they go on re-
peating themselves as fiercely as if they had never happened before.
—WILLA CATHER, *O Pioneers!*

That it will never come again
Is what makes life so sweet.     —EMILY DICKINSON, poem

What we anticipate seldom occurs; what we least expected generally happens.     —BENJAMIN DISRAELI, *Henrietta Temple*

I have measured out my life with coffee spoons.
—T. S. ELIOT, *Love Song of J. Alfred Prufrock*

✗ Birth, copulation, and death.
That's all the facts when you come to brass tacks.
—T. S. ELIOT, *Sweeney Agonistes*

We are always getting ready to live but never living.
—RALPH WALDO EMERSON, *Journals*, 1834

Life consists in what a man is thinking of all day.     —*Ibid*., 1847

Only connect . . .     —E. M. FORSTER, *Howards End*, epigraph
[What Forster had in mind is conveyed in this passage in the book:
"Only connect! That was the whole of her sermon. Only connect
the prose and the passion, and both will be exalted, and human love
will be seen at its height. Live in fragments no longer. Only connect,
and the beast and the monk, robbed of the isolation that is life to
either, will die."]

Life is a jest; and all things show it.
I thought so once; but now I know it.
—JOHN GAY, *My Own Epitaph*

A useless life is an early death.     —GOETHE, *Iphigenie auf Tauris*

Life is short, art long, opportunity fleeting, experience treacher-
ous, judgment difficult.
—HIPPOCRATES, *Aphorisms*
[For the proverbial version, see under ART.]

The condition of man . . . is a condition of war of everyone against everyone.                              —Thomas Hobbes, *Leviathan*

. . . the life of man, solitary, poor, nasty, brutish, and short.
                              —*Ibid.*

Life is just one damn thing after another.
                    —Elbert Hubbard, *Thousand and One Epigrams*
[For Edna St. Vincent Millay's response, see below.]

Life is an abnormal business.       —Eugène Ionesco, *Rhinoceros*

How small it's all.             —James Joyce, *Finnegans Wake*

There is always inequity in life. Some men are killed in a war and some men are wounded, and some men never leave the country. . . . Life is unfair.                    —John F. Kennedy,
                    press conference, March 23, 1962

For men must work and women must weep,
And the sooner it's over, the sooner to sleep.
                    —Charles Kingsley, *The Three Fishers*

Ships that pass in the night, and speak each other in passing;
Only a signal shown and a distant voice in the darkness;
So on the ocean of life we pass and speak one another,
Only a look and a voice; then darkness again and a silence.
                    —Henry Wadsworth Longfellow,
                    *The Theologian's Tale*, in *Tales of a Wayside Inn*

Life is one long struggle in the dark.
                    —Lucretius, *De Rerum Natura*

The world has always been the same; and there has always been as much good fortune as bad in it.
                    —Machiavelli, *Discorsi*, introduction

It is not true that life is one damned thing after another—it is one damn thing over and over.
                    —Edna St. Vincent Millay, *Letters of
                    Edna St. Vincent Millay*, edited by Allen R. Macdougal

The value of life lies not in the length of days, but in the use we make of them; a man may live long yet live very little.
                    —Montaigne, *Essays*

Those who have compared life to a dream were right. . . . We sleep when we are awake, and awake when sleeping.          —*Ibid.*

*La vie est vaine:*
*Un peu d'amour,*
*Un peu de haine . . .*
*Et puis—bonjour!*

*La vie est brève:*
*Un peu d'espoir,*
*Un peu de rêve*
*Et puis—bon soir!*

Life is aimless: a little love, a little hate, and then—good day! Life is short: A little hope; a little dreaming, and then—goodnight!
—LÉON MONTENAEKEN, *Peu de chose*

Human life is but a series of footnotes to a vast obscure unfinished masterpiece.          —VLADIMIR NABOKOV, *Pale Fire*

To burn always with this hard gem-like flame, to maintain this ecstasy, is success in life.
—WALTER PATER, *The Renaissance*, "Conclusion"

The world itself is but a large prison out of which some daily are led to execution.          —SIR WALTER RALEGH
[Sir Walter made this comment while being led back to prison after his trial.]

There is no wealth but life.          —JOHN RUSKIN, *Unto This Last*

There must be more to life than having everything!
—MAURICE SENDAK, *Higglety Pigglety Pop!*

All the world's a stage,
And all the men and women merely players.
—SHAKESPEARE, *As You Like It*, II, vii

Life is as tedious as a twice-told tale
Vexing the dull ear of a drowsy man.
—SHAKESPEARE, *King John*, III, iv

When we are born, we cry that we are come
To this great stage of fools.          —SHAKESPEARE, *King Lear*, IV, vi

Life's but a walking shadow, a poor player
That struts and frets his hour upon the stage
And then is heard no more. It is a tale
Told by an idiot, full of sound and fury,
Signifying nothing. —Shakespeare, *Macbeth*, V, v

Old and young, we are all on our last cruise.
—Robert Louis Stevenson, *Crabbed Age and Youth*

While there's life, there's hope.
—Terence, *Heauton Timoroumenos*

The mass of men lead lives of quiet desperation.
—Thoreau, *Walden*

The world is a comedy to those that think, a tragedy to those that
feel. —Horace Walpole, letter to the Countess of Upper
Ossory, Aug. 16, 1776

Life is an offensive, directed against the repetitious mechanism of
the universe. —Alfred North Whitehead, *Adventures of Ideas*

Life imitates art far more than art imitates life.
—Oscar Wilde, *The Decay of Lying* in *Intentions*
[Cf. Seneca on art, under ART.]

The world is too much with us; late and soon,
Getting and spending, we lay waste our powers:
Little we see in nature that is ours.
We have given our hearts away.
—William Wordsworth
*The World Is Too Much With Us*

**LITERATURE** See ARTS entries;
BOOKS & READING

**LITTLE THINGS** See DETAILS & OTHER
SMALL THINGS; THINGS
& POSSESSIONS

**LIVING WELL** See GRACE; HEDONISM; LIFE

**LOGIC**                               See MIND; PHILOSOPHY;
                                    REASONABLE & UNREASONABLE PEOPLE

**LONDON**                                       See CITIES

**LONELINESS**                                 See SOLITUDE

**LOSERS**                            See HAVES AND HAVE-NOTS;
                                           WINNING & LOSING,
                                            VICTORY & DEFEAT

**LOVE**              See also HEART; JEALOUSY; LOVE, EXPRESSIONS OF;
                      LOVE & CHARITY: BIBLICAL REFERENCES;
                      MARRIAGE; SEX; WOMEN & MEN

Love teaches even asses to dance.
                            —ANONYMOUS (FRENCH PROVERB)

The heart that loves is always young.
                            —ANONYMOUS (GREEK PROVERB)

It is impossible to love and be wise.      —FRANCIS BACON, *Of Love*

Absence makes the heart grow fonder.
                            —T. H. BAYLY, *Isle of Beauty*

Where love is concerned, too much is not even enough.
                            —PIERRE-AUGUSTIN DE BEAUMARCHAIS,
                            *The Marriage of Figaro*

Who can give law to lovers? Love is a greater law to itself.
                            —BOETHIUS, *De Consolatione Philosophiae*
[See also John Lyly, below.]

Man's love is of man's life a thing apart,
'Tis woman's whole existence.          —LORD BYRON, *Don Juan*

In her first passion woman loves her lover,
In all the others, all she loves is love.
                                                      —*Ibid.*
[Byron might have credited La Rochefoucauld, see below.]

Love, such as it is in society, is only the exchange of two fantasies,
and the contact of two bodies.
                            —SÉBASTIEN R. N. CHAMFORT, *Maximes et pensées*

Great loves too must be endured.
> —Coco Chanel, quoted in Marcel Haedrich,
> *Coco Chanel, Her Life, Her Secrets*

Love is blind.     —Geoffrey Chaucer, *The Merchant's Tale*, in
> *The Canterbury Tales*

[Essentially proverbial; see variations by Menander and Shakespeare, below.]

Can there be a love which does not make demands on its object?
> —Confucius, *Analects*

Love and murder will out.
> —William Congreve, *The Double Dealer*

[For more on the alleged tendency of murder to be discovered, see under CRIME.]

Love, all alike, no season knows, nor clime,
Nor hours, days, months, which are the rags of time.
> —John Donne, *The Sun Rising*

For heaven be thanked, we live in such an age,
When no man dies for love, but on the stage.
> —John Dryden, *Mithridates*, Epilogue

All mankind love a lover.     —Ralph Waldo Emerson, *Love*

Love is all we have, the only way that each can help the other.
> —Euripides, *Orestes*

She who has never loved has never lived.     —John Gay, *Captives*

It's love that makes the world go round!
> —W. S. Gilbert, *Iolanthe*

[Probably proverbial. The French say, "*L'amour fait tourner le monde.*"]

Love knows nothing of order.     —St. Jerome, letter 7

Love is swift, sincere, pious, pleasant, generous, strong, patient, faithful, prudent, long-suffering, manly, and never seeking her own; for wheresoever a man seeketh his own, there he falleth from love.
> —Thomas à Kempis, *Imitation of Christ*

A fool there was and he made his prayer
(Even as you and I!)
To a rag and a bone and a hank of hair
(We called her the woman who did not care)
But the fool he called her his lady fair—
Even as you and I.          —RUDYARD KIPLING, *The Vampire*

If one judges love by the majority of its effects, it is more like hatred than friendship.          —LA ROCHEFOUCAULD, *Maxims*

There is no disguise which can hide love for long where it exists, or simulate it where it does not.          —*Ibid.*

In their first passion, women love their lovers; in all the others, they love love.

—*Ibid.*

[See also Byron, above.]

It requires far more genius to make love than to command armies.
          —NINON DE LENCLOS, ascribed

Two souls with but a single thought,
Two hearts that beat as one.
          —MARIA LOVELL, *Ingomar the Barbarian*

Love is a product of habit.          —LUCRETIUS, *De Rerum Natura*
[A similar thought occurred to Jane Austen: "I am pleased that you have learned to love a hyacinth, the mere habit of learning to love is the thing."]

Love knoweth no laws.
[See also Boethius, above.]          —JOHN LYLY, *Euphues*

Delicacy is to love what grace is to beauty.
          —MADAME DE MAINTENON, *Maximes de
          Mme. de Maintenon*

It is love, not reason, that is stronger than death.
          —THOMAS MANN, *Magic Mountain*

Who ever loved that loved not at first sight?
          —CHRISTOPHER MARLOWE, *Hero and Leander*

When you have loved as she has loved, you grow old beautifully.
          —W. SOMERSET MAUGHAM, *The Circle*

Love blinds all men alike, both the reasonable and the foolish.
—Menander, *Andria*

We are easily duped by those we love. —Molière, *Tartuffe*

No, there's nothing half so sweet in life
As love's young dream. —Thomas Moore, *Love's Young Dream*

This is the hardest of all: to close the open hand out of love, and
to keep modest as a giver.
—Friedrich Nietzsche, *Thus Spake Zarathustra*

Love is a kind of warfare. —Ovid, *Ars Amatoria*

Oh, life is a glorious cycle of song,
A medley of extemporanea;
And love is a thing that can never go wrong,
And I am Marie of Roumania. —Dorothy Parker, *Comment*

By the time you swear you're his
Shivering and sighing,
And he vows his passion is
Infinite, undying—
Lady make a note of this:
One of you is lying. —Dorothy Parker,
*Unfortunate Coincidence*

[Love is] the joy of the good, the wonder of the wise, the amazement of the gods. —Plato, *The Symposium*

There can be no peace of mind in love since the advantage one has
secured is never anything but a fresh starting point for further desire.
—Proust, *Remembrance of Things Past:
Within a Budding Grove*

Love means never having to say you're sorry.
—Erich Segal, *Love Story*

Men have died from time to time and worms have eaten them, but
not for love. —Shakespeare, *As You Like It*, IV, i

Love is a familiar. Love is a devil. There is no evil angel but Love.
—Shakespeare, *Love's Labour's Lost*, I, ii

But love is blind, and lovers cannot see
The pretty follies that themselves commit.
                    —SHAKESPEARE, *The Merchant of Venice*, II, vi

The course of true love never did run smooth.
                    —SHAKESPEARE, *A Midsummer Night's Dream*, I, i

Speak low, if you speak love.
                    —SHAKESPEARE, *Much Ado About Nothing*, II, 1

Speak of me as I am . . . one that loved not wisely but too well.
                    —SHAKESPEARE, *Othello*, V, ii

They do not love that do not show their love.
                    —SHAKESPEARE, *The Two Gentlemen of Verona*, I, ii
[An old saying; Shakespeare freely used proverbial comments in
writing dialogue.]

Let me not to the marriage of true minds
Admit impediments. Love is not love
Which alters when it alteration finds,
Or bends with the remover to remove.
Oh no! It is an ever-fixèd mark
That looks on tempests and is never shaken. It is the star to every
    wandering bark,
Whose worth's unknown, although his height be taken.
                    —SHAKESPEARE, sonnet 116

Love comforteth like sunshine after rain.
                    —SHAKESPEARE, *Venus and Adonis*

Familiar acts are beautiful through love.
                    —PERCY BYSSHE SHELLEY, *Prometheus Unbound*

All love is sweet,
Given or returned. Common as light is love,
And its familiar voice wearies not ever.          —*Ibid.*

One word frees us of all the weight and pain of life: That word is
love.                    —SOPHOCLES, *Oedipus at Colonus*

'Tis better to have loved and lost
Than never to have loved at all.
                    —ALFRED, LORD TENNYSON, *In Memoriam*

O, tell her, brief is life but love is long.
—ALFRED, LORD TENNYSON, *The Princess*

All, everything that I understand, I understand only because I love.
—LEO TOLSTOY, *War and Peace*

*Omnia vincit Amor: et nos cedamus Amori.* —VIRGIL, *Eclogues*
Love conquers all: and let us too surrender to love.

Love those who love you.
—VOLTAIRE, letter to d'Alembert, Nov. 28, 1762
[This is the last, often overlooked phrase in the noted *écrasez l'infâme* exhortation, cited in full at RELIGION.]

'Tis said that some have died for love.
—WILLIAM WORDSWORTH, *'Tis said that some have died*

A pity beyond all telling
Is hid in the heart of love.
—WILLIAM BUTLER YEATS, *The Pity of Love*

**LOVE & CHARITY:** See also LOVE
**BIBLICAL REFERENCES**

Thou shalt love thy neighbor as thyself.
—BIBLE, *Leviticus* 19:18
[Also found in several other places in the Bible, including most notably *Matthew* 22:39, where in the next verse it is described as one of the two essential commandments, along with the commandment to love God—see under GOD.]

A new commandment I give unto you, that you love one another.
—BIBLE, *John* 13:34

Though I speak with the tongues of men and of angels, and have not charity, I am become as sounding brass, or a tinkling cymbal.
—BIBLE, *I Corinthians* 13:1

Charity suffereth long and is kind; charity envieth not; charity vaunteth not itself, is not puffed up. —*Ibid.*, 13:4

And now abideth faith, hope, and charity, these three; but the greatest of these is charity. —*Ibid.*, 13:13

There is no fear in love; but perfect love casteth out fear.

—BIBLE, *I John* 4:18

He that loveth not his brother whom he hath seen, how can he love God whom he hath not seen?                    —*Ibid.*, 4:20

**LOVE, EXPRESSIONS OF**                    See also HEDONISM; LOVE;
WOMEN, BEAUTIFUL & HOMELY

Western Wind, when wilt thou blow,
That the small rain down can rain?
Christ if my love were in my arms
And I in my bed again.                    —ANONYMOUS

Arise, my love, my fair one, and come away.
—BIBLE, *The Song of Solomon* 2:10–13
[The quote is given in full at NATURE: SEASONS.]

If ever two were one, then surely we.
If ever man were loved by wife, then thee.
—ANNE BRADSTREET, *To My Dear and Loving Husband*

These I have loved:
White plates and cups, clean-gleaming,
Ringed with blue lines.          —RUPERT BROOKE, *The Great Lover*

Then, the cool kindliness of sheets, that soon
Smooth away trouble; and the rough male kiss
Of blankets; grainy wood; live hair that is
Shining and free; blue massing clouds; the keen
Unpassioned beauty of a great machine.                    —*Ibid.*

How do I love thee? Let me count the ways.
I love thee to the depth and breadth and height
My soul can reach, when feeling out of sight
For the ends of being and ideal grace.
—ELIZABETH BARRETT BROWNING,
*Sonnets from the Portuguese*, 43

I love thee with the breath,
Smiles, tears, of all my life!—and, if God choose,
I shall but love thee better after death.                    —*Ibid.*

But to see her was to love her,
Love but her, and love for ever.
—ROBERT BURNS, *Ae Fond Kiss*
[Yes, Burns wrote almost identical lines in another poem:
To see her is to love her,
And love but her for ever:
For Nature made her what she is, and never made sic anither!
*Bonnie Lesley.*]


O, my luve's like a red red rose
That's newly sprung in June:
O my luve's like the melodie
That's sweetly played in tune.
—ROBERT BURNS, *My Love is Like a Red Red Rose*


O whistle an' I'll come to ye, my lad,
O whistle an' I'll come to ye, my lad,
Tho' father an' mother an' a' should gae mad,
O whistle an' I'll come to ye, my lad.
—ROBERT BURNS, *O Whistle an' I'll Come to Ye, My Lad*


Come live with me, and be my love,
And we will some new pleasures prove
Of golden sands, and crystal brooks,
With silken lines, and silver hooks.    —JOHN DONNE, *The Bait*
[The similar but more famous verse is by Christopher Marlowe, see below.]


I have found it impossible to carry the heavy burden of responsibility and to discharge my duties as king as I would wish without the help and support of the woman I love.
—EDWARD VIII, abdication speech, Dec. 11, 1936


A book of verses underneath the bough
A jug of wine, a loaf of bread—and thou
Beside me singing in the wilderness.
—EDWARD FITZGERALD, *The Rubáiyát of Omar Khayyám*


Why don't you speak for yourself, John?
—HENRY WADSWORTH LONGFELLOW,
*The Courtship of Miles Standish*
[Priscilla Mullins to John Alden, who had been speaking for his friend Miles Standish. Longfellow was descended from John and Priscilla.]

Come live with me and be my love,
And we will all the pleasures prove
That valleys, groves, hills, and fields,
Woods or steepy mountain yields.
                —CHRISTOPHER MARLOWE,
                    *The Passionate Shepherd to his Love*
[Cf. John Donne, above.]


I was a child and she was a child,
In this kingdom by the sea;
But we loved with a love that was more than love—
I and my Annabel Lee.        —EDGAR ALLAN POE, *Annabel Lee*


What's mine is yours, and what is yours is mine.
                —SHAKESPEARE, *Measure for Measure*, V, i
[Plautus used the same line.]


But, soft! What light through yonder window breaks?
It is the east, and Juliet is the sun.
                —SHAKESPEARE, *Romeo and Juliet*, II, ii


See how she leans her cheek upon her hand!
Oh, that I were a glove upon that hand,
That I might touch that cheek!                —*Ibid.*


O Romeo, Romeo, wherefore art thou Romeo?
Deny thy father and refuse thy name,
Or, if thou wilt not, be but sworn my love
And I'll no longer be a Capulet.                —*Ibid.*


Goodnight! goodnight!
Parting is such sweet sorrow
That I shall say goodnight till it be morrow.        —*Ibid.*


When he shall die,
Take him and cut him out in little stars,
And he will make the face of heaven so fine
That all the world will be in love with night.        —*Ibid.*, III, ii


Kiss me, Kate!        —SHAKESPEARE, *The Taming of the Shrew*, II, i


Shall I compare thee to a summer's day?
Thou art more lovely and more temperate.
                —SHAKESPEARE, sonnet 18

Nothing in the world is single;
All things by a law divine
In one spirit meet and mingle.
Why not I with thine?
—PERCY BYSSHE SHELLEY, *Love's Philosophy*

One can't live on love alone; and I am so stupid that I can do nothing but think of him. —SOPHIE TOLSTOY, *A Diary*

When you are old and gray and full of sleep
And nodding by the fire, take down this book,
And slowly read. —WILLIAM BUTLER YEATS, *When You Are Old*

How many loved your moments of glad grace,
And loved your beauty with love false or true;
But one man loved the pilgrim soul in you,
And loved the sorrows of your changing face. —*Ibid.*

## LOYALTY
See UNITY AND LOYALTY

## LUCK
See also FATE

Throw a lucky man in the sea, and he will come up with a fish in his mouth. —ANONYMOUS (ARAB PROVERB)

The race is not to the swift, nor the battle to the strong, neither yet bread to the wise, nor yet riches to men of understanding, nor yet favor to men of skill; but time and chance happeneth to them all. —BIBLE, *Ecclesiastes* 9:11

Who has good luck is good. Who has bad luck is bad. —BERTOLT BRECHT, *The Exception and the Rule*

Heaven's help is better than early rising. —CERVANTES, *Don Quixote*
[Probably proverbial—Mencken cites as an Irish proverb, "Good luck beats early rising."]

Luck is not chance—
It's toil—
Fortune's expensive smile
Is earned. —EMILY DICKINSON, poem

The lucky person passes for a genius. —EURIPIDES, *Herakleidai*

Have but luck, and you will have the rest; be fortunate, and you
will be thought great.          —Victor Hugo, *Les Misérables*

A lucky man is rarer than a white cow.          —Juvenal, *Satires*

Now and then
there is a person born
who is so unlucky
that he runs into accidents
which started out to happen to somebody else.
          —Don Marquis, *archy says*

Luck is the Residue of Design.
          —Branch Rickey, lecture title, 1950
[At the time, Mr. Rickey was running the Brooklyn Dodgers.]

Luck never made a man wise.          —Seneca, *Letters to Lucilius*

Fortune favors the brave.          —Terence, *Phormio*

'Tis better to be fortunate than wise.
          —John Webster, *The White Devil*

Luck is not something you can mention in the presence of self-
made men.          —E. B. White, *Control* in *One Man's Meat*

**L Y I N G**          See DISHONESTY

**M A C H I N E S**          See TECHNOLOGY

**M A D N E S S**          See also ILLNESS & REMEDIES; SCIENCE:
          PSYCHOLOGY & PSYCHOANALYSIS

We are all born mad. Some remain so.
          —Samuel Beckett, *Waiting for Godot*

My name is Legion: for we are many.
          —Bible, *Mark* 5:9
[The speaker is a devil inhabiting a madman of the Gadarenes. Jesus
sent the devils to enter a herd of two thousand swine.]

There is a pleasure sure
In being mad, which none but madmen know.
          —John Dryden, *The Spanish Friar*

Those whom God wishes to destroy, he first makes mad.

—Euripides, fragment

[This became a proverbial comment, and is found in several other sources.]

Everyone is more or less mad on one point.

—Rudyard Kipling, *On the Strength of a Likeness* in
*Plain Tales from the Hills*

As I was going up the stair,
I met a man who wasn't there.
He wasn't there again today.
I wish, I wish he'd stay away.   —Hughes Mearns, *The Psychoed*

From childhood's hour I have not been
As others were—I have not seen
As others saw.           —Edgar Allan Poe, *Alone*

Madness in great ones must not unwatched go.

—Shakespeare, *Hamlet*, III, i

Is this a dagger which I see before me,
The handle toward my hand? Come let me clutch thee.

—Shakespeare, *Macbeth*, II, i

Art thou but
A dagger of the mind, a false creation
Proceeding from the heat-oppressed brain?           —*Ibid.*

It is an accustomed action with her to seem thus washing her hands. I have known her continue in this a quarter of an hour.

—*Ibid.*, V, i

Out, damned spot! Out, I say! One, two, why, then 'tis time to do't. Hell is murky!           —*Ibid.*
[Poor Lady Macbeth also appears under GUILT.]

When we remember that we are all mad, the mysteries disappear and life stands explained.           —Mark Twain, *Notebook*

My apprehensions come in crowds;
I dread the rustling of the grass;
The very shadows of the clouds
Have power to shake me as they pass:
I question things and do not find
One that will answer to my mind;
And all the world appears unkind.

—William Wordsworth, *The Affliction of Margaret*

**MAJORITY**                                            See PEOPLE, THE

**MALAYA**                                              See ORIENT, THE

**MANDALAY**                                            See ORIENT, THE

**MANKIND**                                     See HUMANS & HUMAN NATURE;
                                                MEN; WOMEN & MEN

**MANNERS**                                     See also GRACE; HOSPITALITY;
                                                INSULTS & PUT-DOWNS

An injury is much sooner forgotten than an insult.
                                        —EARL OF CHESTERFIELD, letter to his son,
                        Oct. 9, 1746

Take the tone of the company you are in.     —*Ibid*., Oct. 9, 1747
[See also St. Ambrose at TRAVEL.]

*O tempora! O mores!*
O the times! O the manners!                     —CICERO, *In Catilinam*

Tact consists in knowing how far we may go too far.
                                        —JEAN COCTEAU, *Le coq et l'Harlequin*

It is good manners which make the excellence of a neighborhood.
No wise man will settle where they are lacking.
                                        —CONFUCIUS, *Analects*

The trouble with treating people as equals is that the first thing
you know they may be doing the same thing to you.
                                        —PETER DE VRIES, *The Prick of Noon*

The art of pleasing consists in being pleased.
                                        —WILLIAM HAZLITT, *On Manners*
[See also Johnson, below.]

You never want to give a man a present when he's feeling good.
You want to do it when he's down.
                                        —LYNDON B. JOHNSON, quoted in Doris Kearns,
                        *Lyndon Johnson and the Amazing Dream*

He who endeavors to please must appear to be pleased.
                                        —SAMUEL JOHNSON, *The Rambler*, Aug. 31, 1751

Punctuality is the politeness of kings.    —Louis XVIII, attributed

My father used to say
"Superior people never make long visits."
                              —Marianne Moore, *Silence*

It is almost a definition of a gentleman to say that he is one who
never inflicts pain.    —Cardinal Newman, *The Idea of a University*

Manners go on deteriorating.                    —Plautus, *Mercator*

Etiquette can be at the same time a means of approaching people
and of staying clear of them.  —David Riesman, *The Lonely Crowd*

Rudeness is better than any argument; it totally eclipses intellect.
                              —Arthur Schopenhauer, *Position*

Is there no respect of place, persons, nor time, in you?
                              —Shakespeare, *Twelfth Night*, II, iii

Do not do unto others as you would they should do unto you.
Their tastes may not be the same.
                              —George Bernard Shaw, *Man and Superman*,
                              "Maxims for Revolutionists"

Good breeding consists in concealing how much we think of ourselves and how little we think of the other person.
                              —Mark Twain, *Notebooks*


## MARRIAGE                              See also FAMILY; HOME;
                                         LOVE; WOMEN & MEN

Those marriages generally abound most with love and constancy
that are preceded by a long courtship.
                              —Joseph Addison, *The Spectator*, Dec. 29, 1711

When a match has equal partners, then I fear not.
                              —Aeschylus, *Prometheus Bound*

*Autant de mariages, autant ménages.*
As many as there are marriages, so many living arrangements.
                              —Anonymous (French Proverb)

Marriage, to woman as to men, must be a luxury, not a necessity;
an incident of life, not all of it.    —Susan B. Anthony, speech, 1875

I married beneath me—all women do.
　　　　　　—NANCY ASTOR, speech, Oldham, England, 1951

It is a truth universally acknowledged, that a single man in possession of good fortune, must be in want of a wife.
　　　　　　—JANE AUSTEN, *Pride and Prejudice*
[For more on this line, see Austen at WOMEN & MEN.]

It is better to marry than to burn.　　—BIBLE, *I Corinthians* 7:9

One was never married, and that's his hell; another is, and that's his plague.　　—ROBERT BURTON, *The Anatomy of Melancholy*

Polygamy may well be held in dread,
Not only as a sin but as a bore.　　—LORD BYRON, *Don Juan*

Marriage is a result of the longing for the deep, deep peace of the double bed after the hurly-burly of the chaise-longue.
　　　　　　—MRS. PATRICK CAMPBELL, quoted in
　　　　　　Ralph G. Martin, *Jenny*

I am not against hasty marriages, where a mutual flame is fanned by an adequate income.　　—WILKIE COLLINS, *No Name*

Married in haste, we may repent at leisure.
　　　　　　—WILLIAM CONGREVE, *The Old Bachelor*
[The proverb—"Marry in haste, repent at leisure"—predates Congreve.]

A single man . . . is an incomplete animal. He resembles the odd half of a pair of scissors.
　　　　　　—BENJAMIN FRANKLIN, letter to a young man, June 25, 1745

Where there's marriage without love, there will be love without marriage.　　—BENJAMIN FRANKLIN, *Poor Richard's Almanac*

I think it can be stated without denial that no man ever saw a man he would be willing to marry if he were a woman.
　　　　　　—GEORGE GIBBS, *How To Stay Married*

Let there be spaces in your togetherness.
　　　　　　—KAHLIL GIBRAN, *The Prophet*

A wife loves out of duty, and duty leads to constraint, and constraint kills desire.　　—JEAN GIRADOUX, *Amphitryon 38*

Faithful women are all alike. They think only of their fidelity and not of their husbands. **—*Ibid.***

When a woman gets married, it's like jumping into a hole in the ice in the middle of winter: you do it once and you remember it the rest of your days. **—MAXIM GORKY, *The Lower Depths***

A gentleman who had been very unhappy in marriage, married immediately after his wife died: Johnson said it was the triumph of hope over experience. **—SAMUEL JOHNSON, quoted in James Boswell, *Life of Johnson*, 1770**

Marriage has many pains, but celibacy has no pleasures. **—SAMUEL JOHNSON, *Rasselas***

There are some good marriages, but no delightful ones. **—LA ROCHEFOUCAULD, *Maxims***

There is no more lovely, friendly, and charming relationship, communion, or company than a good marriage. **—MARTIN LUTHER, *Table Talk***

Marriages are made in heaven. **—JOHN LYLY, *Euphues and His England***

"That's bigamy."
"Yes and it's big of me, too. It's big of all of us. I'm sick of these conventional marriages. One woman and one man was good enough for your grandmother. But who wants to marry your grandmother?" **—GROUCHO MARX, *Animal Crackers***

Marriage, to tell the truth, is an evil, but it is a necessary evil. **—MENANDER, fragment**

It [marriage] is like a cage; one sees the birds outside desperate to get in, and those inside desperate to get out. **—MONTAIGNE, *Essays***

Not louder shrieks to pitying heaven are cast,
When husbands or when·lapdogs breathe their last. **—ALEXANDER POPE, *The Rape of the Lock***

A good marriage is that in which each appoints the other the guardian of his solitude. **—RAINER MARIA RILKE, *Letters***

It doesn't much signify whom one marries, for one is sure to find out the next morning that it was someone else. **—SAMUEL ROGERS, *Table Talk***

Love, the quest; marriage, the conquest; divorce, the inquest.
                    —HELEN ROWLAND, *A Guide to Men*

Marriage is for woman the commonest mode of livelihood, and the total amount of undesired sex endured by women is probably greater in marriage than in prostitution.
                    —BERTRAND RUSSELL, *Marriage and Morals*

It takes patience to appreciate domestic bliss; volatile spirits prefer unhappiness.        —GEORGE SANTAYANA, *The Life of Reason*

To marry is to halve your rights and double your duties.
                    —ARTHUR SCHOPENHAUER, *The World as Will and Idea*

Marriage is a desperate thing.        —JOHN SELDEN, *Marriage*

The ancient saying is no heresy,
Hanging and wiving goes by destiny.
                    —SHAKESPEARE, *The Merchant of Venice*, II, ix
[Another form of this proverb was cited by John Heywood:
Wedding is destiny,
And hanging likewise.]

A light wife doth make a heavy husband.        —*Ibid.*, V, i

*Item*: I give unto my wife my second best bed.
                    —SHAKESPEARE, his will

It is a woman's business to get married as soon as possible, and a man's to keep unmarried as long as he can.
                    —GEORGE BERNARD SHAW, *Man and Superman*

Marriage is popular because it combines the maximum of temptation with the maximum of opportunity.
                    —*Ibid.*, "Maxims for Revolutionists"

In marriage, a man becomes slack and selfish, and undergoes a fatty degeneration of his moral being.
                    —ROBERT LOUIS STEVENSON, *Virginibus Puerisque*

In married life, three is company and two is none.
                    —OSCAR WILDE, *The Importance of Being Earnest*

The world has grown suspicious of anything that looks like a happy married life.        —OSCAR WILDE, *Lady Windermere's Fan*

MARXISM                                    See COMMUNISM

MASSES                                     See PEOPLE, THE

MATHEMATICS         See SCIENCE: MATHEMATICS & STATISTICS

MAXIMS              See QUOTATIONS, MAXIMS & PROVERBS

MAY                                        See NATURE: SEASONS

MEDIA                                      See also ADVERTISING;
                                                      PRESS, THE

One picture is worth more than a thousand words.
                              —ANONYMOUS (CHINESE PROVERB)

The printing press is either the greatest blessing or the greatest
curse of modern times, one sometimes forgets which.
                              —J. M. BARRIE, *Sentimental Tommy*

Some television programs are so much chewing gum for the eyes.
                              —JOHN MASON BROWN, interview, July 28, 1955
[Also has been attributed to Frank Lloyd Wright.]

Now Barabbas was a publisher.
                              —LORD BYRON, traditional attribution
[Some feel that a more likely source is Thomas Campbell.]

Television is a form of soliloquy.
                              —SIR KENNETH CLARK, in the *Guardian*, Nov. 26, 1977

The hand that rules the press, the radio, the screen, and the far-
spread magazine rules the country.
                              —LEARNED HAND, speech, Dec. 21, 1942

[Television:] a medium, so called because it is neither rare nor
well done.              —ERNIE KOVACS, quoted in Leslie Halliwell,
                              *The Filmgoer's Book of Quotes*

The new electronic interdependence recreates the world in the
image of a global village.
                              —MARSHALL MCLUHAN, *The Gutenberg Galaxy*

The medium is the message.
                              —MARSHALL MCLUHAN, *Understanding Media*

[If you watch television from morning to night] I can assure you that you will observe a vast wasteland.
—NEWTON MINOW, speech to the
National Association of Broadcasters, 1961

It is not enough to cater to the nation's whims—you must also serve the nation's needs.                                        —*Ibid.*

The more we elaborate our means of communication, the less we communicate.          —J. B. PRIESTLEY, *Televiewing* in
*Thoughts in the Wilderness*

I believe television is going to be the test of the modern world, and that in this new opportunity to see beyond the range of our vision we shall discover either a new and unbearable disturbance of the general peace or a saving radiance in the sky. We shall stand or fall by television.          —E. B. WHITE, *One Man's Meat*
[This particular essay, *Removal*, was written in 1938 for *Harper's* magazine.]

## MEDICINE

See DOCTORS & THE PRACTICE OF
MEDICINE; ILLNESS & REMEDIES;
MADNESS; SCIENCE: PSYCHOLOGY
& PSYCHOANALYSIS

## MEDIOCRITY

Be not righteous over much; neither make thyself over wise.
—BIBLE, *Ecclesiastes* 7:16

The world is a republic of mediocrities, and always was.
—THOMAS CARLYLE, letter to Emerson,
May 13, 1853

The only sin is mediocrity.
—MARTHA GRAHAM, quoted in *The New York Times*,
March 31, 1985

The way to get on in the world is to be neither more nor less wise, neither better nor worse than your neighbors.
—WILLIAM HAZLITT, *On Knowledge of the World*

Some men are born mediocre, some men achieve mediocrity, and some men have mediocrity thrust upon them. With Major Major it had been all three.          —JOSEPH HELLER, *Catch-22*

There are certain things in which mediocrity is insupportable—
poetry, music, painting, public speaking.
—LA BRUYÈRE, *Les Caractères*

## MEMORY
See also PAST, THE

Memory is the mother of all wisdom.
—AESCHYLUS, *Prometheus Bound*

I have more memories than if I were a thousand years old.
—CHARLES BAUDELAIRE, *Spleen et idéal*

Some memories are realities, and are better than anything that can
ever happen to one again.     —WILLA CATHER, *My Ántonia*

Memory is the treasury and guardian of all things.
—CICERO, *De Oratore*

Good memories are lost jewels.
—PAUL VALÉRY, *Mauvaises pensées*

In memory everything seems to happen to music.
—TENNESSEE WILLIAMS, *The Glass Menagerie*

## MEN
See also HUMANS &
HUMAN NATURE; WOMEN & MEN

If there is anything disagreeable going on, men are sure to get
out of it.     —JANE AUSTEN, *Northanger Abbey*

As long as you know that most men are like children, you know
everything.     —COCO CHANEL, attributed

A man is a god in ruins.     —RALPH WALDO EMERSON, *Nature*

Every man has a wild animal in him.
—FREDERICK THE GREAT, letter to Voltaire, 1759

There's nothing so stubborn as a man when you want him to do
something.     —JEAN GIRADOUX, *The Madwoman of Chaillot*

What a piece of work is a man! How noble in reason! How
infinite in faculty! In form, in moving, how express and admirable!
In action how like an angel! In apprehension how like a god! The
beauty of the world! The paragon of animals!
—SHAKESPEARE, *Hamlet*, II, ii

Sigh no more, ladies, sigh no more,
Men were deceivers ever;
One foot in sea, and one on shore,
To one thing constant never.
—SHAKESPEARE, *Much Ado About Nothing*, II, iii

Every man over forty is a scoundrel.
—GEORGE BERNARD SHAW, *Man and Superman*,
"Maxims for Revolutionists"

A man in the house is worth two in the streets.
—MAE WEST, *Belle of the Nineties*

## MERCY

See FORGIVENESS &
MERCY; JUSTICE

## METAPHYSICS

See ETHICS &
MORALITY; PHILOSOPHY

## MIDDLE AGE & MID-LIFE CRISIS

Midway in our life's journey, I went astray from the straight road
and woke to find myself alone in a dark wood.
—DANTE, *Inferno*, in *The Divine Comedy*

After thirty, a man wakes up sad every morning, excepting perhaps five or six, until the day of his death.
—RALPH WALDO EMERSON, *Journals*, 1834

By the time a person has achieved years adequate for choosing a
direction, the die is cast and the moment has long since passed which
determined the future.     —ZELDA FITZGERALD, *Save Me the Waltz*

Whoever, in middle age, attempts to realize the wishes and hopes
of his early youth invariably deceives himself. Each ten years of a
man's life has its own fortunes, its own hopes, its own desires.
—GOETHE, *Elective Affinities*

Men, like peaches and pears, grow sweet a little while before they
begin to decay.          —OLIVER WENDELL HOLMES, SR.,
*The Autocrat of the Breakfast Table*

The long dull monotonous years of middle-aged prosperity or
middle-aged adversity are excellent campaigning weather for the
Devil.             —C. S. LEWIS, *The Screwtape Letters*

[Middle age is] the time when a man is always thinking that in a week or two he'll feel just as good as ever.
—Don Marquis, quoted in B. Wilcox,
*A Little Book of Aphorisms*

Maturity hath her defects, as well as greenness, or worse.
—Montaigne, *Essays*

From forty to fifty, a man is at heart either a stoic or a satyr.
—A. W. Pinero, *The Second Mrs. Tanqueray*
One's prime is elusive.
—Muriel Spark, *The Prime of Miss Jean Brodie*

# MIGHT

See STRENGTH;
VIOLENCE & FORCE

# MILITARY, THE

See also MILITARY BATTLES; WAR

If it moves, salute it. If it doesn't move, pick it up. If you can't pick it up, paint it. —Anonymous

Don't talk to me about naval tradition. It's nothing but rum, sodomy, and the lash. —Winston Churchill, quoted by
Sir Peter Gretton, *Former Naval Person*

The services in wartime are fit only for desperadoes, but in peace are fit only for fools. —Benjamin Disraeli, *Vivian Grey*

There are all sorts of things to be done in this country. . . . I see no reason why the sums which are now going into these sterile, negative mechanisms that we call war munitions shouldn't go into something positive.
—Dwight D. Eisenhower, quoted in
Stephen E. Ambrose, *Eisenhower: The President*
[For the renowned "military-industrial establishment" speech, see AMERICAN HISTORY: MEMORABLE MOMENTS.]

A large army is always disorderly. —Euripides, *Hecuba*

Stick close to your desks and *never go to sea,*
And you all may be Rulers of the Queen's Navee!
—W. S. Gilbert, *H. M. S. Pinafore*

Ask any soldier. To kill a man is to merit a woman.
—Jean Giradoux, *Tiger at the Gates*

For a people who are free, and who mean to remain so, a well-organized and armed militia is their best security.
—THOMAS JEFFERSON, message to Congress, Nov. 1808

Every citizen [should] be a soldier. This was the case with the Greeks and the Romans, and must be that of every free state.
—THOMAS JEFFERSON, letter to James Monroe, 1813

The people are like water and the army is like fish.
—MAO TSE-TUNG, *Aspects of China's Anti-Japanese Struggle*

The greatest general is he who makes the fewest mistakes.
—NAPOLEON BONAPARTE, *Maxims*

Soldiers generally win battles; generals generally get credit for them.
—NAPOLEON BONAPARTE, to Gaspard Gourgaud at St. Helena

An army marches on its stomach.
—NAPOLEON BONAPARTE, traditional attribution

Russia has two generals whom she can trust—Generals Janvier and Février [Generals January and February].
—NICHOLAS I, quoted in *Punch*, March 10, 1853

I never expect a soldier to think.
—GEORGE BERNARD SHAW, *The Devil's Disciple*

The British soldier can stand up to anything except the British War Office.
—*Ibid.*

To fight and conquer in all your battles is not supreme excellence; supreme excellence consists in breaking the enemy's resistance.
—SUN TZE, *Sun Tze Ping Fa*

Theirs is not to reason why,
Theirs is but to do and die.
—ALFRED, LORD TENNYSON, *The Charge of the Light Brigade*

[For more, see under MILITARY BATTLES, below.]

The strength of an army lies in strict discipline and undeviating obedience to its officers.
—THUCYDIDES, *The History of the Peloponnesian War*

The chief attraction of military service has consisted and will consist in this compulsory and irreproachable idleness.
—Leo Tolstoy, *War and Peace*

God is always on the side of the big battalions.
—Marshal Turenne, attributed
[Sometimes also attributed to Voltaire, Frederick the Great, and others, but the saying was already established by then. *Bartlett* suggests that it may date from Tacitus; see under strength.]

The army is a nation within the nation: it is a vice of our time.
—Alfred de Vigny, *Servitude et grandeur militaires*

Military intelligence—a contradiction in terms.
—Oswald Garrison Villard, lecture, about 1920,
personal report by a member of the audience

In this country we find it pays to shoot an admiral from time to time to encourage the others. —Voltaire, *Candide*

Discipline is the soul of an army. It makes small numbers formidable; procures success to the weak and esteem to all.
—George Washington, letter to the
Captains of the Virginia Regiments, July 1759

Who is this happy warrior? Who is he
That every man in arms should wish to be?
—William Wordsworth,
*Character of the Happy Warrior*

**MILITARY BATTLES**          See also AMERICAN HISTORY:
MEMORABLE MOMENTS; ENGLAND;
MILITARY, THE; WAR

*Veni, vidi, vici.*
I came, I saw, I conquered. —Julius Caesar, quoted in Suetonius,
*Lives of the Caesars*

Gentlemen, we are being killed on the beaches. Let's go inland and be killed. —General Norman Cota, Omaha Beach, 1944

My center is giving way, my right is in retreat; situation excellent. I am attacking. —Ferdinand Foch, attributed
[Sources vary as to the date; it is most often reported as Sept. 1914, the Battle of the Marne. The quote is probably apocryphal but does reflect Foch's characteristic approach to warfare.]

Sighted sub, sank same.          —DONALD F. MASON, radio dispatch,
                                          Jan. 28, 1942


Soldiers, consider that from the summit of these pyramids, forty
centuries look down upon you.
                              —NAPOLEON BONAPARTE, address to the troops
                                    before the Battle of the Pyramids, July 1798


*Ils ne passeront pas.*
They shall not pass.      —ROBERT-GEORGES NIVELLE, Verdun, 1916
[In this form, the order became a slogan; however, the actual wording was, "*Vous ne laisserez pas passer*"—"You shall not let them
pass." In the Spanish Civil War, the Republicans used *No pasarán*.]


One more such victory, and we are undone.
                              —KING PYRRHUS OF EPIRUS, after fighting the
                                    Romans at Asculum, 279 B.C.


Go, tell the Spartans, thou who passeth by:
Carrying out their orders, here we lie.
                              —SIMONIDES, epitaph for the Spartan dead at
                                    Thermopylae, quoted in Herodotus, *Histories*


It is the beginning of the end.
                              —TALLEYRAND, after the Battle of Borodino, 1812


Half a league, half a league,
Half a league onward,
All in the valley of Death
Rode the six hundred.              —ALFRED, LORD TENNYSON,
                                          *The Charge of the Light Brigade*


Cannon to right of them
Cannon to left of them,
Cannon behind them
Volleyed and thundered.                                     —*Ibid.*


Into the jaws of death,
Into the mouth of hell
Rode the six hundred.                                       —*Ibid.*


Nothing except a battle lost can be half so melancholy as a battle
won.        —DUKE OF WELLINGTON, dispatch from Waterloo, 1815

The battle of Waterloo was won on the playing fields of Eton.
> —DUKE OF WELLINGTON, traditional attribution,
> but apparently invented several years after
> Wellington's death

**MIND, THOUGHT,**                     See also GENIUS;
**& UNDERSTANDING**            IDEAS & IDEALS; MADNESS;
                                        REASONABLE & UNREASONABLE
                                        PEOPLE; SOUL; VISION & VISIONARIES

Reason is the ruler and queen of all things.
> —CICERO, *Tusculanae Disputationes*

*Cogito ergo sum.*
I think therefore I am.   —RENÉ DESCARTES, *Discourse on Method*

Being and thought are one.
> —JEAN DUBUFFET, quoted in his obituary,
> *The New York Times*, May 15, 1985

What once was thought can never be undone.
> —FRIEDRICH DÜRRENMATT, *The Physicists*

Imagination is more important than knowledge.
> —ALBERT EINSTEIN, *On Science*

Reason can wrestle and overthrow terror.
> —EURIPIDES, *Iphigenia in Aulis*

On earth there is nothing great but man; in man there is nothing
great but mind.                      —SIR WILLIAM HAMILTON,
                                        *Lectures on Metaphysics*

What we call a mind is nothing but a heap or collection of
different perceptions, united together by certain relations, and supposed, though falsely, to be endowed with a perfect simplicity and
identity.        —DAVID HUME, *A Treatise of Human Nature*

Sooner or later, false thinking brings wrong conduct.
> —JULIAN HUXLEY, *Essays of a Biologist*

Meditation is not a means to an end. It is both the means and the
end.    —KRISHNAMURTI, *The Second Penguin Krishnamurti Reader*

Intelligence forbids tears.
—Doris Lessing, *To Room 19* in *A Man and Two Women*

Stone walls do not a prison make
Nor iron bars a cage.
—Richard Lovelace, *To Althea, From Prison*

Our life is what our thoughts make it.
—Marcus Aurelius, *Meditations*

The mind is its own place, and in itself
Can make a heaven of Hell, a hell of Heaven.
—John Milton, *Paradise Lost*

[There is no] Ghost in the Machine.
—Gilbert Ryle, *The Concept of Mind*

Our dignity is not in what we do but what we understand. The whole world is doing things.
—George Santayana, *Winds of Doctrine*

A good mind is a lord of a kingdom.     —Seneca, *Thyestes*

There is nothing either good or bad but thinking makes it so.
—Shakespeare, *Hamlet*, II, ii

Thy wish was father, Harry, to that thought.
—Shakespeare, *Henry IV*, *Part II*, IV, v
[Prince Henry has just said to his aged father, the king, who appeared to have died in his sleep, "I never thought to hear you speak again."]

He gave man speech, and speech created thought,
Which is the measure of the universe.
—Percy Bysshe Shelley, *Prometheus Unbound*

Reason is God's crowning gift to man.     —Sophocles, *Antigone*

It is the mind that maketh good or ill,
That maketh wretch or happy, rich or poor.
—Edmund Spenser, *The Faerie Queene*

Intellect does not attain its full force until it attacks power,
—Madame de Staël, *De la littérature considerée
dans ses rapports avec les institutions sociales*

Intellectual passion drives out sensuality.
—Leonardo da Vinci, *Notebooks*

**MINORITIES** See RACES & PEOPLES

**MIRACLES**

Rise, take up thy bed, and walk. —BIBLE, *John* 5:8

The distance is nothing. It's only the first step that's important.
—MARQUISE DU DEFFAND [commenting on the legend that
St. Denis walked six miles holding his head in his hand],
letter to d'Alembert, July 7, 1763

Everything is miraculous. It is miraculous that one does not melt
in one's bath. —PICASSO, attributed
[*The Penguin Dictionary of Modern Quotations* suggests that Cocteau reported this delightful observation.]

Miracles are propitious accidents, the natural causes of which are
too complicated to be readily understood.
—GEORGE SANTAYANA, *The Ethics of Spinoza*

They say miracles are past.
—SHAKESPEARE, *All's Well That Ends Well*, II, iii

Macbeth shall never vanquished be until
Great Birnam Wood to High Dunsinane Hill
Shall come against him. —SHAKESPEARE, *Macbeth*, IV, i
[Macbeth, bolstered by this prophecy, later boasts,
   I will not be afraid of death and bane
   Till Birnham Forest come to Dunsinane.
He expects neither a miracle nor a trick. For more on wonders and
the weird sisters, see OCCULT, THE.]

**MISANTHROPY**

I do not want people to be very agreeable, as it saves me the
trouble of liking them a great deal.
—JANE AUSTEN, letter to her sister Cassandra,
   Dec. 24, 1798
[The date suggests the author may have been suffering a holiday
depression.]

I do not love thee, Doctor Fell.
The reason why I cannot tell.
But this alone I know full well.
I do not love thee, Doctor Fell. —THOMAS BROWN

I wish I loved the human race;
I wish I loved its silly face;
I wish I loved the way it walks;
I wish I loved the way it talks;
And when I'm introduced to one,
I wish I thought *What jolly fun.*
> —SIR WALTER A. RALEIGH, *Wishes of an Elderly Man*

Any man who hates dogs and babies can't be all bad.
> —LEO C. ROSTEN, speaking of W. C. Fields,
> Masquer's Club, 1939

[Often attributed to Fields in the form: "Anyone who hates children and dogs can't be all bad." Williams Safire, thanks to a correspondent, unearthed an earlier version, from *Harper's* magazine, 1937, penned by Cedric Worth: "No man who hates dogs and children can be all bad."]

*Plus je connais les hommes, plus j'aime mon chien.*
The more I know men, the more I like my dog.
> —MADAME DE SÉVIGNÉ, attributed

Man delights not me; no, nor woman either.
> —SHAKESPEARE, *Hamlet*, II, ii

**MISERY**                    See DESPAIR, DEPRESSION,
                              MISERY; TROUBLE

**MISFORTUNE**                    See LUCK; RUIN; TROUBLE

**MISTAKES**                    See also FAILINGS

He is always right who suspects that he makes mistakes.
> —ANONYMOUS (SPANISH PROVERB)

*C'est pire qu'un crime, c'est une faute.*
It's worse than a crime, it's a blunder.
> —ANTOINE BOULAY DE LA MEURTHE,
> on the execution of the Duc d'Enghien, 1804

[Attributed also to Talleyrand and Joseph Fouché.]

It is the true nature of mankind to learn from mistakes, not from example.
> —FRED HOYLE, *Into Deepest Space*

When I make a mistake, it's a beaut!
> —FIORELLO LA GUARDIA, attributed remark
> referring to a bad appointment

A life spent in making mistakes is not only more honorable but more useful than a life spent doing nothing.
—GEORGE BERNARD SHAW, *The Doctor's Dilemma*, preface

Mistakes live in the neighborhood of truth and therefore delude us. —RABINDRANATH TAGORE, *Fireflies*

**MODERATION** See PRUDENCE & PRACTICAL WISDOM

**MODERN TIMES** See also CIVILIZATION; ENVIRONMENT; MEDIA; TECHNOLOGY; TURBULENT TIMES

In the nightmare of the dark
All the dogs of Europe bark,
And the living nations wait,
Each sequestered in its hate.
—W. H. AUDEN, *In Memory of W. B. Yeats*

We have grasped the mystery of the atom and rejected the Sermon on the Mount.
—OMAR BRADLEY, speech, Armistice Day, 1948

The age of chivalry is gone. That of sophisters, economists, and calculators has succeeded, and the glory of Europe is extinguished forever. —EDMUND BURKE, *Reflections on the Revolution in France*

The age of miracles is forever here!
—THOMAS CARLYLE, *The Hero as Priest*

Perfection of means and confusion of goals seem, in my opinion, to characterize our age. —ALBERT EINSTEIN, *Out of My Later Years*

I saw the best minds of my generation destroyed by madness.
—ALLEN GINSBERG, *Howl*

The lamps are going out all over Europe; we shall not see them lit again in our lifetime.
—VISCOUNT GREY OF FALLODEN, Aug. 3, 1914
[The remark was made while Grey was standing at a window in the Foreign Office, London, watching lamplighters at work. War was declared the next day.]

One of the crying needs of the time is for a suitable burial service for the admittedly damned. —H. L. MENCKEN, *Prejudices*

There are evidently limits to the achievements of science; and there are irresolvable contradictions both between prosperity and virtue, and between happiness and "the good life," which had not been anticipated in our philosophy. The discovery of these contradictions threatens our culture with despair.
> —REINHOLD NIEBUHR, *The Irony of American History*

Morality in Europe today is herd morality.
> —FRIEDRICH NIETZSCHE, *Beyond Good and Evil*

Today violence is the rhetoric of the period.
> —ORTEGA Y GASSET, *The Revolt of the Masses*

We are suffering today from a greed for knowledge of evil.
> —CHRISTABEL PANKHURST, speech, 1930, quoted in David Mitchell, *The Fighting Pankhursts*

All the modern inconveniences.
> —MARK TWAIN, *Life on the Mississippi*

The century on which we are entering can be and must be the century of the common man.
> —HENRY A. WALLACE, speech, May 8, 1942

Plain living and high thinking are no more.
> —WILLIAM WORDSWORTH, *Written in London*, Sept. 1802

Things fall apart; the center cannot hold;
Mere anarchy is loosed upon the world.
> —WILLIAM BUTLER YEATS, *The Second Coming*

The best lack all conviction, while the worst
Are full of passionate intensity.
> —*Ibid.*

**MONEY**                    See also ECONOMICS; HAVES & HAVE-NOTS;
                                                POVERTY & HUNGER

Money disappears like magic.    —ANONYMOUS (ARAB PROVERB)

Every man thinks God is on his side. The rich and powerful know he is.
> —JEAN ANOUILH, *The Lark*

It is very difficult for the prosperous to be humble.
> —JANE AUSTEN, *Emma*

[Cf. Epictetus, below.]

A large income is the best recipe for happiness I ever heard of.
—JANE AUSTEN, *Northanger Abbey*

Money is like muck, not good except it be spread.
—FRANCIS BACON, *Of Seditions and Troubles*

Money, it turned out, was exactly like sex. You thought of nothing else if you didn't have it and thought of other things if you did.
—JAMES BALDWIN, *The Black Boy Looks at the White Boy* in *Nobody Knows My Name*

If you want to know what the Lord God thinks of money, you have only to look at those to whom he gives it.
—MAURICE BARING, quoted by Dorothy Parker, *Writers at Work: First Series*

Wealth maketh many friends.          —BIBLE, *Proverbs* 19:4

He that maketh haste to be rich shall not be innocent.
—*Ibid.*, 28:20

A feast is made for laughter, and wine maketh merry: but money answereth all things.          —BIBLE, *Ecclesiastes* 10:19

It is easier for a camel to go through the eye of a needle, than for a rich man to enter into the kingdom of God.
—BIBLE, *Matthew* 19:24
[Also *Mark* 10:25, and *Luke* 18:25. The "needle" was actually a narrow city gate—too narrow for a camel loaded with baggage.]

The love of money is the root of all evil.  —BIBLE, *I Timothy* 6:10

*Money, n.* A blessing that is of no advantage to us excepting when we part with it.          —AMBROSE BIERCE, *The Devil's Dictionary*

A rich man's joke is always funny.
—THOMAS E. BROWNE, *The Doctor*

It has been said that the love of money is the root of all evil. The want of money is so quite as truly.          —SAMUEL BUTLER, *Erewhon*
[Cf. George Bernard Shaw, below.]

Ready money is Aladdin's lamp.          —LORD BYRON, *Don Juan*

Money you know will hide many faults.
—CERVANTES, *Don Quixote*

I knew once a very covetous, sordid fellow, who used to say, "Take care of the pence, for the pounds will take care of themselves."   —EARL OF CHESTERFIELD, letter to his son, Nov. 6, 1747

To be clever enough to get all the money, one must be stupid enough to want it.
—G. K. CHESTERTON, *The Innocence of Father Brown*

Annual income twenty pounds, annual expenditure nineteen pounds six, result happiness. Annual income twenty pounds, annual expenditure twenty pounds ought and six, result misery.
—CHARLES DICKENS, *David Copperfield*

A billion here and a billion there and pretty soon you're talking big money.   —SEN. EVERETT DIRKSEN, attributed
[*The Wall Street Journal* reported on January 1, 1985, that the curator of the Dirksen Congressional Center could not track down the quote, but had noted, "That doesn't mean he didn't say it."]

All heiresses are beautiful.   —JOHN DRYDEN, *King Arthur*

It is difficult for a rich person to be modest, or a modest person rich.   —EPICTETUS, *Enchiridion*
[Cf. Jane Austen, above.]

Money's the wise man's religion.   —EURIPIDES, *The Cyclops*

Money is far more persuasive than logical arguments.
—EURIPIDES, *Medea*

Ah, take the Cash, and let the Credit go,
Nor heed the rumble of a distant Drum.
—EDWARD FITZGERALD, *The Rubáiyát of Omar Khayyám*

Let me tell you about the very rich. They are different from you and me.   —F. SCOTT FITZGERALD, *The Rich Boy*
[Later, Hemingway recorded a rejoinder, "Yes, they have more money."]

Money is like an arm or leg: use it or lose it.
—HENRY FORD, *The New York Times*, Nov. 8, 1931

Money is a singular thing. It ranks with love as man's greatest source of joy. And with his death as his greatest source of anxiety.
—JOHN KENNETH GALBRAITH, *The Age of Uncertainty*

Honesty is incompatible with amassing a large fortune.
—MOHANDAS GANDHI, *Non-Violence in Peace and War*

I am indeed rich since my income is superior to my expenses, and my expense is equal to my wishes.  —EDWARD GIBBON, *Memoirs*

He is almost always a slave who cannot live on little.
—HORACE, *Satires*

The almighty dollar, that great object of universal devotion throughout our land.  —WASHINGTON IRVING, *Wolfert's Roost*

There are few ways in which a man can be more innocently employed than in getting money.
—SAMUEL JOHNSON, letter to William Strahan,
March 27, 1775

The human species, according to the best theory I can form of it, is composed of two distinct races, the men who borrow and the men who lend.  —CHARLES LAMB, *The Two Races of Men*

Nothing hurts worse than the loss of money.
—LIVY, *History of Rome*

All wealth is the product of labor.
—JOHN LOCKE, *Two Treatises on Government*

When a man tells you that he got rich through hard work, ask him: "Whose?"  —DON MARQUIS, quoted in Edward Anthony,
*O Rare Don Marquis*

What's a thousand dollars? Mere chicken feed. A poultry matter.
—GROUCHO MARX, *The Cocoanuts*,
screenplay by George S. Kaufman

Money is like a sixth sense without which you cannot make a complete use of the other five.
—W. SOMERSET MAUGHAM, *Of Human Bondage*

He must have killed a lot of people to have gotten so rich.
—MOLIÈRE, *La Malade imaginaire*

You can never be too skinny or too rich.
—BARBARA "BABE" PALEY, attributed

The rich have many consolations.  —PLATO, *The Republic*

The tears of an heir are masked laughter.
                              —PUBLILIUS SYRUS, *Moral Sayings*

I believe the power to make money is a gift of God.
          —JOHN D. ROCKEFELLER, quoted in Matthew Josephson,
          *The Robber Barons*

A full pocketbook often groans more loudly than an empty
stomach.          —FRANKLIN D. ROOSEVELT, speech, Nov. 1, 1940

Neither a borrower nor a lender be.   —SHAKESPEARE, *Hamlet*, I, iii

Lack of money is the root of all evil.
               —GEORGE BERNARD SHAW, *Man and Superman*,
               "Maxims for Revolutionists"
[Cf. Samuel Butler, above.]

The universal regard for money is the one hopeful fact in our
civilization.      —GEORGE BERNARD SHAW, *Major Barbara*, preface

There are few sorrows, however poignant, in which a good income is of no avail.      —LOGAN PEARSALL SMITH, *Afterthoughts*

For money you would sell your soul.      —SOPHOCLES, *Antigone*

There is nothing in the world so demoralizing as money.     —*Ibid.*

That man is the richest whose pleasures are the cheapest.
                         —THOREAU, *Journal*, March 3, 1856

In order to stand well in the eyes of the community, it is necessary
to come up to a certain, somewhat indefinite, conventional standard
of wealth.     —THORSTEIN VEBLEN, *The Theory of the Leisure Class*

All those men have their price.
                    —SIR ROBERT WALPOLE, referring to certain
                    members of Parliament, *Memoirs*
[The popular version is: "Every man has his price."]

Money should circulate like rainwater.
                    —THORNTON WILDER, *The Matchmaker*

**MOON, THE**              See NATURE: THE HEAVENS, THE SKY

MORNING                          See NATURE: TIMES OF DAY

MORALITY                          See ETHICS & MORALITY

MORTALITY                        See DEATH; GENERATIONS; LIFE

MOTHERS                          See PARENTS & PARENTHOOD

MURDER                                          See CRIME

MUSIC                               See ARTS: MUSIC & DANCE

MYSTICISM

The most beautiful thing we can experience is the mysterious. It is the source of all true art and science.
—ALBERT EINSTEIN, *What I Believe*

Without mysticism man can achieve nothing great.
—ANDRÉ GIDE, *The Counterfeiters*

The dark night of the soul through which the soul passes on its way to the Divine Light.
—ST. JOHN OF THE CROSS, *The Ascent of Mount Carmel* [He also used the phrase "The Dark Night of the Soul" as the title of a treatise. The metaphor is the most famous expression of the despair that often precedes intense mystical experience.]

The Way [Tao] that can be told is not the eternal way.
—LAO-TZU, *Tao Te Ching*

The Way is like an empty vessel that yet may be drawn from.
—*Ibid.*

Mysticism is, in essence, little more than a certain intensity and depth of feeling in regard to what is believed about the universe.
—BERTRAND RUSSELL, *Mysticism and Logic*, title essay

The more mysterious, the more imperfect: that which is mystically spoken is but half spoken.
—BENJAMIN WHICHCOTE, *Moral and Religious Aphorisms*

**NAPLES**                                    See CITIES

**NATIONS**                        See also AMERICA & AMERICANS;
                                   CITIES; ENGLAND; ORIENT, THE;
                                   RACES & PEOPLES; TRAVEL

My heart's in the Highlands, my heart is not here,
My heart's in the Highlands a-chasing the deer.
                    —ROBERT BURNS, *My Heart's in the Highlands*

England is a paradise for women, and hell for horses; Italy is a
paradise for horses, hell for woman, as the diverb [proverb] goes.
                    —ROBERT BURTON, *Anatomy of Melancholy*

*Gallia est omnis divisa in partes tres.*
All Gaul is divided in three parts.
                    —JULIUS CAESAR, *De Bello Gallico*

France was a long despotism tempered by epigrams.
                    —THOMAS CARLYLE, *History of the French Revolution*

I am rather inclined to believe that this is the land God gave to
Cain.                        —JACQUES CARTIER, speaking of Canada,
                                   *La première relation*

It [Russia] is a riddle wrapped in a mystery inside an enigma.
                    —WINSTON CHURCHILL, radio speech, Oct. 1, 1939

Very big, China.                        —NOËL COWARD, *Private Lives*

How can you be expected to govern a country that has two
hundred and forty-six kinds of cheese?
                    —CHARLES DE GAULLE, *Newsweek*, Oct. 1, 1962

Our fatal troika [modern Russia] dashes on in her headlong flight,
perhaps to destruction.                        —FËDOR DOSTOEVSKI,
                                   *The Brothers Karamazov*

The Swiss are not a people so much as a neat clean quite solvent
business.                    —WILLIAM FAULKNER, *Intruder in the Dust*

They [the Greeks] were the first Westerners; the spirit of the
West, the modern spirit, is a Greek discovery.
                    —EDITH HAMILTON, *The Greek Way*

The Irish are a fair people;—they never speak well of one another.
—SAMUEL JOHNSON, quoted in Boswell's
*Life of Johnson*, March 20, 1775

A man who has not been in Italy is always conscious of an inferiority.                    —*Ibid.*, April 1776

Ireland is the old sow that eats her farrow.
—JAMES JOYCE, *Portrait of the Artist as a Young Man*

The wind of change is blowing through this Continent, and whether we like it or not, this growth of national consciousness is a political fact.        —HAROLD MACMILLAN, speech in Cape Town,
Feb. 3, 1960

Greece is the home of the gods.
—HENRY MILLER, *The Colossus of Maroussi*

I'm troubled, I'm dissatisfied. I'm Irish.
—MARIANNE MOORE, *Spenser's Ireland*

Everything ponderous, viscous, and solemnly clumsy, all long-winded and boring types of style are developed in profuse variety among Germans.     —FRIEDRICH NIETZSCHE, *Beyond Good and Evil*

There is always something new out of Africa.
—PLINY THE ELDER, *Natural History*

While we spend energy and imagination on new ways of cleaning the floors of our houses, the Japanese solve the problem by not dirtying them in the first place.        —BERNARD RUDOFSKY,
*The Kimono Mind*

The Japanese have perfected good manners and made them indistinguishable from rudeness.
—PAUL THEROUX, *The Great Railway Bazaar*

We [Greeks] are lovers of the beautiful, yet simple in our tastes, and we cultivate the mind without loss of manliness.
—THUCYDIDES, *The Peloponnesian War*

I fear the Greeks even when they bring gifts.   —VIRGIL, *Aeneid*

This agglomeration which was called and still calls itself the Holy Roman Empire was neither holy, nor Roman, nor an empire in any way.        —VOLTAIRE, *Essai sur le moeurs et l'esprit des nations*

In Italy for thirty years under the Borgias, they had warfare, terror, murder, bloodshed. They produced Michelangelo, Leonardo da Vinci, and the Rennaissance. In Switzerland, they had brotherly love, five hundred years of democracy and peace, and what did they produce? The cuckoo clock.   —ORSON WELLES, *The Third Man* [The script writer was Graham Greene, but Welles reportedly added this passage himself.]

Romantic Ireland's dead and gone,
It's with O'Leary in the grave.
      —WILLIAM BUTLER YEATS, *Responsibilities*,
      preliminary poem

**N A T U R E**         See also COUNTRY, THE; CREATION, DIVINE;
ENVIRONMENT; SEAS & SHIPS, SAILING & BOATING;
UNIVERSE; and NATURE subcategories, below

*Natura genetrix.*
Nature is our mother.       —ANONYMOUS (Latin Proverb)

Nature, to be commanded, must be obeyed.
      —FRANCIS BACON, *Novum Organum*

What I know of the divine science and Holy Scripture I learnt in woods and fields.       —ST. BERNARD, *Epistle 106*

Listen to a man of experience: thou wilt learn more in the woods than in books.       —*Ibid.*

Speak to the earth, and it shall teach thee.       —BIBLE, *Job* 12:8

For the earth is the Lord's, and the fulness thereof.
      —BIBLE, *I Corinthians* 10:26

To see a world in a grain of sand
And a heaven in a wild flower,
Hold infinity in the palm of your hand
And eternity in an hour.
      —WILLIAM BLAKE, *Auguries of Innocence*

There is a pleasure in the pathless woods,
There is a rapture on the lonely shore,
There is a society where none intrudes,
By the deep sea, and music in its roar:
I love not man the less, but nature more.
      —LORD BYRON, *Childe Harold's Pilgrimage*

The works of nature must all be accounted good.
—Cicero, *De Senectute*

Earth, with her thousand voices, praises God.
—Samuel Taylor Coleridge, *Hymn Before Sunrise*

Whatever nature has in store for mankind, unpleasant as it may be, men must accept, for ignorance is never better than knowledge.
—Enrico Fermi, quoted in Laura Fermi,
*Atoms in the Family*

Nature goes her own way, and all that to us seems an exception is really according to order.
—Goethe, quoted in Johann Peter Eckermann,
*Conversations with Goethe*

Glory be to God for dappled things.
—Gerard Manley Hopkins, *Pied Beauty*

The world is charged with the grandeur of God.
—Gerard Manley Hopkins, *God's Grandeur*

Though you drive away nature with a pitchfork, she always returns.
—Horace, *Epistles*, I, x

Never does nature say one thing and wisdom another.
—Juvenal, *Satires*

The poetry of earth is never dead.
—John Keats, *On the Grasshopper and the Cricket*

The roaring of the wind is my wife and the stars through the window pane are my children.
—John Keats, letter to
George and Georgina Keats, Oct. 14, 1818

I demonstrate by means of philosophy that the earth is round, and is inhabited on all sides; that it is insignificantly small, and is borne through the stars.
—Johann Kepler, *Astronomia nova*

Nature is not human-hearted.
—Lao-tzu, *Tao Te Ching*

The clearest way into the universe is through a forest wilderness.
—John Muir, *John of the Mountains*

Nature is an infinite sphere of which the center is everywhere and the circumference nowhere.                    —PASCAL, *Pensées*

It were happy if we studied nature more in natural things, and acted according to nature, whose rules are few, plain, and most reasonable.                    —WILLIAM PENN, *Some Fruits of Solitude*

All nature is but art, unknown to thee;
All chance, direction, which thou canst not see;
All discord, harmony not understood;
All partial evil, universal good.
                    —ALEXANDER POPE, *An Essay on Man*

Perhaps nature is our best assurance of immortality.
                    —ELEANOR ROOSEVELT, *My Day*, newspaper column,
                    April 24, 1945

What else is nature but God?                    —SENECA, *De Beneficiis*

One touch of nature makes the whole world kin.
                    —SHAKESPEARE, *Troilus and Cressida*, III, iii
[George Eliot offered this variant: "One touch of biliousness makes the whole world kin," Gordon S. Haight, ed., *Selections from George Eliot's Letters*.]

The earth and ocean seem
To sleep in one another's arms, and dream
Of waves, flowers, clouds, woods, rocks, and all that we
Read in their smiles, and call reality.
                    —PERCY BYSSHE SHELLEY, *Epipsychidion*

In nature, there is less death and destruction than death and trans-mutation.                    —EDWIN WAY TEALE, *Circle of the Seasons*

For men may come and men may go,
But I go on forever.                    —ALFRED, LORD TENNYSON, *The Brook*

Nature, red in tooth and claw.
                    —ALFRED, LORD TENNYSON, *In Memoriam*

I have learned
To look on nature, not as in the hour
Of thoughtless youth; but hearing oftentimes
The still, sad music of humanity.
                    —WILLIAM WORDSWORTH, *Tintern Abbey*

Nature never did betray the heart that loved her.                    —*Ibid.*

## NATURE: ANIMALS

The dog was created especially for children. He is the god of frolic.   —HENRY WARD BEECHER, *Proverbs from Plymouth Pulpit*

Hast thou given the horse strength? hast thou clothed his neck with thunder? . . .

He paweth in the valley, and rejoiceth in his strength; he goeth on to meet the armed men. . . .

He saith among the trumpets, Ha, ha; and he smelleth the battle afar off, the thunder of the captains, and the shouting.
                                        —BIBLE, *Job* 39: 19, 21, 25

A robin red breast in a cage
Puts all heaven in a rage.
                          —WILLIAM BLAKE, *Auguries of Innocence*

Tiger! Tiger! burning bright
In the forests of the night,
What immortal hand or eye
Could frame thy fearful symmetry?

In what distant deeps or skies
Burnt the fire of thine eyes?
On what wings dare he aspire?
What the hand dare seize the fire?

                                   —WILLIAM BLAKE, *The Tiger*

When the stars threw down their spears,
And watered heaven with their tears,
Did he smile his work to see?
Did he who made the Lamb make thee?                       —*Ibid.*

That's the wise thrush; he sings each song twice over,
Lest you think he never could recapture
The first fine careless rapture!
           —ROBERT BROWNING, *Home Thoughts From Abroad*

An animal's eyes have the power to speak a great language.
                            —MARTIN BUBER, *I and Thou*

Wee, sleekit, cow'ring, tim'rous beastie,
O what a panic's in thy breastie!   —ROBERT BURNS, *To a Mouse*

A hen is only an egg's way of making another egg.
                            —SAMUEL BUTLER, *Life and Habit*

The greatest pleasure of a dog is that you may make a fool of yourself with him and not only will he not scold you, but he will make a fool of himself too.
—SAMUEL BUTLER, *Higgledy-Piggledy*, in *Notebooks*

A canter is the cure for every evil.
—BENJAMIN DISRAELI, *The Young Duke*

Animals are such agreeable friends—they ask no questions, they pass no criticisms.     —GEORGE ELIOT, *Mr. Gilfil's Love Story* in *Scenes of Clerical Life*

The Cat. He walked by himself, and all places were alike to him.
—RUDYARD KIPLING, *The Cat That Walked by Himself*

I never saw a wild thing
Sorry for itself.
A small bird will drop frozen dead
From a bough
Without ever having felt sorry for itself.
—D. H. LAWRENCE, *Self Pity*

A wonderful bird is the pelican,
His bill will hold more than his belican.
He can take in his beak
Enough food for a week,
But I'm darned if I know how the helican.
—DIXON MERRITT, *The Pelican*

When I play with my cat, who knows whether she is not amusing herself with me more than I with her.     —MONTAIGNE, *Essays*

Dogs display reluctance and wrath
If you try to give them a bath
They bury bones in hideaways
And half the time they trot sideaways.
—OGDEN NASH, *An Introduction to Dogs*

The trouble with a kitten is
That
Eventually it becomes a
Cat.                    —OGDEN NASH, *The Kitten*

The song of canaries
Never varies,
And when they're moulting
They're pretty revolting.          —OGDEN NASH, *The Canary*

There is something about the unselfish and self-sacrificing love of a brute, which goes directly to the heart of him who has had frequent occasion to test the paltry friendship and gossamer fidelity of mere man. —EDGAR ALLAN POE, *The Black Cat*

A horse! A horse! my kingdom for a horse!
—SHAKESPEARE, *Richard III*, V, iv

Hail to thee, blithe Spirit!
Bird thou never wert,
That from Heaven, or near it,
Pourest thy full heart
In profuse strains of unpremeditated art.
—PERCY BYSSHE SHELLEY, *To a Skylark*

So, naturalists observe, a flea
Hath smaller fleas that on him prey;
And these have smaller fleas to bite 'em
and so proceed *ad infinitum*. —JONATHAN SWIFT, *On Poetry*

[Swift's conclusion, less well-known, is:
Thus every poet, in his kind,
Is bit by him that comes behind.]

He clasps the crag with crooked hands;
Close to the sun in lonely lands,
Ringed with the azure world, he stands.
The wrinkled sea beneath him crawls;
He watches from his mountain walls,
And like a thunderbolt he falls.
—ALFRED, LORD TENNYSON, *The Eagle*

Cheerfulness is proper to the cock, which rejoices over every little thing, and crows with varied and lively movements.
—LEONARDO DA VINCI, *Notebooks*

If a dog jumps in your lap, it is because he is fond of you; but if a cat does the same thing, it is because your lap is warmer.
—ALFRED NORTH WHITEHEAD, *Dialogues*

I think I could turn and live with animals, they are so placid and
self-contained,
I stand and look at them long and long.
—WALT WHITMAN, *Song of Myself*

The best thing about animals is that they don't talk much.
—THORNTON WILDER, *The Skin of Our Teeth*

## NATURE: GARDENS, FLOWERS & TREES

God almighty first planted a garden. —Francis Bacon, *Of Gardens*

Flowers are the sweetest things that God ever made, and forgot to put a soul into.　　　—Henry Ward Beecher, *Life Thoughts*

The Lord God planted a garden eastward in Eden.
　　　　　　　　　　　　　　　—Bible, *Genesis* 2:8

Consider the lilies of the field, how they grow; they toil not neither do they spin:
And yet I say unto you, That even Solomon in all his glory was not arrayed like one of these.　　　—Bible, *Matthew* 6:28

A garden is a lovesome thing, God wot!
　　　　　　　　　　—T. E. Brown, *My Garden*

The dandelion's pallid tube
Astonishes the grass,
And winter instantly becomes
An infinite alas.　　　　　—Emily Dickinson, poem

There are fairies at the bottom of our garden.
　　　　　　　　　　—Rose Fyleman, *Fairies*

*Verde que te quiero verde*
*Verde viento. Verde ramas.*
Green I love you green.
Green wind. Green branches.
　　　　—Gabriel García Lorca, *Romance sonámbulo*

The kiss of the sun for pardon,
The song of the birds for mirth.
One is nearer God's heart in a garden
Than anywhere else on earth.
　　　　　　—Dorothy Gurney, *God's Garden*

But though I am an old man, I am but a young gardener.
　　　　　　—Thomas Jefferson, letter to
　　　　　　Charles Willson Peale, Aug. 20, 1811

I think that I shall never see
A poem lovely as a tree.　　　　—Joyce Kilmer, *Trees*

Poems are made by fools like me,
But only God can make a tree.             *—Ibid.*

I want death to find me planting my cabbages.
          —MONTAIGNE, *To the Reader*, in *Essays*

Woodman, spare that tree!
Touch not a single bough!
In youth it sheltered me,
And I'll protect it now.
        —GEORGE POPE MORRIS, *Woodman Spare That Tree*

Each flower is a soul opening out to nature.
          —GÉRARD DE NERVAL, *Vers Dorés*

Where'er you walk, cool glades shall fan the glade,
Trees where you sit shall crowd into a shade:
Where'er you tread, the blushing flowers shall rise,
And all things flourish where you turn your eyes.
        —ALEXANDER POPE, *Summer*, in *Pastorals*

There is material enough in a single flower for the ornament of a
score of cathedrals.         —JOHN RUSKIN, *Stones of Venice*

There's rosemary, that's for remembrance—pray you love, remember. And there is pansies, that's for thoughts.
        —SHAKESPEARE, *Hamlet*, IV, v

For you there's rosemary and rue, these keep
Seeming and savor all the winter long.
        —SHAKESPEARE, *The Winter's Tale*, IV, iii

The summer's flower is to the summer sweet,
Though to itself it only live and die.     —SHAKESPEARE, sonnet 94

Rose is a rose is a rose.     —GERTRUDE STEIN, *Sacred Testimony*

Flower in the crannied wall,
I pluck you out of the crannies,
I hold you here, root and all, in my hand,
Little flower—but *if* I could understand
What you are, root and all, and all in all,
I should know what God and man is.
        —ALFRED, LORD TENNYSON, *Flower in the Crannied Wall*

I wandered lonely as a cloud
That floats on high o'er vales and hills,
When all at once I saw a crowd,
A host of golden daffodils.
—WILLIAM WORDSWORTH, *I Wandered Lonely as a Cloud*

A primrose by a river's brim
A yellow primrose was to him,
And it was nothing more.    —WILLIAM WORDSWORTH, *Peter Bell*

## NATURE: THE HEAVENS, THE SKY

See also SCIENCE: PHYSICS & COSMOLOGY

I do set my bow in the cloud, and it shall be for a token of a covenant between me and the earth.    —BIBLE, *Genesis* 9:13

The heavens declare the glory of God; and the firmament showeth his handiwork.    —BIBLE, *Psalms* 19:1

The moon like a flower
In heaven's high bower,
With silent delight,
Sits and smiles on the night.    —WILLIAM BLAKE, *Night*

The moon is a different thing to each one of us.
—FRANK BORMAN, from Apollo VIII, Dec. 24, 1968

The heavens call to you, and circle around you, displaying to you their eternal splendours, and your eye gazes only to earth.
—DANTE, *Purgatorio*, in *The Divine Comedy*

Space is the stature of God.    —JOSEPH JOUBERT, *Pensées*

Now the bright morning star, day's harbinger,
Comes dancing from the east. —JOHN MILTON, *On May Morning*

The evening star,
Love's harbinger, appeared.    —JOHN MILTON, *Paradise Lost*

The moon was a ghostly galleon tossed upon cloudy skies.
—ALFRED NOYES, *The Highwayman*

The eternal silence of these infinite spaces frightens me.
—PASCAL, *Pensées*

I have a horror of sunsets, they're so romantic, so operatic.
—PROUST, *Remembrance of Things Past:
The Guermantes Way*

My heart leaps up when I behold
A rainbow in the sky.
—WILLIAM WORDSWORTH, *My Heart Leaps Up*

And pluck till time and times are done
The silver apples of the moon,
The golden apples of the sun.
—WILLIAM BUTLER YEATS, *The Song of Wander Aengus*

## NATURE: THE OCEAN

See also SEAS & SHIPS,
SAILING & BOATING

Roll on, thou deep and dark blue ocean—roll!
Ten thousand fleets sweep over thee in vain;
Man marks the earth with ruin—his control
Stops with the shore. —LORD BYRON, *Childe Harold's Pilgrimage*

For all at last returns to the sea.
—RACHEL CARSON, *The Sea Around Us*

The sea never changes and its works, for all the talk of men, are
wrapped in mystery. —JOSEPH CONRAD, *Typhoon*

## NATURE: SEASONS

Sumer is icumen in,
Lhude sing cuccu!
Groweth sed, and bloweth med,
And springth the wude nu—
Sing cuccu! —ANONYMOUS
[Cf. Ezra Pound, below.]

Rise up, my love, my fair one, and come away.
  For lo, the winter is past, the rain is over and gone;
  The flowers appear on the earth; the time of the singing of birds
is come, and the voice of the turtle is heard in our land;
  The fig tree putteth forth her green figs, and the vines with the
tender grape give a good smell. Arise, my love, my fair one, and
come away. —BIBLE, *The Song of Solomon* 2:10–13

Autumn arrives in the early morning, but spring at the close of a
winter day. —ELIZABETH BOWEN, *The Death of the Heart*

The years at the spring
And day's at the morn;
Morning's at seven;
The hillside's dew-pearled;
The lark's on the wing;
The snail's on his thorn:
God's in his heaven—
All's right with the world.          —ROBERT BROWNING, *Pippa Passes*

Hard is the heart that loved naught in May.
                    —GEOFFREY CHAUCER, *The Romance of the Rose*

April is the cruellest month, breeding
Lilacs out of the dead land, mixing
Memory and desire, stirring
Dull roots with spring rain.          —T. S. ELIOT, *The Waste Land*

Alas, that Spring should vanish with the Rose!
          —EDWARD FITZGERALD, *The Rubáiyát of Omar Khayyám*
[More of this is at YOUTH.]

Sweet spring, full of sweet days and roses.
                    —GEORGE HERBERT, *Virtue*, in *The Temple*

I saw old autumn in the misty morn
Stand shadowless like silence, listening
To silence.                    —THOMAS HOOD, *Autumn*

Summer afternoon—summer afternoon; to me those have always
been the two most beautiful words in the English language.
                    —HENRY JAMES, quoted in Edith Wharton,
                    *A Backward Glance*

His soul swooned slowly as he heard the snow falling faintly
through the universe and faintly falling, like the descent of their
last end, upon all the living and the dead.
                    —JAMES JOYCE, *The Dead* in *Dubliners*

Season of mists and mellow fruitfulness.
                    —JOHN KEATS, *To Autumn*

What is so rare as a day in June?
Then, if ever, come perfect days.
                    —JAMES RUSSELL LOWELL, *The Vision of Sir Launfal*,
                    Prelude

'Tis the last rose of summer
Left blooming alone;
All her lovely companions
Are faded and gone.　　—THOMAS MOORE, *'Tis the Last Rose*


It snowed and snowed, the whole world over,
Snow swept the world from end to end.
A candle burned on the table;
A candle burned.　　—BORIS PASTERNAK, *Doctor Zhivago*


Winter is icumen in,
Lhude sign Goddamm,
Raineth drop and staineth slop,
And how the wind doth ramm!
Sing: Goddamm.　　—EZRA POUND, *Ancient Music*
[For the original ancient music, see above, author anonymous.]


O, it sets my heart a-clickin' like the tickin' of a clock,
When the frost is on the punkin and the fodder's in the shock.
　　—JAMES WHITCOMB RILEY, *When the Frost Is on the Punkin*


The seasons . . . are authentic; there is no mistake about them,
they are what a symphony ought to be: four perfect movements in
intimate harmony with one another.
　　—ARTHUR RUBINSTEIN, *My Young Years*


Summer makes a silence after spring.
　　—VITA SACKVILLE-WEST, *The Land*


November's sky is chill and drear,
November's leaf is red and sear.
　　—SIR WALTER SCOTT, *Marmion*, Introduction


Why, this is very midsummer madness.
　　—SHAKESPEARE, *Twelfth Night*, III, iv


A sad tale's best for winter.　　—SHAKESPEARE, *The Winter's Tale*


Rough winds do shake the darling buds of May,
And summer's lease hath all too short a date.
　　—SHAKESPEARE, sonnet 18


If winter comes, can spring be far behind?
　　—PERCY BYSSHE SHELLEY, *Ode to the West Wind*

In winter I get up by night
And dress by yellow candlelight.
In summer quite the other way,
I have to go to bed by day.
　　　　　　　—ROBERT LOUIS STEVENSON, *Bed in Summer* in
　　　　　　　　　　　*A Child's Garden of Verses*

In the spring a young man's fancy lightly turns to thoughts of
love.　　　　　　—ALFRED, LORD TENNYSON, *Locksley Hall*

## NATURE: TIMES OF DAY

The morning is wiser than the evening.
　　　　　　　　　—ANONYMOUS (RUSSIAN PROVERB)

The night
Hath been to me a more familiar face
Than that of man; and in her starry shade
Of dim and solitary loveliness
I learned the languages of another world.
　　　　　　　　　　　—LORD BYRON, *Manfred*

Night is the mother of thoughts.　　—JOHN FLORIO, *First Frutes*

Awake! for Morning in the Bowl of Night
Has flung the Stone that puts the Stars to Flight.
　　　　—EDWARD FITZGERALD, *The Rubáiyát of Omar Khayyám*

Night is the other half of life, and the better half.
　　　　　　—GOETHE, *Wilhelm Meisters Lehrjahre*

The curfew tolls the knell of parting day,
The lowing herd wind slowly o'er the lea,
The plowman homeward plods his weary way,
And leaves the world to darkness and to me.
　　　—THOMAS GRAY, *Elegy Written in a Country Churchyard*

The day is done, and the darkness
Falls from the wings of night,
As a feather is wafted downward
From an eagle in his flight.
　　　　—HENRY WADSWORTH LONGFELLOW, *The Day Is Done*

Night hath a thousand eyes.　—JOHN LYLY, *Maides Metamorphose*

Is not the night mournful, sad, and melancholy?
—RABELAIS, *Gargantua*

Night, when words fade and things come alive.
—ANTOINE DE SAINT-EXUPÉRY, *Flight to Arras*

Each day is a little life; every waking and rising a little birth; every fresh morning a little youth; every going to rest and sleep a little death.     —ARTHUR SCHOPENHAUER, *Our Relation to Ourselves*

'Tis now the very witching time of night,
When churchyards yawn and hell itself breathes out
Contagion to this world.     —SHAKESPEARE, *Hamlet*, III, ii

I arise from dreams of thee
In the first sweet sleep of night
When the winds are breathing low,
And the stars are shining bright.
—PERCY BYSSHE SHELLEY, *The Indian*

Never greet a stranger in the night, for he may be a demon.
—THE TALMUD

## NATURE:  WIND  &  WEATHER

See also NATURE:
TIMES OF DAY

A cloudy day, or a little sunshine have as great an influence on many constitutions as the most real blessings or misfortunes.
—JOSEPH ADDISON, *The Spectator*, no. 162

It ain't a fit night out for man or beast.
—W. C. FIELDS, *The Fatal Glass of Beer*

Not snow, no, nor rain, nor heat, nor night keeps them from accomplishing their appointed courses with all speed.
—HERODOTUS, *Histories*
[The version inscribed on the main Post Office in Manhattan is: "Neither snow, nor rain, nor gloom of night stays these couriers from the swift completion of their appointed rounds."]

Who has seen the wind?
Neither you nor I:
But when the trees bow down their heads
The wind is passing by.     —CHRISTINA ROSSETTI, *Sing-Song*

There is really no such thing as bad weather, only different kinds of good weather.                    —JOHN RUSKIN, attributed

The fog comes in on little cat feet.        —CARL SANDBURG, *Fog*

O Wild West Wind, thou breath of Autumn's being,
Thou from whose unseen presence the leaves dead
Are driven like ghosts from an enchanter fleeing,
Yellow and black, and pale, and hectic red,
Pestilence-stricken multitude.
                    —PERCY BYSSHE SHELLEY, *Ode to the West Wind*

Thank heaven, the sun has gone in, and I don't have to go out and enjoy it.                    —LOGAN PEARSALL SMITH, *Last Words*

Sweet and low, sweet and low,
Wind of the western sea.
                    —ALFRED, LORD TENNYSON, *The Princess*

Everybody talks about the weather, but nobody does anything about it.                    —MARK TWAIN, attributed
[The aphorism appeared in print in an unsigned editorial in the *Hartford Courant*, Aug. 24, 1897. Twain lived in Hartford, so although the attribution is uncertain, the saying may very well have originated with him. *Bartlett* notes that Charles Dudley Warner was associate editor of the paper at the time; so he, too, might have coined the saying.]

**NAVY**                                   See MILITARY, THE

**NEUROSIS**                               See ILLNESS & REMEDIES

**NEWS**                              See MEDIA; PRESS, THE; RUMOR

**NEW THINGS**          See also CHANGE; SCIENCE: DISCOVERY;
                                   TECHNOLOGY; VARIETY

He that will not apply new remedies must expect new evils; for time is the greatest innovator.        —FRANCIS BACON, *Of Innovations*

There is nothing new except that which has been forgotten.
                    —MLLE BERTIN, ascribed
[She was the dressmaker of Marie Antoinette.]

There is no new thing under the sun.        —BIBLE, *Ecclesiastes* 1:9

Neither do men put new wine into old bottles.
—BIBLE, *Matthew* 9:17

Men love . . . newfangledness.
—GEOFFREY CHAUCER, *The Squire's Tale*, in
*The Canterbury Tales*

Nothing quite new is perfect. —CICERO, *Brutus*

Mr. and Mrs. Veneering were bran-new people in a bran-new house in a bran-new quarter of London. Everything about the Veneerings was spick-and-span new. All their furniture was new, all their friends were new, all their servants were new, their plate was new, their carriage was new, their harness was new, their horses were new, their pictures were new, they themselves were new, they were as newly married as was lawfully compatible with having a bran-new baby, and if they had set up a great-grandfather, he would have come in matting from the Pantechnicon, without a scratch upon him, French polished to the crown of his head.
—CHARLES DICKENS, *Our Mutual Friend*

If a man write a better book, preach a better sermon, or make a better mousetrap than his neighbor, tho' he build his house in the woods, the world will make a beaten path to his door.
—RALPH WALDO EMERSON,
quoted by Sarah S. B. Yule, *Borrowings*
[*The Concise Oxford Dictionary of Quotations* reports that she took down this remark while listening to a lecture by Emerson; later Elbert Hubbard claimed that he originated the quote.]

It is always the latest song that an audience applauds the most.
—HOMER, *Odyssey*

New opinions are always suspected, and usually opposed, without any other reason but because they are not already common.
—JOHN LOCKE, *Essay Concerning Human Understanding*

All good things which exist are the fruit of originality.
—JOHN STUART MILL, *On Liberty*

The true creator is necessity, which is the mother of our invention.
—PLATO, *The Republic*

Nothing can be said nowadays which has not already been said.
—TERENCE, *Eunuchus*

# NEW YEAR

Now the New Year reviving old Desires,
The thoughtful Soul to Solitude retires.
—EDWARD FITZGERALD, *The Rubáiyát of Omar Khayyám*

Ring out, wild bells, to the wild sky,
The flying cloud, the frosty light:
The year is dying in the night;
Ring out wild bells and let him die.

Ring out the old, ring in the new,
Ring, happy bells, across the snow:
The year is going, let him go;
Ring out the false, ring in the true.
—ALFRED, LORD TENNYSON, *In Memoriam*

**NEW YORK** See CITIES

**NIGHT** See NATURE: TIMES OF DAY

**NONVIOLENCE** See PACIFISM

**NOVELTY** See NEW THINGS

**NOVEMBER** See NATURE: SEASONS

**OBEDIENCE** See also APPEASEMENT VS. RESISTANCE;
RESIGNATION

Obedience is the mother of success, and the wife of security.
—AESCHYLUS, *The Seven Against Thebes*

Obedience is in a way the mother of all virtues.
—ST. AUGUSTINE, *On the Good of Marriage*

Nevertheless, not my will, but thine, be done.
—BIBLE, *Luke* 22:42

Obedience is a hard profession.    —PIERRE CORNEILLE, *Nicomède*

It is much safer to obey than to rule.
—THOMAS À KEMPIS, *Imitation of Christ*

It is right that what is just should be obeyed; it is necessary that what is strongest should be obeyed. —PASCAL, *Pensées*

He who yields a prudent obedience exercises a partial control. —PUBLILIUS SYRUS, *Moral Sayings*

Let them obey that know not how to rule. —SHAKESPEARE, *Henry VI, Part II*, V, i

Obedience,
Bane of all genius, virtue, freedom, truth,
Makes slaves of men, and, of the human frame,
A mechanized automaton. —PERCY BYSSHE SHELLEY, *Queen Mab*

Learn to obey before you command. —SOLON, quoted in Diogenes Laërtius, *Lives of Eminent Philosophers*

## OBJECTS See THINGS & POSSESSIONS

## OCCULT, THE

To deny the possibility, nay, the actual existence of witchcraft and sorcery is flatly to contradict the revealed word of God. —WILLIAM BLACKSTONE, *Commentaries on the Laws of England*

The constellations were consulted for advice, but no one understood them. —ELIAS CANETTI, *Aufzeichungen*

Go and catch a falling star,
Get a child with mandrake root. —JOHN DONNE, *Song: Go and Catch a Falling Star*

Nature has given us astrology as an adjunct and ally to astronomy. —JOHANNES KEPLER, *De Fundamentis*

Astrology is framed by the devil. —MARTIN LUTHER, *Table-Talk*

Millions of spiritual creatures walk the earth
Unseen, both when we wake, and when we sleep. —JOHN MILTON, *Paradise Lost*

Once upon a midnight dreary, while I pondered, weak and weary,
Over many a quaint and curious volume of forgotten lore—
While I nodded, nearly napping, suddenly there came a tapping,
As of someone gently rapping, rapping at my chamber door.
　　　　　　　　　　　—EDGAR ALLAN POE, *The Raven*

Quoth the Raven, "Nevermore."　　　　　　　　　—*Ibid.*

GLENDOWER: I can call spirits from the vasty deep.
HOTSPUR: Why so can I, or so can any man;
But will they come when you do call for them?
　　　　　　　　　—SHAKESPEARE, *Henry IV, Part I*, III, i

Double, double toil and trouble,
Fire burn and caldron bubble.　　　—SHAKESPEARE, *Macbeth*, IV, i

Eye of newt and toe of frog,
Wool of bat and tongue of dog,
Adder's fork and blindworm's sting,
Lizard's leg and owlet's wing,
For a charm of powerful trouble,
Like a hell broth boil and bubble.　　　　　　　　—*Ibid.*

I'll break my staff,
Bury it certain fathoms in the earth,
And deeper than did ever plummet sound
I'll drown my book.　　　—SHAKESPEARE, *The Tempest*, V, i

**OCEAN**　　　　　　　See NATURE: THE OCEAN; SEAS & SHIPS,
　　　　　　　　　　　　　　　　　　　　SAILING & BOATING

**OLD　AGE**　　　　See AGE & AGING; OLD THINGS, OLD FRIENDS

**OLD　THINGS,　OLD　FRIENDS**　　See also AGE; PAST, THE

I love everything that's old: old friends, old times, old manners,
old books, old wines.　—OLIVER GOLDSMITH, *She Stoops to Conquer*

Is not old wine wholesomest, old pippins toothsomest, old wood
burn brightest, old linen wash whitest? Old soldiers, sweethearts, are
surest, and old lovers are soundest.
　　　　　　　　　　　　—JOHN WEBSTER, *Westward Hoe*

**OPTIMISM & PESSIMISM**    See also DESPAIR, DEPRESSION, MISERY; HOPE

The optimist proclaims that we live in the best of all possible worlds; and the pessimist fears this is true.
—JAMES BRANCH CABELL, *The Silver Stallion*

Cheer up, the worst is yet to come.
—PHILANDER JOHNSON, *Shooting Stars*

A pessimist is a person who has had to listen to too many optimists.
—DON MARQUIS, quoted in Frederick B. Wilcox, *A Little Book of Aphorisms*

An optimist is a guy that never has had much experience.
—DON MARQUIS, *archy and mehitabel*

To fear the worst oft cures the worse.
—SHAKESPEARE, *Troilus and Cressida*, III, ii

In this best of all possible worlds . . . all is for the best.
—VOLTAIRE, *Candide*

**ORIENT, THE**    See also NATIONS; TRAVEL

In Xanadu did Kubla Khan
A stately pleasure dome decree:
Where Alph, the sacred river ran
Through caverns measureless to man
Down to a sunless sea.  —SAMUEL TAYLOR COLERIDGE, *Kubla Khan*

The mysterious East, perfumed like a flower, silent like death, dark like a grave.                —JOSEPH CONRAD, *Youth*

This is Malaya. Everything takes a long, a very long time in Malaya. Things get done, occasionally, but more often they don't, and the more in a hurry you are, the quicker you break down.
—HAN SUNYIN, *And the Rain My Drink*

Oh, East is East, and West is West, and never the twain shall meet,
Till Earth and Sky stand presently at God's great Judgment Seat.
—RUDYARD KIPLING, *The Ballad of East and West*

On the road to Mandalay,
Where the flyin'-fishes play,
An' the dawn comes up like thunder outer China 'crost the Bay!
—RUDYARD KIPLING, *Mandalay*

**PACIFISM**
See also APPEASEMENT VS. RESISTANCE;
PEACE; RESIGNATION; VIOLENCE; WAR

Resist not evil: but whosoever shall smite thee on thy right cheek, turn to him the other also.　　　—BIBLE, *Matthew* 5:39

Be ye therefore wise as serpents, and harmless as doves.
　　　—*Ibid.*, 10:16

Non-violence is the first article of my faith. It is also the last article of my creed.
　　　—MOHANDAS K. GANDHI, speech in defense against a charge of sedition, March 23, 1922

Man lives freely only by his readiness to die, if need be, at the hands of his brother, never by killing him.
　　　—MOHANDAS K. GANDHI, quoted in S. Hobhouse, ed., *True Patriotism: Some Sayings of Mahatma Gandhi*

Pacifism is simply undisguised cowardice.
　　　—ADOLF HITLER, speech, Aug. 21, 1926

**PAINTING**
See ARTS: PAINTING

**PARENTS & PARENTHOOD**
See also CHILDREN & CHILDHOOD;
FAMILY; GENERATIONS

The joys of parents are secret, and so are their griefs and fears: they cannot utter the one, nor will they utter the other.
　　　—FRANCIS BACON, *Of Parents and Children*

There is no slave out of heaven like a loving woman; and, of all loving women, there is no such slave as a mother.
　　　—HENRY WARD BEECHER, *Proverbs from Plymouth Pulpit*

What the mother sings to the cradle goes all the way down to the coffin.　　　—*Ibid.*

Honor they father and they mother.　　　—BIBLE, *Exodus* 22:12, and elsewhere

He that spareth his rod hateth his son.　　　—BIBLE, *Proverbs* 13:24

Train up a child in the way he should go: and when he is old, he will not depart from it.                                   —*Ibid.*, 22:6

Who doesn't desire his father's death?
                      —FËDOR DOSTOEVSKI, *The Brothers Karamazov*

Happy that man whose children make his happiness in life and not his grief.                                   —EURIPIDES, *Orestes*

A man who has been the indisputable favorite of mother keeps for life the feeling of a conqueror, that confidence of success that often induces real success.
                      —FREUD, quoted in Ernest Jones, *Life and Works*
[For the opposite view, in the English tradition, see Maugham below.]

You are the bows from which your children are as living arrows sent forth.                           —KAHLIL GIBRAN, *The Prophet*

There are some extraordinary fathers who seem, during the whole course of their lives, to be giving their children reasons for being consoled at their death.             —LA BRUYÈRE, *Les Caractères*

He that will have his son have respect for him and his orders, must himself have a great reverence for his son.
                      —JOHN LOCKE, *Some Thoughts Concerning Education*

wot in hell
have I done to deserve
all these kittens.             —DON MARQUIS, *archy and mehitabel*

Few misfortunes can befall a boy which bring worse consequence than to have a really affectionate mother.
                      —W. SOMERSET MAUGHAM, *A Writer's Notebook*
[Cf. Freud, above.]

People are always rather bored with their parents. That's human nature.             —W. SOMERSET MAUGHAM, *The Bread-Winner*

How sharper than a serpent's tooth it is
To have a thankless child!             —SHAKESPEARE, *King Lear*, I, iv

It is a wise father that knows his own child.
                      —SHAKESPEARE, *The Merchant of Venice*, II, ii

If parents would only realize how they bore their own children!
—GEORGE BERNARD SHAW, *Misalliance*

You know more than you think you do.
—DR. BENJAMIN SPOCK, opening line of *Baby and Child Care*, addressed to new parents

Most American children suffer too much mother and too little father.              —GLORIA STEINEM, in
*The New York Times*, Aug. 26, 1971

Happy he
With such a mother! faith in womankind
Beats with his blood.      —ALFRED, LORD TENNYSON, *The Princess*

I have found the best way to give advice to your children is to find out what they want and then advise them to do it.
—HARRY S. TRUMAN, television interview, May 27, 1955

Children begin by loving their parents. After a time they judge them. Rarely, if ever, do they forgive them.
—OSCAR WILDE, *A Woman of No Importance*
[In *Dorian Gray*, Wilde concludes the same thought more optimistically: "*Sometimes* they forgive them (italics added)"]

All women become like their mothers. That is their tragedy. No man does. That's his.      —OSCAR WILDE,
*The Importance of Being Earnest*

There are no illegitimate children—only illegitimate parents.
—JUDGE LÉON R. YANKWICH,
decision in *Zipkin* v. *Mozon*, June 1928
[J. M. and M. J. Cohen, in *The Penguin Dictionary of Modern Quotations*, say that Yankwich was quoting the columnist O. O. McIntyre.]

**PARIS**                                                            See CITIES

**PARTIES**                                        See CONVERSATION; HOSPITALITY

**PASSION**                                        See ENTHUSIASM, ENERGY, ZEAL;
LOVE; SEX

**PAST, THE**                    See also HISTORY; MEMORY; REGRET

Of one power even God is deprived, and that is the power of
making what is past never to have been.
                    —AGATHON, quoted in Aristotle, *The Nicomachean Ethics*

In the carriages of the past you can't go anywhere.
                    —MAXIM GORKY, *The Lower Depths*

Yesterday
A night-gone thing
A sun-down name.
                    —LANGSTON HUGHES, *Youth* in *From My People*

The past is the present, isn't it? It's the future too.
                    —EUGENE O'NEILL, *Long Day's Journey Into Night*

Only the past when you were happy is real.          —*Ibid.*

Don't look back. Something may be gaining on you.
                    —SATCHEL PAIGE, *How to Keep Young*

I tell you the past is a bucket of ashes.  —CARL SANDBURG, *Prairie*

Those who cannot remember the past are condemned to repeat it.
                    —GEORGE SANTAYANA, *The Life of Reason*

What's past is prologue.          —SHAKESPEARE, *The Tempest*, II, i

The world is weary of the past,
Oh, might it die or rest at last.          —PERCY BYSSHE SHELLEY, *Hellas*

All things are taken from us, and become
Portions and parcels of the dreadful past.
                    —ALFRED, LORD TENNYSON, *The Lotus Eaters*

*Mais où sont les neiges d'antan?*
Where are the snows of yesteryear?
                    —FRANÇOIS VILLON, *Ballade des dames du temps jadis*

We live in reference to past experience and not to future events,
however inevitable.  —H. G. WELLS, *Mind at the End of Its Tether*
[See also Auden, at HISTORY.]

**PATIENCE**                    See also PERSEVERANCE & ENDURANCE

Patience is bitter but its fruit is sweet.
                              —ANONYMOUS (FRENCH PROVERB)

Sit on the bank of a river and wait: your enemy's corpse will
soon float by.                —ANONYMOUS (INDIAN PROVERB)

Patience is the companion of wisdom.
                              —ST. AUGUSTINE, *On Patience*

The end is not yet.                    —BIBLE, *Matthew* 24:6

*Patience, n.* A minor form of despair disguised as a virtue.
                              —AMBROSE BIERCE, *The Devil's Dictionary*

Everything comes if a man will only wait.
                              —BENJAMIN DISRAELI, *Tancred*

Beware the fury of a patient man.
                              —JOHN DRYDEN, *Absalom and Achitophel*

Patience and delay achieve more than force and rage.
                              —LA FONTAINE, *Fables*

They also serve who only stand and wait.
                              —JOHN MILTON, *On his Blindness*

How poor are they that have not patience!
What wound did ever heal but by degrees?
                              —SHAKESPEARE, *Othello*, II, iii

**PATRIOTISM**                    See also AMERICA & AMERICANS;
                                        AMERICAN HISTORY:
                                  MEMORABLE MOMENTS; HEROES

Patriotism is in political life what faith is in religion.
                              —LORD ACTON, *Nationality* in
                              *The Home and Foreign Review*, July, 1862

*Plus je vis d'étrangers, plus j'aimai ma patrie.*
The more I saw of foreigners, the more I loved my country.
                              —P. L. DE BELLOY, *Le Siège de Calais*
[Madame de Staël later slightly rephrased the thought in *Corinne*:
"The more I see of other countries, the more I love my own."]

"My country, right or wrong," is a thing no patriot would think of saying except in a desperate case. It is like saying, "My mother, drunk or sober."        —G. K. CHESTERTON, *The Defendant*
[He is referring to Decatur; see below.]

Our country: In her intercourse with foreign nations, may she always be in the right; but our country right or wrong.
                    —STEPHEN DECATUR, toast at Norfolk, April 1816
[Cf. Chesterton above. Carl Schurz also offered a correction, in a speech on Oct. 17, 1899: "Our country, right or wrong. When right, to be kept right; when wrong, to be put right."]

When a whole nation is roaring Patriotism at the top of its voice, I am fain to explore the cleanness of its hands and purity of its heart.
                    —RALPH WALDO EMERSON, *Journals*

*Dulce et decorum est pro patria mori.*
It is a sweet and seemly thing to die for one's country.
                                        —HORACE, *Odes*

Patriotism is the last refuge of a scoundrel.
                    —SAMUEL JOHNSON, quoted in James Boswell,
                    *Life of Johnson*

Ask not what your country can do for you, ask what you can do for your country.
                    —JOHN F. KENNEDY, inaugural address, 1961
[*The Concise Oxford Dictionary of Quotations* notes that a similar exhortation was used in the funeral oration for John Greenleaf Whittier (died 1892). And *Bartlett* cites several predecessors, not including Whittier but going back to an even earlier address by Oliver Wendell Holmes on May 30, 1884: ". . . we pause . . . to recall what our country has done for each of us, and to ask ourselves what we can do for our country in return."]

You're not supposed to be so blind with patriotism that you can't face reality. Wrong is wrong no matter who does it or who says it.
                    —MALCOLM X, *Malcolm X Speaks Out*

Patriotism is a kind of religion; it is the egg from which wars are hatched.        —GUY DE MAUPASSANT, *My Uncle Sosthenes*

Breathes there the man, with soul so dead,
Who never to himself has said,
This is my own, my native land!
                    —SIR WALTER SCOTT, *The Lay of the Last Minstrel*

No one loves his country for its size or eminence, but because it is his own. —SENECA, *Letter to Lucilius*

"Shoot, if you must, this old gray head,
But spare your country's flag," she said.
—JOHN GREENLEAF WHITTIER, *Barbara Frietchie*

## PATTERNS

Perfumes, colors, and sounds echo one another.
—CHARLES BAUDELAIRE, *Correspondances*

We all of us live too much in circles.    —DISRAELI, *Sybil*

The life of man is a self-evolving circle.
—RALPH WALDO EMERSON, *Circles*

*Network, n.* Any thing reticulated or decussated at equal distances, with interstices between the intersections.
—SAMUEL JOHNSON, *Dictionary*

Christ! What are patterns for?    —AMY LOWELL, *Patterns*

The wheel is come full circle.   —SHAKESPEARE, *King Lear*, V, iii

## PEACE                              See also PACIFISM; WAR

They shall beat their swords into plowshares, and their spears into pruning hooks: nation shall not lift up sword against nation, neither shall they learn war any more.    —BIBLE, *Isaiah* 2:4;
also *Micah* 4:3

The wolf also shall dwell with the lamb, and the leopard shall lie down with the kid; and the calf and the young lion and the fatling together; and a little child shall lead them.    —*Ibid.*, 11:6

Blessed are the peacemakers: for they shall be called the children of God.    —BIBLE, *Matthew* 5:9
[For other verses from the Sermon on the Mount, see VIRTUE.]

Peace is liberty in tranquillity.    —CICERO, *Philippics*

Peace cannot be kept by force. It can only be achieved by understanding.    —ALBERT EINSTEIN, *Notes on Pacifism*

The most disadvantageous peace is better than the most just war.
                                    —ERASMUS, *Adagia* ·

You and me, we've made a separate peace.
                        —ERNEST HEMINGWAY, *A Very Short Story*

Better to live in peace than to begin a war and lie dead.
            —CHIEF JOSEPH, quoted in Time-Life Books, *The Indians*

First keep peace within yourself, then you can also bring peace to others.                    —THOMAS À KEMPIS, *Imitation of Christ*

Arms alone are not enough to keep the peace. It must be kept by men.        —JOHN F. KENNEDY, State of the Union message, 1963

Certain peace is better than anticipated victory.
                                    —LIVY, *Ab Urbe Condita*

Peace hath her victories
No less renowned than war.        —JOHN MILTON, *To Cromwell*

The only alternative to co-existence is co-destruction.
        —JAWAHARLAL NEHRU, quoted in the *Observer*, Aug. 29, 1954

It isn't enough to talk about peace. One must believe in it. And it isn't enough to believe in it. One must work at it.
                —ELEANOR ROOSEVELT, Voice of America, Nov. 11, 1951

Peace, like charity, begins at home.
                —FRANKLIN DELANO ROOSEVELT, speech, Aug. 14, 1936

A peace is of the nature of a conquest;
For then both parties nobly are subdued,
And neither party loser.   —SHAKESPEARE, *Henry IV, Part II*, IV, ii

They make a desert and call it peace.        —TACITUS, *Agricola*

Ring out the thousand wars of old,
Ring in the thousand years of peace.
                        —ALFRED, LORD TENNYSON, *In Memoriam*

Peace hath higher tests of manhood
Than battle ever knew.   —JOHN GREENLEAF WHITTIER, *The Hero*

Only a peace between equals can last.
                —WOODROW WILSON, speech to U.S. Senate, 1917

**PEOPLE**                    See HUMANS & HUMAN NATURE;
                              PEOPLE, THE; RACES & PEOPLES;
                              REASONABLE & UNREASONABLE PEOPLE

**PEOPLE, NOT LIKING**        See MISANTHROPY

**PEOPLE, THE**               See also DEMOCRACY

*Vox populi, vox Dei.*
The voice of the people is the voice of God.
                    —ALCUIN, letter to Charlemagne, 800 A.D.
[Alexander Pope was rather less sure of this:
   The people's voice is odd,
   It is, and is not, the voice of God
—*Imitations of Horace.* William Tecumseh Sherman simply dis-
agreed: "*Vox populi, vox humbug,*" letter to his wife, June 2, 1863.]

Who builds upon the people, builds upon sand.
                    —ANONYMOUS (ITALIAN PROVERB)

The people want to be deceived.
                    —ANONYMOUS (ROMAN EPIGRAPH)

In the common people there is no wisdom, no penetration, no
power of judgment.                    —CICERO, *Pro Planchio*

If it has to choose who is to be crucified, the crowd will always
save Barabbas.        —JEAN COCTEAU, *Le rappel à l'ordre*

Nor is the people's judgment always true;
The most may err as grossly as the few.
                    —JOHN DRYDEN, *Absalom and Achitophel*

All the world over, I will back the masses against the classes.
                    —WILLIAM GLADSTONE, speech, June 6, 1886

There is not a more mean, stupid, dastardly, pitiful, selfish, spite-
ful, envious, ungrateful animal than the public. It is the greatest of
cowards, for it is afraid of itself.   —WILLIAM HAZLITT, *Table Talk*

The wealth of a country is its working people.
                    —THEODOR HERZL, *Altneuland*

The great masses of the people will more easily fall victims to a
big lie than to a small one.     —ADOLF HITLER, *Mein Kampf*

The people are a many-headed beast.
—HORACE, *Epistles*, first epistle

The people are the only sure reliance for the preservation of our liberty.    —THOMAS JEFFERSON, letter to James Madison, 1787

About things on which the public thinks long it commonly thinks right.    —SAMUEL JOHNSON, *Addison*, in *Lives of the English Poets*

Why should there not be a patient confidence in the ultimate justice of the people? Is there any better or equal hope in the world?
—ABRAHAM LINCOLN, *First Inaugural Address*, 1861

You may fool all the people some of the time; you can even fool some of the people all the time; but you can't fool all of the people all the time.
—ABRAHAM LINCOLN, attributed but possibly apocryphal
[*Bartlett* cites Alexander K. McClure, *Lincoln's Yarns and Stories*.]

Every man a king!    —HUEY LONG, slogan

The people, and the people alone, are the motive force in the making of world history.    —MAO TSE-TUNG, *Quotations from Chairman Mao Tse-tung*

I am the people—the mob—the crowd—the mass.
Do you know that all the great work of the world is done
    through me?    —CARL SANDBURG, *I Am the People, the Mob*

**PEOPLES**    See NATIONS; RACES & PEOPLES

**PERSEVERANCE**    See also PATIENCE;
**& ENDURANCE**    SURVIVAL; WORK

Slow and steady wins the race.
—AESOP, *The Hare and the Tortoise*

He that can't endure the bad will not live to see the good.
—ANONYMOUS (JEWISH PROVERB)

He that endureth to the end shall be saved.
—BIBLE, *Matthew* 10:22

Be there a will, and wisdom finds a way.
—GEORGE CRABBE, *The Birth of Flattery*

To persevere, trusting in what hopes he has, is courage in a man.
The coward despairs. —EURIPIDES, *Heracles*

Much effort, much prosperity.
—EURIPIDES, *The Suppliant Women*

'Tis a lesson you should heed,
Try, try again.
If at first you don't succeed,
Try, try again. —WILLIAM E. HICKSON, *Try and Try Again*

Great works are performed not by strength, but by perseverance.
—SAMUEL JOHNSON, *Rasselas*

God helps those who persevere. —KORAN

Sorrow and silence are strong, and patient endurance is godlike.
—HENRY WADSWORTH LONGFELLOW, *Evangeline*

Endurance is the crowning quality,
And patience all the passion of great hearts.
—JAMES RUSSELL LOWELL, *Columbus*

Perseverance is more prevailing than violence; and many things
which cannot be overcome when they are taken together, yield
themselves up when taken little by little.
—PLUTARCH, *Life of Sertorius*, in *Parallel Lives*

**PESSIMISM** See DESPAIR, DEPRESSION, MISERY;
OPTIMISM & PESSIMISM

**PETS** See NATURE: ANIMALS

**PHILADELPHIA** See CITIES; INSULTS & PUT-DOWNS

**PHILANTHROPY** See CHARITY; PHILANTHROPY

**PHILOSOPHY** See also ETHICS & MORALITY

A metaphysician is a man who goes into a dark cellar at midnight
without a light, looking for a black cat that is not there.
—LORD BOWEN, attributed

There is but one truly serious philosophical problem, and that is suicide. Judging whether life is or is not worth living amounts to answering the fundamental question of philosophy.
—ALBERT CAMUS, *The Myth of Sisyphus*

There is nothing so ridiculous but some philosopher has said it.
—CICERO, *De Divinatione*
[Matters did not improve in the next seventeen hundred years; see Descartes, below.]

There is nothing so strange and so unbelievable that it has not been said by one philosopher or another.
—RENÉ DESCARTES, *Discourse on Method*
[For Descartes' own fundamental dictum, the *cogito* argument, see under MIND, THOUGHT & UNDERSTANDING.]

The test of a religion or philosophy is the number of things it can explain.     —RALPH WALDO EMERSON, *Journals*, 1836

What is it to be a philosopher? Is it not to be prepared against events?     —EPICTETUS, *Discourses*

You can't do without philosophy, since everything has its hidden meaning which we must know.     —MAXIM GORKY, *The Zykovs*

Philosophy will clip an angel's wing.     —JOHN KEATS, *Lamia*

Do not all charms fly
At the mere touch of cold philosophy?     *—Ibid.*

Logic is the art of making truth prevail.
—LA BRUYÈRE, *Les Caractères*

Metaphysics is almost always an attempt to prove the incredible by an appeal to the unintelligible.     —H. L. MENCKEN,
*Minority Report*

Most philosophical treatises show the human cerebrum loaded far beyond its Plimsoll mark.     —H. L. MENCKEN, *Prejudices*

To philosophize is to doubt.     —MONTAIGNE, *Essays*

Wonder is the foundation of all philosophy, inquiry the process, ignorance the end.     *—Ibid.*

Wonder is the feeling of a philosopher, and philosophy begins in wonder.                                                —PLATO, *Theaetetus*

To teach how to live without certainty and yet without being paralyzed by hesitation is perhaps the chief thing that philosophy, in our age, can do for those who study it.
—BERTRAND RUSSELL, *History of Western Philosophy*

Philosophy arises from an unusually obstinate attempt to arrive at real knowledge.   —BERTRAND RUSSELL, *An Outline of Philosophy*

There are more things in heaven and earth, Horatio,
Than are dreamt of in your philosophy.
—SHAKESPEARE, *Hamlet*, I, v

Adversity's sweet milk, philosophy.
—SHAKESPEARE, *Romeo and Juliet*, III, iii

The unexamined life is not worth living.
—SOCRATES, quoted in Plato, *Apology*

I am a citizen, not of Athens or Greece, but of the world.
—SOCRATES, quoted in Plutarch, *De Exilio*

Nero's mother turned him from the study of philosophy, warning that it was contrary to the needs of one destined to rule.
—SUETONIUS, *Nero*, in *Lives of the Caesars*

The safest general characterization of the European philosophical tradition is that it consists of a series of footnotes to Plato.
—ALFRED NORTH WHITEHEAD, *Process and Reality*

Philosophy begins in wonder, and at the end, when philosophic thought has done its best, the wonder remains.
—ALFRED NORTH WHITEHEAD, *Modes of Thought*

Philosophy is not a body of doctrine but an activity.
—LUDWIG WITTGENSTEIN, *Tractatus logico-philosophicus*

Most propositions and questions that have been written about philosophical matters are not false but senseless.        —*Ibid.*

[The reader may decide whether this also applies to Wittgenstein's own celebrated proposition in the *Tractatus*, "The world is everything that is the case."]

**PHYSICIANS**                See DOCTORS & THE PRACTICE
                                                 OF MEDICINE

**PITY**                              See FORGIVENESS & MERCY

**PLANS**

The best-laid schemes o' mice an' men
Gang aft a-gley.                    —ROBERT BURNS, *To a Mouse*

It's a bad plan that can't be changed.
                        —PUBLILIUS SYRUS, *Moral Sayings*

**PLANTS**                          See NATURE: GARDENS,
                                              FLOWERS & TREES

**PLEASURE**                              See HEDONISM

**POETRY & POETS**          See ARTS: POETRY & POETS

**POLITICS**                    See also CAPITALISM; COMMUNISM;
                        DEMOCRACY; DIPLOMACY; FREEDOM; GOVERNMENT;
                              HIGH POSITION: RULERS & LEADERS;
                              POWER; REVOLUTION; SOCIALISM

Politics, as a practice, whatever its professions, has always been
the systematic organization of hatreds.
        —HENRY BROOKS ADAMS, *The Education of Henry Adams*

Knowledge of human nature is the beginning and end of political
education.                                          —*Ibid.*

My country has in its wisdom contrived for me the most insignificant office [the vice-presidency] that ever the invention of
man contrived or his imagination conceived.
        —JOHN ADAMS, letter to Abigail Adams, Dec. 19, 1793

A liberal is a man who tells other people how to spend their
money.                                          —ANONYMOUS
[Mencken traces this to Carter Glass, 1938; but it's not clear that it
was original with him.]

You have all the characteristics of a popular politician: a horrible voice, bad breeding, and a vulgar manner.

—ARISTOPHANES, *Knights*

Man is by nature a political animal.      —ARISTOTLE, *Politics*

We know what happens to people who stay in the middle of the road. They get run over.

—ANEURIN BEVAN, *Observer*, Dec. 9, 1953, Saying of the Week

Politics is a blood sport.

—ANEURIN BEVAN, quoted in Jennie Lee, *My Life with Nye*

Politics is not an exact science.

—OTTO VON BISMARCK, speech, Dec. 1863

Politics is the art of the possible, the attainable . . . , the art of the next best.      —OTTO VON BISMARCK, conversation with
Meyer von Waldeck, Aug. 11, 1867
[The saying "politics is the art of compromise" derives in part from a speech by Burke on conciliation with America, made on March 22, 1775. The relevant passage is: "All government—indeed, every human benefit and enjoyment, every virtue and every prudent act—is founded on compromise and barter.]

Politics ruins the character.

—OTTO VON BISMARCK, quoted by Bernhard Brige,
*Berlin Tägliche Rundschau*, 1881

Politics are not the task of a Christian.

—DIETRICH BONHOEFFER, *No Rusty Swords*
[An opinion of venerable age; see Tertullian, below.]

Vain hope to make people happy by politics!

—THOMAS CARLYLE, *Journal*, Oct. 10, 1831

Persistence in one opinion has never been considered a merit in political leaders.      —CICERO, *Ad Familiares*

Politics are impossible without spoils. . . . You have to deal with men as they are . . . you must bribe the masses with spoils.

—"Boss" RICHARD CROKER, quoted in Richard Norton Smith,
*Thomas E. Dewey*

No government can long be secure without a formidable opposition.　　　　　　　　　　　—BENJAMIN DISRAELI, *Coningsby*

Finality is not the language of politics.
　　　　　　　　—BENJAMIN DISRAELI, speech, Feb. 28, 1859

A conservative government is an organized hypocrisy.
　　　　　　　　—BENJAMIN DISRAELI, speech, March 1845

A party is perpetually corrupted by personality.
　　　　　　　　—RALPH WALDO EMERSON, *Politics*

Politics is not the art of the possible. It consists in choosing between the disastrous and the unpalatable.
　　　　　　　　—JOHN KENNETH GALBRAITH, *Ambassador's Journal*
[He is updating Bismarck; see above.]

Since a politician never believes what he says, he is surprised when others believe him.
　　　　　　　　—CHARLES DE GAULLE, quoted in *Newsweek*, Oct. 1, 1962

Treason doth never prosper: what's the reason?
For if it prosper, none dare call it treason.
　　　　　　　　—SIR JOHN HARINGTON, *Of Treason* in *Epigrams*

You can't adopt politics as a profession and remain honest.
　　　　　　　　—LOUIS MCHENRY HOWE, speech, Jan. 17, 1933
[Howe was Franklin Delano Roosevelt's invaluable aide and adviser.]

When a man assumes a public trust, he should consider himself as public property.
　　　　　　　　—THOMAS JEFFERSON, quoted in Rayner, *Life of Jefferson*

Political action is the highest responsibility of a citizen.
　　　　　　　　—JOHN F. KENNEDY, speech, Oct. 20, 1960

Politicians are the same all over. They promise to build bridges, even where there are no rivers.
　　　　　　　　—NIKITA KHRUSHCHEV, to the press, Oct. 1960,
　　　　　　　　in Glen Cove, L.I.

What is conservatism? Is it not adherence to the old and tried, against the new and untried?
　　　　　　　　—ABRAHAM LINCOLN, speech, Feb. 27, 1860

A politician must often talk and act before he has thought and read.                                    —THOMAS BABINGTON MACAULAY,
*Gladstone on Church and State*

In every age, the vilest specimens of human nature are to be found among demagogues.
—THOMAS BABINGTON MACAULAY, *History of England*

Politics is war without bloodshed, while war is politics with bloodshed.
—MAO TSE-TUNG, *Quotations from Chairman Mao Tse-tung*
[For his observation on the source of political power, see under POWER.]

All reactionaries are paper tigers.
—MAO TSE-TUNG, conversation with
Anna Louise Strong, 1946

Liberal institutions straightway cease from being liberal the moment they are soundly established.
—FRIEDRICH NIETZSCHE, *Twilight of the Idols*

In our time, political speech and writing are largely the defense of the indefensible.
—GEORGE ORWELL, *Politics and the English Language*

Never lose your temper with the press or the public is a major rule of political life.     —CHRISTABEL PANKHURST, *Unshackled Woman*

It is now known . . . that men enter local politics solely as a result of being unhappily married.
—C. NORTHCOTE PARKINSON, *Parkinson's Law*

Party-spirit . . . at best is but the madness of many for the gain of a few.          —ALEXANDER POPE, letter to E. Blount, Aug. 27, 1714

All politics are based on the indifference of the majority.
—JAMES RESTON, *The New York Times*, June 12, 1968

Politicians, after all, are not over a year behind public opinion.
—WILL ROGERS, *Autobiography*

I tell you folks, all politics is applesauce.
—WILL ROGERS, *The Illiterate Digest*

A radical is a man with both feet firmly planted in the air.
—FRANKLIN D. ROOSEVELT, radio speech, Oct. 26, 1939

A conservative is a man with two perfectly good legs who, however, has never learned how to walk forward.   —*Ibid.*

A reactionary is a somnambulist walking backward.   —*Ibid.*

A politician . . . one that would circumvent God.
—SHAKESPEARE, *Hamlet*, V, i

He knows nothing and thinks he knows everything. That points clearly to a political career.
—GEORGE BERNARD SHAW, *Major Barbara*

Politics is perhaps the only profession for which no preparation is thought necessary.   —ROBERT LOUIS STEVENSON,
*Familiar Studies of Men and Books*

Nothing is more foreign to us Christians than politics.
—TERTULLIAN, *The Christian's Defense*

In politics, if you want anything said, ask a man; if you want anything done, ask a woman.
—MARGARET THATCHER, quoted in Anthony Sampson,
*The Changing Anatomy of Britain*

A statesman is a politician who's been dead ten or fifteen years.
—HARRY S. TRUMAN, *New York World-Telegram &
Sun*, April 12, 1958
[Probably not original with Truman. The authors heard this from James F. Byrnes at least ten years earlier, and it seemed to have been around for a while even then.]

There is no distinctly native American criminal class except Congress.   —MARK TWAIN, *Pudd'nhead Wilson*

Politics is the art of preventing people from taking part in affairs which properly concern them.   —PAUL VALÉRY, *Tel quel*

Politics makes strange bedfellows.
—CHARLES DUDLEY WARNER, *My Summer in a Garden*

Among politicians, the esteem of religion is profitable, the principles of it are troublesome.
—BENJAMIN WHICHCOTE, *Moral and Religious Aphorisms*

Prosperity is necessarily the first theme of a political campaign.
—WOODROW WILSON, speech, Sept. 4, 1912

**POOR, THE**                          See HAVES & HAVE-NOTS;
                                       MONEY; POVERTY & HUNGER

**POPULAR OPINION**                    See PEOPLE, THE

**POSSESSIONS**                        See THINGS & POSSESSIONS

**POVERTY & HUNGER**                   See also HAVES &
                                       HAVE-NOTS; MONEY

Hunger knows no friend but its feeder.
—ARISTOPHANES, *The Wasps*

Poverty is the parent of revolution and crime.
—ARISTOTLE, *Politics*

The poor man's wisdom is despised, and his words are not heard.
—BIBLE, *Ecclesiastes* 9:16

For the poor always ye have with you.        —BIBLE, *John* 12:8

Poverty makes you sad as well as wise.
—BERTOLT BRECHT, *The Threepenny Opera*

Eats first, morals after.                              —*Ibid.*

Poverty demoralizes.        —RALPH WALDO EMERSON, *Wealth*

There is something about poverty that smells like death. Dead dreams dropping off the heart like leaves in a dry season and rotting around the feet.        —ZORA NEALE HURSTON, *Dust Tracks*

A decent provision for the poor is the true test of civilization.
—SAMUEL JOHNSON, quoted in Boswell's
*Life of Johnson*, 1770

A man who has nothing can whistle in a robber's face.
—JUVENAL, *Satires*

Love in a hut, with water and a crust,
Is—Love, forgive us—cinders, ashes, dust.    —John Keats, *Lamia*

If a free society cannot help the many who are poor, it cannot save the few who are rich.
—John F. Kennedy, *Inaugural Address*, 1961

Anticipate charity by preventing poverty.
—Maimonides, *Charity's Eight Degrees*

The more humanity owes him [the poor man], the more society denies him. Every door is shut against him, even when he has a right to its being opened: and if he ever obtains justice, it is with much greater difficulty than others obtain favors.
—Jean Jacques Rousseau,
*A Discourse on Political Economy*

The greatest of evils and the worst of crimes is poverty.
—George Bernard Shaw, *Major Barbara*, preface

I have been a common man and a poor man; and it has no romance for me.                                  —*Ibid.*

Pickering: Have you no morals, man?
Doolittle: Can't afford them, Governor. Neither could you if you was as poor as me.    —George Bernard Shaw, *Pygmalion*

Poverty is no disgrace to a man, but it is profoundly inconvenient.
—Reverend Sydney Smith, *His Wit and Wisdom*

A hungry man is not a free man.
—Adlai Stevenson, speech, Sept. 6, 1952

No one can worship God or love his neighbor on an empty stomach.          —Woodrow Wilson, speech, May 23, 1912

# POWER
See also HIGH POSITION:
RULERS & LEADERS; STRENGTH;
TYRANNY & TOTALITARIANISM

Power tends to corrupt and absolute power corrupts absolutely. . . . Great men are almost always bad men.
—Lord Acton, letter to
Bishop Mandell Creighton, April 1887

I am more and more convinced that man is a dangerous creature and that power, whether vested in many or a few, is ever grasping, and like the grave, cries, "Give, give."
—ABIGAIL ADAMS, letter to John Adams, Nov. 27, 1775

A friend in power is a friend lost.
—HENRY BROOKS ADAMS,
*The Education of Henry Adams*

Power always thinks it has a great soul and vast views beyond the comprehension of the weak; and that it is doing God's service, when it is violating all His laws.
—JOHN ADAMS, letter to Thomas Jefferson, quoted by James Reston, *The New York Times*, Nov. 21, 1984

There is no power but of God.          —BIBLE, *Romans* 13:1

The greater the power, the more dangerous the abuse.
—EDMUND BURKE, speech on the Middlesex election, 1771

Power is the first good.     —RALPH WALDO EMERSON, *Inspiration*

You shall have joy, or you shall have power, said God: you shall not have both.     —RALPH WALDO EMERSON, *Journals*, 1842

Life is a search after power.     —RALPH WALDO EMERSON, *Power*

Power is precarious.                    —HERODOTUS, *Histories*

This is the bitterest pain among men, to have much knowledge but no power.                    —*Ibid.*

Power is the supreme law.     —ADOLF HITLER, *Mein Kampf*

An honest man can feel no pleasure in the exercise of power over his fellow citizens.     —THOMAS JEFFERSON, letter to John Melish, Jan. 13, 1813

All power, of whatever sort, is desirable.
—SAMUEL JOHNSON, quoted in Boswell,
*Life of Johnson*

Power is the great aphrodisiac.
—HENRY KISSINGER, quoted in
*The New York Times*, Jan. 19, 1971

Power never takes a back step—only in the face of more power.
—MALCOLM X, *Malcolm X Speaks*

Every Communist must grasp the truth: political power grows out of the barrel of a gun. —MAO TSE-TUNG, *Quotations from Chairman Mao Tse-tung*

Political power is merely the organized power of one class to oppress another. —KARL MARX and FRIEDRICH ENGELS, *Communist Manifesto*

We cannot all be masters. —SHAKESPEARE, *Othello*, I, i

Power, like a desolating pestilence,
Pollutes whate'er it touches.
—PERCY BYSSHE SHELLEY, *Queen Mab*

Power takes as ingratitude the writhing of its victims.
—RABINDRANATH TAGORE, *Stray Birds*

In order to obtain and hold power, a man must love it.
—LEO TOLSTOY, *The Kingdom of God Is Within You*

We have, I fear, confused power with greatness.
—STEWART UDALL, Commencement speech, Dartmouth College, 1965

## PRACTICAL WISDOM

See PRUDENCE & PRACTICAL WISDOM

## PRAYER

See also PRAYERS

Ask the gods nothing excessive.
—AESCHYLUS, *The Suppliant Women*

It is in vain to expect our prayers to be heard, if we do not strive as well as pray. —AESOP, *Hercules and the Waggoner*

*Orare est laborare, laborare est orare.*
To pray is to work, to work is to pray.
—BENEDICTINE ORDER, motto

The wish to pray is a prayer in itself.
—GEORGES BERNANOS, *The Diary of a Country Priest*

God is in heaven, and thou upon earth: therefore let thy words be few.                                                                —BIBLE, *Ecclesiastes* 5:5

When thou prayest, thou shalt not be as the hypocrites are: for they love to pray standing in the synagogues and in the corners of the streets that they may be seen of men. Verily I say unto you, they have their reward.                                            —BIBLE, *Matthew* 6:6

Watch and pray.                                                     —BIBLE, *Mark* 13:33

*Pray, v.* To ask that the rules of the universe be annulled in behalf of a single petitioner, confessedly unworthy.
                            —AMBROSE BIERCE, *The Devil's Dictionary*

Prayer is conversation with God.
                            —CLEMENT OF ALEXANDRIA, *Stromateis*

He prayeth well, who loveth well
Both man and bird and beast.
                            —SAMUEL TAYLOR COLERIDGE, *The Rime
                            of the Ancient Mariner*

He prayeth best, who loveth best
All things both great and small;
For the dear God who loveth us,
He made and loveth all.                                             —*Ibid.*

Prayer is the little implement
Through which men reach
Where presence—is denied them.        —EMILY DICKINSON, poem

Prayer is the contemplation of the facts of life from the highest point of view.             —RALPH WALDO EMERSON, *Self-Reliance*

You pray in your distress and in your need: would that you might pray also in the fullness of your joy and in your days of abundance.
                            —KAHLIL GIBRAN, *The Prophet*

And fools, who came to scoff, remained to pray.
                            —OLIVER GOLDSMITH, *The Deserted Village*

Prayer indeed is good, but while calling on the gods, a man should himself lend a hand.                        —HIPPOCRATES, *Regimen*

Pray, for all men need the aid of the gods.      —HOMER, *Odyssey*

Certain thoughts are prayers. There are moments when, whatever be the attitude of the body, the soul is on its knees.
—Victor Hugo, *Les Misérables*

A single grateful thought raised to heaven is the most perfect prayer. —Gotthold Ephraim Lessing, *Minna von Barnhelm*

There are few men who would dare publish to the world the prayers they make to almighty God. —Montaigne, *Essays*

My words fly up; my thoughts remain below.
Words without thoughts never to heaven go.
—Shakespeare, *Hamlet*, III, iii

His worst fault is that he is given to prayer. He is something peevish that way. —Shakespeare, *The Merry Wives of Windsor*, I, iv

Complaint is the largest tribute Heaven receives, and the sincerest part of our devotion. —Jonathan Swift, *Thoughts on Various Subjects*

Pray for my soul. More things are wrought by prayer
Than this world dreams of.
—Alfred, Lord Tennyson, *The Passing of Arthur*, in *Idylls of the King*

Whatever a man prays for, he prays for a miracle. Every prayer reduces itself to this: "Great God, grant that twice two be not four."
—Ivan Turgenev, *Prayer*

**PRAYERS** See also PRAYER

Matthew, Mark, Luke, and John,
The bed be blest that I lie on.
Four angels to my bed,
Four angels round my head,
One to watch, and one to pray,
And two to bear my soul away.
—Thomas Ady, *A Candle in the Dark*

Now I lay me down to sleep;
I pray the Lord my soul to keep.
If I should die before I wake,
I pray the Lord my soul to take. —Anonymous

From ghoulies and ghosties and long-leggety beasties
And things that go bump in the night,
Good Lord deliver us!                                   —ANONYMOUS


O Lord! thou knowest how busy I must be this day; if I forget thee, do not thou forget me.
                              —SIR JACOB ASTY, prior to the Battle of Edgehill,
                                       quoted in Sir Philip Warwick, *Memoirs*


Give me chastity and continency, but not yet.
                                   —ST. AUGUSTINE, *Confessions*


The Lord bless thee, and keep thee:
    The Lord make his face shine upon thee, and be gracious unto thee:
    The Lord lift up his countenance upon thee, and give thee peace.
                                   —BIBLE, *Numbers* 6:24–26


Out of the depths have I cried unto thee, O Lord.
                                   —BIBLE, *Psalms* 130:1


Glory to God in the highest, and on earth peace, good will toward men.                              —BIBLE, *Luke* 2:14


As it was in the beginning, is now, and ever shall be; world without end. Amen.                    —BOOK OF COMMON PRAYER


Teach me, my God and king,
In all things thee to see;
And what I do in anything,
To do it as for thee.
                              —GEORGE HERBERT, *The Elixir* in *The Temple*


And help us, this and every day,
To live more nearly as we pray.
                                   —JOHN KEBLE, *The Christian Year*


Would to God that we might spend a single day really well.
                              —THOMAS À KEMPIS, *Imitation of Christ*


Lord God of Hosts, be with us yet,
Lest we forget—lest we forget.    —RUDYARD KIPLING, *Recessional*

Sabrina fair,
Listen where thou art sitting
Under the glassy, cool, translucent wave,
In twisted braids of lilies knitting
The loose train of thy amber-dropping hair;
Listen for dear honor's sake,
Goddess of the silver lake,
Listen and save.                    —JOHN MILTON, *Comus*

What in me is dark
Illumine, what is low raise and support;
That to the height of this great argument
I may assert eternal Providence,
And justify the ways of God to men.
                         —JOHN MILTON, *Paradise Lost*

God, give us grace to accept with serenity the things that cannot
be changed, courage to change the things which should be changed,
and the wisdom to distinguish the one from the other.
              —REINHOLD NIEBUHR, *The Serenity Prayer*

Angels and ministers of grace defend us.
                         —SHAKESPEARE, *Hamlet*, I, iv

Good night, sweet prince,
And flights of angels sing thee to thy rest.        —*Ibid.*, V, ii

Mount, mount my soul! thy seat is up on high,
Whilst my gross flesh sinks downward, here to die.
                    —SHAKESPEARE, *King Richard II*, V, v

Wild Spirit, which art moving everywhere;
Destroyer and preserver;
Hear, oh, hear! —PERCY BYSSHE SHELLEY, *Ode to the West Wind*

**PREJUDICE**                        See RACES & PEOPLES

**PRESENT, THE**                  See also MODERN TIMES;
                                              TIME

Take therefore no thought for the morrow: for the morrow shall
take thought for the things of itself. Sufficient unto the day is the
evil thereof.                        —BIBLE, *Matthew* 6:34

Happy the man, and happy he alone,
He, who can call today his own:
He who, secure within, can say,
Tomorrow do thy worst, for I have lived today.
　　　　　　　　　—JOHN DRYDEN, *Imitation of Horace*


We want to live in the present, and the only history that is worth
a tinker's damn is the history we make today.
　　　　　　　　　—HENRY FORD, *Chicago Tribune*, May 25, 1916


Every situation—no, every moment—is of infinite worth; for it is
the representative of a whole eternity.
　　　　　　　　　—GOETHE, quoted in Johann Peter Eckermann,
　　　　　　　　　*Conversations with Goethe*


*Carpe diem, quam minimum credula a postero.*
Seize the day, and put the least possible trust in tomorrow.
　　　　　　　　　—HORACE, *Odes*


No mind is much employed upon the present; recollection and
anticipation fill up almost all our moments.
　　　　　　　　　—SAMUEL JOHNSON, *Rasselas*


Each day the world is born anew
For him who takes it rightly.
　　　　　　　　　—JAMES RUSSELL LOWELL, *Gold Egg: A Dream-Fantasy*


Tomorrow's life is too late. Live today.　　　—MARTIAL, *Epigrams*


Each day provides its own gifts.　　　　　　　　　*—Ibid.*


The only living life is in the past and future—the present is an
interlude—strange interlude in which we call on past and future to
bear witness we are living.　　　—EUGENE O'NEILL, *Strange Interlude*


Let others praise ancient times. I am glad that I was born in these.
　　　　　　　　　—OVID, *Ars amatoria*


Past, and to come, seems best; things present, worst.
　　　　　　　　　—SHAKESPEARE, *Henry IV, Part II*, I, iii


Do not say, "It is morning," and dismiss it with a name of yesterday. See it for the first time as a newborn child that has no name.
　　　　　　　　　—RABINDRANATH TAGORE, *Stray Birds*

Life is all memory except for the one present moment that goes by so quick you can hardly catch it going.
—TENNESSEE WILLIAMS, *The Milk Train Doesn't Stop Here Anymore*


**PRESS, THE**          See also CENSORSHIP; FREE SPEECH; MEDIA


What the proprietorship of these newspapers is aiming at is power, and power without responsibility—the prerogative of the harlot through the ages.          —PRIME MINISTER STANLEY BALDWIN, referring to press barons Beaverbrook and Rothermere, quoted in D. Butler and A. Sloman, *British Political Facts*
[J. M. and M. J. Cohen, in *The Penguin Dictionary of Modern Quotations*, note that Lord Birkenhead, Kipling's biographer, credits Kipling with originating the key phrase here. Baldwin was Kipling's cousin.]


When a dog bites a man, that is not news. But when a man bites a dog, that is news.     —JOHN B. BOGART, quoted in Frank M. O'Brien, *The Story of the Sun*
[Bogart was the city editor of *The New York Sun*. It is not clear whether this quote originated with him or with his boss, Charles Henry Dana.]


The pen is mightier than the sword.
—EDWARD GEORGE BULWER-LYTTON, *Richelieu*


A free press can, of course, be good or bad, but, most certainly without freedom, the press will never be anything but bad.
—ALBERT CAMUS, *Resistance, Rebellion, and Death*


The press must be free; it has always been so and much evil has been corrected by it. If Government finds itself annoyed by it, let it examine its own conduct and it will find the cause.
—LORD CHANCELLOR THOMAS ERSKINE, *Rex* v. *Paine*, 1792


Madame, we are the press. You know our power. We fix all values. We set all standards. Your entire future depends on us.
—JEAN GIRADOUX, *The Madwoman of Chaillot*


Our liberty depends on the freedom of the press, and that cannot be limited without being lost.
—THOMAS JEFFERSON, letter to James Currie, 1786

Were it left to me to decide whether we should have a government without newspapers, or newspapers without a government, I should not hesitate a moment to prefer the latter.
—THOMAS JEFFERSON, letter to
Colonel Edward Carrington, June 16, 1787

Why should any man be allowed to buy a printing press and disseminate pernicious opinions calculated to embarrass the government?
—V. I. LENIN, speech, Moscow, 1920

The gallery in which the reporters sit has become a fourth estate of the realm.   —THOMAS BABINGTON MACAULAY,
*Hallam's Constitutional History* in *Historical Essays*
[Often attributed to Edmund Burke, because of the following passage from Thomas Carlyle's *Heroes and Hero-Worship*: "Burke said that there were three estates in Parliament; but in the reporters' gallery yonder, there sat a fourth estate more important far than them all." But the phrase has not been found in Burke's works, and Carlyle actually may have had Macaulay in mind. William Safire notes that the phrase was used earlier to refer to "the mob," and credits its application to the press to William Hazlitt, who used it this way in an 1821 essay.]

All I know is just what I read in the papers.
—WILL ROGERS, saying used as a lead-in
to his routines

There aren't any embarrassing questions—only embarrassing answers.
—CARL ROWAN, saying

Nobody likes the bringer of bad news.   —SOPHOCLES, *Antigone*

I don't care what the papers say about me as long as they spell my name right.   —"BIG TIM" SULLIVAN, attributed

The report of my death was an exaggeration.
—MARK TWAIN, cable from London to the
Associated Press, 1897

Possible? Is anything impossible? Read the newspapers.
—DUKE OF WELLINGTON, quoted in
*Words of Wellington*

Publish and be damned.        —DUKE OF WELLINGTON, attributed
[The woman threatening to publish Wellington's letters to her, and
her own memoirs, was Harriette Wilson.]

In old days, men had the rack. Now they have the press.
                    —OSCAR WILDE, *The Soul of Man Under Socialism*
[For a final negative view of journalism, see George Bernard Shaw
at INSULTS & PUT-DOWNS.]

## PRIDE & VANITY        See also AMBITION; SELF-CONFIDENCE

It's a fine thing to rise above pride, but you must have pride in
order to do so.
                    —GEORGES BERNANOS, *The Diary of a Country Priest*

The Lord will destroy the house of the proud.
                                        —BIBLE, *Proverbs* 15:25

Pride goeth before destruction, and an haughty spirit before a fall.
                                        —BIBLE, *Proverbs* 16:18

Vanity of vanities, saith the Preacher, vanity of vanities; all is
vanity.                                —BIBLE, *Ecclesiastes* 1:2

Half of the harm that is done in this world
Is due to people who want to feel important.
                                    —T. S. ELIOT, *The Cocktail Party*

Pride ruined the angels.        —RALPH WALDO EMERSON, *The Sphinx*

Who does not detest a haughty man?        —EURIPIDES, *Hippolytus*

Pride is said to be the last vice the good man gets clear of.
                            —BENJAMIN FRANKLIN, *Poor Richard's Almanac*

I'm the straw that stirs the drink.        —REGGIE JACKSON, saying

Vanity is the greatest of all flatterers.
                                    —LA ROCHEFOUCAULD, *Maxims*

The most violent passions sometimes leave us at rest, but vanity
agitates us constantly.                                —*Ibid.*

I never wanted to be a crumb. If I had to be a crumb, I'd rather be dead.                    —Salvatore "Lucky" Luciano, quoted in Richard Norton Smith, *Thomas E. Dewey*

Better to reign in hell than serve in heaven.
                              —John Milton, *Paradise Lost*

For he will never follow anything
That other men begin.          —Shakespeare, *Julius Caesar*, II, i

He that is proud eats up himself.
                              —Shakespeare, *Troilus and Cressida*

Nobody holds a good opinion of a man who has a low opinion of himself.                    —Anthony Trollope, *Orley Farm*

Vanity is only being sensitive to what other people probably think of us.          —Paul Valéry, *Mauvaises pensées*

I have nothing to declare except my genius.
                              —Oscar Wilde, remark at the New York Customs House, quoted in F. Harris, *Oscar Wilde*


**PRINCES**                                    See HIGH POSITION:
                                                  RULERS & LEADERS


**PRINCIPLES**                                 See ETHICS & MORALITY;
                                                  IDEAS & IDEALS


**PRISONS**                                    See PUNISHMENT


**PRIVACY**                                    See also SOLITUDE

The right to be alone—the most comprehensive of rights and the most valued by civilized men.
                              —Justice Louis D. Brandeis, *Olmstead v. the U.S.*
[For another observation on civilization and privacy, see Ayn Rand, at CIVILIZATION.]

"If everybody minded their own business," said the Duchess in a hoarse growl, "the world would go round a deal faster than it does."
                              —Lewis Carroll, *Alice's Adventures in Wonderland*

A man's house is his castle.          —Sir Edward Coke, *Institutes*
[Americans may be more familiar with the reference by James Otis;
see below.]

The saint and poet seek privacy.
                              —Ralph Waldo Emerson, *Culture*

One of the most essential branches of English liberty is the freedom of one's house. A man's house is his castle; and whilst he is quiet,
he is as well guarded as a prince in his castle.
                    —James Otis, argument on the Writs of Assistance,
                         Boston, 1761
[See also Coke, above.]

**PROBLEMS**                                          See TROUBLE

**PROCRASTINATION**                              See also TIME

Never do today what you can do as well tomorrow.
                              —Aaron Burr, quoted in James Parton,
                                   *Life and Times of Aaron Burr*
[See Rands, below, for a British variant.]

Delay always breeds danger, and to protract a great design is
often to ruin it.                    —Cervantes, *Don Quixote*

No idleness, no laziness, no procrastination; never put off till
tomorrow what you can do today.
                              —Earl of Chesterfield, letter to his son,
                                   Dec. 26, 1749
[This intolerable piece of advice is at least as old as Hesiod; see
below.]

Don't put things off till tomorrow or the day after!
                              —Hesiod, *Works and Days*

Delay is preferable to error.
                              —Thomas Jefferson, letter to
                                   George Washington, May 16, 1792

The time to repair the roof is when the sun is shining.
                              —John F. Kennedy, State of the Union address, 1962

Never do today what you can
Put off till tomorrow.
                    —WILLIAM BRIGHTY RANDS, *Lilliput Levee*
[The witticism has occurred to many. We also cite Aaron Burr,
above.]

Delays have dangerous ends.
                    —SHAKESPEARE, *Henry VI, Part I*, III, ii

He who hesitates is sometimes saved.
                    —JAMES THURBER, *The Glass in the Field* in
                    *The Thurber Carnival*

Procrastination is the thief of time.
                    —EDWARD YOUNG, *Night Thoughts*


**PROGRESS**                    See also CHANGE; CIVILIZATION;
                                FUTURE, THE; TECHNOLOGY


*Quo vadis?*
Whither goest thou?
[The Latin is in the Vulgate version.]        —BIBLE, *John* 16:5

Progress, man's distinctive mark alone,
Not God's and not the beasts'.
                    —ROBERT BROWNING, *A Death in the Desert*

Progress is
The law of life, man is not man as yet.
                    —ROBERT BROWNING, *Paracelsus*

The march of the human mind is slow.
                    —EDMUND BURKE, speech, March 22, 1775

All progress is based upon a universal innate desire of every
organism to live beyond its means.    —SAMUEL BUTLER, *Notebooks*

Change is certain. Progress is not.
                    —E. H. CARR, *From Napoleon to Stalin,
                    and Other Essays*

As natural selection works solely by and for the good of each
being, all corporeal and mental endowments will tend to progress
toward perfection.    —CHARLES DARWIN, *The Origin of Species*

All that is human must retrograde if it does not advance.
—EDWARD GIBBON, *Decline and Fall of the Roman Empire*

We still dream what Adam dreamt.     —VICTOR HUGO, *Horror*

All progress is precarious, and the solution of one problem brings us face to face with another problem.
—MARTIN LUTHER KING, JR., *Strength to Love*

Is it progress if a cannibal uses a fork?
—STANISLAW J. LEC, *Unkempt Thoughts*

Human progress is furthered, not by conformity, but by aberration.     —H. L. MENCKEN, *Prejudices: Third Series*

The desire to understand the world and the desire to reform it are the two great engines of progress.
—BERTRAND RUSSELL, *Marriage and Morals*

All progress means war with society.
—GEORGE BERNARD SHAW, *Getting Married*

Progress, therefore, is not an accident, but a necessity. . . . It is a part of nature.     —HERBERT SPENCER, *Social Statics*

Yet I doubt not through the ages one increasing purpose runs,
And the thoughts of men are widened,
With the process of the suns.
—ALFRED, LORD TENNYSON, *Locksley Hall*

Progress imposes not only new possibilities for the future but new restrictions. —NORBERT WIENER, *The Human Use of Human Beings*

**PROPERTY**                                    See CAPITALISM;
                                       THINGS & POSSESSIONS

**PROPHETS**                              See VISION & VISIONARIES

**PROVERBS**                                see QUOTATIONS,
                                        MAXIMS & PROVERBS

## PROVIDENCE, DIVINE

The Lord is my shepherd; I shall not want.

He maketh me to lie down in green pastures; he leadeth me beside the still waters.

He restoreth my soul: he leadeth me in the paths of righteousness for his name's sake,

Yea, though I walk through the valley of the shadow of death, I will fear no evil: for thou art with me; thy rod and thy staff they comfort me.

Thou preparest a table before me in the presence of mine enemies: thou anointest my head with oil; my cup runneth over.

Surely goodness and mercy shall follow me all the days of my life: and I will dwell in the house of the Lord forever.

—BIBLE, *Psalms* 23

For he shall give his angels charge over thee, to keep thee in all thy ways.

They shall bear thee up in their hands, lest thou dash thy foot against a stone. —*Ibid.*, 91:11–12

The Lord shall preserve thy going out and thy coming in.
—*Ibid.*, 121:8

We degrade Providence too much by attributing our ideas to it out of annoyance at being unable to understand it.
—FËDOR DOSTOEVSKI, *The Idiot*

Know from the bounteous heaven all riches flow.
—HOMER, *Odyssey*

## PRUDENCE & PRACTICAL WISDOM
See also CRAFTINESS; WISDOM

Don't count your chickens before they are hatched.
—AESOP, *The Milkmaid and Her Pail*

Slow and steady wins the race.
—AESOP, *The Hare and the Tortoise*

Never eat at a place called Mom's. Never play cards with a man named Doc. And never lie down with a woman who's got more troubles than you.
—NELSON ALGREN, *What Every Young Man Should Know*

One swallow does not make a spring.
                              —ARISTOTLE, *Nicomachean Ethics*

Prudence is a rich, ugly old maid courted by
Incapacity.  —WILLIAM BLAKE, *The Marriage of Heaven and Hell*

A wise man does not trust all his eggs to one basket.
                              —CERVANTES, *Don Quixote*
[But see Mark Twain, below.]

The cautious seldom err.                    —CONFUCIUS, *Analects*

Trust everybody, but cut the cards.
                    —FINLEY PETER DUNNE, *Mr. Dooley's Philosophy*

You will go most safely in the middle.      —OVID, *Metamorphoses*

Be not the first by whom the new are tried,
Nor yet the last to lay the old aside.
                    —ALEXANDER POPE, *An Essay on Criticism*

Be wisely worldly, be not worldly wise.
                              —FRANCIS QUARLES, *Emblems*

If you want to get along, go along.
                    —[Speaker of the House] SAM RAYBURN, saying

The better part of valor is discretion.
                    —SHAKESPEARE, *Henry IV, Part I*, V, iv

Moderation in all things.                    —TERENCE, *Andria*

Put all your eggs in one basket—and watch that basket.
                    —MARK TWAIN, *Pudd'nhead Wilson*
[Cf. Cervantes, above.]

Common sense is not so common.
                    —VOLTAIRE, *Dictionnaire philosophique*, "Self-Love"


**PUBLIC, THE**                              See PEOPLE, THE

**PUBLIC OFFICE**          See GOVERNMENT; HIGH POSITION:
                              RULERS & LEADERS; POLITICS

**PUBLISHING**                    See BOOKS & READING;
                                    MEDIA; PRESS, THE


**PUNISHMENT**                    See also JUSTICE; REVENGE

Eye for eye, tooth for tooth, hand for hand, foot for foot.
Burning for burning, wound for wound, stripe for stripe.
                              —BIBLE, *Exodus* 21:24–25


Let the punishment match the offense.      —CICERO, *De Legibus*


To punish and not prevent is to labor at the pump and leave open
the leak.                        —THOMAS FULLER, *Gnomologia*


If a man destroy the eye of another man, they shall destroy his eye.
                              —CODE OF HAMMURABI


Distrust all in whom the impulse to punish is powerful.
                   —FRIEDRICH NIETZSCHE, *Thus Spake Zarathustra*


Punishment brings wisdom. It is the healing art of wickedness.
                              —PLATO, *Gorgias*


Frequent punishments are always a sign of weakness or laziness
on the part of the government.
                   —JEAN JACQUES ROUSSEAU, *Social Contract*


The reformative effect of punishment is a belief that dies hard,
chiefly I think, because it is so satisfying to our sadistic impulses.
                              —BERTRAND RUSSELL,
                              *Ideas That Have Harmed Mankind*


While we have prisons, it matters little which of us occupy the
cells.              —GEORGE BERNARD SHAW, *Man and Superman*,
                   "Maxims for Revolutionists"


I am all for bringing back the birch but only between consenting
adults.          —GORE VIDAL, television interview with David Frost


The vilest deeds like poison weeds
Bloom well in prison air:
It is only what is good in man
That wastes and withers there.
                   —OSCAR WILDE, *The Ballad of Reading Gaol*

## QUOTATIONS, MAXIMS, & PROVERBS

A proverb is the child of experience.
—ANONYMOUS (ENGLISH PROVERB)

The maxims of men disclose their hearts.
—ANONYMOUS (FRENCH PROVERB)

Despise not the discoveries of the wise, but acquaint thyself with their proverbs.            —BIBLE, *Ecclesiasticus* 8:8

It is a good thing for an uneducated man to read books of quotations.            —WINSTON CHURCHILL, *Roving Commission* in *My Early Life*

Proverbs are the sanctuary of the intuitions.
—RALPH WALDO EMERSON, *Compensation*

Next to the originator of a good sentence is the first quoter of it.
—RALPH WALDO EMERSON, *Quotation and Originality*

I hate quotations, tell me what you know.
—RALPH WALDO EMERSON, *Journal*, Dec. 20, 1822

A book that furnishes no quotations is, *me judice*, no book—it is a plaything.            —LADY CAROLINE LAMB, *Crotchet Castle*

Some, for renown, on scraps of learning dote,
And think they grow immortal as they quote.
—EDWARD YOUNG, *Love of Fame*

## RACES & PEOPLES                    See also NATIONS

The most certain test by which we judge whether a country is really free is the amount of security enjoyed by minorities.
—LORD ACTON, *The History of Freedom in Antiquity*

The Pilgrim Fathers landed on the shores of America and fell upon their knees. Then they fell upon the aborigines.
—ANONYMOUS, cited in H. L. Mencken, *A New Dictionary of Quotations*

Am I not a man and a brother?
—ANONYMOUS, inscription on the seal of the Antislavery Society of London, c. 1770

We shall overcome, we shall overcome,
We shall overcome some day.
Oh, deep in my heart, I do believe
We shall overcome some day.
> —ANONYMOUS, song associated with the Civil Rights
> movement of the 1960s, adapted from a
> Baptist hymn

Black is beautiful.                    —ANONYMOUS, slogan, ca. 1967
[Cf. *The Song of Solomon*, Douay version 1:5, "I am black but
beautiful."]

If we do not now dare everything, the fulfillment of that prophecy,
recreated from the Bible in song by a slave, is upon us:
God gave Noah the rainbow sign,
No more water, the fire next time!
> —JAMES BALDWIN, *The Fire Next Time*

It is not healthy when a nation lives within a nation, as colored
Americans are living inside America. A nation cannot live confident
of its tomorrow if its refugees are among its own citizens.
> —PEARL S. BUCK, *What America Means To Me*

Yes, I am a Jew, and when the ancestors of the right honorable
gentleman were brutal savages in an unknown island, mine were
priests in the temple of Solomon.
> —BENJAMIN DISRAELI, reply to Daniel O'Connell, in
> the House of Commons

The destiny of the colored American . . . is the destiny of America.
> —FREDERICK DOUGLASS, speech, Feb. 12, 1862

To be a poor man is hard, but to be a poor race in a land of dollars
is the very bottom of hardships.
> —W. E. B. DU BOIS, *The Souls of Black Folk*

However painful it may be for me to accept this conclusion, I am
obliged to state it: for the black man there is only one destiny. And
it is white.              —FRANTZ FANON, *Black Skin, White Masks*

Death is a slave's freedom.
> —NIKKI GIOVANNI, speech at the funeral of
> Martin Luther King, Jr.

The American economy, the American society, the American un-
conscious are all racist.
> —MICHAEL HARRINGTON, *The Other America*

I swear to the Lord
I still can't see
Why democracy means
Everybody but me.   —LANGSTON HUGHES, *The Black Man Speaks*

We will not be satisfied until justice rolls down like waters and righteousness like a mighty stream.
                    —MARTIN LUTHER KING, JR., speech, June 15, 1963

You're a better man than I am, Gunga Din!
                    —RUDYARD KIPLING, *Gunga Din*

All I ask for the Negro is that if you do not like him, let him alone. If God gave him but little, that little let him enjoy.
                    —ABRAHAM LINCOLN, speech, July 17, 1858

No democracy can long survive which does not accept as fundamental to its very existence the recognition of the rights of minorities.
                    —FRANKLIN DELANO ROOSEVELT,
                    letter to the NAACP, June 25, 1938

We don't have to be what you want us to be.
                    —BILL RUSSELL, quoted by George Vecsey,
                    *The New York Times*, 1985

When the last red man shall have become a myth among the white man . . . when your children's children think themselves alone in the fields or the pathless woods, they will not be alone . . . your lands will throng with the returning hosts that once filled them and still love this beautiful land. The white man will never be alone.
                    —SEATTLE, quoted in Joseph Epes Brown,
                    *The Spiritual Legacy of the American Indian*

Hath not a Jew eyes? Hath not a Jew hands, organs, dimensions, senses, affections, passions? Fed with the same food, hurt with the same weapons, subject to the same diseases, healed by the same means, warmed and cooled by the same winter and summer as a Christian is? If you prick us, do we not bleed? If you tickle us, do we not laugh? If you poison us, do we not die? And if you wrong us, shall we not revenge?
                    —SHAKESPEARE, *The Merchant of Venice*, III, i

"Do you know who made you?" "Nobody, as I knows on," said the child, with a short laugh. . . . "I 'spect I grow'd. Don't think nobody never made me."
                    —HARRIET BEECHER STOWE, *Uncle Tom's Cabin*

We have ground the manhood out of them, and the shame is ours not theirs, and we should pay for it.
> —MARK TWAIN, letter to Francis Wayland,
> Dean of the Yale Law School,
> offering to pay the tuition and board
> of a black student

The slave system on our place, in large measure, took the spirit of self-reliance and self-help out of the white people.
> —BOOKER T. WASHINGTON, *Up From Slavery*

J'accuse.
I accuse you.        —ÉMILE ZOLA, title of a letter to the president of the French Republic, accusing the government of wrongdoing in the Dreyfus case, published Jan. 13, 1898

**RAIN**                                    See NATURE: SEASONS;
                                            NATURE: WIND & WEATHER

**RAINBOW**                                 See NATURE: THE HEAVENS,
                                                         THE SKY

**REALITY  &  ILLUSIONS**

Every age is fed on illusions, lest men should renounce life early and the human race come to an end.        —JOSEPH CONRAD, *Victory*

⊢ Humankind
Cannot bear very much reality.
> —T. S. ELIOT, *Murder in the Cathedral*

"Real life" often appears, at least, to be an imitation of art. Today, it is poster art.        —MARSHALL McLUHAN, *Cokes and Cheesecake*, in *The Mechanical Bride*

We live in a fantasy world, a world of illusion. The great task in life is to find reality.
> —IRIS MURDOCH, quoted by Rachel Billington,
> interview in *The Times*, London, April 15, 1883

Reality is a staircase going neither up nor down; we don't move, today is today, always is today. —OCTAVIO PAZ, *The Endless Instant*

All that we see or seem
Is but a dream within a dream.
                    —EDGAR ALLAN POE, *A Dream within a Dream*


In the American metaphysic, reality is always material reality, hard, resistant, unformed, impenetrable, unpleasant.
                    —LIONEL TRILLING, *Reality* in *The Liberal Imagination*


**REASON**                    See MIND; PHILOSOPHY; REASONABLE
                                        & UNREASONABLE PEOPLE


**REASONABLE &**                    See also MIND
**UNREASONABLE PEOPLE**


When a man begins to reason, he ceases to feel.
                    —ANONYMOUS (FRENCH PROVERB)


Come now, and let us reason together.        —BIBLE, *Isaiah* 1:18


Falling in love is one of the activities forbidden that tiresome person, the consistently reasonable man.
                    —SIR ARTHUR EDDINGTON, *News Chronicle*,
                    London, March 2, 1932


Who reasons wisely is not therefore wise;
His pride in reasoning, not in acting, lies.
                    —ALEXANDER POPE, *Moral Essays*


*Tout par raison.*
Everything according to reason.
                    —CARDINAL RICHELIEU, *Mirame*


Pure logic is the ruin of the spirit.
                    —ANTOINE DE SAINT-EXUPÉRY, *Flight to Arras*


The reasonable man adapts himself to the world; the unreasonable one persists in trying to adapt the world to himself. Therefore all progress depends on the unreasonable man.
                    —GEORGE BERNARD SHAW, *Man and Superman*,
                    "Maxims for Revolutionists"


A mind all logic is like a knife all blade. It makes the hand bleed that uses it.        —RABINDRANATH TAGORE, *Stray Birds*

Passion and prejudice govern the world; only under the name of reason.      —JOHN WESLEY, letter to Joseph Benson, Oct. 5, 1770

**REGRET**                                                See also PAST, THE

If you board the wrong train, it is no use running along the corridor in the other direction.
                        —DIETRICH BONHOEFFER, *The Way to Freedom*

We have left undone those things which we ought to have done; and we have done those things which we ought not to have done; and there is no health in us.          —BOOK OF COMMON PRAYER

Of all the horrid, hideous notes of woe,
Sadder than owl songs or the midnight blast,
Is that portentous phrase, "I told you so."
                        —LORD BYRON, *Don Juan*

Footfalls echo in the memory
Down the passage which we did not take
Towards the door we never opened
Into the rosegarden.
                        —T. S. ELIOT, *Burnt Norton* in *Four Quartets*

I shall be telling this with a sigh
Somewhere ages and ages hence:
Two roads diverged in a wood, and I—
I took the one less traveled by,
And that has made all the difference.
                        —ROBERT FROST, *The Road Not Taken*

God has little patience with remorse.
                        —MALCOLM LOWRY, *Under the Volcano*

When I am dead and opened, you shall find "Calais" written on my heart.          —MARY I, quoted in Holinshed's *Chronicles*
[In some versions, it is "Philip and Calais" that is written.]

Why should I mourn at the untimely fate of my people? Tribe follows tribe, and nation follows nation, and regret is useless.
                        —SEATTLE, quoted in Joseph Epes Brown,
                        *The Spiritual Legacy of the American Indian*

What's done is done.          —SHAKESPEARE, *Macbeth*, III, ii

Oh, call back yesterday, bid time return.
—SHAKESPEARE, *Richard II*, III, ii

What's gone and what's past help
Should be past grief.        —SHAKESPEARE, *Winter's Tale*, III, ii

To regret deeply is to live afresh.
—HENRY DAVID THOREAU, *Journal*, Nov. 13, 1839

For all sad words of tongue or pen,
The saddest are these: "It might have been!"
—JOHN GREENLEAF WHITTIER, *Maud Muller*

**RELIGION**        See also FAITH; GOD; MYSTICISM; PRAYER

Man doth not live by bread only, but by every word that proceedeth out of the mouth of the Lord doth man live.
—BIBLE, *Deuteronomy* 8:3
[Also *Matthew* 4:4: "Man shall not live by bread alone . . ."—and *Luke* 4:4.]

No man can serve two masters.        —BIBLE, *Matthew* 6:24

Ye cannot serve God and mammon.        —*Ibid.*

Thou art Peter, and upon this rock I will build my church; and the gates of hell shall not prevail against it.        —*Ibid.*, 16:18

*Heathen, n.* A benighted creature who has the folly to worship something that he can see and feel.
—AMBROSE BIERCE, *The Devil's Dictionary*

To die for a religion is easier than to live it absolutely.
—JORGE LUIS BORGES, *Deutsches Requiem* in *Labyrinths*

How very hard it is
To be a Christian!        —ROBERT BROWNING, *Easter-Day*

Every day, people are straying away from the church and going back to God.        —LENNY BRUCE, *The Essential Lenny Bruce*

This Ariyan Eightfold Path, that is to say: Right view, right aim, right speech, right action, right living, right effort, right mindfulness, right contemplation.        —BUDDHA, from F. L. Woodward,
*Some Sayings of the Buddha*

One religion is as true as another.
                              —ROBERT BURTON, *Anatomy of Melancholy*

Wonder is the basis of worship.
                              —THOMAS CARLYLE, *Sartor Resartus*

Religion is by no means a proper subject of conversation in mixed
company.              —EARL OF CHESTERFIELD, letter to his godson,
                              # 112, undated

The all-male religions have produced no religious imagery. . . .
The great religious art of the world is deeply involved with the
female principle.              —SIR KENNETH CLARK, *Civilization*

In my religion, there would be no exclusive doctrine; all would
be love, poetry, and doubt.  —CYRIL CONNOLLY, *The Unquiet Grave*

Science without religion is lame; religion without science is blind.
                              —ALBERT EINSTEIN, quoted in
                              *The Reader's Digest*, Nov. 1973

I like the silent church before the service begins, better than any
preaching.              —RALPH WALDO EMERSON, *Self-Reliance*

God builds his temple in the heart on the ruins of churches and
religions.              —RALPH WALDO EMERSON, *Worship*

Religion is an illusion and it derives its strength from the fact that
it falls in with our instinctual desires.
                              —FREUD, *A Philosophy of Life* in
                              *Lectures in Psychoanalysis*

The Bible shows the way to go to heaven, not the way the heavens
go.                              —GALILEO, fragment

All religions are ancient monuments to superstitions, ignorance,
ferocity; and modern religions are only ancient follies rejuvenated.
                              —BARON D'HOLBACH, *Le bons sens . . .*

Writing for a penny a word is ridiculous. If a man really wants to
make a million dollars, the best way would be to start his own
religion.              —L. RONALD HUBBARD, the founder of Scientology,
                              lecture 1949, quoted in *The New York Times*,
                              July 11, 1984

It does me no injury for my neighbor to say there are twenty Gods, or no God.                        —Thomas Jefferson,
*Notes on the State of Virginia*

The church must be reminded that it is not the master or the servant of the state, but rather the conscience of the state.
—Martin Luther King, Jr., *Strength to Love*

Here I stand, I cannot do otherwise.
—Martin Luther, speech, Diet of Worms, 1521

Religion is the sign of the oppressed creature, the sentiment of a heartless world, and the soul of soulless conditions. It is the opium of the people.          —Karl Marx, *Criticism of Hegel's Philosophy of Right*

What mean and cruel things men do for the love of God.
—W. Somerset Maugham, *A Writer's Notebook*

We must respect the other fellow's religion, but only in the sense and to the extent that we respect his theory that his wife is beautiful and his children smart.          —H. L. Mencken, *Minority Report*

Fear of death and fear of life both become piety.          *—Ibid.*

A nation must have a religion, and that religion must be under the control of the government.
—Napoleon Bonaparte, to Count Thibaubeau, June 6, 1801

I want nothing to do with any religion concerned with keeping the masses satisfied to live in hunger, filth, and ignorance.
—Jawaharlal Nehru, quoted in Edgar Snow, *Journey to the Beginning*

Dogma has been the fundamental principle of my religion. . . . Religion, as mere sentiment, is to me a mockery.
—Cardinal Newman, *Apologia pro Vita Sua*

Any system of religion that has anything in it that shocks the mind of a child, cannot be a true system.
—Thomas Paine, *The Age of Reason*

Men despise religion; they hate it, and they fear it is true.
—Pascal, *Pensées*

Religion is so great a thing that it is right that those who will not take the trouble to seek it if it be obscure, should be deprived of it.
—*Ibid.*

To be like Christ is to be a Christian.
—WILLIAM PENN, last words

The world would be poorer without the antics of clergymen.
—V. S. PRITCHETT, *The Dean* in *My Good Books*

Religion is something infinitely simple, ingenuous. . . . In the infinite extent of the universe, it is a direction of the heart.
—RAINER MARIA RILKE, letter to
Ilse Blumenthal-Weiss, Dec. 28, 1921

The Bible is literature, not dogma.
—GEORGE SANTAYANA, *The Ethics of Spinoza*

Religion is the love of life in the consciousness of impotence.
—GEORGE SANTAYANA, *Winds of Doctrine*

He worships God who knows him.   —SENECA, *Letters to Lucilius*

The devil can cite Scripture for his purpose.
—SHAKESPEARE, *The Merchant of Venice*, I, iii

There is only one religion though there are a hundred versions of it.                        —GEORGE BERNARD SHAW, *Arms and the Man*

How many divisions has the Pope?        —STALIN, attributed

I never saw, heard, nor read that the clergy were beloved in any nation where Christianity was the religion of the country. Nothing can render them popular but some degree of persecution.
—JONATHAN SWIFT, *Thoughts on Religion*

We have just enough religion to make us hate, but not enough to make us love one another.
—JONATHAN SWIFT, *Thoughts on Various Subjects*

*Quoi que vous fassiez, écrasez l'infâme, et aimez qui vous aime.*
Whatever you do, crush this infamy, and love those who love you.
—VOLTAIRE, letter to d'Alembert, Nov. 28, 1762
[The "infamy," or "infamous thing," is usually interpreted as referring to superstition.]

Orthodoxy is my doxy; heterodoxy is another man's doxy.
—WILLIAM WARBURTON, quoted in
Joseph Priestley, *Memoirs*

Religion is love; in no case is it logic.
—BEATRICE POTTER WEBB, *My Apprenticeship*

As society is now constituted, a literal adherence to the moral precepts scattered throughout the Gospels would mean sudden death. —ALFRED NORTH WHITEHEAD, *Adventures in Ideas*

And I could wish my days to be
Bound each to each by natural piety.
—WILLIAM WORDSWORTH, *My Heart Leaps Up*

**REMEDIES**
See ILLNESS &
REMEDIES; TROUBLE

**REMORSE**
See REGRET

**REPENTANCE**
See FORGIVENESS &
MERCY; REGRET

**RESIGNATION**
See also OBEDIENCE

Naked came I out of my mother's womb, and naked shall I return thither: the Lord gave, and the Lord hath taken away; blessed be the name of the Lord. —BIBLE, *Job* 1:21

Teach us to care and not to care.
Teach us to sit still. —T. S. ELIOT, *Ash Wednesday*

Better to accept whatever happens. —HORACE, *Odes*

Hear me, my chiefs, I am tired; my heart is sick and sad. From where the sun now stands, I will fight no more forever.
—CHIEF JOSEPH, speech at the conclusion
of the Nez Percé War

A calm despair, without angry convulsion or reproaches directed to heaven, is the essence of wisdom.
—ALFRED DE VIGNY, *Journal d'un Poète*

**RESISTANCE**                    See APPEASEMENT VS. RESISTANCE;
                                   COURAGE: REVOLUTION

**RESPONSIBILITY**                    See also FATE; SELF;
                                         SELF-RELIANCE

Everybody's business is nobody's business.        —ANONYMOUS
[Sometimes attributed to Macaulay or Izaak Walton, but evidently an ancient byword; see Aristotle, for example, on everybody's property, under COMMUNISM.]

To be a good shepherd is to shear the flock, not skin it!
                         —TIBERIUS, favorite proverbial saying,
                              quoted in Seutonius, *Lives of the Caesars*

Am I my brother's keeper?                    —BIBLE, *Genesis* 4:9

Unto whomsoever much is given, of him shall be much required.
                                        —BIBLE, *Luke* 12:48

Every man is the architect of his own fortune.
                              —APPIUS CLAUDIUS CAECUS,
                                   quoted in Sallust, *De Civitate*

When your neighbor's wall is on fire, it becomes your business.
                                        —HORACE, *Epistles*

Our privileges can be no greater than our obligations. The protection of our rights can endure no longer than the performance of our responsibilities.        —JOHN F. KENNEDY, speech, May 18, 1963

I believe that every right implies a responsibility; every opportunity, an obligation; every possession, a duty.
                         —JOHN D. ROCKEFELLER, speech, July 8, 1941

To be a man is, precisely, to be responsible.
                         —ANTOINE DE SAINT-EXUPÉRY, *Wind, Sand, and Stars*

The fault, dear Brutus, is not in our stars,
But in ourselves, that we are underlings.
                              —SHAKESPEARE, *Julius Caesar*, I, ii

The buck stops here.        —HARRY S. TRUMAN, handwritten sign
                              on his White House desk

**R E V E N G E**   See also JUSTICE; PUNISHMENT

Revenge is a dish that should be eaten cold.
—ANONYMOUS (ENGLISH PROVERB)

Men regard it as their right to return evil for evil—and if they cannot, feel they have lost their liberty.
—ARISTOTLE, *Nicomachean Ethics*

In taking revenge, a man is but even with his enemy; but in passing it over, he is superior.   —FRANCIS BACON, *Of Revenge*

A man that studieth revenge keeps his own wounds green, which otherwise would heal and do well.   —*Ibid.*

Thou shalt not avenge.   —BIBLE, *Leviticus* 19:18

Vengeance is mine; I will repay, saith the Lord.
—BIBLE, *Romans* 12:19

Living well is the best revenge.
—GEORGE HERBERT, *Jacula Prudentum*

Revenge is the poor delight of little minds.   —JUVENAL, *Satires*

**R E V O L U T I O N**   See also APPEASEMENT VS. RESISTANCE; TURBULENT TIMES

I came not to send peace, but a sword.   —BIBLE, *Matthew* 10:34

Revolutions are not made with rosewater.
—EDWARD GEORGE BULWER-LYTTON, *The Parisians*

In the groves of *their* academy, at the end of every walk, you see nothing but the gallows.
—EDMUND BURKE, *Reflections on the French Revolution*

Lay the proud usurpers low!
Tyrants fall in every foe!
Liberty's in every blow!
Let us do or die!   —ROBERT BURNS, *Scots Wha Hae*

What is a rebel? A man who says no. —ALBERT CAMUS, *The Rebel*

All modern revolutions have ended in a reinforcement of the power of the state.   —*Ibid.*

The revolutionary spirit is mighty convenient in this, that it frees
one from all scruples as regards ideas.
—JOSEPH CONRAD, *A Personal Record*

The blow by which kings fall causes a long bleeding.
—PIERRE CORNEILLE, *Cinna*

Plots true or false are necessary things,
To raise up commonwealths and ruin kings.
—JOHN DRYDEN, *Absalom and Achitophel*

When you strike at a king, you must kill him.
—RALPH WALDO EMERSON, attributed
[*Bartlett* traces this to a recollection of Oliver Wendell Holmes, Jr.,
quoted in Max Lerner, *The Mind and Faith of Justice Holmes.*]

Desperate diseases require desperate remedies.
—GUY FAWKES, attributed in connection with
the Gunpowder Plot
[Cf. Shakespeare, below.]

A great revolution is never the fault of the people, but of the
government.          —GOETHE, quoted in Johann Peter Eckermann,
*Conversations with Goethe*

What happens to a dream deferred?
Does it dry up
Like a raisin in the sun? . . .
Or does it explode?          —LANGSTON HUGHES, *Harlem*

Fire in the lake: the image of revolution.          —I CHING, Book I

The tree of liberty must be refreshed from time to time with the
blood of patriots and tyrants. It is its natural manure.
—THOMAS JEFFERSON, letter to Col. William S. Smith,
Nov. 13, 1787

If you feed the people just with revolutionary slogans, they will
listen today, they will listen tomorrow, they will listen the day
after tomorrow, but on the fourth day, they will say "To hell with
you."          —NIKITA KHRUSHCHEV, quoted in
*The New York Times*, Oct. 4, 1964

When smashing monuments, save the pedestals—they always come
in handy.          —STANISLAW LEC, *Unkempt Thoughts*

Inciting to revolution is treason, not only against man, but also against God.                                    —POPE LEO XIII, *Immortale Dei*

Revolution is the proper occupation of the masses.
                              —MAO TSE-TUNG, quoted in Dennis Bloodworth,
                              *The Messiah and the Mandarins*

The workers have nothing to lose in this but their chains. They have a world to gain. Workers of the world, unite!
                              —KARL MARX and FRIEDRICH ENGELS,
                              *The Communist Manifesto*

In revolutions everything is forgotten. . . . Gratitude, friendship, parentage, every tie vanishes, and all that is sought is self-interest.
                              —NAPOLEON BONAPARTE, quoted in Barry E. O'Meara,
                              *Napoleon at St. Helena*

A share in two revolutions is living to some purpose.
                              —THOMAS PAINE, quoted in Eric Foner,
                              *Tom Paine and Revolutionary America*

*Après nous le déluge.*
After us, the flood.                    —MADAME DE POMPADOUR, quoted in
                                        Mme de Hausset, *Mémoires*

I will have no laws. I will acknowledge none. I protest against every law which an authority calling itself necessary imposes upon my free will.                                    —PIERRE-JOSEPH PROUDHON,
                                        *Idée générale de la révolution*

Diseases desperate grown
By desperate appliance are relieved,
Or not at all.
[Cf. Guy Fawkes, above.]                —SHAKESPEARE, *Hamlet*, IV, iii

Revolutions have never lightened the burden of tyranny. They have only shifted it to another shoulder.
                              —GEORGE BERNARD SHAW, *Man and Superman*,
                              "The Revolutionist's Handbook"

All changed, changed utterly:
A terrible beauty is born.
                              —WILLIAM BUTLER YEATS, *Easter 1916*

**RICH, THE**                    See HAVES & HAVE-NOTS; MONEY

**RIGHTEOUSNESS**          See SELF-RIGHTEOUSNESS; VIRTUE

**RIGHTS**                          See also DEMOCRACY; EQUALITY;
                                             FREEDOM; FREE SPEECH;
                                LAW & LAWYERS; PRESS, THE; PRIVACY

A right sometimes sleeps but it never dies.
                                —ANONYMOUS (Legal Maxim)

Rights are lost by disuse.        —ANONYMOUS (Legal Maxim)
[These contradictory maxims cover both sides of the issue, as is
necessary in law.]

The public good is in nothing more essentially interested than in
the protection of every individual's private rights.
                                —WILLIAM BLACKSTONE, *Commentaries*

There is no such thing as rights anyhow. It is a question of whether
you can put it over. In any legal sense or practical sense, whatever
is, is "a right."        —CLARENCE DARROW, debate on Prohibition,
                                quoted in Kevin Tierney, *Darrow*

[All men] are endowed by their Creator with certain inalienable
rights.        —THOMAS JEFFERSON, *The Declaration of Independence*
[A full citation is given under AMERICAN HISTORY: MEMORABLE
MOMENTS.]

A bill of rights is what the people are entitled to against every
government on earth.
                                —THOMAS JEFFERSON, letter to James Madison,
                                Dec. 1787

Nobody talks more passionately of his rights than he who, in the
depths of his soul, is doubtful about them.
                —FRIEDRICH NIETZSCHE, *Human, All Too Human*

**ROME**                                              See CITIES

**RUDENESS**                                        See MANNERS;
                                            INSULTS & PUT-DOWNS

**RUIN**
See also POVERTY & HUNGER;
TROUBLE; WINNING & LOOSING,
VICTORY & DEFEAT

The road to ruin is always kept in good repair.   —ANONYMOUS

He bears the seed of ruin in himself.   —MATTHEW ARNOLD,
*Merope*

How are the mighty fallen in the midst of the battle!
—BIBLE, *II Samuel* 1:25

MENE, MENE, TEKEL, UPHARSIN.   —BIBLE, *Daniel* 5:25
[The writing on the wall announcing the destruction of Babylon.]

But the children of the kingdom shall be cast out into outer darkness: there shall be weeping and gnashing of teeth.
—BIBLE, *Matthew* 8:12

All men that are ruined are ruined on the side of their natural
propensities.   —EDMUND BURKE, *Letters on a Regicide Peace*

Let everyone witness how many different cards fortune has up her
sleeve when she wants to ruin a man.
—BENVENUTO CELLINI, *Autobiography*

There is no loneliness greater than the loneliness of failure. The
failure is a stranger in his own house.
—ERIC HOFFER, *The Passionate State of Mind*

There is not a fiercer hell than the failure in a great object.
—JOHN KEATS, *Endymion*, preface

Men fall from great fortune because of the same shortcomings
that led to their rise.   —LA BRUYÈRE, *Les Caractères*

From the sublime to the ridiculous there is only one step.
—NAPOLEON BONAPARTE, remark to the Polish ambassador
De Pradt after the retreat from Moscow, 1812

Men shut their doors against a setting sun.
—SHAKESPEARE, *Timon of Athens*, I, ii

**RULER**
See HIGH POSITION:
RULERS & LEADERS

# RUMOR

There is a demon who puts wings on certain stories and who launches them like eagles in the air.
—ALEXANDRE DUMAS, *La Dame du Monsoreau*

I know nothing swifter in life than the voice of rumor.
—PLAUTUS, fragment

Rumor travels faster, but it don't stay put as long as truth.
—WILL ROGERS, *The Illiterate Digest*

Rumor is not always wrong.   —TACITUS, *Life of Agricola*

# RUSSIA   See COMMUNISM; NATIONS

# SAILING   See NATURE: THE OCEAN;
SEAS & SHIPS, SAILING & BOATING

# SCOTLAND   See NATIONS

# SCIENCE   See also SCIENCE entries below;
TECHNOLOGY; UNIVERSE

Enough research will tend to support your theory.
—ANONYMOUS, quoted in A. Bloch, *Murphy's Law*, and titled "Murphy's Law of Research"

What is now proved was once only imagined.
—WILLIAM BLAKE, *The Marriage of Heaven and Hell*

\ It is a capital mistake to theorize before one has data.
—A. CONAN DOYLE, *Scandal in Bohemia*

Most of the fundamental ideas of science are essentially simple, and may, as a rule, be expressed in a language comprehensible to everyone.   —ALBERT EINSTEIN, *The Evolution of Physics*

The whole of science is nothing more than a refinement of everyday thinking.   —ALBERT EINSTEIN, *Out of My Later Years*

Men love to wonder, and that is the seed of science.
—RALPH WALDO EMERSON, *Society and Solitude*

Science is the knowledge of consequences and the dependence of one fact upon another.          —THOMAS HOBBES, *Leviathan*

Science says the first word on everything, and the last word on nothing.          —VICTOR HUGO, *Things of the Infinite*

The great tragedy of science—the slaying of a beautiful hypothesis by an ugly fact.          —T. H. HUXLEY, *Biogenesis and Abiogenesis*

It is the first duty of a hypothesis to be intelligible.
          —T. H. HUXLEY,
          *Evidence as to Man's Place in Nature*

I am sorry to say that there is too much point to the wisecrack that life is extinct on other planets because their scientists were more advanced than ours.          —JOHN F. KENNEDY, speech, Dec. 11, 1959

Science without conscience is but the death of the soul.
          —MONTAIGNE, *Essays*
[Or, Rabelais: "Science without conscience is but the ruin of the soul," Gargantua's Letter to Pantagruel.]

If I have seen further, . . . it is by standing upon the shoulders of giants.          —ISAAC NEWTON, letter to Robert Hooke,
          Feb. 5, 1675/76
[Robert K. Merton has written a little book on this quotation, in which among other things, he demonstrates that it was a commonplace of the period. He traces it back to Bernard of Chartres; see under VISION.]

*Hypotheses non fingo.*
I feign no hypotheses.
          —ISAAC NEWTON, *Principia Mathematica*, scholium

I know not what I may appear to the world, but to myself I seem to have been only like a boy playing on the sea-shore, and diverting myself in now and then finding a smoother pebble or a prettier shell than ordinary, whilst the great ocean of truth lay all undiscovered before me.          —ISAAC NEWTON, quoted in David Brewster,
          *Memoirs of Newton*

*Entia non sunt multiplicanda praeter necessitatem.*
Entities should not be multiplied unnecessarily.
          —WILLIAM OF OCKHAM, *Quodlibeta*
[This is known as "Ockham's razor." A modern version is the KISS Principle: Keep It Simple, Stupid.]

I am become Death, the shatterer of worlds.

> —J. ROBERT OPPENHEIMER, quoting a line from
> the Bhagavad Gita that came to his mind
> at the test of the first atom bomb,
> July 16, 1945; cited in N. P. Davis,
> *Lawrence and Oppenheimer*

Science is built of facts the way a house is built of bricks; but an accumulation of facts is no more a science than a pile of bricks is a house. —HENRI POINCARÉ, *La Science et l'hypothèse*

Nature and nature's laws lay hid in night:
God said, "Let Newton be!" and all was light.

> —ALEXANDER POPE, epitaph written for
> Sir Isaac Newton

The simplest schoolboy is now familiar with facts for which Archimedes would have sacrificed his life.
—ERNEST RENAN, *Souvenirs d'enfance et de jeunesse*

The work of science is to substitute facts for appearances, and demonstration for impressions. —JOHN RUSKIN,
*The Stones of Venice*

Even if the open windows of science at first make us shiver . . . in the end, the fresh air brings vigor, and the great spaces have a splendor of their own. —BERTRAND RUSSELL, *What I Believe*

Science is always simple and profound. It is only the half truths that are dangerous. —GEORGE BERNARD SHAW,
*The Doctor's Dilemma*

Science is the great antidote to the poison of enthusiasm and superstition. —ADAM SMITH, *Wealth of Nations*

The religions disperse, kingdoms fall apart, but works of science remain for all ages.

> —ULUGH-BEG

[Words carved on stone astronomical observatory erected by Ulugh-Beg, Tamerlane's grandson, in Samarkand in 1528–29.]

Science is a cemetery of dead ideas.
—MIGUEL DE UNAMUNO, *The Tragic Sense of Life*

Happy is he who has been able to learn the causes of things.
—VIRGIL, *Georgics*

Familiar things happen, and mankind does not bother about them. It requires a very unusual mind to undertake the analysis of the obvious.                    —ALFRED NORTH WHITEHEAD,
                    *Science and the Modern World*

## SCIENCE: BIOLOGY

Is man an ape or an angel? Now I am on the side of the angels.
                    —BENJAMIN DISRAELI, speech, Nov. 25, 1864

*Ex ovo omnia.* Everything from an egg.
                    —WILLIAM HARVEY, *De Generatione Animalium*,
                    frontispiece.

Species do not evolve to perfection, but quite the contrary. The weak, in fact, always prevail over the strong, not only because they are in the majority, but also because they are the more crafty.
                    —FRIEDRICH NIETZSCHE, *The Twilight of the Idols*
[For the opposing view, see Darwin at PROGRESS.]

This survival of the fittest . . . I have here sought to express in mechanical terms.          —HERBERT SPENCER, *Principles of Biology*
[This phrase, "survival of the fittest," became identified with Darwinism, but was not used by Darwin himself.]

## SCIENCE: DISCOVERY & EXPLORATION

*Eureka!*
I have found it!          —ARCHIMEDES, quoted in Vitruvius Polla,
                    *De Architectura*
[What he had found is what is now called Archimedes' principle, which relates the density of a body to the quantity of fluid it will displace. This enabled him to solve a problem posed, according to tradition, by King Hiero II: was the king's crown pure gold or a gold and silver alloy?]

That's one small step for [a] man, one giant leap for mankind.
                    —NEIL A. ARMSTRONG, disembarking from
                    the Eagle moon lander, July 20, 1969,
                    mission of Apollo 11
["*A* man . . ." is the official version; but he said "for man," according to recordings of the landing.]

Then I felt like some watcher of the skies
When a new planet swims into his ken;
Or like stout Cortez, when with eagle eyes
He stared at the Pacific—and all his men
Looked at each other with a wild surmise—
Silent, upon a peak in Darien.
> —JOHN KEATS, *On First Looking into Chapman's Homer*

What hath God wrought!
> —SAMUEL F. B. MORSE, first electric telegraph
> message, May 24, 1844

[Morse was quoting the Bible, *Numbers* 23:23; he had asked Annie Ellsworth, daughter of the U.S. Commissioner of Patents, to provide a suitable first message for him, and the Biblical text was her suggestion.]

Doctor Livingstone, I presume?
> —SIR HENRY MORTON STANLEY, on finding
> David Livingstone at Lake Tanganyika,
> Nov. 10, 1871; cited in Stanley's book
> *How I Found Livingstone*

It was wonderful to find America, but it would have been still more wonderful to miss it.     —MARK TWAIN, *Pudd'nhead Wilson*

## SCIENCE: MATHEMATICS & STATISTICS

Mathematics is the door and the key to the sciences.
> —ROGER BACON, *Opus Majus*

Numbers are intellectual witnesses that belong only to mankind.
> —HONORÉ DE BALZAC, *Louis Lambert*

A witty statesman said, you might prove anything by figures.
> —THOMAS CARLYLE, *Chartism*

There are three kinds of lies—lies, damned lies, and statistics.
> —BENJAMIN DISRAELI, quoted in Mark Twain,
> *Autobiography*

I don't believe in mathematics.
> —ALBERT EINSTEIN, quoted in Carl Seelig,
> *Albert Einstein*

It is here [in mathematics] that the artist has the fullest scope of his imagination. —HAVELOCK ELLIS, *The Dance of Life*

The mathematician has reached the highest rung on the ladder of human thought. —*Ibid.*

There is no royal road to geometry.
—EUCLID, quoted in Proclus' *Commentaries*

It has been said that figures rule the world. Maybe. But I am sure that figures show us whether it is being ruled well or badly.
—GOETHE, quoted in Johann Peter Eckermann,
*Conversations with Goethe*

I tell them that if they will occupy themselves with the study of mathematics, they will find in it the best remedy against the lusts of the flesh. —THOMAS MANN, *The Magic Mountain*

To understand God's thoughts, we must study statistics, for these are the measure of his purpose.
—FLORENCE NIGHTINGALE, quoted in K. Pearson,
*Life . . . of Francis Galton*

Let no one ignorant of geometry enter my door.
—PLATO, *The Republic*
[Plato's interest, however, had its limits; see below.]

The ludicrous state of solid geometry made me pass over this branch. —*Ibid.*

Order is heaven's first law. —ALEXANDER POPE, *An Essay on Man*

Mathematics possesses not only truth, but supreme beauty—a beauty cold and austere, like that of sculpture.
—BERTRAND RUSSELL, *The Study of Mathematics* in
*Mysticism and Logic*

Prayers for the condemned man will be offered on an adding machine. Numbers constitute the only universal language.
—NATHANAEL WEST, *Miss Lonelyhearts*

The science of pure mathematics . . . may claim to be the most original creation of the human spirit.
—ALFRED NORTH WHITEHEAD,
*Science and the Modern World*

**SCIENCE:**                          See also NATURE: THE HEAVENS,
**PHYSICS & COSMOLOGY**                          THE SKY; UNIVERSE

Give me a firm spot on which to stand, and I will move the earth.
—ARCHIMEDES, commenting on the principle of the lever,
quoted in Pappus of Alexandria, *Collectio*

Nothing exists except atoms and empty space; everything else is
opinion.                          —DEMOCRITUS, fragment

Everything existing in the universe is the fruit of chance and
necessity.                          —DEMOCRITUS, fragment

God does not play dice with the universe.
—ALBERT EINSTEIN, saying
[See Hawking's response, below; and there is a related observation
by Einstein, under GOD.]

Physical concepts are free creations of the human mind, and are
not, however it may seem, uniquely determined by the external
world.                          —ALBERT EINSTEIN, *Evolution of Physics*

God not only plays dice, He also sometimes throws the dice where
they cannot be seen.           —STEPHEN WILLIAM HAWKING, in
*Nature* 257, 1975
[He was commenting on Einstein's famous saying, see above.]

Space isn't remote at all. It's only an hour's drive away if your car
could go straight upwards.           —FRED HOYLE, in the *Observer*,
Sept. 9, 1979

Nothing puzzles me more than time and space; and yet nothing
troubles me less as I never think about them.
—CHARLES LAMB, letter to Thomas Manning,
Jan. 2, 1806

Every body continues in its state of rest, or of uniform motion in
a right [straight] line, unless it is compelled to change that state by
forces impressed upon it.
—ISAAC NEWTON, the first law of motion,
*Principia Mathematica*, A. Motte, transl.

To every action there is always opposed an equal reaction.
—ISAAC NEWTON, third law of motion, *Ibid.*

We have no right to assume that any physical laws exist, or if they have existed up to now, that they will continue to exist in a similar manner in the future.

—MAX PLANCK, *The Universe
in the Light of Modern Physics*

Astronomy compels the soul to look upwards and leads us from this world to another. —PLATO, *The Republic*

*Natura vacuum abhorret.*
Nature abhors a vacuum. —RABELAIS, *Gargantua*
[He is quoting a Latin proverb. Another citation often given is Spinoza, *Ethics*.]

Water is the principle, or the element, of all things. All things are water. —THALES OF MILETUS, quoted in Plutarch,
*Placita Philosophorum*

## SCIENCE: PSYCHOLOGY & PSYCHOANALYSIS

See also MADNESS;
SELF-KNOWLEDGE

Of course "behaviorism" works. So does torture.
—W. H. AUDEN, *Behaviorism* in *A Certain World*

The true science and study of man is man.
—PIERRE CHARRON, *De le sagesse*, preface

It might be said of psychoanalysis that if you give it your little finger, it will soon have your whole hand.
—FREUD, *Introductory Lectures on Psychoanalysis*

Freud is the father of psychoanalysis. It has no mother.
—GERMAINE GREER, *The Female Eunuch*

I am still more frightened by the fearless power in the eyes of my fellow psychiatrists than by the powerless fear in the eyes of their patients. —R. D. LAING, *Wisdom, Madness, and Folly*

Dreams are the true interpreters of our inclinations; but there is art required to sort and understand them. —MONTAIGNE, *Essays*

Psychology which explains everything
explains nothing,
and we are still in doubt. —MARIANNE MOORE, *Marriage*

MACBETH: Canst thou not minster to a mind diseased,
Pluck from memory a rooted sorrow,
Raze out the written troubles of the brain . . . ?

DOCTOR: Therein the patient
Must minister to himself. —*Ibid.*, V, iii

If you talk to God, you are praying; if God talks to you, you have
schizophrenia. —THOMAS SZASZ, *Schizophrenia* in *The Second Sin*

## SEAS & SHIPS, SAILING & BOATING

See also NATURE: THE OCEAN

They that go down to the sea in ships, that do business in great
waters;
These see the works of the Lord, and his wonders in the deep.
—BIBLE, *Psalms* 107:23-24

What is a ship but a prison?
—ROBERT BURTON, *The Anatomy of Melancholy*
[The thought was elaborated by Samuel Johnson; see below.]

Water, water, every where,
And all the boards did shrink;
Water, water, every where,
Nor any drop to drink. —SAMUEL TAYLOR COLERIDGE,
*The Rime of the Ancient Mariner*

There is nothing more enticing, disenchanting, and enslaving than
the life at sea. —JOSEPH CONRAD, *Lord Jim*

The life of a sailor is very unhealthy.
—FRANCIS GALTON, *Inquiries into Human Faculty*

There is *nothing*—absolutely nothing—half so much worth doing
as simply messing about in boats.
—KENNETH GRAHAME, *The Wind in the Willows*

He that will learn to pray, let him go to sea.
—GEORGE HERBERT, *Jacula Prudentum*

His heart was mailed with oak and triple brass who first committed a frail ship to the wild seas. —HORACE, *Odes*

Being in a ship is being in jail, with the chance of being drowned.
—SAMUEL JOHNSON, quoted in Boswell's
*Life of Johnson*, 1759

The Owl and the Pussycat went to sea
In a beautiful pea-green boat,
They took some honey, and plenty of money,
Wrapped up in a five-pound note.
—EDWARD LEAR, *The Owl and the Pussycat*

I must down to the seas again, to the lonely sea and the sky,
And all I ask is a tall ship and a star to steer her by,
And the wheel's kick and the wind's song and the white sail's
shaking,
And a grey mist on the sea's face and a grey dawn breaking.
—JOHN MASEFIELD, *Sea Fever*

Call me Ishmael.   —HERMAN MELVILLE, *Moby-Dick*, opening line
[In the Bible, Ishmael is the son of Abraham and the bondservant
Hagar, and the older half-brother of Isaac. He was disinherited and
sent away, and the name came to stand for an outcast.]

A man who is not afraid of the sea will soon be drowned.
—J. M. SYNGE, *The Aran Islands*

O Captain! my Captain! our fearful trip is done,
The ship has weathered every rack, the prize we sought is won.
—WALT WHITMAN, *O Captain! My Captain!*

**SEASONS IN LIFE**                    See GENERATIONS; LIFE

**SEASONS OF THE YEAR**               See NATURE: SEASONS

**SELF**                    See also HONESTY & SINCERITY;
PRIDE & VANITY; SELF entries below

Resolve to be thyself: and know that he
Who finds himself, loses his misery.
—MATTHEW ARNOLD, *Self-Dependence*

The kingdom of God is within you.          —BIBLE, *Luke* 17:21

Angels can fly because they take themselves lightly.
—G. K. CHESTERTON, *Orthodoxy*

The man who masters himself is delivered from the force that binds all creatures.  —GOETHE, *Die Geheimnisse*

What other dungeon is so dark as one's own heart! What jailer so inexorable as one's self!  —NATHANIEL HAWTHORNE,
*The House of the Seven Gables*

The least pain in our little finger gives more concern and uneasiness than the destruction of millions of our fellow beings.
—WILLIAM HAZLITT, *Dr. Channing* in
*American Literature*

There is only one corner of the universe you can be certain of improving, and that's your own self.
—ALDOUS HUXLEY, *Time Must Have a Stop*

Self-love is the greatest of all flatterers.
—LA ROCHEFOUCAULD, *Maxims*

He that would govern others first should be
The master of himself.  —PHILIP MASSINGER, *The Bondman*

The greatest thing in the world is to know how to belong to oneself.  —MONTAIGNE, *Essays*, "To the Reader"

The worst of all deceptions is self-deception.  —PLATO, *Cratylus*

To understand oneself is the classic form of consolation; to elude oneself is the romantic.  —GEORGE SANTAYANA, *Winds of Doctrine*

Our remedies oft in ourselves do lie.
—SHAKESPEARE, *All's Well That Ends Well*, I, i

This above all: To thine own self be true,
And it must follow, as the night the day,
Thou canst not then be false to any man.
—SHAKESPEARE, *Hamlet*, I, iii

My closest relation is myself.  —TERENCE, *Andria*

I celebrate myself, and sing myself.
—WALT WHITMAN, *Song of Myself*
[For Whitman on self-contradiction, see under CONSISTENCY.]

To love oneself is the beginning of a life-long romance.
—OSCAR WILDE, *An Ideal Husband*

Men can starve from a lack of self-realization as much as they can from a lack of bread.          —RICHARD WRIGHT, *Native Son*

**SELF-CONFIDENCE**          See also AMBITION;
BOLDNESS & INITIATIVE;
PRIDE & VANITY

Be always sure you're right, then go ahead.
          —DAVY CROCKETT, motto, quoted in Maria Leach, ed.,
          *Standard Dictionary of Folklore, Mythology,*
          *and Legend*

Who has self-confidence will lead the rest.          —HORACE, *Epistles*

The bullet that will kill me is not yet cast.
          —NAPOLEON BONAPARTE, attributed remark from 1814

I bear a charmed life.          —SHAKESPEARE, *Macbeth*, V, viii

They can do all because they think they can.          —VIRGIL, *Aeneid*

**SELF-INTEREST**          See also CAPITALISM

Everyone believes that what suits him is the right thing to do.
          —GOETHE, *Tasso*

If I am not for myself, who is for me?
          —HILLEL "THE ELDER," quoted in C. Taylor, ed.,
          *Sayings of the Jewish Fathers*

It makes a difference whose ox is gored.
          —MARTIN LUTHER, *Works*

**SELF-KNOWLEDGE**          See also SCIENCE:
PSYCHOLOGY & PSYCHOANALYSIS

*Gnóthi seautón.*
Know thyself.          —ANONYMOUS, inscription at the temple of
          Apollo at Delphi
[An axiom of ancient wisdom, repeated often.]

The questions which one asks oneself begin, at last, to illuminate the world, and become one's key to the experience of others.
          —JAMES BALDWIN, *Nobody Knows My Name*

To know oneself, one should assert oneself.
—ALBERT CAMUS, *Notebooks*

The humble knowledge of thyself is surer way to God than the deepest search after science.
—THOMAS À KEMPIS, *Imitation of Christ*

Know then thyself, presume not God to scan;
The proper study of mankind is man.
—ALEXANDER POPE, *An Essay on Man*

We know what we are, but know not what we may be.
—SHAKESPEARE, *Hamlet*, IV, v

To know oneself is not necessarily to improve oneself.
—PAUL VALÉRY, *Choses Tués*

To enter one's own self, it is necessary to go armed to the teeth.
—PAUL VALÉRY, *Quelques Pensées de Monsieur Teste*

## SELF-RELIANCE

See also BOLDNESS & INITIATIVE;
FATE; RESPONSIBILITY; WORK

The gods help them that help themselves.
—AESOP, *Hercules and the Waggoner*
[Appears in other works, including Benjamin Franklin's *Poor Richard's Almanac*.]

If the hill will not come to Mahomet, Mahomet will come to the hill.
—FRANCIS BACON, *Of Boldness*

Put your trust in God, my boys, and keep your powder dry!
—VALENTINE BLACKER, *Oliver Cromwell's Advice*

He was a self-made man who owed his lack of success to nobody.
—JOSEPH HELLER, *Catch-22*

I am the master of my fate;
I am the captain of my soul.
—W. E. HENLEY, *Invictus* in
*In Memoriam R. T. Hamilton Bruce*

Never depend on anyone except yourself.   —LA FONTAINE, *Fables*

Help yourself and heaven will help you.                    —*Ibid.*

If you want a thing done well, do it yourself.
—NAPOLEON BONAPARTE, *Maxims*

**SELF-RIGHTEOUSNESS**                     See also VIRTUE

Righteous people terrify me. . . . Virtue is its own punishment.
—ANEURIN BEVAN, quoted in
Michael Foot, *Aneurin Bevan*

God, I thank thee, that I am not as other men are.
—BIBLE, *Luke* 18:11

God hates those who praise themselves.
—ST. CLEMENT, *First Epistle to the Corinthians*

Moral indignation is in most cases two percent moral, forty-eight percent indignation, and fifty percent envy.
—VITTORIO DE SICA, quoted in the *Observer*, 1961

The louder he talked of his honor, the faster we counted our spoons.                     —RALPH WALDO EMERSON, *Worship* in
*The Conduct of Life*

**SEX**                     See also HEDONISM; LOVE;
SIN, VICE, & NAUGHTINESS

*Post coitum omne animal triste.*
After coition every animal is sad.          —ANONYMOUS, Latin saying

Bed is the poor man's opera.
—ANONYMOUS (ITALIAN PROVERB), quoted in
Aldous Huxley, *Heaven and Hell*

To many, total abstinence is easier than perfect moderation.
—ST. AUGUSTINE, *On the Good of Marriage*
[On the other hand, see Augustine's ambivalence, under PRAYERS.]

Sexuality is the lyricism of the masses.
—CHARLES BAUDELAIRE, *Intimate Journal*

Men make love more intensely at twenty, but make love better, however, at thirty.     —CATHERINE THE GREAT, letter to Voltaire, in
*The Complete Works of Catherine II*,
Evdokimov, ed.

License my roving hands, and let them go,
Before, behind, between, above, below.
                    —JOHN DONNE, *To His Mistress Going to Bed*

I am the Love that dare not speak its name.
                    —LORD ALFRED DOUGLAS, *Two Loves*

Sex lies at the root of life, and we can never learn to reverence
life until we know how to understand sex.
                    —HAVELOCK ELLIS, *Studies in the Psychology of Sex*

If your life at night is good, you think you have everything.
                    —EURIPIDES, *Medea*

While a person does not give up on sex, sex does not give up on
the person.     —GABRIEL GARCÍA MÁRQUEZ, on sex and growing old,
                    *The New York Times*, April 7, 1985

People will insist . . . on treating the *mons Veneris* as though it
were Mount Everest.          —ALDOUS HUXLEY, *Eyeless in Gaza*

and his heart was going like mad and yes I said yes I will Yes.
                    —JAMES JOYCE, *Ulysses*, the ending

A man who has not passed through the inferno of his passions has
never overcome them.  —CARL JUNG, *Memories, Dreams, Reflections*

Most mothers think that to keep young people away from love-
making it is enough never to speak of it in their presence.
                    —MARIE MADELEINE DE LA FAYETTE,
                    *La Princesse de Clèves*

If we resist our passions, it is due more to their weakness than our
own strength.          —LA ROCHEFOUCAULD, *Maxims*

Sex and beauty are inseparable, like life and consciousness.
                    —D. H. LAWRENCE, *Sex Versus Loneliness*

You mustn't force sex to do the work of love or love to do the
work of sex.          —MARY MCCARTHY, *The Group*

Contraceptives should be used on all conceivable occasions.
                    —SPIKE MILLIGAN, *The Last Goon Show of All*

The daughter-in-law of Pythagoras said that a woman who goes to
bed with a man ought to lay aside her modesty with her skirt, and
put it on again with her petticoat.          —MONTAIGNE, *Essays*

Whether a pretty woman grants or withholds her favors, she always likes to be asked for them.          —Ovid, *Ars Amatoria*

Men seldom make passes
At girls who wear glasses.          —Dorothy Parker, *News Item*

Sex Is Never an Emergency.
          —Dr. Elaine Pierson, title of guide for college students

Civilized people cannot fully satisfy their sexual instinct without love.          —Bertrand Russell, *Marriage and Morals*

As I grow older and older
And totter towards the tomb,
I find I care less and less
Who goes to bed with whom.
          —Dorothy Sayers,
          *That's Why I Never Read Modern Novels*

Is it not strange that desire should so many years outlive performance.          —Shakespeare, *Henry IV, Part II*, II, iv

She is a woman, therefore may be wooed;
She is a woman, therefore may be won.
          —Shakespeare, *Titus Andronicus*, II, i

There are worse occupations in this world than feeling a woman's pulse.          —Laurence Sterne, *A Sentimental Journey*

## SHIPS

See SEAS & SHIPS,
SAILING & BOATING

## SILENCE

Loose lips sink ships.          —Anonymous, World War II poster

The silent dog is the first to bite.
          —Anonymous (German Proverb)

Drawing on my fine command of language, I said nothing.
          —Robert Benchley, *Chips off the Old Benchley*

Try as we may to make a silence, we cannot.  —John Cage, *Silence*

Speech is of time, silence is of eternity.  —Carlyle, *Sartor Resartus*

When you're leading, don't talk.
—THOMAS E. DEWEY, remark during
presidential campaign, 1948, quoted in
Richard Norton Smith, *Thomas E. Dewey*

Blessed is the man who, having nothing to say, abstains from
giving in words evidence of the fact.
—GEORGE ELIOT, *Impressions of Theophrastus Such*

Silence gives consent.
—OLIVER GOLDSMITH, *The Good-Natured Man*

The silence of the mind is the true religious mind, and the silence
of the gods is the silence of the earth.
—KRISHNAMURTI, quoted in
*The Second Penguin Krishnamurti Reader*

Do you wish people to believe good of you? Don't speak.
—PASCAL, *Pensées*

A sage thing is timely silence, and better than any speech.
—PLUTARCH, *The Education of Children*

An absolute silence leads to sadness: it is the image of death.
—JEAN JACQUES ROUSSEAU, *Reveries of a Solitary Walker*

Wise men say nothing in dangerous times.
—JOHN SELDEN, *Table Talk*

The silence often of pure innocence
Persuades when speaking fails.  —SHAKESPEARE, *The Winter's Tale*

God is the friend of silence. Trees, flowers, grass grow in silence.
See the stars, moon, and sun, how they move in silence.
—MOTHER TERESA, *For the Brotherhood of Man*

Only silence is great; all else is weakness.
—ALFRED DE VIGNY, *La Mort du Loup*

Whereof one cannot speak, thereof one must be silent.
—LUDWIG WITTGENSTEIN, *Tractatus logico-philosophicus*

SIMPLICITYSee also INNOCENCE;
THINGS & POSSESSIONS

Less is more.                    —ROBERT BROWNING, *Andrea del Sarto*
[Also a saying of the architect Mies Van Der Rohe.]

Everything should be made as simple as possible, but not simpler.
                    —ALBERT EINSTEIN, *Reader's Digest*, Oct. 1977
[This is similar to "Ockham's razor"; see under SCIENCE.]

*O sancta simplicitas!*
O holy simplicity!                    —JOHN HUSS, last words before
                                        burning at the stake

Manifest plainness,
Embrace simplicity,
Reduce selfishness,
Have few desires.                    —LAO-TZU, *Tao Te Ching*

Simplicity, most rare in our age.                    —OVID, *Ars Amatoria*

Beauty of style and harmony and grace and good rhythm depend
on simplicity.                    —PLATO, *The Republic*

Simplify, simplify.                    —THOREAU, *Walden*

The art of art, the glory of expression, and the sunshine of the light
of letters, is simplicity.    —WALT WHITMAN, *Leaves of Grass*,
                                        preface

SINSee EVIL; SIN, VICE, &
NAUGHTINESS

SIN, VICE, & NAUGHTINESSSee also EVIL; EXCESS;
HEDONISM; SEX; TEMPTATION

The vice is not in entering, but in not coming out again.
                    —ARISTIPPUS, remark to pupils who saw him
                        entering the house of a prostitute,
                        cited in Montaigne, *Essays*

Never practice two vices at once.
                    —TALLULAH BANKHEAD, *Tallulah*

I'm as pure as the driven slush.   —TALLULAH BANKHEAD, attributed

I once was a maid, tho' I cannot tell when,
And still my delight is in proper young men:
Some one of a troop of dragoons was my daddie,
No wonder I'm fond of a sodger laddie.
> —ROBERT BURNS, *The Jolly Beggars*

It is the function of vice to keep virtue within reasonable bounds.
> —SAMUEL BUTLER, *Notebooks*

What men call gallantry, and gods adultery,
Is much more common where the climate's sultry.
> —LORD BYRON, *Don Juan*

Pleasure's a sin, and sometimes sin's a pleasure.           —*Ibid.*

Vice is it's own reward.
> —QUENTIN CRISP, *The Naked Civil Servant*

Do you think your mother and I should have lived comfortably so long together if ever we had been married?
> —JOHN GAY, *The Beggar's Opera*

The probable fact is that we are descended not only from monkeys but from monks.     —ELBERT HUBBARD, *Roycroft Dictionary
and Book of Epigrams*

Really to sin you have to be serious about it.
> —HENRIK IBSEN, *Peer Gynt*

You know, of course, that the Tasmanians, who never committed adultery, are now extinct.     —W. SOMERSET MAUGHAM,
*The Breadwinner*

All fashionable vices pass for virtues.     —MOLIÈRE, *Don Juan*

Of course heaven forbids certain pleasures, but one finds means of compromise.     —MOLIÈRE, *Tartuffe*

Men are more easily governed through their vices than through their virtues.     —NAPOLEON BONAPARTE, *Maxims*

If all the girls attending it [the Yale prom] were laid end to end—I wouldn't be at all surprised.
> —DOROTHY PARKER, quoted in
> Alexander Woollcott, *While Rome Burns*

Enjoyed it! One more drink and I'd have been under the host.
> —DOROTHY PARKER, on being asked if she
> enjoyed a cocktail party; quoted in
> Howard Teichmann, *George S. Kaufman*

[See also Parker at ALCOHOL & DRINKING.]

When the passions become masters, they are vices.
> —PASCAL, *Pensées*

For lawless joys a bitter ending waits.    —PINDAR, *Odes*

Every vice has its excuse ready.  —PUBLILIUS SYRUS, *Moral Sayings*

Vices can be learnt even without a teacher.
> —SENECA, *Natural Questions*

Commit
The oldest sins the newest kind of ways.
> —SHAKESPEARE, *Henry IV, Part II*, IV, v

It's a bawdy planet.    —SHAKESPEARE, *The Winter's Tale*, I, ii

Certainly nothing is unnatural that is not physically impossible.
> —RICHARD SHERIDAN, *The Critic*

[On baseball players who break curfew:] It ain't getting it that
hurts them, it's staying up all night looking for it. They got to
learn that if you don't get it by midnight, you ain't gonna get it,
and if you do, it ain't worth it.
> —CHARLES DILLON "CASEY" STENGEL, quoted in
> Robert Creamer, *Stengel*

There is a charm about the forbidden that makes it unspeakably
desirable.    —MARK TWAIN, *Notebooks*

When I'm good I'm very, very good, but when I'm bad I'm better.
> —MAE WEST, *I'm No Angel*

"Goodness, what beautiful diamonds!"
"Goodness had nothing to do with it dearie."
> —MAE WEST, *Diamond Lil*

There is nothing in the world like the devotion of a married
woman. It's a thing no married man knows anything about.
> —OSCAR WILDE, *Lady Windermere's Fan*

All the things I really like to do are either immoral, illegal, or fattening. —ALEXANDER WOOLLCOTT, quoted in
Howard Teichmann, *George S. Kaufman*

**S I N C E R I T Y**                     See HONESTY & SINCERITY

**S K E P T I C I S M**                   See also ATHEISM; FAITH

O thou of little faith, wherefore didst thou doubt?
—BIBLE, *Matthew* 14:31

Except I shall see in his hands the print of the nails, and put my finger into the print of the nails, and thrust my hand into his side, I will not believe.                     —BIBLE, *John* 20:25
["Doubting Thomas" is speaking.]

He that doubteth is damned.                     —BIBLE, *Romans* 14:23

Mock on, mock on Voltaire, Rousseau;
Mock on, mock on; 'tis all in vain!
You throw the sand against the wind,
And the wind blows it back again.
—WILLIAM BLAKE, *Mock on, Mock on*

If you would be a real seeker after truth, you must at least once in your life doubt, as far as possible, all things.
—DESCARTES, *Discourse on Method*

Skepticism is the first step toward truth.
—DIDEROT, *Pensées philosophiques*

Do we, holding that the gods exist, deceive ourselves with unsubstantial dreams and lies, while random careless chance and change alone control the world?                     —EURIPIDES, *Hecuba*

Ignorance is preferable to error; and he is less remote from the truth who believes nothing, than he who believes what is wrong.
—THOMAS JEFFERSON, *Notes on the State of Virginia*

*Que sais-je?*
What do I know?                     —MONTAIGNE, motto

Great intellects are skeptical.
—FRIEDRICH NIETZSCHE, *The Antichrist*

The pragmatist knows that doubt is an art which has to be acquired with difficulty. —C. S. PEIRCE, *Collected Papers*

Of the gods I know nothing, whether they exist or do not exist, nor what they are like in form. Many things stand in the way of knowledge—the obscurity of the subject, the brevity of human life. —PROTAGORAS, quoted in Diogenes Laërtius, *Lives of Eminent Philosophers*

Modest doubt is called
The beacon of the wise. —SHAKESPEARE, *Troilus and Cressida*, II, ii

Life is doubt, and faith without doubt is nothing but death. —MIGUEL DE UNAMUNO, *Poesías*

One never knows, do one?
—"FATS" WALLER, saying, quoted by Roger Angell, *The New Yorker*, Aug. 5, 1985

## SKY

See NATURE: THE HEAVENS, THE SKY

## SLEEP & DREAMS

See also SCIENCE: PSYCHOLOGY & PSYCHOANALYSIS

The beginning of health is sleep. —ANONYMOUS (IRISH PROVERB)

Dreaming men are haunted men.
—STEPHEN VINCENT BENÉT, *John Brown's Body*

He giveth his beloved sleep. —BIBLE, *Psalms* 127:2

Sleep hath its own world,
And a wide realm of wild reality. —LORD BYRON, *The Dream*

Now blessings light on him that first invented this same sleep! It covers a man all over, thoughts and all, like a cloak. . . . 'Tis the current coin that purchases all the pleasures of the world cheap; and the balance that sets the king and the shepherd, the fool and the wise man even. —CERVANTES, *Don Quixote*

Men have conceived a twofold use of sleep: that it is a refreshing of the body in this life; that it is a preparing of the soul for the next. —JOHN DONNE, *Meditation xv*

Wynken, Blynken, and Nod one night
Sailed off in a wooden shoe—
Sailed on a river of crystal light
Into a sea of dew.    —EUGENE FIELD, *Wynken, Blynken, and Nod*

We are not hypocrites in our sleep.
                              —WILLIAM HAZLITT, *On Dreams*

Sleep is the twin of death.                    —HOMER, *The Iliad*

Preserve me from unseasonable and immoderate sleep.
              —SAMUEL JOHNSON, *Prayers and Meditations*

Methought I heard a voice cry "Sleep no more!
Macbeth does murder sleep"—the innocent sleep,
Sleep that knits up the ravelled sleeve of care,
The death of each day's life, sore labor's bath,
Balm of hurt minds, great nature's second course,
Chief nourisher in life's feast.    —SHAKESPEARE, *Macbeth*, II, ii

Sleep my little one, sleep my pretty one, sleep.
              —ALFRED, LORD TENNYSON, *The Princess*

## SMALL THINGS          See DETAILS & OTHER SMALL THINGS;
                                             THINGS & POSSESSIONS

## SNOW                                    See NATURE: SEASONS;
                                      NATURE: WIND & WEATHER

## SOCIALISM

I am for socialism because I am for humanity.
              —EUGENE V. DEBS, speech, Jan. 1, 1897

We are all socialists nowadays.
                              —EDWARD VII, speech, 1895,
                              when he was still Prince of Wales

Socialism is . . . not only a way of life, but a certain scientific
approach to social and economic problems.
                              —JAWAHARLAL NEHRU, *Credo*

All socialism involves slavery.
                  —HERBERT SPENCER, *The Coming Slavery*

Any man who is not something of a socialist before he is forty has no heart. Any man who is still a socialist after he is forty has no head.
—WENDELL L. WILLKIE, quoted in
Thomas Norton Smith, *Thomas E. Dewey*

## SOLITUDE

He who is unable to live in society, or who has no need because he is sufficient for himself, must be either a beast or a god.
—ARISTOTLE, *Politics*

Woe to him that is alone when he falleth; for he hath not another to help him up.
—BIBLE, *Ecclesiastes* 4:10

'Tis solitude should teach us how to die;
... alone—man with his God must strive.
—LORD BYRON, *Childe Harold's Pilgrimage*

We live, as we dream—alone.
—JOSEPH CONRAD, *Heart of Darkness*

I want to be alone.     —GRETA GARBO, saying, and also one of her lines in *Grand Hotel*

Full many a flower is born to blush unseen,
And waste its sweetness on the desert air.  —THOMAS GRAY, *Elegy*

Pray that your loneliness may spur you into finding something to live for, great enough to die for.     —DAG HAMMARSKJÖLD, *Diaries*

The strongest man in the world is he who stands most alone.
—HENRIK IBSEN, *An Enemy of the People*

In solitude pride quickly creeps in.
—ST. JEROME, letter to Rusticus

Then on the shore
Of the wide world I stand alone, and think
Till love and fame to nothingness do sink.
—JOHN KEATS, *When I Have Fears*

Solitude is the playfield of Satan.  —VLADIMIR NABOKOV, *Pale Fire*

If you would live innocently, seek solitude.
—PUBLILIUS SYRUS, *Moral Sayings*

To be adult is to be alone.
—JEAN ROSTAND, *Thoughts of a Biologist*

I love all waste
And solitary places; where we taste the pleasure of believing what
    we see
Is boundless, as we wish our souls to be.
—PERCY BYSSHE SHELLEY, *Julian and Maddalo*

I never found the companion that was so companionable as
solitude. —THOREAU, *Walden*

The happiest of all lives is a busy solitude.
—VOLTAIRE, letter to Frederick the Great, Aug. 1751

She dwelt among the untrodden ways
Beside the springs of Dove,
A maid whom there were none to praise
And very few to love. —WILLIAM WORDSWORTH, *Ruth*

Avoid the reeking herd,
Shun the polluted flock,
Live like that stoic bird
The eagle of the rock. —ELINOR WYLIE, *The Eagle and the Mole*

The wind blows out of the gates of the day,
The wind blows over the lonely of heart,
And the lonely of heart is withered away.
—WILLIAM BUTLER YEATS, *The Land of Heart's Desire*

**SORROW** See TROUBLE

**SOUL** See also MIND, THOUGHT, &
UNDERSTANDING

What shall it profit a man, if he shall gain the whole world, and
lose his own soul? —BIBLE, *Mark* 8:36

The human soul develops up to the time of death.
—HIPPOCRATES, *Aphorisms*

The soul is the mirror of an indestructible universe.
—G. W. LEIBNIZ, *The Monadology*

The wealth of the soul is the only true wealth.
—Lucian, *Dialogues*

Every soul is a melody which needs renewing.
—Stéphane Mallarmé, *Crise de vers*

Those things that nature denied to human sight, she revealed to the eyes of the soul.
—Ovid, *Metamorphoses*

A beautiful soul has no other merit than its own existence.
—J. F. C. von Schiller, *Über Anmut und Würde*

The soul alone raises us to nobility.
—Seneca, *Epistles*

Throughout this varied and eternal world
Soul is the only element.
—Percy Bysshe Shelley, *Queen Mab*

Teach me, like you, to drink creation whole
And casting out my self, become a soul.
—Richard Wilbur, *The Aspen and the Stream* in *Advice to a Prophet*

**SPACE**

See NATURE: THE HEAVENS, THE SKY; SCIENCE: PHYSICS & COSMOLOGY

**SPEAKING & SPEECH**

See LANGUAGE

**SPEECH, FREE**

See FREE SPEECH

**SPIRIT**

See COURAGE; SOUL

**SPIRITS, OTHER-WORLDLY**

See OCCULT, THE

**SPORTS**

See also GAMES; WINNING & LOSING, VICTORY & DEFEAT

Float like a butterfly,
Sting like a bee!
Rumble young man! Rumble!
Waaa!
—Muhammad Ali and Drew "Bundini" Brown, their "war cry," *The Greatest: My Own Story*

*Ave Caesar, morituri te salutant.*
Hail Caesar, we who are about to die salute you.
> —ANONYMOUS, gladiators' salute,
> quoted in Suetonius, *Life of Claudius*

In America, it is sport that is the opiate of the masses.
> —RUSSELL BAKER, *The New York Times*, Oct. 3, 1967

Whoever wants to know the heart and mind of America had better learn baseball.          —JACQUES BARZUN, *God's Country and Mine*

The game isn't over till it's over.
> —LAWRENCE PETER "YOGI" BERRA, remark in 1973

The bigger they come, the harder they fall.
> —BOB FITZSIMMONS, remark before losing his fight
> with Jim Jeffries, 1899
[Also attributed to John L. Sullivan, and probably of ancient origin.]

Because it's there.
> —G. H. L. MALLORY, explaining why he wanted to
> climb Mt. Everest, quoted in John Hunt,
> *The Ascent of Everest*

Serious sport has nothing to do with fair play. It is bound up with hatred, jealousy, boastfulness, disregard of all rules, and sadistic pleasure in witnessing violence: in other words, it is war minus the shooting.          —GEORGE ORWELL, *Shooting an Elephant*

Win this one for the Gipper.
> —KNUTE ROCKNE, exhortation to the
> Notre Dame football team
[Rockne seems to have used this line more than once to urge on the team. According to *The Fireside Book of Football*, the first occasion was prior to the Indiana game in 1921, a year after Notre Dame player George Gipp died from a streptococcus infection.]

+ The race is not always to the swift nor the battle to the strong—but that's the way to bet it.          —DAMON RUNYON,
> *More Than Somewhat*

A hit, a very palpable hit.          —SHAKESPEARE, *Hamlet*, V, ii

Oh! somewhere in this favored land the sun is shining bright;
The band is playing somewhere, and somewhere hearts are light;
And somewhere men are laughing and somewhere children shout,
But there is no joy in Mudville—mighty Casey has struck out.
          —ERNEST LAWRENCE THAYER, *Casey at the Bat*

I love any discourse of rivers, and fish and fishing.
          —IZAAK WALTON, *Compleat Angler*

The English country gentleman galloping after a fox—the un-
speakable in full pursuit of the uneatable.
          —OSCAR WILDE, *A Woman of No Importance*

**SPRING**                          See NATURE: SEASONS

**STARS**                    See NATURE: THE HEAVENS, THE SKY;
          OCCULT, THE; SCIENCE: PHYSICS & COSMOLOGY

**STATISTICS**                          See SCIENCE:
          MATHEMATICS & STATISTICS

**STRENGTH**                          See also POWER;
          VIOLENCE & FORCE

When the going gets tough, the tough get going.
          —ANONYMOUS, popularized by John N. Mitchell,
          Attorney General under Richard M. Nixon

*Kraft durch Freude.*
Strength through joy.
          —ROBERT LEY, slogan for the German Labor Front, 1933

If we must choose between them, it is far better to be feared than
loved.                          —MACHIAVELLI, *The Prince*

A nation does not have to be cruel to be tough.
          —FRANKLIN D. ROOSEVELT, radio speech, Oct. 13, 1940

Physical strength can never permanently withstand the impact of
spiritual force.          —FRANKLIN D. ROOSEVELT, speech, May 4, 1941

There is a homely adage which runs: "Speak softly and carry a big stick; you will go far." —THEODORE ROOSEVELT, speech, Sept. 2, 1901 [Stephen Jay Gould has traced this adage back to an African proverb; see *Natural History*, May 1985.]

The strongest is never strong enough always to be master, unless he transforms strength into right, and obedience into duty.
　　　　　—JEAN JACQUES ROUSSEAU, *The Social Contract*

O! it is excellent
To have a giant's strength, but it is tyrannous
To use it like a giant.　—SHAKESPEARE, *Measure for Measure*, II, ii

The Gods are on the side of the stronger.　—TACITUS, *Histories*

If you can't stand the heat, get out of the kitchen.
　　　　　—HARRY S. TRUMAN, *Mr. Citizen*

There is no need to fear the strong. All one needs to know is the method of overcoming them. There is a special jujitsu for every strong man.　　　　　—YEVGENY YEVTUSHENKO,
　　　　　*A Precocious Autobiography*

**STUPIDITY**　　　　　　　　　　　See FOOLS & STUPIDITY

**STYLE**　　　　　　　　　　See also APPEARANCES; ARTS:
　　　　　　　　　　STYLE IN WRITING & EXPRESSION;
　　　　　　　　　　FASHION & CLOTHES; GRACE

Our style betrays us.　　　—ANONYMOUS (LATIN PROVERB)

*Le style est l'homme même.*
The style is the man himself.
　　　　　—GEORGES LOUIS DE BUFFON, *Discours sur le style*

To achieve harmony in bad taste is the height of elegance.
　　　　　—JEAN GENET, *The Thief's Journal*

In matters of great importance, style, not sincerity, is the vital thing.　　　—OSCAR WILDE, *The Importance of Being Earnest*

**SUCCESS & FAME**     See also ACCOMPLISHMENT; GREATNESS;
HIGH POSITION: RULERS & LEADERS;
MONEY; POWER

*Sic transit gloria mundi.*
So passes away the glory of this world.     —ANONYMOUS
[Used in papal coronations since the fifteenth century but probably
of earlier origin. Essentially the same phrase is found in *The Imitation
of Christ*; see Thomas à Kempis, below.]

The desire for fame tempts even noble minds.
—ST. AUGUSTINE, *The City of God*

Fame is like a river, that beareth up things light and swollen, and
drowns things weighty and solid.
—FRANCIS BACON, *Of Ceremonies and Respects*

Fame always brings loneliness. Success is as ice cold and lonely as
the North Pole.     —VICKI BAUM, *Grand Hotel*

Let us now praise famous men.     —BIBLE, *Ecclesiasticus* 44:1

The celebrity is a person who is known for his well-knownness.
—DANIEL BOORSTIN, *The Image*

A sign of a celebrity is often that his name is worth more than his
services.     —*Ibid.*

Success produces success, just as money produces money.
—SÉBASTIEN R. N. CHAMFORT, *Maximes et pensées*

That's what fame is: solitude.
—COCO CHANEL, quoted in Marcel Haedrich,
*Coco Chanel: Her Life, Her Secrets*

We are all motivated by a keen desire for praise, and the better a
man is, the more he is inspired by glory.     —CICERO, *Pro Archia*

Fame is a bee.
It has a song—
It has a sting—
Ah, too, it has a wing.     —EMILY DICKINSON, poem

Nothing succeeds like success.  —ALEXANDRE DUMAS, *Ange Pitou*
[For Oscar Wilde's variations, see EXCESS.]

Along with success comes a reputation for wisdom.
                              —EURIPIDES, *Hippolytus*

Success has ruined many a man.
            —BENJAMIN FRANKLIN, *Poor Richard's Almanac*

Fame hath sometimes created something of nothing.
        —THOMAS FULLER, *Of Fame* in *Holy and Profane State*

The paths of glory lead but to the grave.  —THOMAS GRAY, *Elegy*

Success has killed more men than bullets.
                —TEXAS GUINAN, saying used in nightclub act

It is better to be envied than pitied.       —HERODOTUS, *Histories*

The moral flabbiness born of the bitch goddess Success. That—
with the squalid cash interpretation put on the word success—is our
national disease.       —WILLIAM JAMES, letter to H. G. Wells,
                              Sept. 11, 1906

Oh how quickly the world's glory passes away.
            —THOMAS À KEMPIS, *The Imitation of Christ*
[A variation of the anonymous *sic transit gloria munde*; see above.]

There is no business in the world so troublesome as the pursuit of
fame: life is over before you have hardly begun your work.
                              —LA BRUYÈRE, *Les Caractères*.

Be nice to people on your way up because you'll need them on
your way down.       —WILSON MIZNER, quoted in A. Johnson,
                              *The Incredible Mizners*
[Also attributed to Jimmy Durante.]

Success is like a liberation or the first phase of a love affair.
            —JEANNE MOREAU, quoted in Oriana Fallaci, *The Egoists*

There is only one success—to be able to spend your life in your
own way.       —CHRISTOPHER MORLEY, *Where the Blue Begins*

What rage for fame attends both great and small!
Better be damned than mentioned not at all.
                      —"PETER PINDAR" (John Walcot),
                      *To the Royal Academicians*

Fame can never make us lie down contentedly on a deathbed.
>—ALEXANDER POPE, letter to William Trumbell,
> March 12, 1713

The highest form of vanity is love of fame.
>—GEORGE SANTAYANA, *Reason in Society*

There's hope a great man's memory may outlive his life half a year. —SHAKESPEARE, *Hamlet*, III

There are two tragedies in life. One is to lose your heart's desire. The other is to gain it. —GEORGE BERNARD SHAW,
>*Man and Superman*

All you need in this life is ignorance and confidence, and then success is sure. —MARK TWAIN, letter to Mrs. Foote, Dec. 2, 1887

In the future, everyone will be famous for fifteen minutes.
>—ANDY WARHOL, *Andy Warhol's Exposures*

There is always room at the top. —DANIEL WEBSTER, attributed

## SUICIDE

As soon as one does not kill oneself, one must keep silent about life.
>—ALBERT CAMUS, *Notebooks*
[For his view of suicide and philosophy, see PHILOSOPHY.]

When all the blandishments of life are gone,
The coward sneaks to death, the brave live on.
>—MARTIAL, *Epigrams*

A suicide kills two people . . . that's what it's for.
>—ARTHUR MILLER, *After the Fall*

It is always consoling to think of suicide: in that way one gets through many a bad night.
>—FRIEDRICH NIETZSCHE, *Beyond Good and Evil*

Razors pain you;
Rivers are damp;
Acids stain you;
And drugs cause cramp;
Guns aren't lawful;
Nooses give;
Gas smells awful;
You might as well live.
>—DOROTHY PARKER, *Resumé* in *Enough Rope*

Amid the sufferings of life on earth, suicide is God's best gift to man.                                    —PLINY THE ELDER, *Natural History*

There is nothing in the world to which every man has a more unassailable title than to his own life and person.
                                    —SCHOPENHAUER, *On Suicide*

To be, or not to be—that is the question:
Whether 'tis nobler in the mind to suffer
The slings and arrows of outrageous fortune,
Or to take arms against a sea of troubles,
And by opposing end them.        —SHAKESPEARE, *Hamlet*, III, i

It is silliness to live when to live is torment.
                                    —SHAKESPEARE, *Othello*, I, iii

The man who, in a fit of melancholy, kills himself today, would have wished to live had he waited a week.
                —VOLTAIRE, *Philosophical Dictionary*, "Cato"

**S U M M E R**                                    See NATURE: SEASONS

**S U R V I V A L**                         See also APPEASEMENT VS. RESISTANCE;
                                          CRAFTINESS; PERSEVERANCE &
                                                          ENDURANCE

He that fights and runs away
May live to fight another day.
              —ANONYMOUS, in *Musarium Deliciae*, 17th century

To all the living there is hope; for a living dog is better than a dead lion.                        —BIBLE, *Ecclesiastes* 9:4

It isn't important to come out on top. What matters is to be the one who comes out alive.        —BERTOLT BRECHT, *Jungle of Cities*

Happiness in the ordinary sense is not what one needs in life, though one is right to aim at it. The true satisfaction is to come through and see those whom one loves come through.
              —E. M. FORSTER, letter, 1922, in *Selected Letters*,
              Vol. II (1921–1970)

In the clutch of circumstance,
I have not winced or cried aloud;
Under the bludgeoning of chance
My head is bloody but unbowed.
—WILLIAM E. HENLEY, *Invictus*, in
*In Memoriam R. T. Hamilton Bruce*

I bend but do not break.
—LA FONTAINE, *The Oak and the Reed* in *Fables*

We shall live to fight again and to strike another blow.
—ALFRED, LORD TENNYSON, *The Revenge*

Endure, and preserve yourselves for better things.
—VIRGIL, *Aeneid*

## SWITZERLAND
See NATIONS

## TAXES

Render therefore unto Caesar the things which are Caesar's; and
unto God the things that are God's.　　—BIBLE, *Matthew* 22:21

To tax and to please, no more than to love and be wise, is not given
to man.　　—EDMUND BURKE, speech, Apr. 9, 1774

The art of taxation consists in so plucking the goose as to obtain
the largest possible amount of feathers with the least possible amount
of hissing.　　—JEAN BAPTISTE COLBERT, attributed

In this world, nothing can be said to be certain except death and
taxes.　　—BENJAMIN FRANKLIN, letter to J.-B. LeRoy,
Nov. 13, 1789

The wisdom of man never yet contrived a system of taxation that
operates with perfect equality.　　—ANDREW JACKSON, *Proclamation
to the People of South Carolina*

*Excise, n.* A hateful tax levied upon commodities, and adjudged
not by the common judges of property, but by wretches hired by
those to whom the excise is paid.　　—SAMUEL JOHNSON, *Dictionary*

The power to tax involves the power to destroy.
—JOHN MARSHALL, *McCulloch* v. *Maryland*

Taxation without representation is tyranny.

—JAMES OTIS, attributed

Where there is an income tax, the just man will pay more and the unjust less on the same income.   —PLATO, *The Republic*

The income tax has made more liars out of the American people than golf has.   —WILL ROGERS, *The Illiterate Digest*

Taxes, after all, are dues that we pay for the privileges of membership in an organized society.

—FRANKLIN D. ROOSEVELT, speech, Oct. 21, 1936

## TECHNOLOGY                    See also MEDIA; SCIENCE

Garbage in, garbage out.

—ANONYMOUS, on why computer findings may be unsatisfactory

To err is human, but to really foul things up requires a computer.

—ANONYMOUS

The "control of nature" is a phrase conceived in arrogance, born of the Neanderthal age of biology and the convenience of man.

—RACHEL CARSON, *The Silent Spring*

Machines, from the Maxim gun to the computer, are for the most part means by which a minority can keep free men in subjection.

—SIR KENNETH CLARK, *Civilization*

Any sufficiently advanced technology is indistinguishable from magic.   —ARTHUR C. CLARKE, *The Lost Worlds of 2001*

If true computer music were ever written, it would only be listened to by other computers.   —MICHAEL CRICHTON, *Electronic Life*

Technology . . . the knack of so arranging the world that we don't have to experience it.

—MAX FRISCH, quoted in Daniel J. Boorstin, *The Image*

Is it a fact, or have I dreamt it—that, by means of electricity, the world of matter has become a great nerve, vibrating thousands of miles in a breathless point of time?

—NATHANIEL HAWTHORNE, *The House of the Seven Gables*

Have you heard of the wonderful one-hoss shay,
That was built in such a logical way
It ran a hundred years to a day?
　　　　　—OLIVER WENDELL HOLMES, *The Deacon's Masterpiece*

The automobile changed our dress, manners, social customs, vacation habits, the shape of our cities, consumer purchasing patterns, common tastes, and positions in intercourse.
　　　　　—JOHN KEATS, *The Insolent Chariots*

Our scientific power has outrun our spiritual power. We have guided missiles and misguided men.
　　　　　—MARTIN LUTHER KING, JR., *Strength to Love*

To George F. Babbitt . . . his motor-car was poetry and tragedy, love and heroism.　　　　　—SINCLAIR LEWIS, *Babbitt*

It is critical vision alone which can mitigate the unimpeded operation of the automatic.
　　　　　—MARSHALL MCLUHAN, *The Mechanical Bride*

The electric age . . . establishes a global network that has much the character of our central nervous system.
　　　　　—MARSHALL MCLUHAN, *Understanding Media*

The car has become the carapace, the protective and aggressive shell, of urban and suburban man.　　　　　—*Ibid.*

Machines are worshipped because they are beautiful and valued because they confer power; they are hated because they are hideous and loathed because they impose slavery.
　　　　　—BERTRAND RUSSELL, *Sceptical Essays*

The machine does not isolate man from the great problems of nature but plunges him more deeply into them.
　　　　　—ANTOINE DE SAINT-EXUPÉRY, *Wind, Sand, and Stars*

The machine yes the machine
never wastes anybody's time
never watches the foreman
never talks back.　　　　　—CARL SANDBURG, *The People, Yes*

The real problem is not whether machines think, but whether men do.　　　　　—B. F. SKINNER, *Contingencies of Reinforcement*

Men have become the tools of their tools.    —THOREAU, *Walden*

Everything in life is somewhere else, and you get there in a car.
                        —E. B. WHITE, *One Man's Meat*
[For E. B. White on television, see under MEDIA.]

In the past, human life was lived in a bullock cart; in the future, it will be lived in an aeroplane; and the change of speed amounts to a difference in quality.    —ALFRED NORTH WHITEHEAD,
                        *Science and the Modern World*

## TELEVISION                                    See MEDIA

## TEMPTATION                        See also SIN, VICE, & NAUGHTINESS

Opportunity can often sway even an honest man.
                        —ANONYMOUS (LATIN PROVERB)

Saintliness is also a temptation.        —JEAN ANOUILH, *Becket*

Lead us not into temptation.
[Also *Luke*, 11:4.]                        —BIBLE, *Matthew* 6:13

Get thee behind me, Satan.                    —*Ibid.*, 16:23

Watch and pray, that ye enter not into temptation: the spirit indeed is willing, but the flesh is weak.        —*Ibid.*, 26:41

Blessed is the man that endureth temptation.    —BIBLE, *James* 1:12

For to tempt and to be tempted are things very nearly allied, and in spite of the finest maxims of morality impressed upon the mind, whenever feeling has anything to do in the matter, no sooner is it excited than we have already gone vastly farther than we are aware of.                        —CATHERINE THE GREAT, *Memoirs*

Tempt not a desperate man.
                        —SHAKESPEARE, *Romeo and Juliet*, V, iii

I generally avoid temptation unless I can't resist it.
                        —MAE WEST, *My Little Chickadee*, movie

I can resist everything except temptation.
                        —OSCAR WILDE, *Lady Windermere's Fan*

**THEATER**  See ARTS: DRAMA & ACTING

**THEORY**  See SCIENCE

**THINGS**  See DETAILS & OTHER SMALL THINGS;
NEW THINGS; OLD THINGS, OLD FRIENDS;
SIMPLICITY; THINGS & POSSESSIONS

**THINGS &**  See also NEW THINGS; OLD THINGS,
**POSSESSIONS**  OLD FRIENDS; SIMPLICITY

The goal of all inanimate objects is to resist man and ultimately to defeat him.　　—RUSSELL BAKER, *The New York Times*, June 18, 1968

Inanimate objects are classified scientifically into three major categories—those that don't work, those that break down, and those that get lost.　　—*Ibid.*

Things have their laws as well as men; things refuse to be trifled with.　　—RALPH WALDO EMERSON, *Politics*

We are the slaves of objects around us.
　　—GOETHE, quoted in Johann Peter Eckermann, *Conversations with Goethe*

Every increased possession loads us with a new weariness.
　　—JOHN RUSKIN, *The Eagle's Nest*

An ill-favored thing, sir, but mine own.
　　—SHAKESPEARE, *As You Like It*, V, iv

A place for everything and everything in its place.
　　—SAMUEL SMILES, *Thrift*

How many things I can do without!
　　—SOCRATES, in a marketplace, quoted in Diogenes Laërtius, *Lives of Eminent Philosophers*

A coin, sleeve button, or a collar button dropped in a bedroom will hide itself and be hard to find. A handkerchief in bed *can't* be found.　　—MARK TWAIN, *Notebook*

**THINKING & THOUGHT**    See MIND, THOUGHT, &
UNDERSTANDING

**TIME**    See also PRESENT, THE;
PROCRASTINATION

Time brings all things to pass.  —AESCHYLUS, *The Libation Bearers*

Time and tide wait for no man.
—ANONYMOUS (ENGLISH PROVERB)

What then is time? If no one asks me, I know what it is. If I wish
to explain it to him who asks, I do not know.
—ST. AUGUSTINE, *Confessions*

Time is a great teacher, but unfortunately it kills all its pupils.
—HECTOR BERLIOZ, quoted in
*Almanach des lettres françaises*

Men talk of killing time, while time quietly kills them.
—DION BOUCICAULT, *London Assurance*
[Also, from about the same period, Herbert Spencer in *Definitions:
Time:* That which man is always trying to kill, but which ends in
killing him.]

Time ripens all things. No man's born wise.
—CERVANTES, *Don Quixote*

Time is the great physician.
—BENJAMIN DISRAELI, *Henrietta Temple*

Time present and time past
Are both perhaps present in time future,
And time future contained in time past.
—T. S. ELIOT, *Burnt Norton*, in *Four Quartets*

The Moving Finger writes; and having writ,
Moves on: nor all your Piety nor Wit
Shall lure it back to cancel half a Line,
Nor all your Tears wash out a Word of it.
—EDWARD FITZGERALD, *The Rubáiyát of Omar Khayyám*

Time is money.
—BENJAMIN FRANKLIN, *Advice to a Young Tradesman*

Dost thou love life? Then do not squander time, for that's the stuff life is made of.   —BENJAMIN FRANKLIN, *The Way to Wealth*

Time flies over us, but leaves its shadow behind.
                    —NATHANIEL HAWTHORNE, *The Marble Faun*

But at my back I always hear
Time's wingèd chariot hurrying near.
                    —ANDREW MARVELL, *To His Coy Mistress*
[For more, see under HEDONISM.]

I must govern the clock, not be governed by it.
                    —GOLDA MEIR, quoted in Oriana Fallaci,
                    *L'Europeo*

Time is the best medicine.         —OVID, *Remedia amoris*

In theory, one is aware that the earth revolves, but in practice one does not perceive it; the ground upon which one treads seems not to move, and one can live undisturbed. So it is with time in one's life.
                    —PROUST, *Remembrance of Things Past:
                    Within a Budding Grove*

Everything is a matter of chronology.
                    —PROUST, *Remembrance of Things Past:
                    The Past Recaptured*

Time, which changes people, does not alter the image we have retained of them.                    —*Ibid.*

To realize the unimportance of time is the gate of wisdom.
                    —BERTRAND RUSSELL, *Mysticism and Logic*, title essay

Nothing is ours except time.         —SENECA, *Epistles*

Ah! the clock is always slow;
It is later than you think.
                    —ROBERT W. SERVICE, *Songs of a Sourdough*

Come what come may,
Time and the hour runs through the roughest day.
                    —SHAKESPEARE, *Macbeth*, I, iii

I wasted time, and now doth time waste me.
                    —SHAKESPEARE, *Richard II*, V, v

Time eases all things.                    —SOPHOCLES, *Oedipus Rex*
[Or, from his *Electra*, "Gentle time will heal our sorrows."]

The butterfly counts not months but moments, and has time
enough.                    —RABINDRANATH TAGORE, *Stray Birds*

Oh as I was young and easy in the mercy of his means,
Time held me green and dying
Though I sang in my chains like the sea.
                    —DYLAN THOMAS, *Fern Hill*

As if you could kill time without injuring eternity.
                    —THOREAU, *Walden*

Time bears away all things, even the mind.    —VIRGIL, *Eclogues*

The years like great black oxen tread the world,
And God the herdsman goads them on behind,
And I am broken by their passing feet.
                    —WILLIAM BUTLER YEATS, *The Countess Cathleen*

## TIMES                    See FUTURE; GENERATIONS; MODERN TIMES;
PAST, THE; PRESENT, THE; TURBULENT TIMES

## TIMES OF DAY                    See NATURE: TIMES OF DAY

## TOBACCO

Tobacco, divine, rare, superexcellent tobacco . . . a sovereign
remedy to all diseases. . . . But, as it is commonly abused by most
men, which take it as tinkers do ale, 'tis a plague, a mischief, a
violent purger of goods, lands, health, hellish, devilish, and damned
tobacco, the ruin and overthrow of body and soul.
                    —ROBERT BURTON, *Anatomy of Melancholy*

The believing we do something when we do nothing is the first
illusion of tobacco.    —RALPH WALDO EMERSON, *Journals*, 1859

A custom [smoking] loathsome to the eye, harmful to the brain,
dangerous to the lungs, and in the black stinking fume thereof,
nearest resembling the horrible Stygian smoke of the pit that is
bottomless.    —JAMES I OF ENGLAND, *Counterblaste to Tobacco*

A woman is only a woman, but a good cigar is a smoke.
—RUDYARD KIPLING, *The Betrothed* in
*Departmental Ditties*

What this country needs is a good five-cent cigar.
—THOMAS R. MARSHALL, remark c. 1920 to
John Crockett, chief clerk of the Senate

There's nothing like tobacco; it is the passion of all decent men;
a man who lives without tobacco does not deserve to live.
—MOLIÈRE, *Don Juan*

I have never smoked in my life and look forward to a time when
the world will look back in amazement and disgust to a practice so
unnatural and offensive.   —GEORGE BERNARD SHAW, *The New York
Herald Tribune*, April 14, 1946

**TODAY**                              See MODERN TIMES;
                                       PRESENT, THE

**TOLERANCE**                    See also FORGIVENESS & MERCY
**& UNDERSTANDING**

Live and let live.            —ANONYMOUS (SCOTTISH PROVERB)

Judge not, that ye be not judged.
[See also *Luke*, below.]                    —BIBLE, *Matthew* 7:1

Why beholdest thou the mote that is in thy brother's eye, but
considerest not the beam that is in thine own eye?        —*Ibid.*, 7:3

Judge not, and ye shall not be judged: condemn not, and ye shall
not be condemned: forgive, and ye shall be forgiven.
—BIBLE, *Luke* 6:37

He that is without sin among you, let him first cast a stone at her.
—BIBLE, *John* 8:7

There is so much good in the worst of us,
And so much bad in the best of us,
That it hardly becomes any of us
To talk about the rest of us.
—EDWARD WALLIS HOCH, *Good and Bad*

The highest result of education is tolerance.
　　　　　　　　　　　　　—HELEN KELLER, *Optimism*

No law or ordinance is mightier than understanding.
　　　　　　　　　　　　　　　—PLATO, *Laws*

*Tout comprendre rend très indulgent.*
To understand everything makes one very tolerant.
　　　　　　　　　　—MADAME DE STAËL, *Corinne*
[Commonly quoted as, *Tout comprendre, c'est tout pardonner*, "To understand everything is to forgive everything."]

**TOMORROW**　　　　　　　　　　　　See FUTURE

**TOO　MUCH**　　　　　　　　　　　See EXCESS

**TOTALITARIANISM**　　　　　　See TYRANNY &
　　　　　　　　　　　　　　　TOTALITARIANISM

**TRAGEDY**　　　　　　　　　See ARTS entries

**TRAINING**　　　　　　　　See EDUCATION &
　　　　　　　　　　　　　　　　LEARNING

**TRAVEL**　　　　　　　　　See also CITIES;
　　　　　　　　　　　　　ESCAPE; NATIONS

When I am here [Milan], I do not fast on the Sabbath; when I am at Rome, I do fast on the Sabbath.
　　　　　　　　—ST. AMBROSE, *Letters to Augustine*
[Often rephrased as, "When in Rome do as the Romans do, when elsewhere live as they live elsewhere."]

Travelling is the ruin of all happiness. There's no looking at a building here after seeing Italy.　　　—FANNY BURNEY, *Cecilia*

Travellers, like poets, are mostly an angry race.
　　　　　　—SIR RICHARD BURTON, *Narrative of a Trip to Harar*

All places are distant from heaven alike.
　　　　　　—ROBERT BURTON, *Anatomy of Melancholy*

Why do people so love to wander? I think the civilized parts of the world will suffice for me in the future.
—MARY CASSATT, letter to Louisine Havemeyer,
Feb. 11, 1911

Men travel faster now, but I do not know if they go to better things. —WILLA CATHER, *Death Comes for the Archbishop*

Travelling is almost like talking with men of other centuries.
—RENÉ DESCARTES, *Discourse on Method*

I want to travel in Europe . . . I know that I am only going to a graveyard, but it's a most precious graveyard.
—FËDOR DOSTOEVSKI, *The Brothers Karamazov*

No man should travel until he has learned the language of the country he visits. Otherwise he voluntarily makes himself a great baby,—so helpless and ridiculous.
—RALPH WALDO EMERSON, *Journals*

Travelling is a fool's paradise.
—RALPH WALDO EMERSON, *Self-Reliance*

The woods are lovely, dark and deep,
But I have promises to keep,
And miles to go before I sleep,
And miles to go before I sleep.
—ROBERT FROST, *Stopping by Woods on a Snowy Evening*

He that travels much knows much.
—THOMAS FULLER, *Gnomologia*

One of the pleasantest things in the world is going a journey; but I like to go by myself. —WILLIAM HAZLITT, *On Going a Journey*

There is nothing worse for mortals than a wandering life.
—HOMER, *The Odyssey*

Those who go overseas find a change of climate, not a change of soul. —HORACE, *Epistles*

He travels fastest who travels alone.
—RUDYARD KIPLING, *The Winners*

Ship me somewheres east of Suez, where the best is like the worst,
Where there aren't no Ten Commandments, an' a man can raise a
thirst.                                   —RUDYARD KIPLING, *Mandalay*

I love to sail forbidden seas, and land on barbarous coasts.
                              —HERMAN MELVILLE, *Moby-Dick*

Travel is the most private of pleasures. There is no greater bore
than the travel bore. We do not in the least want to hear what he
has seen in Hong Kong.
                    —VITA SACKVILLE-WEST, *Passenger to Teheran*

He who would travel happily must travel light.
              —ANTOINE DE SAINT-EXUPÉRY, *Wind, Sand, and Stars*

When I was at home, I was in a better place.
                    —SHAKESPEARE, *As You Like It*, II, iv

Foreigners can always tempt one to abandon any sensible habit.
                    —C. P. SNOW, *Strangers and Brothers*,
                              television broadcast, 1985

A man should know something of his own country, too, before
he goes abroad.        —LAURENCE STERNE, *Tristram Shandy*

I travel not to go anywhere but to go. I travel for travel's sake.
The great affair is to move.
                    —ROBERT LOUIS STEVENSON, *Travels with a Donkey*

To travel hopefully is better than to arrive.
                    —ROBERT LOUIS STEVENSON, *Virginibus Puerisque*
[More of this is given at WORK.]

Three things are weakening: fear, sin, and travel.     —TALMUD

I never travel without my diary. One should always have something sensational to read in the train.
              —OSCAR WILDE, *The Importance of Being Earnest*

**TROUBLE**                        See also DESPAIR, DEPRESSION,
                                          & MISERY; RUIN

Who except the gods can live time through forever without any
pain?                          —AESCHYLUS, *Prometheus Bound*

Many are the troubles of mankind.

—AESCHYLUS, *The Suppliant Maidens*

If anything can go wrong, it will.

—ANONYMOUS, Murphy's Law

[This appears in many versions, and has apparently a military origin.]

If fortune turns against you, even jelly breaks your tooth.

—ANONYMOUS (PERSIAN PROVERB)

You can't have more bedbugs than a blanket-full.

—ANONYMOUS (SPANISH PROVERB)

Man is born unto trouble, as the sparks fly upward.

—BIBLE, *Job* 5:7

Weeping may endure for a night, but joy cometh in the morning.

—BIBLE, *Psalms* 30:5

Take us the foxes, the little foxes, that spoil the vines: for our vines have tender grapes.     —BIBLE, *Song of Solomon* 2:15

[In her book *Little Foxes*, Harriet Beecher Stowe explained that by "little foxes" she meant "those unsuspected, unwatched, insignificant *little* causes that nibble away domestic happiness." Lillian Hellman later used this to title a play about a family quite eaten away by little foxes.]

If it be possible, let this cup pass from me.

—BIBLE, *Matthew* 26:39

Whom the Lord loveth he chasteneth.     —BIBLE, *Hebrews* 12:6

I am convinced that we have a degree of delight, and that no small one, in the real misfortunes and pains of others.

—EDMUND BURKE, *On the Sublime and Beautiful*

[The thought, horrid as it may be, has occurred to many, including Le Rochefoucauld, quoted below. The Germans call it *Schaden freude*.]

Adversity is the first path to truth.     —LORD BYRON, *Don Juan*

If there were no tribulation, there would be no rest; if there were no winter, there would be no summer.

—ST. JOHN CHRYSOSTOM, *Homilies*

A *wounded* deer—leaps highest.     —EMILY DICKINSON, poem

Suffering is the sole origin of consciousness.
　　　　　—FËDOR DOSTOEVSKI, *Notes from Underground*

Every calamity is a spur and valuable hint.
　　　　　—RALPH WALDO EMERSON, *Fate*

Everything has two handles: one by which it may be borne, another by which it cannot.　　　　　—EPICTETUS, *Enchiridion*

There is no wind that always blows a storm.　—EURIPIDES, *Alcestis*
[The classical version of the proverbial, "It's an ill wind that blows no good."]

Problems are only opportunities in work clothes.
　　　　　—HENRY J. KAISER, saying

When written in Chinese, the word *crisis* is composed of two characters. One represents danger and the other represents opportunity.　　　　　—JOHN F. KENNEDY, speech, April 12, 1959

Our problems are man-made; therefore they may be solved by man.　　　　　—JOHN F. KENNEDY, speech, June 10, 1963

If we can really understand the problem, the answer will come out of it, because the answer is not separate from the problem.
　　　　　—KRISHNAMURTI, *The Penguin Krishnamurti Reader*

In the misfortunes of our best friends, we find something that is not unpleasing.　　　　　—LA ROCHEFOUCAULD, *Maxims*
[Cf. Edmund Burke, above.]

The cares that infest the day
Shall fold their tents, like the Arabs,
And as silently steal away.
　　　　　—HENRY WADSWORTH LONGFELLOW, *The Day is Done*

Know how sublime a thing it is
To suffer and be strong.
　　　　　—HENRY WADSWORTH LONGFELLOW, *The Light of the Stars*

Into each life some rain must fall,
Some days must be dark and dreary.
　　　　　—HENRY WADSWORTH LONGFELLOW, *The Rainy Day*

If you are distressed by anything external, the pain is not due to the thing itself, but to your own estimate of it; and this you have the power to revoke at any moment.　—MARCUS AURELIUS, *Meditations*

It is not true that suffering ennobles the character; happiness does that sometimes, but suffering, for the most part, makes men petty and vindictive. —W. SOMERSET MAUGHAM,
*The Moon and Sixpence*

The world is quickly bored by the recital of misfortune, and willingly avoids the sight of distress. —*Ibid.*

Care
Sat on his faded cheek. —JOHN MILTON, *Paradise Lost*

That which does not kill me makes me stronger.
—FRIEDRICH NIETZSCHE, *Twilight of the Idols*

I never knew any man in my life who could not bear another's misfortunes perfectly like a Christian.
—ALEXANDER POPE, *Thoughts on Various Subjects*

Happiness is beneficial for the body, but it is grief that develops the powers of the mind. —PROUST, *Remembrance of Things Past: The Past Recaptured*

Fire is the test of gold, adversity of strong men.
SENECA, *On Providence*

Sweet are the uses of adversity.
—SHAKESPEARE, *As You Like It*, II, i

When sorrows come, they come not single spies,
But in battalions! —SHAKESPEARE, *Hamlet*, IV, v

One woe doth tread upon another's heel,
So fast they follow. —*Ibid.*, IV, vii

The worst is not
So long as we can say, "This is the worst."
—SHAKESPEARE, *King Lear*, IV, i

There's small choice in rotten apples.
—SHAKESPEARE, *The Taming of the Shrew*, I, i

Misery acquaints a man with strange bedfellows.
—SHAKESPEARE, *The Tempest*, II, ii

We have seen better days.
—SHAKESPEARE, *Timon of Athens*, IV, ii

Grief teaches the steadiest minds to waver. —SOPHOCLES, *Antigone*

The greatest griefs are those we cause ourselves.
                                —SOPHOCLES, *Oedipus Rex*

The worst is yet to come. —ALFRED, LORD TENNYSON, *Sea Dreams*

Pure and complete sorrow is as impossible as pure and complete
joy.                                —LEO TOLSTOY, *War and Peace*

Suffering is permanent, obscure, and dark,
And shares the nature of infinity.
                —WILLIAM WORDSWORTH, *The Borderers*

Too long a sacrifice
Can make a stone of the heart.
                —WILLIAM BUTLER YEATS, *Easter 1916*

## TRUTH                        See also HONESTY & SINCERITY

Truth brings forth hatred.        —ANONYMOUS (LATIN PROVERB)

The truth shall make you free.            —BIBLE, *John* 8:32

Pilate saith unto him, What is truth?            —*Ibid.*, 18:38

Great is truth and mighty above all things.    —BIBLE, *I Esdras* 4:41

'Tis strange—but true; for truth is always strange;
Stranger than fiction.            —LORD BYRON, *Don Juan*

Truth ever lovely—since the world began,
The foe of tyrants and the friend of man.
                —THOMAS CAMPBELL, *The Pleasures of Hope*

The aim of the superior man is truth.      —CONFUCIUS, *Analects*

The truth is always modern, and there never comes a time when
it is safe to give it voice.
                —CLARENCE DARROW, writing on Voltaire, cited
                in George Seldes, *The Great Quotations*

Nature has buried truth at the bottom of the sea.
                —DEMOCRITUS, attributed

We swallow greedily any lie that flatters us, but we sip only little by little at a truth we find bitter.
> —DENIS DIDEROT, *Le Neveu de Rameau*

I can be expected to look for truth, but not to find it.
> —DENIS DIDEROT, *Pensées philosophiques*

When you have eliminated the impossible, whatever remains, however improbable, must be the truth.
> —A. CONAN DOYLE, *The Sign of Four*

God offers to every mind its choice between truth and repose.
> —RALPH WALDO EMERSON, *Intellect*

To love the truth is to refuse to let oneself be saddened by it.
> —ANDRÉ GIDE, *Journals*

There are truths which can kill a nation. —JEAN GIRADOUX, *Electra*

Political truth is a libel—religious truth, blasphemy.
> —WILLIAM HAZLITT, *Commonplaces* in *The Round Table*

Truth is tough.    —OLIVER WENDELL HOLMES, *The Professor at the Breakfast Table*

It is the customary fate of new truths to begin as heresies and to end as superstitions.    —T. H. HUXLEY, *The Coming of Age of "The Origin of Species"*

There is not a truth existing which I fear, or would wish unknown to the whole world.    —THOMAS JEFFERSON, letter to Henry Lee, 1826

What the imagination seizes as beauty must be truth.
> —JOHN KEATS, letter to Benjamin Bailey, Nov. 22, 1817

[See Keats also under BEAUTY.]

The exact opposite of what is generally believed is often the truth.
> —LA BRUYÈRE, *Les Caractères*

Truth is often eclipsed but never extinguished.
> —LIVY, *History of Rome*

Truth, like gold, is not less so for being newly brought out of the mine.        —JOHN LOCKE, *An Essay Concerning Understanding*

To love truth is the principal part of human perfection in this world, and the seed-plot of all other virtues.
                        —JOHN LOCKE, letter to Anthony Collins,
                        Oct. 29, 1703

A great truth is a truth whose opposite is also a truth.
                        —THOMAS MANN, *Essay on Freud*

The love of truth has its reward in heaven and even on earth.
                        —FRIEDRICH NIETZSCHE, *Beyond Good and Evil*

We arrive at truth, not by reason only, but also by the heart.
                        —PASCAL, *Pensées*

Truth is the beginning of every good thing, both in heaven and on earth; and he who would be blessed and happy should be from the first a partaker of truth, for then he can be trusted.   —PLATO, *Laws*

Truth is no road to fortune.
                        —JEAN JACQUES ROUSSEAU, *The Social Contract*

Life is short, but truth works far and lives long; let us speak the truth.                 —ARTHUR SCHOPENHAUER, *The World as Will and Idea*

How dreadful knowledge of the truth can be when there's no help in truth.                 —SOPHOCLES, *Oedipus Rex*

Truth is the only safe ground to stand upon.
                        —ELIZABETH CADY STANTON, *The Woman's Bible*

Rather than love, than money, than fame, give me truth.
                        —THOREAU, *Walden*

I never give them hell. I just tell the truth, and they think it's hell.
                        —HARRY S. TRUMAN, cited in William Safire,
                        *Safire's Political Dictionary*

Truth is mighty and will prevail. There is nothing the matter with this, except that it ain't so.        —MARK TWAIN, *Notebook*

Truth confronts us, and we can no longer understand anything.
                        —PAUL VALÉRY, *Eupalinos*

Truth is rarely pure and never simple.
—OSCAR WILDE, *The Importance of Being Earnest*

Truth is on the march; nothing can stop it now.
—ÉMILE ZOLA, *J'accuse*

## TURBULENT TIMES

See also MODERN TIMES; REVOLUTION; TROUBLE

Chaos often breeds life, when order breeds habit.
—HENRY BROOKS ADAMS, *The Education of Henry Adams*

Dictators ride to and fro on tigers from which they dare not dismount. And the tigers are getting hungry.
—WINSTON CHURCHILL, *While England Slept*
[Churchill wrote that the observation, "Dictators ride tigers from which they are afraid to dismount," is a Hindustani proverb. There is a similar proverb among the Chinese: "He who rides a tiger is afraid to dismount."]

It was the best of times, it was the worst of times, it was the age of wisdom, it was the age of foolishness, it was the epoch of belief, it was the epoch of incredulity, it was the season of Light, it was the season of Darkness, it was the spring of hope, it was the winter of despair, we had everything before us, we had nothing before us, we were all going direct to Heaven, we were all going direct the other way. —CHARLES DICKENS, *A Tale of Two Cities*

The time is out of joint; O cursèd spite,
That ever I was born to set it right!
—SHAKESPEARE, *Hamlet*, I, v

So foul and fair a day I have not seen.
—SHAKESPEARE, *Macbeth*, III, iii

Lechery, lechery; still wars and lechery; nothing else holds fashion.
—SHAKESPEARE, *Troilus and Cressida*

## TWENTIETH CENTURY

See MODERN TIMES

## TYRANNY & TOTALITARIANISM

Death is preferable—it is a milder fate than tyranny.
—AESCHYLUS, *Agamemnon*

Any excuse will serve a tyrant. —Aesop, *The Wolf and the Lamb*

Dictators ride to and fro on tigers from which they dare not dismount. —Anonymous (Hindustani Proverb)
[More is given at TURBULENT TIMES, under Churchill.]

Government by a tyrant is the worst form of rule.
—St. Thomas Aquinas, *On Princely Government*

Under conditions of tyranny, it is far easier to act than to think.
—Hannah Arendt, quoted in W. H. Auden,
*A Certain World*

When a nation has allowed itself to fall under a tyrannical regime,
it cannot be absolved from the faults due to the guilt of that regime.
—Winston Churchill, speech, July 28, 1944

All men would be tyrants if they could.
—Daniel Defoe, *The History of the
Kentish Petition*, addenda

Resistance to tyrants is obedience to God.
—Thomas Jefferson, motto on his seal,
original author not known

I am the state—I alone am here the representative of the people.
—Napoleon Bonaparte, in the French Senate, 1814
[For Louis XIV's similar assertion, see HIGH POSITION: RULERS &
LEADERS.]

Big Brother is watching you. —George Orwell, *1984*

Who controls the past controls the future. Who controls the present controls the past. —*Ibid.*

Tyranny is always better organized than freedom.
—Charles Péguy, *War and Peace* in *Basic Virtues*

Necessity is the plea for every infringement of human freedom. It
is the argument of tyrants; it is the creed of slaves.
—William Pitt, speech, Nov. 18, 1783

The face of tyranny is always mild at first. —Racine, *Britannicus*

Man was born free, and everywhere he is in chains.
—Jean Jacques Rousseau, *The Social Contract*

Why, man, he doth bestride the narrow world like a Colossus.
—SHAKESPEARE, *Julius Caesar*, I, ii

They squeeze the orange and throw away the peel.
—VOLTAIRE, describing his experience
in the court of Frederick the Great,
letter to Mme. Denis, Sept. 9, 1751

The despot, be assured, lives night and day like one condemned to
death by the whole of mankind for his wickedness.
—XENOPHON, *Hiero*

UNDERSTANDING                   See MIND, THOUGHT, &
                                 UNDERSTANDING; TOLERANCE
                                 & UNDERSTANDING; VISION &
                                 VISIONARIES; WISDOM

UNHAPPINESS                      See DESPAIR, DEPRESSION, MISERY;
                                 HAPPINESS; TROUBLE

UNITED STATES                    See AMERICA & AMERICANS;
                                 AMERICAN HISTORY:
                                 MEMORABLE MOMENTS

UNITY & LOYALTY

United we stand, divided we fall.
—AESOP, *The Four Oxen and the Lion*
[For Benjamin Franklin's similar observation on hanging together,
see AMERICAN HISTORY: MEMORABLE MOMENTS.]

Union gives strength.            —AESOP, *The Bundle of Sticks*

Whose bread I eat, his song I sing.
—ANONYMOUS, German saying

No man can serve two masters.            —BIBLE, *Matthew* 6:24

He that is not with me is against me.    —*Ibid.* [also *Luke* 11:23]

I have kept the faith.                   —BIBLE, *II Timothy* 4:7
[The full verse is given at ACCOMPLISHMENT.]

If a house be divided against itself, that house cannot stand.
—BIBLE, *Mark* 3:25

When bad men combine, the good must associate; else they will
fall, one by one, an unpitied sacrifice in a contemptible struggle.
—EDMUND BURKE, *Thoughts on the Cause of
the Present Discontents*

All for one, one for all.
—ALEXANDRE DUMAS, *The Three Musketeers*

Something there is that doesn't love a wall.
—ROBERT FROST, *Mending Wall*

There are only two forces that unite men—fear and interest.
—NAPOLEON BONAPARTE, *Maxims*

He may be a son of a bitch, but he's our son of a bitch.
—FRANKLIN D. ROOSEVELT, referring to
Anastasio Somoza of Nicaragua,
cited by William Pfaff in
*The New Yorker*, May 27, 1985

**UNIVERSE**                    See also CREATION, DIVINE; NATURE;
SCIENCE: PHYSICS & COSMOLOGY;
WORLD, END OF

The universe . . . is a machine for making deities.
—HENRI BERGSON, *Les deux sources de la
morale et de la religion*

I don't pretend to understand the universe—it's a great deal bigger
than I am. . . . People ought to be modester.
—THOMAS CARLYLE, quoted in D. A. Wilson and
D. Wilson McArthur, *Carlyle in Old Age*

Law rules throughout existence, a Law which is not intelligent,
but Intelligence.         —RALPH WALDO EMERSON, *Fate*

Ah Love! Could thou and I with Fate conspire
To grasp this sorry Scheme of Things entire,
Would we not shatter it to bits—and then remold it nearer to the
Heart's Desire!         —EDWARD FITZGERALD, *The Rubáiyát of
Omar Khayyám*

The universe begins to look more like a great thought than like a
great machine.         —SIR JAMES JEANS, *The Mysterious Universe*

All are but parts of one stupendous whole,
Whose body nature is, and God the soul.
— ALEXANDER POPE, *An Essay on Man*

The universe is a spiraling Big Band in a polka-dotted speakeasy,
effusively generating new light every one-night stand.
— ISHMAEL REED, cited in Jim Haskins,
*The Cotton Club*

Don't let me catch anyone talking about the Universe in my de-
partment.   — LORD ERNEST RUTHERFORD, quoted by John Kendrew,
BBC broadcast, July 3, 1968

Let the great world spin forever down the ringing grooves of
change.        — ALFRED, LORD TENNYSON, *Locksley Hall*

Thou canst not stir a flower
Without the troubling of a star.
— FRANCIS THOMPSON, *The Mistress of Vision*

O amazement of things—even the least particle!
— WALT WHITMAN, *Song at Sunset*

**UNREASONABLE PEOPLE**        See REASONABLE &
UNREASONABLE PEOPLE

**VALUE**

Neither cast ye your pearls before swine, lest they trample them
under their feet, and turn again and rend you. — BIBLE, *Matthew* 7:6
[T. H. White, in *The Bestiary*, notes that "pearls," written in Latin
*margarites*, may be a mistranslation of the Latin *marguerites*, which
means "flowers."]

Things are only worth what you make them worth.
— MOLIÈRE, *Les Précieuses ridicules*

Good merchandise, even when hidden, soon finds buyers.
— PLAUTUS, *Poenulus*

[A cynic:] a man who knows the price of everything and the value
of nothing.        — OSCAR WILDE, *Lady Windermere's Fan*

**VANITY**                                    See PRIDE & VANITY

**VARIETY**                                    See also CHANGE;
                                                    NEW THINGS

Variety's the very spice of life,
That gives it all its flavor.          —WILLIAM COWPER, *The Task*

What is food to one is to another bitter poison.
                              —LUCRETIUS, *De Rerum Natura*
[This is an early version of the English proverb, "One man's meat is
another man's poison."]

Letting a hundred flowers blossom and a hundred schools of
thought contend is the policy.
                        —MAO TSE-TUNG, speech, May 2, 1956
[Usually shortened to, "Let a hundred flowers blossom."]

No pleasure lasts long unless there is variety in it.
                              —PUBLILIUS SYRUS, *Moral Sayings*

It were not best that we should all think alike; it is difference of
opinion that makes horse races.              —MARK TWAIN,
                                              *Pudd'nhead Wilson*

**VENGEANCE**                                    See REVENGE

**VICE**                                    See EVIL; EXCESS; SIN,
                                              VICE, & NAUGHTINESS

**VIOLENCE & FORCE**                        See also ANGER;
                                              REVOLUTION; WAR

They have sown the wind, and they shall reap the whirlwind.
                                    —BIBLE, *Hosea* 8:7

All they that take the sword shall perish with the sword.
                                    —BIBLE, *Matthew* 26:52
[But see also *Matthew* at REVOLUTION.]

A whiff of grapeshot.
          —THOMAS CARLYLE, *History of the French Revolution*

God hates violence. He has ordained that all men fairly possess their property, not seize it. —EURIPIDES, *Helen*

It is better to be violent, if there is violence in our hearts, than to put on the cloak of non-violence to cover impotence.
—MOHANDAS GANDHI, *Non-Violence* in *Peace and War*

Where wisdom is called for, force is of little use.
—HERODOTUS, *Histories*

Force without wisdom falls of its own weight.    —HORACE, *Odes*

Force cannot give right.
—THOMAS JEFFERSON, *The Rights of British America*

It is far more convenient to commit an act of violence, and afterwards excuse it, than laboriously to consider convincing arguments, and lose time listening to objections. This very boldness itself indicates a sort of conviction of the legitimacy of the action, and the God of success is afterwards the best advocate.
—IMMANUEL KANT, *Perpetual Peace*, appendix

Be peaceful, be courteous, obey the law, respect everyone; but if someone puts his hand on you, send him to the cemetery.
—MALCOLM X, *Malcolm X Speaks*

In violence, we forget who we are.
—MARY McCARTHY, *On the Contrary*

Who overcomes
By force, hath overcome but half his foe.
—JOHN MILTON, *Paradise Lost*

If aggressors are wrong above, they are right here below.
—NAPOLEON BONAPARTE, *Maxims*

Violence is good for those who have nothing to lose.
—JEAN-PAUL SARTRE, *Le Diable et le bon Dieu*

Uncontrolled violence is a fault of youth.    —SENECA, *Troades*

Lay on, Macduff,
And damn'd be him that first cries "Hold, enough!"
—SHAKESPEARE, *Macbeth*, V, viii

Not believing in force is the same as not believing in gravity.
—LEON TROTSKY, *What Next?*


**VIRGIN MARY**                                      See JESUS CHRIST

**VIRTUE**                                    See also COURAGE; GRACE;
HONESTY & SINCERITY; INNOCENCE;
SELF-RIGHTEOUSNESS; STRENGTH; WISDOM


Virtue is not always amiable.   —JOHN ADAMS, *Diary*, Feb. 9, 1779

The happiness of man, as well as his dignity, consists in virtue.
—JOHN ADAMS, *Thoughts on Government*

No act of kindness, no matter how small, is ever wasted.
—AESOP, *The Lion and the Mouse*

Kindness effects more than severity.
—AESOP, *The Wind and the Sun*

Righteousness exalteth a nation.        —BIBLE, *Proverbs* 14:34

What doth the Lord require of thee, but to do justly, and to love
mercy, and to walk humbly with thy God?      —BIBLE, *Micah* 6:8

Blessed are the poor in spirit: for theirs is the kingdom of heaven.
Blessed are they that mourn: for they shall be comforted.
Blessed are the meek: for they shall inherit the earth.
Blessed are they which do hunger and thirst after righteousness:
for they shall be filled.
Blessed are the merciful: for they shall obtain mercy.
Blessed are the pure in heart: for they shall see God.
Blessed are the peacemakers: for they shall be called the children
of God.
Blessed are they which are persecuted for righteousness sake: for
theirs is the kingdom of heaven.        —BIBLE, *Matthew* 5:3–10,
The Sermon on the Mount


Strait is the gate, and narrow is the way, which leadeth unto life,
and few there be that find it.                    —*Ibid.*, 7:14

If thine eye offend thee, pluck it out, and cast it from thee: it is
better for thee to enter into life with one eye, rather than having
two eyes to be cast into hell fire.              —*Ibid.*, 18:9

Unto the pure, all things are pure.     —BIBLE, *Titus* 1:15

The souls of the righteous are in the hand of God, and there shall no torment touch them.     —BIBLE, *Wisdom of Solomon* 3:1

There is no road or ready way to virtue.
    —THOMAS BROWNE, *Religio Medici*

The humblest citizen of all the land, when clad in the armor of a righteous cause, is stronger than all the hosts of error.
    —WILLIAM JENNINGS BRYAN, speech at the
    Democratic National Convention, 1896

The upright, honest-hearted man
Who strives to do the best he can,
Need never fear the church's ban
Or hell's damnation.
    —ROBERT BURNS, *Epistle to the Rev. John McMath*

In my experience, good deeds usually do not go unpunished.
    —WILLIAM SLOANE COFFIN, speech, Oct. 1984,
    in behalf of the Sanctuary Program
    for protecting refugees
[This bit of sharp cynicism seems to have been around a while in various forms. Clare Boothe Luce was credited by H. Farber, in *The Book of Laws*, with the even harsher, "No good deed goes unpunished."]

It is a far, far better thing that I do, than I have ever done; it is a far, far better rest that I go to, than I have ever known.
    —CHARLES DICKENS, *A Tale of Two Cities*

The essence of greatness is the perception that virtue is enough.
    —RALPH WALDO EMERSON, *Heroism*
[But for Emerson's view of people who *talk* about their integrity, see SELF-RIGHTEOUSNESS.]

Life is mostly froth and bubble,
Two things stand like stone,
Kindness in another's trouble,
Courage in your own.
    —ADAM LINDSAY GORDON, *Ye Wearie Wayfarer*

I shall pass through this world but once. If therefore there be any kindness I can show, or any good thing I can do, let me do it now; let me not defer it or neglect it.     —ÉTIENNE DE GRELLET, attributed
[Also attributed to others.]

Be good, sweet maid, and let who will be clever;
Do noble things, not dream them, all day long.
—CHARLES KINGSLEY, *A Farewell*

If you can keep your head when all about you
Are losing theirs and blaming it on you.
If you can trust yourself when all men doubt you
And make allowance for their doubting, too.
—RUDYARD KIPLING, *If*
[In *Please Don't Eat the Daisies*, Jean Kerr observed, "If you can keep your head when all about you are losing theirs, it is just possible that you haven't grasped the situation."]

If you can meet with Triumph and Disaster, and treat those two
impostors just the same.                                    —*Ibid.*

If you can talk with crowds and keep your virtue
Or walk with Kings—nor lose the common touch.            —*Ibid.*

If you can fill the unforgiving minute
With sixty seconds' worth of distance run,
Yours is the earth and everything that's in it,
And—which is more—you'll be a Man, my son!               —*Ibid.*

Very often our virtues are only vices in disguise.
—LA ROCHEFOUCAULD, *Maxims*

Virtue would not go to such lengths if vanity did not keep her
company.                                                    —*Ibid.*

Virtue is harder to be got than knowledge of the world; and, if
lost in a young man, is seldom recovered.
—JOHN LOCKE, *Some Thoughts
Concerning Education*

I could not love thee, dear, so much,
Loved I not honor more.          —RICHARD LOVELACE, *To Lucasta,
Going to the Wars*

I cannot praise a fugitive and cloistered virtue, unexercised and
unbreathed, that never sallies out and sees her adversary, but slinks
out of the race, where that immortal garland is to be run for, not
without dust and heat.          —JOHN MILTON, *Aeropagitica*

Virtue may be assailed, but never hurt,
Surprised by unjust force, but not enthralled.
—JOHN MILTON, *Comus*

I prefer an accommodating vice to an obstinate virtue.
—MOLIÈRE, *Amphitryon*

Virtue in this world should be malleable.
—MOLIÈRE, *Le Misanthrope*

There may be guilt when there is too much virtue.
—PASCAL, *Pensées*

Do good by stealth, and blush to find it fame.
—ALEXANDER POPE, *Epilogue to the Satires*

Charms strike the sight, but merit wins the soul.
—ALEXANDER POPE, *The Rape of the Lock*

When men grow virtuous in their old age, they only make a sacrifice to God of the devil's leavings.
—ALEXANDER POPE, *Thoughts on Various Subjects*

Nature does not bestow virtue, it is an art.
—SENECA, *Letters to Lucilius*

Assume a virtue, if you have it not.
—SHAKESPEARE, *Hamlet*, III, iv

Virtue is bold, and goodness never fearful.
—SHAKESPEARE, *Measure for Measure*, III, i

How far that little candle throws his beams!
So shines a good deed in a naughty world.
—SHAKESPEARE, *The Merchant of Venice*, V, i

Mine honor is my life.        —SHAKESPEARE, *Richard II*, I, i

He lives in fame that died in virtue's cause.
—SHAKESPEARE, *Titus Andronicus*, I, i

He profits most who serves best.
—A. F. SHELDON, motto for International Rotary

Nothing can harm a good man, either in life or after death.
—SOCRATES, quoted in Plato, *Apology*

True virtue is life under the direction of reason.
—BENEDICT SPINOZA, *Ethics*

She would rather light candles than curse the darkness, and her glow has warmed the world.
                                    —ADLAI STEVENSON, said of Eleanor Roosevelt
                                                after her death, 1962
[Cf. the Christopher Society motto, under DOING.]

My strength is as the strength of ten,
Because my heart is pure.
                                    —ALFRED, LORD TENNYSON, *Sir Galahad*

'Tis only noble to be good.
Kind hearts are more than coronets.
                                    —ALFRED, LORD TENNYSON, *Lady Clara Vere de Vere*

Few things are harder to put up with than the annoyance of a good example.                    —MARK TWAIN, *Pudd'nhead Wilson*

Always do right. This will gratify some people and astonish the rest.                    —MARK TWAIN, speech, Greenpoint Presbyterian
                                            Church, Brooklyn, N.Y., 1901

Virtue, study, and gaiety are three sisters who should not be separated.                    —VOLTAIRE, letter to Frederick the Great, 1737

That best portion of a good man's life,
His little, nameless, unremembered acts
Of kindness and of love.
                                    —WILLIAM WORDSWORTH, *Tintern Abbey*

## VISIONS & VISIONARIES          See also IDEAS & IDEALS;
                                                MYSTICISM; WISDOM

We are like dwarves upon the shoulders of giants, and so able to see more and farther than the ancients.
                                    —BERNARD OF CHARTRES, quoted in
                                        John of Salisbury, *Metalogicon*
[For Newton's version, see SCIENCE. Robert K. Merton, in his entertaining book on this aphorism, offered many examples of variations. A late one is from Coleridge: "The dwarf sees farther than the giant, when he has the giant's shoulder to mount on" (*The Friend*).]

Behold, this dreamer cometh.                    —BIBLE, *Genesis* 37:19

Where there is no vision, the people perish.
                                    —BIBLE, *Proverbs* 29:18

Your sons and your daughters shall prophesy, your old men shall dream dreams, your young men shall see visions.   —BIBLE, *Joel* 2:28

A prophet is not without honor, save in his own country.
—BIBLE, *Matthew* 13:57
[For Matthew on false prophets, see under HYPOCRISY.]

If the blind lead the blind, both shall fall into the ditch.
—*Ibid.*, 15:14

For now we see through a glass, darkly; but then face to face: now I know in part; but then I shall know even as I am known.
—BIBLE, *I Corinthians* 13:11–12

A fool sees not the same tree that a wise man sees.
—WILLIAM BLAKE, *The Marriage of Heaven and Hell*

It isn't that they can't see the solution. It is that they can't see the problem.        —G. K. CHESTERTON, *The Point of a Pin* in
*The Scandal of Father Brown*

People see only what they are prepared to see.
—RALPH WALDO EMERSON, *Journals*, 1863

A danger foreseen is half avoided.
—THOMAS FULLER, *Gnomologia*

Only he who keeps his eye fixed on the far horizon will find his right road.        —DAG HAMMARSKJÖLD, *Markings*

A moment's insight is sometimes worth a life's experience.
—OLIVER WENDELL HOLMES, *The Professor at
the Breakfast Table*

You can only predict things after they've happened.
—EUGÈNE IONESCO, *Rhinoceros*

I have a dream.
—MARTIN LUTHER KING, JR., theme of his speech in
the March on Washington, August 28, 1963

Two men look out through the same bars:
One sees the mud, and one the stars.
—FREDERICK LANGBRIDGE, *Cluster of Quiet Thoughts*

All armed prophets have been victorious, and all unarmed prophets have been destroyed.                    —MACHIAVELLI, *The Prince*

The fellow that can only see a week ahead is always the popular fellow, for he is looking with the crowd. But the one that can see years ahead, he has a telescope but he can't make anybody believe that he has it.   —WILL ROGERS, *The Autobiography of Will Rogers*

Vision is the art of seeing things invisible.
                    —JONATHAN SWIFT, *Thoughts on Various Subjects*

A dreamer is one who can only find his way by moonlight, and his punishment is that he sees the dawn before the rest of the world.
                    —OSCAR WILDE, *The Critic as Artist*


**W A R**                    See also MILITARY, THE; MILITARY BATTLES;
                    PEACE; VIOLENCE & FORCE;
                    WINNING & LOSING, VICTORY & DEFEAT


What Price Glory?        —MAXWELL ANDERSON, title of his play
                    about World War I.

To win a war quickly takes long preparation.
                    —ANONYMOUS (LATIN PROVERB)

The price of pride is high, and paid by the young.
                    —ANONYMOUS, inscription on the
                    German memorial at El Alamein

A bayonet is a weapon with a worker at both ends.
                    —ANONYMOUS, British pacifist slogan

It takes twenty years or more of peace to make a man; it takes only twenty seconds of war to destroy him.
                    —KING BAUDOUIN I, of Belgium, speech in the
                    U.S. Congress, May 12, 1959

It is not merely cruelty that leads men to love war, it is excitement.
                    —HENRY WARD BEECHER, *Proverbs from
                    Plymouth Pulpit*

War is like love, it always finds a way.
                    —BERTOLT BRECHT, *Mother Courage*

God is ordinarily for the big battalions against the little ones.
—COUNT BUSSY-RABUTIN, letter to the
Count of Limoges, Oct. 18, 1677
[A thought also voiced by Voltaire, Napoleon, and others.]

In war, whichever side may call itself the victor, there are no winners, but all are losers.
—NEVILLE CHAMBERLAIN, speech, July 3, 1938

The sinews of war, unlimited money.     —CICERO, *Philippic*, V

Laws are silent in time of war.     —CICERO, *Pro Milone*

All great civilizations, in their early stages, are based on success in war.     —SIR KENNETH CLARK, *Civilization: An Essay*

War is nothing more than the continuation of politics by other means.     —KARL VON CLAUSEWITZ, *On War*

There is nothing that war has ever achieved that we could not better achieve without it.
—HAVELOCK ELLIS, *The Philosophy of Conflict*

War educates the senses, calls into action the will, perfects the physical constitution, brings men into such swift and close collision in critical moments that man measures man.
—RALPH WALDO EMERSON, *War*

Men love war because it allows them to look serious. Because it is the one thing that stops women laughing at them.
—JOHN FOWLES, *The Magus*

There never was a good war or a bad peace.
—BENJAMIN FRANKLIN, letter to Josiah Quincy,
Sept. 11, 1773

Either man is obsolete or war is.
—R. BUCKMINSTER FULLER, *I Seem To be a Verb*

Guns will make us powerful; butter will only make us fat.
—HERMANN GOERING, radio speech, 1936

War is death's feast.     —GEORGE HERBERT, *Outlandish Proverbs*

In starting and waging a war, it is not right that matters but victory.　　　　　—ADOLF HITLER, quoted in William L. Shirer,
*The Rise and Fall of the Third Reich*

Older men declare war. But it is the youth that must fight and die.
　　　　　—HERBERT HOOVER, speech,
Republican National Convention

The first casualty when war comes is truth.
　　　　　—SEN. HIRAM JOHNSON, attributed

The slaying of multitudes should be mourned with sorrow. A victory should be celebrated with the funeral rite.
　　　　　—LAO-TZU, *Tao Te Ching*

War is the greatest plague that can afflict humanity; it destroys religion, it destroys states, it destroys families. Any scourge is preferable to it.　　　　　—MARTIN LUTHER, *Table-Talk*

It is fatal to enter any war without the will to win it.
　　　　　—GEN. DOUGLAS MACAUTHUR, speech,
Republican National Convention, 1952

War is just when it is necessary; arms are permissible when there is no hope except in arms.　　　　　—MACHIAVELLI, *The Prince*

To the ashes of the dead, glory comes too late.
　　　　　—MARTIAL, *Epigrams*

War will never cease until babies begin to come into the world with larger cerebrums and smaller adrenal glands.
　　　　　—H. L. MENCKEN, *Minority Report* in *Notebooks*

For what can war, but endless war still breed?
　　　　　—JOHN MILTON, *To Fairfax*

There will be no veterans of World War III.
　　　　　—WALTER MONDALE, speech, Sept. 5, 1984

An empire founded by war has to maintain itself by war.
　　　　　—MONTESQUIEU, *Considérations sur les causes de la grandeur des Romains et de leur décadence*

Against war it may be said that it makes the victor stupid and the vanquished revengeful.
　　　　　—FRIEDRICH NIETZSCHE, *Human, All Too Human*

He who is the author of a war lets loose the whole contagion of hell and opens a vein that bleeds a nation to death.
—THOMAS PAINE, *The American Crisis*

No one won the last war, and no one will win the next.
—ELEANOR ROOSEVELT, letter to Harry S. Truman, Nov. 5, 1948

War is not an adventure. It is a disease.
—ANTOINE DE SAINT-EXUPÉRY, *Flight to Arras*

Sometime they'll give a war and nobody will come.
—CARL SANDBURG, *The People, Yes*

When the rich wage war, it is the poor who die.
—JEAN-PAUL SARTRE, *Le Diable et le bon Dieu*

We ask the outcome of a war, not the cause.
—SENECA, *Hercules Furens*

O war, thou son of hell!   —SHAKESPEARE, *Henry VI, Part II*, V, ii

Cry "Havoc!" and let slip the dogs of war.
—SHAKESPEARE, *Julius Caesar*, III, i

War is hell.
—WILLIAM TECUMSEH SHERMAN, attributed, graduation speech at the Michigan Military Academy, 1879
[Better known but less well documented than the statement at Columbus, below.]

There is many a boy here today who looks on war as all glory, but, boys, it is all hell.   —WILLIAM TECUMSEH SHERMAN, speech, Columbus, Ohio, 1880

War is cruelty, and you cannot refine it.
—WILLIAM TECUMSEH SHERMAN, letter to James M. Calhoun, Sept. 12, 1864

War is much too serious a thing to be left to military men.
—CHARLES-MAURICE DE TALLEYRAND, attributed
[Also attributed to Clemenceau.]

War is a matter not so much of arms as of expenditure, through which arms may be made of service.        —THUCYDIDES, *Historia*

War is the unfolding of miscalculations.
—BARBARA TUCHMAN, *The Guns of August*

**WASHINGTON, D.C.** See CITIES

**WEALTH** See HAVES & HAVE-NOTS;
MONEY

**WEATHER** See NATURE:
WIND & WEATHER

**WICKEDNESS** See EVIL; SIN,
VICE, & NAUGHTINESS

**WIND** See NATURE:
WIND & WEATHER

**WINE** See ALCOHOL & DRINKING;
FOOD, WINE, & EATING

**WINNING & LOSING,** See also GAMES; MILITARY BATTLES;
**VICTORY & DEFEAT** RUIN; SPORTS; SUCCESS & FAME; WAR

The laugh is always on the loser.
—ANONYMOUS (GERMAN PROVERB)

'Tis better to have loved and lost than never to have lost at all.
—SAMUEL BUTLER, *The Way of All Flesh*

Victory at all costs, victory in spite of all terror, victory however long and hard the road may be; for without victory, there is no survival. —WINSTON CHURCHILL, speech, May 13, 1940

The problems of victory are more agreeable than those of defeat, but they are no less difficult.
—WINSTON CHURCHILL, speech, Nov. 11, 1942

Victory is by nature insolent and haughty.
—CICERO, *Pro Marcello*

The race is to the swift;
The battle to the strong. —JOHN DAVIDSON, *War Song*
[For a concurring opinion, see Damon Runyon, under SPORTS; for the opposing Biblical view, see LUCK.]

Nice guys finish last. —LEO DUROCHER, attributed

All is lost save honor.                    —FRANCIS I, letter referring to his
                                           defeat at Pavia, 1525


All victories breed hate.
                —BALTASAR GRACIÁN, *The Art of Worldly Wisdom*


If you think you can win, you can win. Faith is necessary to
victory.          —WILLIAM HAZLITT, *On Great and Little Things*


Lose as if you like it; win as if you were used to it.
                           —TOMMY HITCHCOCK, saying, passed on by
                              his father, Jonas Hitchcock
[Tommy Hitchcock's sport was polo.]


Victory often changes her side.                    —HOMER, *Iliad*


Victory has a thousand fathers, but defeat is an orphan.
                                    —JOHN F. KENNEDY, saying
[In his *Political Dictionary*, William Safire points out that this expression, in various forms, was current prior to Kennedy's use of it.]


[I feel] somewhat like the boy in Kentucky who stubbed his toe
while running to see his sweetheart. The boy said he was too big to
cry, and far too badly hurt to laugh.
                              —ABRAHAM LINCOLN, reply when asked
                                 how he felt about the Democrats winning
                                 the N.Y. State elections, quoted in
                                 *Leslie's Illustrated Weekly*, Nov. 22, 1862
[Adlai Stevenson, crediting Lincoln, used this same anecdote to
illustrate his feelings after his loss in the presidential election of 1952.]


Winning isn't everything, it's the only thing.
                              —VINCENT LOMBARDI, attributed
[The great coach of the Green Bay Packers may actually not ever
have used these exact words, but they are universally attributed to
him.]


Victory puts us on a level with heaven.
                              —LUCRETIUS, *De Rerum Natura*


There are defeats more triumphant than victories.
                              —MONTAIGNE, *Essays*
[On this subject, see King Pyrrhus at MILITARY BATTLES.]


The loser is always suspicious.   —PUBLILIUS SYRUS, *Moral Sayings*

For when the One Great Scorer comes
To mark against your name,
He writes—not that you won or lost—
But how you played the game.
                              —GRANTLAND RICE, *Alumnus Football*

Show me a good and gracious loser, and I'll show you a failure.
                              —KNUTE ROCKNE, attributed
[According to *Bartlett*, he made this remark to Wisconsin basketball
coach Walter Meanwell.]

Once you hear the details of a victory, it is hard to distinguish it
from a defeat.     —JEAN-PAUL SARTRE, *Le Diable et le bon Dieu*


**WINTER**                              See NATURE: SEASONS


**WISDOM**                  See also MIND, THOUGHT, & UNDERSTANDING;
                            PHILOSOPHY; PRUDENCE & PRACTICAL
                            WISDOM; VISION & VISIONARIES

The hours of a wise man are lengthened by his ideas.
                    —JOSEPH ADDISON, *The Spectator*, June 18, 1711

Wisdom comes only through suffering.
                              —AESCHYLUS, *Agamemnon*

Wonder is the beginning of wisdom.
                              —ANONYMOUS (GREEK PROVERB)

The fox knows many things, but the hedgehog knows one great
thing.                        —ARCHILOCHUS, fragment

The great good is wisdom.      —ST. AUGUSTINE, *Soliloquies*

The price of wisdom is above rubies.      —BIBLE, *Job* 28:18

The fear of the Lord is the beginning of wisdom.
                              —BIBLE, *Psalms* 11:10
[Slightly different is *Proverbs* 1:7, "The fear of the Lord is the
beginning of knowledge."]

Happy is the man that findeth wisdom, and the man that getteth
understanding.                —BIBLE, *Proverbs* 3:13

In much wisdom is much grief: and he that increaseth knowledge, increaseth sorrow. —BIBLE, *Ecclesiastes* 1:18

The children of this world are in their generation wiser than the children of light. —BIBLE, *Luke* 16:8

Be wiser than other people if you can, but do not tell them so.
—EARL OF CHESTERFIELD, letter to his son, Nov. 19, 1745

The function of wisdom is discriminating between good and evil.
—CICERO, *De Officiis*

A sadder and a wiser man
He rose the morrow morn.
—SAMUEL TAYLOR COLERIDGE, *The Ancient Mariner*

Errors, like straws, upon the surface flow;
He who would search for pearls must dive below.
—JOHN DRYDEN, *All for Love*, prologue

Those who are held wise among men, and who search for the reason of things, are those who bring the most sorrow on themselves. —EURIPIDES, *Medea*

How prone to doubt, how cautious are the wise!
—HOMER, *Odyssey*

Wisdom denotes the pursuing of the best ends by the best means.
—FRANCIS HUTCHESON, *Inquiry into the
Original of our Ideas of Beauty and Virtue*

The world is full of people who are not wise enough.
—LA FONTAINE, *Fables*

The Way of the sage is to act but not to compete.
—LAO-TZU, *Tao Te Ching*

To know
That which lies before us in daily life,
Is the prime wisdom. —JOHN MILTON, *Paradise Lost*

Pure reason avoids extremes, and requires one to be wise in moderation. —MOLIÈRE, *Le Misanthrope*

The growth of wisdom may be gauged exactly by the diminution of ill-temper.　　　　　—FRIEDRICH NIETZSCHE,
*The Wanderer and His Shadow*

Wisdom sends us back to our childhood.　　—PASCAL, *Pensées*

No one is wise at all times.　　—PLINY THE ELDER, *Natural History*
[Emerson said it too: "Wise men are not wise at all times" (*Wealth*).]

Nine-tenths of wisdom consists in being wise in time.
　　　　　—THEODORE ROOSEVELT, speech, June 14, 1917

Wisdom comes by disillusionment.
　　　　　—GEORGE SANTAYANA, *Reason in Common Sense*

The wise want love; and those who love want wisdom.
　　　　　—PERCY BYSSHE SHELLEY, *Prometheus Unbound*

Wisdom outweighs any wealth.　　　　—SOPHOCLES, *Antigone*

Knowledge comes, but wisdom lingers.
　　　　　—ALFRED, LORD TENNYSON, *Locksley Hall*

It is a characteristic of wisdom not to do desperate things.
　　　　　—THOREAU, *Walden*

The highest wisdom has but one science—the science of the whole—the science explaining the whole creation and man's place in it.　　　　　—LEO TOLSTOY, *War and Peace*

He who is only wise lives a sad life.
　　　　　—VOLTAIRE, letter to Frederick the Great, 1740

Wisdom is ofttimes nearer when we stoop
Than when we soar.　　—WILLIAM WORDSWORTH, *The Excursion*

Be wise with speed;
A fool at forty is a fool indeed.　　—EDWARD YOUNG, *Love of Fame*

**WIT**　　　　　　　　See ARTS: STYLE IN WRITING &
　　　　　　　　　　　EXPRESSION; HUMOR

**WITCHES**　　　　　　　See OCCULT, THE

**WOMEN**

See also HOME; LOVE; MARRIAGE; WOMEN, BEAUTIFUL & HOMELY; WOMEN & MEN

A whistling girl and a crowing hen never came to a good end.
—ANONYMOUS (IRISH AMERICAN PROVERB)
[Courtesy of the great-grandmother of one of the authors, who hoped with this aphorism to discourage tomboy tendencies in young ladies.]

Join the union, girls, and together say, "Equal Pay for Equal Work!"
—SUSAN B. ANTHONY, in *The Revolution*, March 18, 1869

Women must not depend upon the protection of man, but must be taught to protect herself.
—SUSAN B. ANTHONY, speech, July 1871

With women, the heart argues, not the mind.
—MATTHEW ARNOLD, *Merope*

One is not born a woman, one becomes one.
—SIMONE DE BEAUVOIR, *The Second Sex*

Alas! the love of women! it is known
To be a lovely and a fearful thing.
—LORD BYRON, *Don Juan*

Women never have young minds. They are born three thousand years old.
—SHELAGH DELANEY, *A Taste of Honey*

If I were asked . . . to what the singular prosperity and growing strength of that people [Americans] ought mainly to be attributed, I should reply: to the superiority of their women.
—ALEXIS DE TOCQUEVILLE, *Democracy in America*

A woman's hopes are woven of sunbeams; a shadow annihilates them.
—GEORGE ELIOT, *Felix Holt*

The happiest women, like the happiest nations, have no history.
—GEORGE ELIOT, *The Mill on the Floss*

A sufficient measure of civilization is the influence of good women.
—RALPH WALDO EMERSON, *Civilization*

A woman should always challenge our respect, and never move our compassion.
—RALPH WALDO EMERSON, *Journals*, 1836

Woman is woman's natural ally.                —EURIPIDES, *Alope*

Love's all in all to women.                —EURIPIDES, *Andromache*

Women are but women—tears are their portion.
                                        —EURIPIDES, *Medea*

The great . . . question is, "What does a woman want?"
                        —FREUD, quoted in Charles Rolo,
                        *Psychiatry in American Life*

As men become aware that few have had a fair chance, they are inclined to say that no women have had a fair chance.
        —MARGARET FULLER, *Woman in the Nineteenth Century*

I have been a woman for fifty years, and I've never been able to discover precisely what it is I am.
                —JEAN GIRADOUX, *Tiger at the Gates*

The eternal female draws us onward.        —GOETHE, *Faust*

So few grown women like their lives.
                —KATHERINE GRAHAM, quoted by
                Jane Howard, *Ms.*, Oct. 1974

Women never reason, and therefore they are (comparatively) seldom wrong.        —WILLIAM HAZLITT, *Characteristics*

HELMER: First and foremost, you are a wife and mother.
NORA: That I don't believe any more. I believe that first and foremost, I am an individual, just as much as you are.
                —HENRIK IBSEN, *A Doll's House*

There is in every true woman's heart, a spark of heavenly fire, which lies dormant in the broad daylight of prosperity, but which kindles up and beams and blazes in the dark hour of adversity.
                —WASHINGTON IRVING, *The Wife* in
                *The Sketch Book of Geoffrey Crayon, Gent*

The female of the species is more deadly than the male.
                —RUDYARD KIPLING, *The Female of the Species*

For the Colonel's lady an' Judy O'Grady
Are sisters under their skins!        —RUDYARD KIPLING, *The Ladies*

Women run to extremes; they are either better or worse than men.
—La Bruyère, *Les Caractères*

A woman's best protection is a little money of her own.
—Clare Boothe Luce, attributed

Can we today measure devotion to husband and children by our indifference to everything else? —Golda Meir, *The Plough Woman*

There is nothing worse than a woman—even a good woman!
—Menander, fragment
[This pretty well sums up the great majority of established quotes on women, most of which we did not feel compelled to include. For an observation on this hostility, see Germaine Greer in WOMEN & MEN.]

Women have simple tastes. They can get pleasure out of the conversation of children in arms and men in love.
—H. L. Mencken, *Sententiae* in
*A Book of Burlesques*

When women kiss, it always reminds me of prizefighters shaking hands.
—*Ibid.*

Many women do not recognize themselves as discriminated against; no better proof could be found of the totality of their conditioning.
—Kate Millett, *Sexual Politics*

O fairest of creation! last and best
Of all God's works.　　　　　—John Milton, *Paradise Lost*

Women would rather be right than reasonable.
—Ogden Nash, *Frailty, Thy Name Is a Misnomer*

What one beholds of a woman is the least part of her.
—Ovid, *Love's Cure*

If women are expected to do the same work as men, we must teach them the same things.　　　　—Plato, *The Republic*

Most women have no characters at all.
—Alexander Pope, *Moral Essays*

A free race cannot be born of slave mothers.
—Margaret Sanger, *Women and the New Race*

Frailty, thy name is woman!            —SHAKESPEARE, *Hamlet*, I, ii

Her voice was ever soft,
Gentle and low, an excellent thing in woman.
                          —SHAKESPEARE, *King Lear*, V, iii

She is a woman, therefore may be wooed.
She is a woman, therefore may be won.
                          —SHAKESPEARE, *Titus Andronicus*, II, i

By now you will have discovered that women, too, can be militant.                                          —SOPHOCLES, *Electra*

Women are always eagerly on the lookout for any emotion.
                          —STENDHAL, *On Love*

The woman is so hard
Upon the woman.       —ALFRED, LORD TENNYSON, *The Princess*

[That little man in black says] woman can't have as much rights
as man because Christ wasn't a woman. Where did your Christ come
from? . . . From God and a woman. Man had nothing to do with him.
                    —SOJOURNER TRUTH, Women's Rights Convention,
                          Akron, Ohio, 1851
[She was referring to a clergyman in the audience.]

If the first woman God ever made was strong enough to turn the
world upside down all alone, these women together ought to be able
to turn it back, and get it right side up again!          —*Ibid.*

The hand that rocks the cradle
Is the hand that rules the world.
                    —W. R. WALLACE, *The Hand that Rules the World*

Whatever women do, they must do it twice as well as men to be
thought half as good. Luckily, this is not difficult.
                          —CHARLOTTE WHITTON, quoted in
                          *Canada Month*, June 1963
[She was mayor of Ottawa.]

A woman's work is seldom done.
                    —THORNTON WILDER, *The Skin of Our Teeth*

## WOMEN, BEAUTIFUL & HOMELY   See also BEAUTY

She walks in beauty, like the night
Of cloudless climes and starry skies;
And all that's best of dark and bright
Meet in her aspect and her eyes.
—LORD BYRON, *She Walks in Beauty*

It was a blonde. A blonde to make a bishop kick a hole in a stained
glass window.   —RAYMOND CHANDLER, *Farewell, My Lovely*

Women who are either indisputably beautiful, or indisputably
ugly, are best flattered upon the score of their understanding.
—EARL OF CHESTERFIELD, letter to his son, Sept. 15, 1748

She strode like a grenadier, was strong and upright like an obelisk,
had a beautiful face, a candid brow, and not a thought of her own
in her head.   —JOSEPH CONRAD, *The Return* in *Tales of Unrest*

A beautiful woman is a practical poet.
—RALPH WALDO EMERSON, *Beauty*

Was this the face that launched a thousand ships?
And burnt the topless towers of Ilium?
Sweet Helen, make me immortal with a kiss!
—CHRISTOPHER MARLOWE, *Doctor Faustus*

Oh, thou art fairer than the evening air
Clad in the beauty of a thousand stars.   *—Ibid.*

If the nose of Cleopatra had been a little shorter, the whole face
of the world would have been changed.   —PASCAL, *Pensées*

If to her share some female errors fall,
Look on her face, and you'll forget 'em all.
—ALEXANDER POPE, *The Rape of the Lock*

Age cannot wither her, nor custom stale
Her infinite variety; other women cloy
The appetites they feed.
—SHAKESPEARE, *Antony and Cleopatra*, II, ii

She never yet was foolish that was fair.
—SHAKESPEARE, *Othello*, II, i

A thoroughly beautiful woman and a thoroughly homely woman are creations which I love to gaze upon, and which I cannot tire of gazing upon, for each is perfect in her own line.
—MARK TWAIN, *Autobiography*

**WOMEN & MEN**                          See also LOVE; MARRIAGE;
                                          MEN; WOMEN

Do not put such unlimited power into the hands of husbands. Remember all men would be tyrants if they could. [We ladies] will not hold ourselves bound by any laws in which we have no voice, or representation.          —ABIGAIL ADAMS, letter to John Adams,
                          March 31, 1776
[On the ambition to be tyrants, see Defoe at TYRANNY & TOTALITARIANISM.]

A lady's imagination is very rapid; it jumps from admiration to love, from love to matrimony in a moment.
—JANE AUSTEN, *Pride and Prejudice*

Women are very pleased when you call them cruel.
—P. A. C. DE BEAUMARCHAIS, *The Barber of Seville*

It is not good that the man should be alone; I will make him a help meet for him.          —BIBLE, *Genesis* 2:18

That's the nature of women, not to love when we love them, and to love when we love them not.          —CERVANTES, *Don Quixote*

There's no fury like a woman searching for a new lover.
—CYRIL CONNOLLY, *The Unquiet Grave*
[For the original comment on woman's fury, see Congreve at HATE.]

Women fail to understand how much men hate them.
—GERMAINE GREER, *The Female Eunuch*

Oh what can ail thee, wretched wight,
Alone and palely loitering;
The sedge is withered from the lake,
And no birds sing.          —JOHN KEATS, *La Belle Dame Sans Merci*

The silliest woman can manage a clever man; but it needs a very clever woman to manage a fool.
—RUDYARD KIPLING, *Three and—an Extra* in
*Plain Tales from the Hills*

Women want mediocre men, and men are working hard to be as mediocre as possible.
>—MARGARET MEAD, in *Quote Magazine*, May 15, 1958

For contemplation he and valor formed;
For softness she and sweet attractive grace,
He for God only, she for God in him.
>—JOHN MILTON, *Paradise Lost*

Disguise our bondage as we will,
'Tis woman, woman, rules us still.
>—THOMAS MOORE, *Sovereign Woman*

Woman was God's *second* mistake.
>—FRIEDRICH NIETZSCHE, *The Antichrist*

I can't live either without you or with you.    —OVID, *Amores*

Kindness in women, not their beauteous looks,
Shall win my love.
>—SHAKESPEARE, *The Taming of the Shrew*, IV, ii

The queens in history compare favorably with the kings.
>—ELIZABETH CADY STANTON and SUSAN B. ANTHONY, *History of Woman Suffrage*

We hold these truths to be self-evident, that all men and women are created equal. . . .
>—ELIZABETH CADY STANTON, *Declaration of Sentiment*, First Woman's Rights Convention, 1848

Man for the field and woman for the hearth:
Man for the sword and for the needle she:
Man with the head and woman with the heart:
Man to command and woman to obey;
All else confusion.    —ALFRED, LORD TENNYSON, *The Princess*

The woman's cause is man's: they rise or sink
Together.                                              —*Ibid.*

'Tis strange what a man may do, and a woman yet think him an angel.
>—WILLIAM THACKERAY, *Henry Esmond*

Why are women . . . so much more interesting to men than men are to women?    —VIRGINIA WOOLF, *A Room of One's Own*

Women have served all these centuries as looking-glasses possessing the magic and delicious power of reflecting the figure of man at twice its natural size. —*Ibid.*

**W O R D S**                    See ARTS: STYLE IN WRITING
                                    & EXPRESSION; LANGUAGE

**W O R K**                      See also ACCOMPLISHMENT; DOING;
                                    PERSEVERANCE & ENDURANCE

Work is the curse of the drinking classes.        —ANONYMOUS

Work is not the curse, but drudgery is.
                    —HENRY WARD BEECHER,
                        *Proverbs from Plymouth Pulpit*

What is work? And what is not work? These are questions that perplex the wisest of men.        —BHAGAVAD GITA

Go to the ant, thou sluggard; consider her ways, and be wise:
    Which having no guide, overseer, or ruler,
    Provideth her meat in the summer, and gathereth her food in the harvest.        —BIBLE, *Proverbs* 6:6–8

The laborer is worthy of his hire.        —BIBLE, *Luke* 10:7

All composite things decay. Strive diligently.
                    —BUDDHA, reputed last words

Be not solitary, be not idle.
                    —ROBERT BURTON, *The Anatomy of Melancholy*,
                        the closing words

Blessed is he who has found his work. Let him ask no other blessedness.        —THOMAS CARLYLE, *Past and Present*

"A fair day's wages for a fair day's work": it is as just a demand as governed men ever made of governing. It is the everlasting right of man.        —*Ibid.*

Work is the grand cure of all the maladies and miseries that ever beset mankind.        —THOMAS CARLYLE, speech, April 2, 1886

It is better to wear out than to rust out.
                    —RICHARD CUMBERLAND, quoted in George Horne,
                        *Sermon on the Duty of Contending for the Truth*

Working people have a lot of bad habits, but the worst of them is work.     —CLARENCE DARROW, quoted in Kevin Tierney, *Darrow*

A lot of fellows nowadays have a B.A., M.D., or Ph.D. Unfortunately, they don't have a J.O.B.     —"FATS" DOMINO, attributed

Originality and a feeling of one's own dignity are achieved only through work and struggle.
                    —FËDOR DOSTOEVSKI, *A Diary of a Writer*

There is no substitute for hard work.
                                    —THOMAS ALVA EDISON, *Life*

The bitter and the sweet come from the outside, the hard from within, from one's own efforts.
                    —ALBERT EINSTEIN, *Out of My Later Years*

Farming looks might easy when your plow is a pencil and you're a thousand miles from a cornfield.
                    —DWIGHT D. EISENHOWER, speech, Sept. 25, 1956

To the worker, God himself lends aid.     —EURIPIDES, *Hippolytus*

Men for the sake of getting a living forget to live.
                    —MARGARET FULLER, *Summer on the Lakes*

All work is empty save when there is love.
                    —KAHLIL GIBRAN, *The Prophet*

When work is a pleasure, life is a joy! When work is duty, life is slavery.     —MAXIM GORKY, *The Lower Depths*

It is weariness to keep toiling at the same things so that one becomes ruled by them.     —HERACLITUS, fragment

More men are killed by overwork than the importance of the world justifies.     —RUDYARD KIPLING, *The Phantom 'Rickshaw*

Under the spreading chestnut tree
The village smithy stands;
The smith a mighty man is he
With large and sinewy hands.
And the muscles of his brawny arms
Are strong as iron bands.
He earns what'er he can,
His brow is wet with honest sweat,
And looks the whole world in the face,
For he owes not any man.
                    —HENRY WADSWORTH LONGFELLOW, *The Village Blacksmith*

Constant labor of one uniform kind destroys the intensity and flow of a man's animal spirits, which find recreation and delight in mere change of activity.                    —KARL MARX, *Das Kapital*

The average male gets his living by such depressing devices that boredom becomes a sort of natural state to him.
                    —H. L. MENCKEN, *In Defence of Women*

No one hates his job so heartily as a farmer.
        —H. L. MENCKEN, *What is Going on in the World Now?* in
            *American Mercury*, Nov. 1933

Figure it out. Work a lifetime to pay off a house. You finally own it, and there's no one to live in it.
                    —ARTHUR MILLER, *Death of a Salesman*

Work expands so as to fill the time available for its completion.
                    —C. NORTHCOTE PARKINSON, *Parkinson's Law*

In a hierarchy, every employee tends to rise to his level of incompetence.                    —LAURENCE J. PETER, *The Peter Principle*

When you cease to make a contribution, you begin to die.
        —ELEANOR ROOSEVELT, letter to Mr. Horne, Feb. 19, 1960

Far and away the best prize that life offers is the chance to work hard at work worth doing.
                    —THEODORE ROOSEVELT, Labor Day speech, 1903

Which of us . . . is to do the dirty work for the rest—and for what pay? Who is to do the pleasant and clean work, and for what pay?                    —JOHN RUSKIN, *Of King's Treasuries*, in
                    *Sesame and Life*

If I were a medical man, I should prescribe a holiday to any patient who considered his work important.
                    —BERTRAND RUSSELL, *Autobiography*

Nothing will come of nothing.        —SHAKESPEARE, *King Lear*, I, i

My nature is subdued
To what it works in, like the dyer's hand.
                    —SHAKESPEARE, sonnet 111

You may tempt the upper classes
With your villainous demitasses,
But Heaven will protect the working girl.
     —EDGAR SMITH, *Heaven Will Protect the Working Girl*

To travel hopefully is a better thing than to arrive, and true success is to labor. —ROBERT LOUIS STEVENSON, *Virginibus Puerisque*

Death is the end of life; ah, why
Should life all labor be?
     —ALFRED, LORD TENNYSON, *The Lotus-Eaters*

Where our work is, there let our joy be.
     —TERTULLIAN, *Women's Dress*

A small daily task if it be really daily, will beat the labors of a spasmodic Hercules.     —ANTHONY TROLLOPE, *An Autobiography*

Thou, O God, dost sell us all good things at the price of labor.
     —LEONARDO DA VINCI, *Notebooks*

Work spares us from three evils: boredom, vice, and need.
     —VOLTAIRE, *Candide*

There is as much dignity in tilling a field as in writing a poem.
     —BOOKER T. WASHINGTON, speech, Sept. 9, 1895

How doth the little busy bee
Improve each shining hour,
And gather honey all the day
From every opening flower.
     —ISAAC WATTS, *Against Idleness and Mischief*

**WORKING PEOPLE**         See PEOPLE, THE; WORK

**WORLD**         See CREATION, DIVINE; LIFE; NATURE;
REALITY & ILLUSION; UNIVERSE; WORLD, END OF

**WORLD, END OF**         See also LAST JUDGMENT &
THE HEREAFTER

Overhead without any fuss the stars were going out.
     —ARTHUR C. CLARKE, *The Nine Billion Names of God*,
     final sentence

This is the way the world ends
Not with a bang but a whimper.  —T. S. Eliot, *The Hollow Men*

Some say the world will end in fire,
Some say in ice.
From what I've tasted of desire
I hold with those who favor fire.
But if it had to perish twice
I think I know enough of hate
To say that for destruction ice
Is also great
And would suffice.                         —Robert Frost, *Fire and Ice*

And what rough beast, its hour come round at last,
Slouches towards Bethlehem to be born?
               —William Butler Yeats, *The Second Coming*

When shall the stars be blown about the sky,
Like the sparks blown out of a smithy, and die?
               —William Butler Yeats, *The Secret Rose*

**WRATH**                                           See ANGER

**WRITING**                                  See ARTS: WRITING

**XANADU**                                  See ORIENT, THE

**YESTERDAY**                                  See PAST, THE

**YOUTH**                        See also CHILDREN & CHILDHOOD

The young are permanently in a state resembling intoxication; for youth is sweet and they are growing.
                    —Aristotle, *Nicomachean Ethics*
[Cf. La Rochefoucauld, below.]

Youth is easily deceived because it is quick to hope.
                    —Aristotle, *Rhetoric*

Young men are fitter to invent than to judge, fitter for execution than for counsel, fitter for new projects than settled business.
                    —Francis Bacon, *Of Youth and Age*

Youth is the pollen
That blows through the sky
And does not ask why.
>—STEPHEN VINCENT BENÉT, *John Brown's Body*

Rejoice, O young man in thy youth.    —BIBLE, *Ecclesiastes* 11:9

Youth will be served, every dog has his day, and mine has been a
fine one.                              —GEORGE BORROW, *Lavengro*

Youth means love.    —ROBERT BROWNING, *The Ring and the Book*

Youth is like spring, an overpraised season.
>—SAMUEL BUTLER, *The Way of All Flesh*

Youth is something very new: twenty years ago, no one mentioned it.                  —COCO CHANEL, quoted in Marcel Haedrich,
>*Coco Chanel, Her Life, Her Secrets*

A youth is to be regarded with respect. How do you know that his
future will not be equal to our present?    —CONFUCIUS, *Analects*

Youth is a period of missed opportunities.
>—CYRIL CONNOLLY, *Journal and Memoir*

Youth is the best time to be rich and the best time to be poor.
>—EURIPIDES, *Heracles*

Alas, that Spring should vanish with the Rose!
That Youth's sweet-scented Manuscript should close.
>—EDWARD FITZGERALD, *The Rubáiyát of
>Omar Khayyám*

One could do worse than be a swinger of birches.
>—ROBERT FROST, *Birches*

Youth's the season made for joys,
Love is then our duty.           —JOHN GAY, *The Beggar's Opera*

Give me back my youth!                       —GOETHE, *Faust*

No young man believes he shall ever die.
>—WILLIAM HAZLITT, *On the Feeling of
>Immortality in Youth*

Never trust anyone over thirty.        —ABBIE HOFFMAN, saying

Youth is quick in feeling but weak in judgment.     —HOMER, *Iliad*

*Fugit juventus.*
Youth flies.                           —HORACE, *Epodes*

Youth, even in its sorrows, has a brilliance of its own.
                              —VICTOR HUGO, *Les Misérables*

Be gentle with the young.                   —JUVENAL, *Satires*

When all the world is young, lad,
And all the trees are green;
And every goose a swan, lad,
And every lass a queen;
Then hey for boot and horse, lad,
And round the world away:
Young blood must have its course, lad,
And every dog its day.        —CHARLES KINGSLEY, *Water Babies*

Youth is unending intoxication; it is a fever of the mind.
                          —LA ROCHEFOUCAULD, *Maxims*
[He knew his Aristotle; see above.]

A boy's will is the wind's will,
And the thoughts of youth are long, long thoughts.
              —HENRY WADSWORTH LONGFELLOW, *My Lost Youth*

It is only an illusion that youth is happy, and illusion of those who
have lost it.        —W. SOMERSET MAUGHAM, *Of Human Bondage*

We were very young, we were very merry—
We went back and forth all night on the ferry.
                  —EDNA ST. VINCENT MILLAY, *Recuerdo*

The American ideal is youth—handsome, empty youth.
              —HENRY MILLER, *The Wisdom of the Heart*

No time to marry, no time to settle down;
I'm a young woman, and I ain't done runnin' around.
                  —BESSIE SMITH, *Young Woman's Blues*

Pay attention to the young, and make them just as good as possible.              —SOCRATES, quoted in Plato, *Euthyphro*

Bright youth passes swiftly as a thought.    —THEOGNIS, *Elegies*

Bliss it was that dawn to be alive,
But to be young was very heaven!
   —WILLIAM WORDSWORTH, *The French Revolution*

**ZEAL**        See ENTHUSIASM, ENERGY, ZEAL

# INDEX

ACTON, John Dalberg-Acton,
  [Lord] *(1834–1902)*
  freedom & minorities, 247
  patriotism, 214
  power & great men, 299
ADAMS, Abigail *(1744–1818)*
  frippery, 87
  man & power, 230
  men & women, 342
ADAMS, Henry Brooks, *(1838–1918)*
  chaos vs order, 315
  friend in power, 230
  friends, 96
  learning, 69
  politics (2 quotes), 223
ADAMS, John *(1735–1826)*
  power, 230
  vice-presidency, 223
  virtue (2 quotes), 322
ADAMS, Samuel *(1722–1803)*
  glorious morning for America, 14
ADDISON, Joseph *(1672–1719)*
  die but once (note under Hale) 15
  marriage, 165
  music, 25
  weather, 203
  wisdom, 334
ADLER, Alfred *(1870–1937)*
  principles, 77
ADY, Thomas *(fl. 1655)*
  Matthew, Mark, Luke & John, 233
AESCHYLUS *(525–456 B.C.)*
  gods, requests of, 231
  health & disease, 113
  hospitality, 124
  marriage, 165
  memory, 171
  obedience, 206

AESCHYLUS *(continued)*
  old men, 6
  pain, 308
  time, 302
  trouble, 309
  tyranny, 315
  wisdom 334
AESOP *(fl c. 550 B.C.)*
  appearances, 19
  counting chickens, 244
  familiarity & contempt, 135
  fine feathers, 87
  gods & those who help themselves, 276
  kindness (2 quotes), 322
  prayers, 231
  slow & steady, 219
  tyrants, 316
  union, 317
  united we stand, 317
AGATHON *(c. 448–400 B.C.)*
  past, the, 213
AIKEN, [Senator] George *(1892–1984)*
  Vietnam War, 14
ALCUIN *(735–804)*
  voice of the people, 218
ALEXANDER, Cecil Frances
  *(1818–1895)*
  All things bright & beautiful, 55
ALFIERI, [Count] Vittorio *(1749–1803)*
  courage, 54
ALGREN, Nelson *(1909–1981)*
  food, cards, & women, 244
ALI, Muhammad *(b. 1942)*
  butterfly & bee, 289
ALLEN, Fred *(1894–1956)*
  California, 133
AMBROSE, [Saint] *(c. 340–397*
  when in Rome, 306

ANACHARSIS *(fl. c. 600 B.C.)*
a market, 40
ANDERSON, Maxwell *(1888–1959)*
glory, 328
ANONYMOUS
America, don't sell short, 11
Antislavery Society motto, 247
*ars longa*, 21
bayonets & workers, 328
billiards, 98
black is beautiful, 248
business, everybody's & nobody's, 258
coition & sadness, 277
computers & foul-ups, 298
computers & garbage, 298
dead vs Red, 20
fight & run away, 296
free lunch, 69
gladiators' salute, 290
glory passes, 293
God, 101
hard cases (note under Holmes), 144
if it moves, salute it, 173
know self, 275
learn by doing, 69
liberals, 223
loose lips, 279
loyalty to benefactors, 317
Murphy's law, 309
Murphy's law of research, 264
Pallas Athena, 101
Pilgrim Fathers, 247
people, the (2 quotes), 218
professionals & amateurs, 83
recession, depression, 69
responsible shepherd, 258
rights (2 quotes), 262
ruin, 263
sucker & even break, 112
sumer is icumen in, 199
tough going, 291
war, 328
we shall overcome, 248
Western Wind, 158
wine, women & song, 114
work & the drinking classes, 344
ANONYMOUS (PRAYERS)
ghoulies & ghosties, 234
I lay me down to sleep, 233
See also BOOK OF COMMON
PRAYER

ANONYMOUS (PROVERBS)
bed bugs, 309
beginning, a good, 34
clothes, 87
crime, 56
divide & rule, 104
done well is done quickly (note
under Augustus Caesar), 111
endurance, 219
excuses, 82
fortune, ill, 309
future, 97
gambling, 98
God laughs, 142
hasten slowly, 110
hatred, 111
illness, 131
Jerusalem, 47
joy, sharing, 108
laugh is on the loser, 332
laughing last, 142
laughter, meaningless, 142
laughter & seduction, 142
law, 143
laziness, 146
live & let live, 305
love & dancing, 152
love & youth, 152
luck, 161
marriages, 165
maxims, 247
meat/poison (note under Lucretius),
320
mistakes, 180
money, 182
morning & evening, 202
murder will out, 56
Naples, 48
nature, 190
opportunity & temptation, 300
patience, 214
people, the, 218
picture vs words, 169
proverbs, 247
reason, 251
responsible shepherd (note under
Tiberius), 258
revenge, 259
rich & poor, 112
rose & thorns, 84
sex, 277

ANONYMOUS *(continued)*
  silent dogs bite, 279
  sleep & health, 285
  style, 292
  tigers, riding (note under Churchill),
    315
  time & tide, 302
  truth,, 312
  waiting & your enemy's corpse, 214
  war, winning quickly, 328
  whistling girl, 337
  wine & truth, 9
  wisdom & wonder, 334
ANOUILH, Jean *(b. 1910)*
  art & life, 21
  courage, 54
  God & the rich, 182
  saintliness, 300
ANSELM, [Saint] *(c. 1033–1109)*
  God 101.
ANTHONY, Susan B[rownell]
  *1820–1906)*
  equal pay, equal work, 337
  marriage, 165
  women & men, 337, 343
APPIUS CLAUDIUS CAECUS
  *(fl. late 4th & early 3rd cent. B.C.)*
  architect own fate, 258
AQUINAS, Thomas *(c. 1225–1274)*
  tyranny, 316
ARBUTHNOT, John *(1667–1735)*
  law, 143
ARCHILOCHUS *(early 7th cent. B.C.)*
  fox & hedgehog, 334
ARCHIMEDES *(c. 287–212 B.C.)*
  "Eureka, . . ." 267
  leverage, 270
ARENDT, Hannah *(1906–1975)*
  hypocrisy, 129
  tyranny, 316
ARGENSON, René [Marquis de]
  *(1694–1757)*
  *laissez faire,* 40
ARISTIPPUS *(fl. 399 B.C.)*
  visiting a prostitute, 281
ARISTOPHANES *(c. 450–385 B.C.)*
  hear both sides, 79
  hunger, 228
  politicians, 224
ARISTOTLE *(384–322 B.C.)*
  beauty, 33

ARISTOTLE *(continued)*
  common property, 50
  hope, 123
  just acts, 67
  justice, 137
  law, 143
  living in solitude, 287
  man is political, 224
  metaphor, 29
  one swallow, 245
  poverty, 228
  revenge, 259
  style (3 quotes), 29
  tragedy, pity & terror, 22
  youth (2 quotes), 348
ARMSTRONG, Neil *(b. 1930)*
  giant step (moon landing), 267
ARMY CORPS OF ENGINEERS
  motto, 71
ARNOLD, George *(1834–1865)*
  living need charity, 43
ARNOLD, Matthew *(1822–1888)*
  darkling plain, 147
  be thyself, 273
  seed of ruin, 263
  women, 337
ASTOR, [Lady] Nancy *(1879–1964)*
  fear, 88
  marriage, 166
ASTY, [Sir] Jacob *(1579–1652)*
  his prayer before battle, 234
AUDEN, W[ystan] H[ugh]
  *(1907–1973)*
  behaviorism, 271
  criticism, in arts, 23
  Europe & hate, 182
  evil, 80
  heroes, 116
  man & history, 120
AUGUSTINE, [Saint] *(354–430)*
  abstinence, 277
  chastity, but not yet, 234
  fame, 293
  hear other side, 79
  innocence, 132
  obedience, 206
  pain, 131
  patience, 214
  time, 302
  wisdom, 334

AUGUSTUS CAESAR
  *(63 B.C.–14 A.D.)*
  doing things well, 111
AURELIUS, MARCUS
  See MARCUS AURELIUS
    ANTONINUS
AUSTEN, Jane *(1775–1817)*
  ladies' imagination, 242
  love (note under Lucretius), 154
  marriage, 166
  men, 171
  money & happiness, 183
  money & humility, 182
  parties, large, 124
  people, liking, 179
AYER, [Sir] A[lfred] J[ules] *(b. 1910)*
  morality, 77

BABBAGE, Charles *(1792–1871)*
  birth rate (note under Tennyson),
    100
BACON, Francis *(1561–1626)*
  fame, 293
  God & gardens, 196
  hill & Mahomet, 276
  hope, 124
  knowledge is power, 69
  love, 152
  money, 183
  nature, 190
  parents, 210
  princes, 118
  remedies, new, 204
  remedy & disease (note under
    Publilius Syrus), 131
  revenge (2 quotes), 259
  wife & children, 86
  young man, 348
BACON, Roger *(c. 1214–c. 1294)*
  mathematics, 268
BAKER, Russell *(b. 1925)*
  inanimate objects (2 quotes), 301
  sports, 290
BAKUNIN, Mikhail A. *(1814–1876)*
  law, 143
BALDWIN, James *(b. 1924)*
  fire next time, 248
  money, 183
  questions of oneself, 275
BALDWIN, Stanley *(1867–1947)*
  the press, 237

BALL, John *(d. 1381)*
  Adam delved, Eve span, 75
BALZAC, Honoré de *(1799–1850)*
  numbers, 268
BANKHEAD, Tallulah *(1903–1968)*
  less than meets the eye, 133
  pure as slush, 282
  vices, 281
BARING, Maurice *(1874–1945)*
  money, 183
BARNUM, P[hineas] T[aylor]
    *(1810–1891)*
  suckers, 92
BARRIE, [Sir] James M[atthew]
    *1860–1937)*
  charm, 44
  printing press, 169
BARTH, Karl *(1886–1968)*
  Bach & Mozart, 25
  conscience, 52
BARUCH, Bernard *(1870–1965)*
  cold war, 14
  old age, 6
BARZUN, Jacques [Martin] *b. 1907)*
  baseball, 290
BAUDELAIRE, Charles *(1821–1867)*
  bourgeois, shocking the, 21
  correspondence, 216
  memories, 171
  sexuality & the masses, 277
BAUDOIN [King] *(b. 1930)*
  war, 328
BAUM, Vicki [given name, Hedwig
    Baum] *(1888–1960)*
  fame & success, 293
BAYLY, T[homas] H[aynes]
    *(1797–1839)*
  absence makes heart fonder, 152
BEAUMARCHAIS, Pierre-Augustin
    de *(1732–1799)*
  craftiness, 54
  drinking & sex, 82
  jealousy, 136
  laughter vs weeping, 142
  love, 152
  women, 342
BEAUVOIR, Simone de *(b. 1908)*
  women, 337
BECKETT, Samuel, *(b. 1906)*
  madness, 162

BEECHER, Henry Ward *(1813–1887)*
dogs & children, 193
drudgery, 344
flowers, 196
mother's song, 210
principles, 77
war, 328
women, loving, 210
BEETHOVEN, Ludwig van
*(1770–1827)*
fate, 88
BELLAMY, Edward *(1850–1898)*
buying & selling, 39
BELLOY, P.–L. de *(1727–1775)*
patriotism, 214
BENCHLEY, Robert *(1889–1945)*
dry clothes, wet martini, 9
language & silence, 279
BENEDICTINE ORDER
prayer & work, 231
BENÉT, Stephen Vincent *(1898–1943)*
dreaming men, 285
Wounded Knee, 14
youth, 349
BENTHAM, Jeremy *(1748–1832)*
greatest happiness of greatest
number, 77.
BERENSON, Bernard *(1865–1959)*
age & love of beauty, 6
consistency, 52
BERGSON, Henri *(1859–1941)*
laughter, 142
universe, 318
BERKELEY, [Bishop] George
*(1685–1753)*
America (course of empire), 11
BERLIOZ, Hector *(1803–1869)*
time, 302
BERNANOS, Georges *(1888–1948)*
hell, 115
prayer, 231
pride, 239
BERNARD, [St.] *(1091–1153)*
hell (note under Marx), 116
nature (2 quotes), 190
BERNARD OF CHARTRES
*(d, c. 1130)*
shoulders of giants, 262
BERRA, ("Yogi") Lawrence Peter
b. *1925)*
game isn't over, 290

BERTIN, [Mlle.] *(fl. 1770s)*
nothing new, 204
BEVAN, Aneurin, *(1897–1960)*
middle of the road, 224
politics, a blood sport, 224
righteous people, 277
*BHAGAVADGITA*
work, 344
BIBLE—OLD TESTAMENT
age & wisdom, 7
all have one father, 76
angels have charge over you, 244
ant, not a sluggard, 344
babes & sucklings, 44
bloodthirsty hate the upright, 111
bread alone, 253
brother, do not hate, 111
brother's keeper?, 258
Cain, 56
cast bread upon waters, 43
child, training a, 211
child shall lead them, 45
creation of the world, 55
days spent without hope, 63
do justly, love mercy, 322
do with thy might, 67
dove, wings like, 76
down to the sea in ships, 272
dreamer cometh, 326
earth shall teach thee, 190
eat & drink, 114
eat, drink, be merry, 90
Eden, garden of, 196
end vs beginning, 5
Eve, 342
eye for an eye, 246
falling when alone, 287
famous men, 99
father, one, 76
father & mother, honor thy, 210
fear of Lord & wisdom, 334
feast & wine, 90
fool said no God, 32
fool uttereth his mind, 92
foes, little, 309
generations pass, earth abideth, 99
go to ant, sluggeard, 344
God, being doorkeeper for, 80
God—our refuge & strength, 101
God said I am that I am, 101

BIBLE (*continued*)

God—why hast thou forsaken me?
God's mercy, 101
hate of brother, 111
heavens declare God's glory, 198
help meet, 342
horse, 193
jealousy, 136
joy in morning, 108
lamp unto my feet, 101
living dog vs dead lion, 296
Lord bless thee, 234
Lord gave & hath taken away, 257
Lord is my shepherd, 101, 244
Lord shall preserve you, 244
love & jealousy, 136
love neighbor as self, 157
Lucifer, 65
man is born unto trouble, 309
MENE, MENE, 263
might, do with thy, 67
mighty are fallen, 263
money, 183
no new thing, 204
out of the depths I have cried, 234
poor & rich 112
poor man's wisdom, 228
praise famous men, 99
pray with few words, 232
pride, 239
prophecy, dreams & visions, 327
proud, the house of the, 239
race not to the swift, 161
rainbow, a covenant, 198
reason together, 251
revenge, 259
rich not innocent, 183
righteous & wise, but not over much,
170
righteousness & nations, 322
rise up, my love, 199
season for everything, 147
ships, 272
sleep, 285
soft answer, 106
sow wind, reap whirlwind, 320
sparing the rod, 210
spring (Song of Solomon), 199
stranger in strange land, 10
sun also ariseth, 99
swords into plowshares, 216

BIBLE (*continued*)

training a child, 211
trouble, man born into, 309
vanity of vanities, 63
vision, 326
voice of the turtle, 199
way of an eagle, way of a man, 106
wealth, 183
weeping & joy, 108
weighed & found wanting, 85
what hath God wrought? (note
under Morse), 268
what thy hand does, do with might,
67
wickedness, 80
wine vs money, 183
wings like a dove, 76
winter is past, 199
wisdom above rubies, 334
wisdom & fear of Lord, 334
wisdom and understanding, 334
wisdom & grief, 335
wolf & lamb, 216
woman, creation of, 342
work (2 quotes), 344
writing books, 30
youth, rejoice in, 349

APOCRYPHA

blessings, judging, 108
envy & wrath, 19
friend, old, 96
happiness (judge none blessed . . .),
108
health, 113
joy & long life, 109
medicines, 67
open not thine heart, 55
physician, 67
proverbs, 247
righteous souls, 323
small things, their importance, 64
touch pitch, be defiled, 312

BIBLE—NEW TESTAMENT

alms & hypocrisy, 43
Alpha & Omega, 102
anger, 18, 19
Annunciation, 136
ask & it shall be given, 37
birth of Jesus, 46
blessed are . . . (Sermon on the
Mount), 322

BIBLE (*continued*)
blind leading blind, 327
body, temple of Holy Ghost, 36
bread alone (note under Bible, *Deuteronomy*), 253
camel vs rich man, 183
casting stones, 305
charity, 157
charity to the hungry, thirsty, etc., 44
cheek, turn the other, 210
cheerful giver, 44
child, when I was a, 45
children—become as to enter heaven, 132
children come unto me, 45
children—my little ones, 45
children of this world, 335
Christ's birth, 46
darkness & light, 80
day—its evil is sufficient, 235
death (pale rider), 59
death, where is thy sting?, 59
deny me thrice, 35
doubt & damnation, 284
doubting Thomas, 284
earth is the Lord's, 190
eat & drink, for tomorrow we die (note under Bible, *Isaiah*), 144
end—not yet, 214
enduring to the end, 219
enemies, love thy, 72
everyone that hath shall be given more, 112
evil & good, 80
evil of the day, 235
exalted shall be abased, 141
eye, pluck it out, 322
faith, keeping the, 317
faith, little, 85
faith& works, 85
false prophets, 129
fashion passeth, 87
Father, forgive them, 93
Father's house—many mansions, 102
fatted calf, 90
fight, a good, 5
first shall be last, 141
fool, thou, 18
fools—suffer them gladly, 92
forgive & be forgiven, 93
friends, dying for, 96

BIBLE (*continued*)
fruits—by these you shall know them, 79
gain world, lose soul, 288
give to the poor, 43
giver, cheerful, 44
giving more blessed than receiving, 44
giving to the hungry, 44
glory to God, peace to men, 46
God (if he be for us), 102
God, no respecter of persons, 102
God—thou shalt love, 102
God & all good things, 102
God & mammon, 253
God gave world his only Son, 137
God is love, 102
God makes all things possible, 101
God, why hast thou forsaken me?, 63
go to highways & hedges, 124
good shepherd, 137
grace & faith, 85
haves & have nots, 112
he that is not with me, 317
heaven, treasure in, 43
hospitality, 124, 125
house divided, 317
hypocrites (3 quotes), 129, 232
I am Alpha & Omega, 102
I am not as other men are, 122
I am the resurrection & life, 101
I am the way, truth, & life, 102
I have fought the good fight, 5
I will judge thee out of thine mouth, 79
in the beginning was the Word, 136
Judas, 35
judge not, 305
kingdom of God within you, 273
laborer worthy of hire, 344
law unto themselves, 56
left hand & right hand, 43
Legion, my name is, 162
let cup pass from me, 309
light shineth in the darkness, 137
lilies, 196
little ones—do not offend, 45
Lord chastens whom he loves, 309
lost sheep, 93
love, no fear in, 158
love enemies, 72
love God, 102

BIBLE (*continued*)
love—greater hath no man, 96
love neighbor (note under Bible,
    *Leviticus*), 157
love of brother & God, 158
love one another, 157
loved darkness because evil, 80
mammon of unrighteousness, make
    friends of, 55
man lives not by bread alone (note
    under Bible, *Deuteronomy*), 253
many mansions, 102
marriage better than burning, 166
many are called, 71
measuring & meting, fair, 138
merciful are blessed, 93
millstone on neck, 45
money, love of, 183
more blessed to give, 44
morrow, the, 235
mote vs beam, 305
mouth—judging from; much given,
    much required, 258
new wine, old bottles, 205
pale horse, pale rider, 59
peace, good will to men, 46
peacemakers, 216
pearls before swine, 319
Peter & the church, 253
Peter denies Jesus, 35
physician, heal self, 66
poor always with you, 228
poor in spirit, 93
prayer & hypocrites, 129, 232
prophet honored, 327
prophets, false, 129
pure in heart, 132
purity, 323
Quo vadis?, 242
render unto Caesar, 297
rise, take bed, & walk, 179
Satan, get behind me, 300
separate them like sheep from goats,
    141
Sermon on the Mount, 322
soul—losing, 288
sowing & reaping, 138
spirit willing, flesh weak, 300
stones, casting, 305
strait & narrow, 322
sword, taking the, 320

BIBLE (*continued*)
sword vs peace, 259
temptation, enduring, 300
temptation, lead us not into, 300
through a glass darkly, 327
thy will be done, 206
treasure in heaven, 43
truth & Pilate, 312
truth makes free, 312
turn the other cheek, 210
two masters, 253
vengeance is mine, 259
wages of sin, 80
watch & pray, 232
weeping and gnashing teeth, 263
when I was a child, 45
whitened sepulchres, 129
wide is the gate to destruction, 80
will—thine be done, 206
wine, new, into old bottles, 205
wine vs water, 9
wise as serpents, 210
with me or against me, 317
Word made flesh, 137
words, thy, 139
BIERCE, Ambrose (*1842–c. 1914*)
anger, 19
heathen, 253
history, 120
money, 183
patience, 214
prayer, 232
BISMARCK, Otto von (*1815–1898*)
politics (3 quotes), 224
BLACKER, Valentine, (*1778–1823*)
powder, keep dry, 276
BLACKSTONE, William (*1723–1780*)
law, innocence & guilt, 143
public good, 262
witchcraft, 207
BLAKE, William (*1757–1827*)
anger, 19
cruelty, 125
energy, 74
excess, 82
innocence, 132
law, 143
mercy & love, 125
moon, 198
prudence, 245
robin, 193

BLAKE (*continued*)
  science, 264
  seeing a tree, 327
  tiger (3 quotes), 193
  tigers of wrath, 19
  Voltaire & Rousseau, 284
  world in a grain of sand, 190
BOETHIUS (*480–524*)
  love, 152
BOGART, John B. (*1845–1921*)
  news, 237
BONHOEFFER, Dietrich (*1906–1945*)
  ethics, 77
  politics, 224
  wrong decisions, 252
BOOK OF COMMON PRAYER
  as it was in the beginning, 234
  we have left undone those things we
    ought have done, 252
BOORSTIN, Daniel (*b. 1914*)
  celebrities (2 quotes), 293
BORGES, Jorge Luis (*b. 1899*)
  religion, 253
  writing, 30
BORGIA, Cesare (*1475/6–1507*)
  ambition to be Caesar, 11
BORMAN, Frank (*b. 1928*)
  moon, 198
BORROW, George (*1803–1881*)
  youth, 349
BOSSIDY, John Collins (*1860–1928*)
  Boston, 48
BOUCICAULT, Dion (*1820?–1890*)
  time, 302
BOULAY DE LA MEURTHE,
    Antoine (*1761–1840*)
  blunder vs crime, 180
BOWEN, Charles Synge [Lord]
    (*1835–1894*)
  metaphysicians, 220
BOWEN, Elizabeth (*1899–1973*)
  autumn & spring, 199
BRADLEY, F. H. (*1846–1924*)
  happiness, 109
BRADLEY, Omar (*1893–1981*)
  science & morality, 181
  ethical infants,, 77
BRADSTREET, Anne (*1612?–1672*)
  love of husband, 158
BRAHMS, Johannes (*1833–1897*)
  symphony, 25

BRANCUSI, Constantin (*1876–1957*)
  architecture, 23
BRANDEIS, Louis D. (*1856–1941*)
  bold minds, 143
  right to be alone, 240
BRECHT, Bertolt (*1898–1956*)
  crime & banks, 39
  food & morals, 228
  heroes, 116
  luck, 161
  poverty, 228
  survival, 296
  war, 328
BRIDGES, Robert (*1844–1930*)
  beauty, 33
BRILLAT-SAVARIN, Anthelme
    (*1755–1826*)
  food & nations, 90
  food & identity, 90
BRONOWSKI, Jacob (*1908–1974*)
  genius, 100
BROOKE, Rupert (*1887–1915*)
  death & England, 72
  things I've loved, 158
BROWN, John Mason (*1900–1969*)
  television, 169
BROWN, T[homas] E[dward]
    (*1830–1897*)
  garden, 196
  rich man's jokes, 183
BROWNE, [Sir] Thomas (*1605–1682*)
  charity, 44
  virtue, 323
BROWNING, Elizabeth Barrett
    (*1806–1861*)
  love, 158
BROWNING, Robert (*1812–1889*)
  being Christian, 253
  England, 72
  God's in his heaven, 200
  grow old along with me, 7
  happiness, 109
  heart too soon made glad, 84
  joys of living, 147, 148
  less is more, 281
  progress (2 quotes), 242
  reach & grasp, 11
  Rome, 48
  thrush, singing, 193
  spring, 200

BROWNING (*continued*)
  words, 140
  youth & love, 349
BRUCE, Lenny *(1923–1966)*
  religion, 253
BRUYÈRE, LA
  See LA BRUYÈRE
BRYAN, William Jennings *(1860–1925)*
  cross of gold, 14
  righteous cause, 323
BUBER, Martin *(1878–1965)*
  animals, 193
BUCK, Pearl S[ydenstricker]
    *1892—1973)*
  oppressed people, 242
BUDDHA *(5th cent. B.C.)*
  Eightfold Way, 253
  mortality & work, 344
BUFFON, George Louis Leclerc de
    *1707–1788)*
  style, 292
BULWER-LYTTON, Edward George
    *(1803–1873)*
  pen vs sword, 237
  revolutions, 259
BUÑUEL, Louis *(1900–1983)*
  atheism, 33
BURGON, John William *(1813–1888)*
  rose-red city, 48
BURKE, Edmond *(1729–1797)*
  age of chivalry, 181
  custom, 58
  dangers, 58
  evil, triumph of, 80
  fourth estate (note under Macaulay),
    238
  government, 105
  government & compromise (note
    under Bismarck), 224
  joining forces, 318
  mind, progress of, 242
  others' misfortunes, 309
  power, 230
  revolution & gallows, 259
  ruin, 263
  taxes, 297
BURNEY, Fanny *(1752–1840)*
  travel, 306
BURNS, Robert *(1759–1796)*
  do or die, 259
  domestic life, 121

BURNS (*continued*)
  heart's in Highlands, 188
  honest man's inhumanity, 125
  love at first sight, 159
  Luve's like a rose, 159
  maid who like soldiers, 282
  man's a man, 76
  mouse, 193
  nature & change, 42
  O whistle, 159
  schemes, 223
BURR, Aaron *(1756–1836)*
  procrastination, 241
BURTON [Sir] Richard Francis
    *(1821–1890)*
  travellers, 306
BURTON, Robert *(1577–1640)*
  be not solitary or idle, 344
  England & Italy, 188
  marriage, 166
  poets, 27
  religion, 254
  ships, 272
  tobacco, 304
  travel, 306
  word, cruel, 140
BUSSY-RABUTIN, [Count] Roger
    *(1618–1693)*
  big battalions, 329
BUTLER, Nicholas Murray
    *(1862–1947)*
  experts, 83
BUTLER, Samuel *(1835–1902)*
  Devil, 65
  dogs, 193
  eggs & hens, 193
  faith, 85
  God (note under Ingersoll), 103
  losing, 332
  money, 183
  progress, 242
  vice, 282
  youth, 349
BYRNE, Susan *(b. 1946)*
  capital, 39
BYRON, George Gordon [Lord]
    *(1788–1824)*
  adultery, 282
  adversity, 309
  advice, 6
  Barabbas a publisher, 169

BYRON (*continued*)
 beauty, she walks in, 341
 chess, 98
 hate, 111
 I told you so, 252
 love, 152
 money, 183
 nature, 190
 night, 202
 Ocean, 199
 pleasure & sin, 282
 polygamy, 166
 roving no more, 7
 sleep, 285
 solitude, 287
 truth, 312
 women & love, 152
 women's love, 337

CABELL, James Branch (*1879–1958*)
 optimist & pessimist, 209
CAESAR, Julius (*100–44 B.C.*)
 die cast, 37
 Gaul, 188
 *veni, vidi, vici*, 175
 wife, 118
CAGE, John (*b. 1912*)
 life, 148
 silence, 279
CAMPBELL, [Mrs.] Pat[rick]
 (*1865–1940*)
 marriage, 166
 morals, 77
CAMPBELL, Thomas (*1777–1844*)
 Barabbas, a publisher (note under
  Byron), 169
 truth, 312
CAMUS, Albert (*1913–1960*)
 age & one's face, 36
 charm, 44
 evil, 80
 free press, 237
 Last Judgement, 141
 murderer's soul, 56
 oneself, knowing & asserting, 276
 rebel, 259
 revolution, 259
 suicide & life, 295
 suicide & philosophy, 221
CANETTI, Elias (*b. 1905*)
 constellations, 207

CARYLE, Thomas (*1795–1881*)
 aristocracy, 71
 biography (well written life), 31
 civilization, 49
 dismal science, 69
 duty, 77
 France, 188
 genius, 100
 great men, 120
 history & happiness, 120
 laughter, 142
 man & tools, 125
 mediocrity, 170
 miracles, age of, 181
 politics, 224
 silence vs speech, 279
 statistics, 268
 universe, 318
 whiff of grapeshot, 320
 work, a blessing, 344
 wages & work, 344
 work, a cure, 344
 worship, 254
CARNEY, Julia (*1823–1908*)
 little things, 64
CARR, E. H. (*1892–1982*)
 change vs progress, 242
CARROLL, Lewis (given name,
  Charles L. Dodgson) (*1832–1898*)
 believing in a unicorn, 85
 business, minding own, 240
 Father William, 7
 O frabjous day!, 110
 'Twas brillig 58
 Walrus conversation, 53
 words, 140
CARSON, Rachel (*1907–1964*)
 "control of nature," 298
 the sea, 199
CARTIER, Jacques (*1491–1557*)
 land God gave to Cain, 188
CASALS, Pablo (*1876–1973*)
 melody, 25
CASSATT, Mary (*1844–1926*)
 travel, 307
CATHER, Willa (*1873–1947*)
 hate, 111
 human stories, 148
 memories, 171
 travel, 307

CATHERINE II OF RUSSIA
(CATHERINE THE GREAT)
*(1729–1796)*
men making love, 277
temptation, 300
CATO *(234–149 B.C.)*
Carthage, 48
CATULLUS *(84–54 B.C.)*
silly laughter, 143
CELLINI, Benvenuto *(1500–1571)*
fortune, ruinous, 263
CERVANTES, Miguel de *(1547–1616)*
actors, 24
delay, 241
eggs in one basket, 245
faint heart & fair lady, 37
giving quickly (note under Publilius
Syrus), 44
fear, 89
haves & have nots, 112
heaven's help, 161
honest man, 122
honesty (note at Washington), 123
hunger, 90
money, 183
music, 25
sleep, 285
time, 302
women & love, 342
CHAMBERLAIN, Neville *(1869–1940)*
peace, 20
war, 329
CHAMFORT, Sébastien Roch Nicolas
*(1741–1794)*
laughter, 143
love, 152
success, 293
CHANDLER, Raymond *(1888–1959)*
art, 21
a blonde & a bishop, 341
detective, noble, 116
ideals, 130
CHANEL, Coco (given name,
Gabrielle Bonheur) *(1883–1971)*
fame, 293
love, 153
men, 171
youth, 349
CHARLES V *(1500–1558)*
languages, 140

CHARRON, Pierre *(1541–1603)*
science & study of man, 271
CHAUCER, Geoffrey *(c. 1343–1400)*
guilt, 107
joy & woe, 109
love, 153
May, 200
newfangledness, 205
CHEKHOV, Anton *(1860–1904)*
a gun in act one, 24
CHESTERFIELD, [Earl of] Philip
Stanhope *(1694–1773)*
advice, 6
business, 39
doing things well, 106
flattery, 89
human nature, 125
insult vs injury, 164
laughter, 143
manners & tone, 164
money, 184
procrastination, 241
religion, 254
style (note under Wesley), 30
wisdom, 335
beautiful & ugly, 341
CHESTERTON G[ilbert] K[eith]
*(1874–1936)*
angels, 273
artists, 21
chess players, 98
courage, 54
money, 184
novels, 31
patriotism, 215
problems, 327
CHOU EN LAI *(1898–1976)*
diplomacy, 66
CHRISTOPHER SOCIETY
motto (light one candle), 68
CHRYSOSTOM, [St.] John
*(c. 345–407)*
joy, 109
laughter, 143
tribulation, 309
CHURCHILL, [Sir] Winston
*(1874–1965)*
alcohol, 9
blood, sweat & tears, 72
being shot at, 58

CHURCHILL (*continued*)
democracy, 62
dictators, 315
finest hour, 73
free speech, 96
Iron Curtain, 51
navy, 173
quotations, 247
Russia, 188
so many owe so much, 73
surrender, we shall never, 73
tyranny & national guilt, 316
victory, problems of, 332
victory at all costs, 332
writing style, 29
CICERO, Marcus Tullius (*106–43 B.C.*)
consistency & politicians, 224
justice, 138
laws & war, 329
memory, 171
nature, 191
newness, 205
peace, 216
peace & slavery, 20
people, common, 218
people's good, 143
philosophers, 221
praise & glory, 293
punishment, 246
reason, 177
times & manners, 164
victory, 332
war & money, 329
wisdom, 335
CLARK, [Sir] Kenneth McKenzie
(*b. 1903*)
civilizations & war, 329
machines, 298
opera, 26
religions & female principle, 254
television, 169
CLARKE, Arthur C[harles] (*b. 1917*)
stars were going out, 347
technology, 298
CLAUDIUS CAECUS, Appius.
See APPIUS CLAUDIUS CAECUS
CLAUSEWITZ, Karl von (*1780–1831*)
war, 329
CLAY, Henry (*1777–1852*)
being president, 118

CLEMENCEAU, Georges (*1841–1929*)
being 70 (note under Holmes), 7
war (note under Talleyrand), 331
CLEMENT [St.] (*fl. A.D. 96*)
innocence, 132
praising oneself, 277
CLEMENT OF ALEXANDRIA
(*c. 150–c. 215*)
prayer, 232
CLOUGH, Arthur Hugh (*1819–1861*)
fighting & losing, 20
COCTEAU, Jean (*1891–1963*)
crowd rule, 218
tact, 164
CODE OF HAMMURABI.
See HAMMURABI
COFFIN, William Sloane, Jr. (*b. 1924*)
good deeds, 323
COKE, [Sir] Edward (*1552–1634*)
corporations, 39
home—castle, 241
COLBERT, Jean Baptiste (*1619–1683*)
taxation, 297
COLERIDGE, Samuel Taylor
(*1772–1834*)
dwarf & giants (note under Bernard
of Chartres), 326
the earth, 191
praying (2 quotes), 232
reviewers, 23
sadder but wiser, 335
suspension of disbelief, 22
water, water, 272
Xanadu, 209
COLETTE (given name, Sidonie
Gabrielle Colette) (*1873–1954*)
poetry, 27
COLLINS, [William] F. Wilkie
(*1824–1889*)
marriage & money, 166
COLTON, Charles Caleb (*c. 1780–1832*)
flattery & imitation, 89
CONFUCIUS (*551–479 B.C.*)
caution, 245
friends, 96
gods, 102
habit, 108
love, 153
manners, 164
truth, 312
youth, 349

CONGREVE, William *(1670–1729)*
  love & murder, 153
  marriage in haste, 166
  woman scorned, 111
CONNOLLY, Cyril *(1903–1974)*
  charming people, 44
  religion, 254
  reviewing, 24
  woman & fury, 342
  youth, 349
CONRAD, Joseph *(1857–1924)*
  enemies, 72
  illusions, 250
  loneliness, 287
  Orient, 209
  revolutionary spirit, 260
  sea, the, 199
  life of the, 272
  woman, empty-headed, 341
  work of art, 31
CONRAN, Shirley *(b. 1932)*
  mushroom stuffing, 90
COOLIDGE, Calvin *(1872–1933)*
  business & America, 12
  law, 144
CORBUSIER, Le *(1887–1965)*
  houses, 23
CORNEILLE, Pierre *(1606–1684)*
  danger, 59
  obedience, 206
  regicide, 260
CORNUEL, Anne Bigot de *(1605–1694)*
  man & valet, 135
COTA, [Brig. Gen.] Norman
  *(1893–1971)*
  Omaha Beach, 175
COWARD, Noel *(1899–1973)*
  China, 188
  music, 26
COWPER, William *(1731–1800)*
  variety, 320
CRABBE, George *(1754–1832)*
  will & a way, 219
CRÈVECOEUR, Michel Guillaume
  Jean de *(1735–1813)*
  melting pot (note under Zangwill),
  14
CRICHTON, Michael D. *(b. 1942)*
  computer music, 298

CRISP, Quentin *(b. 1908?)*
  dirt, 50
  vice, 282
CROCKETT, Davy *(1786–1836)*
  be right & go ahead, 275
CROKER, ["Boss"] Richard
  *(1841–1922)*
  spoils, 224
CROMWELL, Oliver *(1599–1658)*
  honesty, 122
CUMBERLAND, [Bishop] Richard
  *(1631–1718)*
  wear out vs rust out, 344
CUMMINGS, e. e. [Edward Estlin]
  *(1894–1962)*
  universe next door, 76
CUMMINGS, William Thomas
  *(1903–1944)*
  atheists & foxholes, 33
CURRAN, John Philpot *(1750–1857)*
  liberty & vigilance, 94

DANA, Charles A. *(1819–1897)*
  news (note under Bogart), 232
DANTE ALIGHIERI *(1265–1321)*
  abandon hope, 115
  heavens, the, 198
  life & losing the way, 172
DARROW, Clarence *(1857–1938)*
  atheism, 33
  freedom, 94
  justice, 138
  law, 144
  rights, 262
  truth, 312
  work, 344
DARWIN, Charles Robert *(1809–1882)*
  natural selection, 242
DAVIDSON, John *(1857–1909)*
  swift & strong, the, 332
DA VINCI, Leonardo
  See VINCI
DAVIS, Bette *(b. 1908)*
  good time had by all, 133
DE BEAUVOIR, Simone
  See BEAUVOIR, Simone de
DEBS, Eugene V[ictor] *(1855–1926)*
  Chicago, 48
  socialism, 286
DECATUR, Stephen *(1779–1820)*
  our country, 215

DE CRÈVECOEUR
See CRÈVECOEUR
DEFFAND, [Marquise] du (1697–1780)
St. Denis' miracle, 179
DEFOE, Daniel (c. 1660–1731)
Devil, 65
tyranny, 316
DE GAULLE, Charles
See GAULLE
DE LA MARE, Walter (1873–1956)
food, 90
DELANEY, Shelagh (b. 1939)
women, 337
DE MAUPASSANT, Guy
See MAUPASSANT
DEMOCRITUS (c. 460–c. 400 B.C.)
atoms, 270
chance & necessity, 270
truth, 312
DENNIS, John (1657–1734)
puns, 127
DESCARTES, René (1596–1650)
books, 37
doubt, 284
philosophy, 221
thought & existence (cogito), 177
travel, 307
DE SICA Vittorio (1901–1974)
moral indignation, 277
DE TOCQUEVILLE
See TOCQUEVILLE, Alexis de
DE VRIES, Peter (b. 1910)
equals, treating people as, 164
God, 102
gluttony, 90
DEWEY, John (1859–1952)
learn by doing (note under
Anonymous), 6
DEWEY, Thomas E. (1902–1971)
ideas, 130
law & money, 144
public office, 105
talking during campaigns, 280
DICKENS, Charles (1812–1870)
annual income, 184
baby, new, 45
best of times & worst of times, 315
butterflies are free, 94
facts, 69, 84
families & accidents, 86

DICKENS (continued)
families & poor relations, 86
far, far better thing, 323
law, 144
murder (note under Eliot), 56
new people, new money, 205
Scrooge (Bah, Humbug), 46
Tiny Tim, 46
DICKINSON, Emily (1830–1886)
death, 59
dandelions, 196
fame, 293
life, 148
luck, 161
prayer, 232
words, 140
wounded deer, 309
DIDEROT, Denis (1713–1784)
death (note under Wittgenstein), 62
flattering lies & harsh truths, 313
hypocrisy, 129
jesting, 127
passion, 74
skepticism, 284
truth, 313
DIOGENES ["The Cynic"]
(412?–323 B.C.)
education, 70
DIRKSEN, [Sen.] Everett McKinley
(1896–1969)
money, 184
DISRAELI, Benjamin (1804–1881)
anecdotage, 7
cantering on horseback, 194
change, 42
conservative government, 225
I am a Jew, 248
justice, 138
little things, 64
living in circles, 216
military, the, 173
opposition creates strength, 225
patience, 214
politics, 225
side of the angels, 267
statistics, 268
time, 302
what we least expect, 148
DODGE, Mabel 1879–1962)
soul & flesh, 36

DODGSON, Charles
See CARROLL, Lewis
DOMINO, Antoine D., Jr., "Fats"
    *(b. 1928)*
    a job, 345
DOMITIAN *(51–96)*
    free speech, 96
DONNE, John *(1572–1631)*
    come live with me, 159
    death, 59
    falling star, 207
    God & distractions, 64
    love, 153
    love and the body, 36
    no man an island, 125, 126
    roving hands, 278
    sleep, 285
DOOLEY, [Mr.]
    See DUNNE, Finley, Peter
DOSTOEVSKI, Fëdor Mikhailovich
    *(1821–1881)*
    father's death, 211
    Providence, 244
    suffering, 310
    travel in Europe, 307
    troika, 188
    work, 345
DOUGLAS, [Lord] Alfred *(1870–1945)*
    homosexuality, 278
DOUGLAS, Norman *(1868–1952)*
    advertisements, 5
DOUGLAS, Frederick *(1817–1895)*
    destiny of colored Americans, 248
DOYLE, [Sir] Arthur Conan
    *(1859–1930)*
    country, the, 53
    crime, 56
    details, 64
    dog didn't bark, 79
    theorizing & facts, 264
    truth, arriving at, 313
DRYDEN, John *(1631–1700)*
    errors, 335
    heiresses, 184
    living for today, 236
    love, 153
    madness, 162
    music, 26
    patient man, 214
    people's judgment, 218
    plots & revolution, 260

DUBOIS, W[illiam] E[dward]
    B[urghardt] *(1868–1963)*
    a poor race, being, 248
DUBUFFET, Jean *(1901–1985)*
    change, 42
    intelligence & being, 177
DUMAS, Alexandre (the Elder)
    *(1802–1870)*
    all for one, 318
    *cherchez la femme* (note under
        Fouché), 56
    rumor, 264
    success, 294
DUNNE, Finley Peter (creator, Mr.
    Dooley) *(1887–1936)*
    trust, 245
DURANT, Will *(1885–1981)*
    hurrying, 111
DUROCHER, Leo *(b. 1906)*
    nice guys, 332
DURRELL, Lawrence *(b. 1912)*
    jealousy, 136
    landscape & people, 75
DURRENMATT, Friedrich *(b. 1921)*
    thought, 177

EDDINGTON, [Sir] Arthur A.
    *(1882–1944)*
    atoms & stars, 126
    love & being reasonable, 251
EDISON, Thomas A[lva] *(1847–1931)*
    genius, 100
    hard work, 345
EDWARD VII *(1841–1910)*
    socialism, 286
EDWARD VIII *(1894–1972)*
    woman I love, 159
EHRLICHMAN, John *(b. 1925)*
    twist in the wind, 14
EINSTEIN, Albert *(1879–1955)*
    God & dice, 270
    God not malicious, 102
    ideas in science, 264
    imagination, 177
    mathematics, 268
    modern times—means & goals, 181
    mystery, 187
    peace, 216
    science, 264
    science concepts, 270

EINSTEIN (*continued*)
  science & religion, 254
  simplicity, 281
EISENHOWER, Dwight D[avid]
    (*1890–1969*)
  farming, 345
  military-industrial complex, 15
  munitions, 173
ELIOT, George (given name, Marian
    Evans Cross) (*1819–1880*)
  animals, 194
  biliousness, touch of (note under
    Shakespeare), 192
  deeds, 68
  having nothing to say, 280
  jokes, 127
  women's hopes, 337
  women, 337
ELIOT, T[homas] S[tearns]
    (*1888–1965*)
  April, 200
  beginning & end, 88
  caring & not caring, 257
  good & evil, 77
  hell, 115
  history, 120
  hollow men, 92
  home, 122
  I grow old, 7
  killing a girl, 56
  life & coffee spoons, 148
  life's facts, 148
  Magi, 47
  memory & regret, 252
  objective correlative, 22
  people who want to feel important,
    239
  poetry, 27
  reality, 250
  time, 302
  way the world ends, 348
  women talking of Michelangelo, 53
ELIZABETH I (*1533–1603*)
  anger, 19
ELIZABETH OF BELGIUM
    (*1876–1965*)
  iron curtain (note under Churchill),
    51
ELLIOTT, Ebenezer (*1781–1849*)
  communism, 51

ELLIS, Havelock (*1859–1939*)
  civilization, 49
  dance, 26
  leadership, 119
  mathematics (2 quotes), 269
  sex, 278
  war, 329
EMERSON, Ralph Waldo (*1803–1882*)
  America & youth, 12
  art, 21
  beautiful women, 341
  books, 37
  calamity, 310
  censorship, 41
  character & crimes, 56
  church, silent, 254
  civilization, 50
  civilization & women, 337
  consistency, foolish, 52
  enthusiasm, 74
  facts, 84
  fashion, 87
  friends (2 quotes), 96, 97
  God builds in the heart, 254
  government, 105
  a great man, 107
  greatness, 107
  greatness & virtue, 323
  haste, 111
  heroes, 116
  honor, boasting of, 277
  hospitality, 125
  Intelligence, universal, 318
  kings, striking at, 260
  language, 140
  life, 148
  laws, obeying, 144
  life, a circle, 216
  living, 148
  lover, all love a, 153
  a man, 171
  mousetrap, better, 205
  murder will speak out, 56
  patriotism, 215
  political party, 225
  poverty, 228
  power (3 quotes), 230
  prayer, 232
  pride, 239
  privacy, 241
  proverbs, 247

EMERSON (*continued*)
  quotations, 247
  quoting, 247
  religion & philosophy, 221
  rulers & advisors, 105
  sadness after thirty, 172
  seeing, 327
  shot heard around the world, 15
  things, 301
  tobacco, 304
  travel & languages, 307
  traveling, 307
  truth vs repose, 313
  virtue & vice, 80
  wagon to a star, 11
  war, 329
  well-dressed, being, 87
  wise men (note under Pliny the
    Elder), 336
  wit, 127
  women & respect, 337
  wonder & science, 264
  writing, 31
EMPEDOCLES (*c. 490–c. 430 B.C.*)
  God, 102
ENGELS, Friedrich (*1820–1895*)
  political power (with Marx), 231
EPICTETUS (*c. 50–120*)
  being what you want to be, 11
  education & freedom, 70
  money, 184
  philosophy, 221
  problems & handles, 310
EPICURUS (*371–170 B. C.*)
  justice (2 quotes), 138
ERASMUS, Desiderius (*1465–1536*)
  peace & war, 217
ERSKINE, Thomas (*1750–1823*)
  free speech, 96, 237
EUCLID (*4th century B.C.*)
  geometry, 269
EURIPIDES (*c. 485–406 B.C.*)
  armies, disorderly, 173
  children, 211
  cities & happiness, 48
  doubting the gods exist, 284
  effort & prosperity, 220
  haughty man is hated, 239
  life at night, 278
  love, 153
  madness, 163

EURIPIDES (*continued*)
  money, (2 quotes), 184
  perseverance vs despair, 220
  reason, 177
  sins of the fathers, 99
  success, 294
  violence, 321
  wind & fortune, 310
  wisdom, 335
  women & love, 338
  women & tears, 338
  women & women, 338
  workers, 345
  youth, 349
EVERETT, David (*1770–1813*)
  oaks & acorns, 65

FANON, Frantz [Omar] (*1925–1961*)
  black man's destiny, 248
FARRAGUT, [Admiral] David
    Glasgow (*1801–1870*)
  damn the torpedoes, 15
FAULKNER, William (*1879–1962*)
  Switzerland, 188
  writers, 31
FAWKES, Guy (*1570–1606*)
  desperate remedies, 260
FERMI, Enrico (*1901–1954*)
  knowledge, 191
FEUERBACH, Ludwig (*1804–1872*)
  food, 90
FIELD, Eugene (*1850–1895*)
  Wynken, Blynken, & Nod, 286
FIELDING, Henry (*1707–1754*)
  dying, 59
  physicians & diseases, 67
FIELDS, W[illiam] C[laude]
    (*1880–1946*)
  bad weather, 203
  children & dogs (note under Rosten),
    180
  Philadelphia, 48, 133
FITZGERALD, Edward (*1809–1883*)
  cash & distant drum, 184
  morning, 202
  moving finger, 302
  New Year, 206
  sorry scheme of things, 318
  spring, 200
  wine, bread, & thou, 159
  youth, 349

FITZGERALD, F[rancis] Scott
  *(1896–1940)*
  American lives, 12
  dark night of the soul, 63
  heroes, 116
  rich, the, 184
FITZGERALD, Zelda *(1900–1948)*
  advertising, 5
  choosing a direction, 172
FITZSIMMONS, Robert ("Bob")
  *(1862–1917)*
  hard falls, 290
FLAUBERT, Gustave *(1812–1880)*
  critics, 24
  idiots, successful, 92
  read to live, 38
FLETCHER, John *(1579–1625)*
  do or die, 5
FLORIO, John *(c. 1553–1625)*
  England, 73
  night, 202
FOCH, Ferdinand *(1851–1929)*
  I am attacking, 175
FONTAINE, Jean de La
  See LA FONTAINE
FORD, Henry *(1863–1947)*
  history, 120
  history & today, 236
  money, 184
FORGY, Howell M[aurice]
  *(1908–1983)*
  pass the ammunition, 15
FORTESCUE, John *(1395–c. 1476)*
  comparisons, 52
FORSTER, E[dward] M[organ]
  *(1879–1970)*
  connect, 148
  friends vs country, 97
  surviving, 296
FOUCHÉ, Joseph *(1763–1820)*
  *cherchez la femme,* 56
FOWLES, John *(b. 1926)*
  war, 329
FRANCE, Anatole *(1844–1924)*
  critic, a good, 24
FRANCIS I *(1494–1547)*
  all lost but honor, 332
FRANK, Anne *(1929–1945)*
  beauty, 34
  people are good, 126

FRANKLIN, Benjamin *(1706–1790)*
  death & taxes, 297
  doctors, 67
  early to bed, 113
  eating & living, 91
  hanging together, 15
  hope, living on, 124
  laziness, 146
  life & time, 303
  man, tool-making (note under
    Carlyle), 125
  marriage & love, 166
  neglect of details, 65
  pride, 239
  single man, 166
  success, 294
  time & life, 303
  time & money, 302
  trade & nations, 39
  war & peace, 329
FREDERICK THE GREAT
  *(1712–1786)*
  man & wild animal within, 171
FREUD, Sigmund *(1856–1939)*
  God, 102
  honest with oneself, 122
  mother's boy, 211
  psychoanalysis, 271
  religion, 254
  self-knowledge & healing, 131
  women, 338
FRIEDMAN, Milton *(b. 1912)*
  free lunch (note under Anonymous),
    69
FRISCH, Max *(b. 1911)*
  technology, 298
FROST, Robert *(1874–1963)*
  aged man & a house, 7
  birches, 349
  home, 122
  miles to go, 307
  two roads, 252
  walls, 318
  world, end of, 348
FROUDE, James A[nthony]
  *(1818–1894)*
  cruelty, 126
FULLER, [Sarah] Margaret
  *(1810–1850)*
  fair chance, 338
  working for a living, 345

FULLER, R[ichard] Buckminster
    *(1895–1983)*
  God, 102
  spaceship earth, 75
  war, 329
FULLER, Thomas *(1608–1661)*
  clothes, 87
  fame, 294
  foreseeing danger, 327
  foxes on juries, 138
  honest man, 122
  hopes, 124
  idleness, 146
  punishment & prevention, 246
  travel, 307
FYLEMAN, Rose *(1877–1957)*
  fairies, 196

GALBRAITH, John Kenneth *(b. 1908)*
  money, 184
  politics, 225
  U.S.—overeating in, 91
GALEN *(129–199)*
  language & clarity, 140
GALILEO, Galilei *(1564–1642)*
  Bible & the heavens, 254
GALSWORTHY, John *(1867–1933)*
  law, 144
GALTON, [Sir] Francis *(1822–1911)*
  sailor's life, 272
GANDHI, Mohandas K. [Mahatma]
    *(1869–1948)*
  honesty & wealth, 185
  nonviolence, 210
  readiness to die, 210
  violence, 321
GARBO, Greta *(b. 1905)*
  to be alone, 287
GARCÍA LORCA, Frederico
    *(1898–1936)*
  greenness, 196
GARCÍA MÁRQUEZ, Gabriel
    *(b. 1928)*
  sex, 278
GARY, Romain *(1914–1980)*
  humor, 127
GAULLE, Charles de *(1890–1970)*
  France & cheese, 188
  politicians, 225
GAY, John *(1688–1732)*
  cohabitation, 282

GAY *(continued)*
  life, 148
  love, 153
  words, fair, 140
  youth, 349
GENET, Jean *(b. 1910)*
  elegance, 292
GETTY, John Paul *(1892–1976)*
  have-nots, 112
GIBBON, Edward *(1737–1794)*
  feeling rich, 185
  history, 121
  humans must advance, 243
GIBBS, George *(1870–1942)*
  marriage, 166
GIBRAN, Kahlil *(1883–1931)*
  parents, 211
  prayer, 232
  togetherness, 166
  work, 345
GIDE, André *(1869–1951)*
  bad writing, 31
  education, 70
  God, 103
  God, aiming toward, 103
  mysticism, 187
  sin, 80
  truth, 313
GILBERT, W[illiam] S[chwenck]
    *(1836–1911)*
  facts, 84
  little list, 57
  love, 153
  policeman's lot, 57
  Queen's Navee, 173
  stoutness, 36
GINSBERG, Allen *(b. 1926)*
  best minds, 181
  poetry, 28
GIOVANNI, Nikki *(b. 1943)*
  death & slavery, 248
GIRADOUX, Jean *(1882–1944)*
  faithful women, 166
  killing, 173
  law, 144
  men, 171
  marriage, 167
  press, the, 237
  success & sincerity, 122
  truths & nations, 313
  a woman, being, 338

GLADSTONE, William Ewart
   *(1809–1898)*
   masses vs classes, 218
GLOUCESTER, William Henry
   [Duke of] *(1743–1805)*
   Gibbon, 133
GOERING, Hermann *(1893–1946)*
   culture (note under Johst), 21
   guns vs butter, 329
GOETHE, Johann Wolfgang von
   *(1749–1842)*
   architecture, 23
   female, eternal, 338
   mathematics, 269
   middle age, 172
   moment, each, 236
   nature, 191
   night, 202
   objects, 301
   revolution, 260
   seize opportunity, 37
   self, mastering, 274
   self, suiting, 275
   useless life, 148
   words, 140
   youth, 349
GOLDBERG, Isaac *(1887–1938)*
   diplomacy, 66
GOLDSMITH, Oliver *(1728–1774)*
   first blow, 37
   hope, 124
   law, 144
   old friends, old things, 208
   praying, 232
   silence, 280
GOLDWATER, Barry *(b. 1909)*
   extremism, 15
   government, 105
GOLDWYN, Samuel *(1882–1974)*
   contracts, 144
   im-possible, 140
GORDON, Adam Lindsay *(1833–1870)*
   kindness & courage, 323
GORDON, George N.
   See BYRON
GORKY, Maxim *(1869–1936)*
   marriage, 167
   past, the, 213
   philosophy, 221
   work, 345

GOURNAY, Vincent de *(1712–1759)*
   *laissez faire* (note under Argenson),
   40
GRACIÁN, Baltasar *(1601–1658)*
   victories & hate, 333
GRAHAM, Katherine *(b. 1917)*
   women, 338
GRAHAM, Martha *(b. 1894)*
   body, 36
   dance, 26
   mediocrity, 170
GRAHAME, Kenneth *(1859–1932)*
   boats, 272
GRANT, Ulysses S[impson]
   fight on the line, 15
GRAY, Thomas *(1716–1771)*
   Elegy, 202
   flower unseen, 287
   paths of glory, 294
GREELEY, Horace *(1811–1872)*
   Go West (note under Soule), 18
GREENE, Grahame *(b. 1904)*
   childhood, 45
GREER, Germaine *(b. 1939)*
   Freud, 271
   women & men, 342
GRELLET, Étienne de *(1773–1855)*
   kindness, 323
GREY, Edward [Viscount of Falloden]
   *(1862–1933)*
   lights out over Europe, 181
GUARESCHI, Giovanni *(1908–1968)*
   sinners
GUINAN, Texas *(1884–1933)*
   success, 294
   sucker & an even break (note under
      Anonymous), 112
GUITRY, Sacha *(1885–1957)*
   wit, 127
GURNEY, Dorothy *(1858–1932)*
   gardens, 196


HALBERSTAM, David *(b. 1934)*
   best & brightest (note under Caryle),
   71
HALE, Nathan *(1755–1776)*
   one life to lose for my country, 15
HAMILTON, Edith *(1867–1963)*
   Greeks, 188

HAMILTON [Sir] William
  (*1788–1856*)
  mind, 177
HÄMMERSKJOLD, Dag (*1905–1961*)
  friendship, 97
  loneliness, 287
  vision, 327
HAMMURABI, Code of (*3rd
  millennium B.C.*)
  eye for an eye, 246
HAN SUNYIN (*b. 1917*)
  Malaya, 209
HAND, Learned (*1872–1961*)
  media, 169
HARINGTON, [Sir] John (*1561–1612*)
  treason, 225
HARRINGTON, Michael (*b. 1928*)
  American racism, 248
HARVEY, William (*1578–1657*)
  egg & life, 267
HAWKING, Stephen William (*b. 1942*)
  God & dice, 270
HAWKINS, [Sir] Anthony Hope
  See HOPE, Anthony
HAWTHORNE, Nathaniel
  (*1804–1864*)
  electricity, 298
  self, 274
  time, 303
HAZLITT, William (*1778–1830*)
  antipathies, 111
  country, visiting the, 53
  fourth estate (note under Macaulay),
    238
  getting on in the world, 170
  grace, 106
  hate, 112
  manners, 164
  painting, 27
  the public, 218
  self-concern, 274
  sleep, 286
  travel, 307
  truth, 313
  winning, 333
  women, 338
  youth, 349
HEBER, Reginald (*1783–1826*)
  brightest and best (note under
    Carlyle), 71

HEGEL, Georg Wilhelm Friedrich
  (*1770–1831*)
  greatness & passion, 74
  history, 121
HEINE, Heinrich (*1797–1856*)
  book burning, 42
  God, 103
HEISENBERG, Werner Karl
  (*1901–1967*)
  experts, 83
HELLER, Joseph (*b. 1923*)
  mediocrity, 170
  self-made man, 276
HELLER, Walter [Wolfgang]
  (*b. 1915*)
  principle vs what's right, 78
HELLMAN, Lillian (*1905–1984*)
  conscience, 52
HEMANS, Felicia (*1739–1835*)
  boy on burning deck, 117
  stately homes, 73
HEMINGWAY, Ernest (*1899–1961*)
  books, 37
  courage & grace, 106
  morality, 78
  Paris, 48
  separate peace, 217
HENLEY, W[illiam] E[rnest]
  (*1849–1903*)
  bloody but unbowed, 297
  master of my fate, 276
HENRY IV (*1553–1610*)
  chicken in every pot, 91
  Paris, 48
HENRY, O. (real name, William
  Sydney Porter) (*1862–1910*)
  New York, 48
  swindles, 57
HENRY, Patrick (*1736–1799*)
  liberty or death, 15
HERACLITUS (*c. 540–c. 480 B.C.*)
  change (3 quotes), 42, 43
  character, 88
  flux (flowing), 42
  river, 42
  toil, 345
  wisdom & particulars, 65
HERBERT, George (*1593–1633*)
  jesting, 127
  law, 144
  living for God, 234

HERBERT (*continued*)
man, 126
prayer & sailing, 272
revenge, 259
spring, 200
war, 329
HERODOTUS (*c. 485–c. 425 B.C.*)
envy vs pity, 294
force, 321
great deeds, 107
haste, 111
knowledge without power, 230
power, 230
seeing vs hearing (note under
Tennyson), 79
snow, rain, etc. & appointed rounds,
203
HERRICK, Robert (*1591–1674*)
disorder in dress, 87
rosebuds, 115
HERZEN, Alexander (*1812–1870*)
history, 121
HERZL, Theodor (*1860–1904*)
working people, 218
HESIOD (*c. 700 B.C.*)
procrastination, 241
HEYWOOD, John (*c. 1497–c. 1580*)
beginnings, hard, 35
marriage and hanging (note under
Shakespeare), 168
HICKSON, William Edward
(*1803–1870*)
try again, 220
HILL, Aaron (*1685–1750*)
nettles, 54
HILLEL "THE ELDER"
(*c. 70 B.C.—c. 10 A.D.*)
self-interest, 275
HIPPOCRATES (*460?–370? B.C.*)
life & art, 148
of medicine, 67
natural forces & healing, 131
patient & doctor, 131
prayer, 232
soul, 288
HITCHCOCK, Tommy (*1900–1944*)
sportsmanship, 333
HITLER, Adolf (*1889–1945*)
enemy, using an, 72
lying to the masses, 218
neutrals, 121

HITLER (*continued*)
pacifism, 210
power, 230
war, 330
HOBBES, Thomas (*1588–1679*)
justice, 138
life (2 quotes), 149
science, 265
HOCH, Edward Wallis (*1849–1925*)
criticizing others, 305
HOFFER, Eric (*b. 1902*)
failure, 263
freedom, 94
holy causes, 85
HOFFMAN, Abbie (*b. 1937*)
anyone over thirty, 350
HOLBACH, Paul Henri Dietrich
[Baron d'] (*1723–1789*)
religions, 254
HOLMES, Oliver Wendell (*1809–1894*)
age & sweetness, 172
insight, 327
one-hoss shay, 299
70 years young, 7
HOLMES, Oliver Wendell, Jr.
(*1841–1935*)
free speech, 96
great cases, 144
law, 144
Oh, to be 70, 7
truth, 313
HOMER (*fl. c. 700 B.C.*)
generations fall like leaves, 99
heaven provides riches, 244
hypocrites, 129
novelty, 205
prayer, 232
sleep, 286
tongue is twisty, 140
victory, 333
wandering, 307
wisdom & doubt, 335
youth, 350
HOOD, Thomas (*1799–1845*)
Autumn, 200
house where born, 122
HOOVER, Herbert (*1874–1964*)
chicken (note under Henry IV), 91
rugged individualism, 12
was, 330

HOPE, Anthony *(1863–1933)*
 good families, 86
HOPKINS, Gerald Manley *(1844–1889)*
 dappled things, 191
 poetical language, 28
 wilderness, 75
 world & God (2 quotes), 103, 191
HORACE *(65–8 B.C.)*
 acceptance, 257
 anger, 19
 beginnings, 35
 force, 321
 Homer nods, 85
 money, needing, 185
 nature, 191
 neighbor's wall, 258
 poet, mediocre, 28
 people, the, 219
 rewriting, 31
 sailing ships, 272
 seize the day, 236
 self-confidence, 275
 to die for one's country, 215
 travel, 307
 wise, courage to be, 35
 words, 140
 writing & erasing, 31
 youth, 350
HOUSEMAN, A[lfred] E[dward]
  *(1859–1936)*
 love, 113
 malt vs Milton, 10
 stranger in world, 10
HOWE, Louis McHenry *(1871–1936)*
 politics, 225
HOYLE, Edmond *(1672–1769)*
 win the trick, 99
HOYLE, [Sir] Fred *(b. 1915)*
 mistakes, 180
 space, 270
HUBBARD, L[afayette] Ron[ald]
  *(1913–1986)*
 religion, founding a, 254
HUBBARD, Elbert *(1859–1915)*
 ancestors, 282
 life, 149
HUGHES, Langston *(1902–1967)*
 democracy for all?, 249
 dream deferred, 260
 Harlem, 48
 yesterday, 213

HUGHIE, Charles
 See under PARKER, Ross
HUGO, Victor *(1802–1885)*
 dreams, 243
 idea whose time has come, 130
 luck, 162
 prayer, 233
 science, 265
 youth, 350
HUME, David *(1711–1776)*
 beauty (note under Hungerford), 34
 custom, 58
 mind, 177
HUNGERFORD, Margaret W.
  *(1855–1897)*
 beauty, 34
HUNT, J. H. Leigh *(1784–1859)*
 Abou Ben Adhem, 141, 142
HURSTON, Zora Neale *(1907–1960)*
 poverty, 228
HUSS, John *(c. 1370–1415)*
 simplicity, 281
HUTCHESON, Francis *(1694–1746)*
 ends & means, 335
HUXLEY, Aldous [Leonard]
  *(1894–1963)*
 excuses, 83
 facts, 84
 *mons veneris*, 278
 self, 274
HUXLEY, Julian [Sorel] *(1887–1975)*
 false thinking, 177
HUXLEY, T[homas] H[enry]
  *(1825–1895)*
 hypotheses (2 quotes), 265
 truths, 313

IBSEN, Henrik *(1828–1906)*
 all or nothing, 11
 debts & home life, 86
 future, 97
 loneliness, 287
 minority always right, 71
 Nora (wife & mother first?), 338
 sinning, 282
 strength & solitude, 287
I CHING
 fire in the lake, 260
IONESCO, Eugène *(b. 1912)*
 civil servants, 105
 life, 149

IONESCO (*continued*)
  predictions, 327
  time, 111
INGERSOLL, R[obert] G[reen]
    (*1833–1899*)
  God & man, 103
IRVING, Washington (*1783–1859*)
  almighty dollar, 185
  women & adversity, 338


JACKSON, Andrew (*1767–1845*)
  taxation, 297
JACKSON, Reggie (*b. 1946*)
  straw that stirs the drink, 239
JACKSON, "Stonewall" [Thomas
    Jonathan] (*1824–1863*)
  pass over river (last words), 59
JAMES, Henry (*1843–1916*)
  art & life, 21
  summer afternoon, 200
JAMES, William (*1842–1910*)
  bitch goddess success, 294
JAMES I (*1566–1625*)
  oysters, 91
  tobacco, 304
JEANS, [Sir] James Hopwood
    (*1877–1946*)
  universe, 318
JEFFERSON, Thomas (*1743–1826*)
  alliances, 15
  American and the military, 16
  bill of rights, 262
  books, 38
  citizen-soldiers, 174
  Declaration of Independence, 15
  delaying, 241
  earth, the, 75
  force, 321
  freedom & militia, 174
  future vs past, 98
  gardener, young, 196
  government & honesty, 105
  government & liberty, 105
  happiness, 109
  ignorance vs error, 284
  inalienable rights, 15
  laws, 144
  living too long, 8
  newspapers, 238
  people, the, 219

JEFFERSON (*continued*)
  power, 230
  press, freedom of, 237
  public trust, 225
  religion, 255
  tree of liberty, 260
  truth, 313
  truths, self-evident, 15
  tyrants, resisting, 316
  U.S. & a just God, 12
  U.S. & the military, 16
JEROME, [St.] (*c. 342–420*)
  love, 153
  solitude & pride, 287
JOHN OF THE CROSS [Saint]
    (*1542–1591*)
  dark night of the soul, 187
JOHNSON, [Sen.] Hiram Warren
    (*1866–1945*)
  war & truth, 330
JOHNSON, Lyndon B[aines]
    (*1908–1973*)
  giving a gift, 164
  president's hardest task, 119
JOHNSON, Philander (*1866–1939*)
  cheer up, 209
JOHNSON, Samuel (*1709–1784*)
  acquaintances, 97
  advertising, 5
  American, cannot love an, 12
  cards, 99
  Chesterfield's letters, 134
  criticism, hostile vs none at all, 24
  criticizing drama, 24
  eating, 91
  editing fine passages, 29
  excise tax, 297
  ignorance of horses, 85
  Irish, 189
  Italy, 189
  hanging & concentration, 60
  language & thought, 140
  lexicographer, 31
  London, 49
  London & Scotchman, 134
  marriage, second, 167
  marriage vs celibacy, 167
  money, 185
  network, 216
  oats, 91
  patriotism, 215

JOHNSON *(continued)*
    patron, 21
    perseverance, 220
    pleasing others, 164
    pleasure & hypocrisy, 129
    poets, 28
    power, 230
    present, the, 236
    provisions for the poor, 228
    public opinion, 219
    ships, 273
    silence, critical, 24
    sleep, 286
    sleeping late, 146
    virtue & vice, 78
    wickedness, 80
    woman preaching, 134
    writing & fine passages, 29
    writing any time, 30
    writing for money, 31
JOHST, Hans *(b. 1890)*
    culture, 21
JOLSON, Al *(1886–1950)*
    ain't heard nothin, 97
JONES, John Paul *(1747–1792)*
    not yet begun to fight, 16
JONSON, Ben *(c. 1573–1637)*
    guilt, 108,
    style, 29
JOSEPH, [Chief of the Nez Percées]
        *(1840–1904)*
    I will fight no more, 257
    peace, 217
JOUBERT, Joseph *(1754–1824)*
    space, 192
JOWETT, Benjamin *(1817–1893)*
    God & clergy, 103
JOYCE, James *(1882–1941)*
    experience & art (Welcome O
        Life . , .), 22
    history, 121
    Ireland, 189
    small it's all, 149
    snow, 200
    yes I will, 278
JULIAN THE APOSTATE *(332–363)*
    Jesus, 137
JULIUS CAESAR
    See CAESAR
JUNG, Carl Gustav *(1875–1961)*
    passions, 278

JUVENAL *(c. 50–c. 130)*
    health, 113
    honesty, 122
    luck, 162
    nature, 191
    poor man & robber, 228
    revenge, 259
    wickedness, 81
    writing, 31
    young, the, 350


KAISER, Henry *(1882–1967)*
    problems, 310
KANT, Immanuel *(1724–1804)*
    categorical imperative, 78
    morality & happiness, 78
    violence, 321
KARR, Alphonse *(1808–1890)*
    *plus ça change,* 43
KAUFMAN, George S. *(1889–1961)*
    satire, 25
KEATS, John *(1795–1821)*
    autumn, 200
    beauty, thing of, 34
    beauty & truth, 34
    discovery (a peak in Darien), 268
    earth, poetry of, 191
    experience, 83
    failure, fiercer hell, 263
    failure vs greatness, 11
    La Belle Dame sans Merci, 342
    love in a hut, 229
    music after the songs of spring, 7
    name writ in water, 63
    philosophy (2 quotes), 221
    poetry (2 quotes), 28
    thought, love & fame, 287
    wind & stars, 191
KEATS, John *(b. 1920)*
    automobile, 299
KEBLE, John *(1792–1866)*
    prayer & behavior, 234
KELLER, Helen *(1880–1968)*
    ancestry, 76
    education & tolerance, 306
    literature, 38
KELLY, Walt *(1913–1973)*
    enemy is us, 126
KEMPIS, Thomas à *(1380–1471)*
    glory of world, 294

KEMPIS *(continued)*
  live the day well, 234
  love, 153
  man & God ,103
  obeying vs ruling, 206
  peace, 217
  self-knowledge, 276
KENNEDY, John F[itzgerald]
    *(1917–1963)*
  Berlin, 16
  communism, 51
  crisis & opportunity, 310
  life is unfair, 149
  negotiation, 66
  peace, 217
  planet, vulnerable, 75
  planning ahead (repairing roof), 241
  poetry, 28
  problems, 310
  political action, 225
  poor, helping the, 229
  responsibility, 258
  scientists, 265
  serving your country (ask not . . .),
    215
  victory & defeat, 333
  Washington, 49
KEPLER, Johannes *(1571–1630)*
  astrology, 207
  planet earth, 191
KERR, Clark *(b. 1911)*
  education, 70
KERR, Jean *(b. 1923)*
  beauty, 84
  keeping your head (note under
    Kipling), 340
KEYNES, John Maynard *(1883–1946)*
  long run, the, 98
KHRUSHCHEV, Nikita *(1894–1971)*
  politicians, 225
  revolutionary slogans, 260
KILMER, Joyce *(1886–1918)*
  trees, 196, 197
KING, Martin Luther, Jr. *(1929–1968)*
  a dream, 327
  evil, 81
  injustice, 138
  justice awaited, 249
  law, 145
  philanthrophy, 44
  progress, 243

KING *(continued)*
  religion, 255
  science, 299
KINGSLEY, Charles *(1819–1875)*
  be good, 324
  do noble things, 68
  men, women & life, 149
  youth, 350
KIPLING, Rudyard *(1865–1936)*
  Cat, 194
  cigars vs women, 305
  Col.'s lady & Judy O'Grady, 338
  Dane-geld, 20
  East & West, 209
  east of Suez, 308
  female of the species, 338
  four greatest things, 107
  freedom, 94
  Gunga Din, 249
  if . . . (4 quotes), 324
  lest we forget, 234
  madness, partial, 163
  rag, bone, hank of hair, 154
  road to Mandalay, 209
  simple things, 132
  traveling alone, 307
  women & men, 342
  work, 345
KISSINGER, Henry A[lfred] *b. 1923)*
  power, 230
*KORAN, THE*
  creation of world, 55
  God, 103
  God & evil, 81
  perseverance, 220
KOVACS, Ernie *(1919–1962)*
  television, 169
KRISHNAMURTI, Jiddu *(1895–1986)*
  belief, 85
  meditation, 177
  problems & answers, 310
  silence, 280

LA BRUYÈRE, Jean de *(1645–1696)*
  Fathers, unloved, 211
  fame, 294
  laughter, 143
  logic, 221
  mediocrity, 171
  ruin, 263
  speaking without thinking, 92

LA BRUYÈRE (*continued*)
  truth & popular beliefs, 313
  women, 339
LA FAYETTE, Marie Madeleine
    [Madame de] (*1634–1692*)
  mothers & sex education, 278
LA FONTAINE, Jean de (*1621–1695*)
  bending vs breaking, 297
  oneself, helping, 276
  oneself, depending on, 276
  patience & delay, 214
  wisdom, lacking, 335
LAGRANGE, [Marquis de]
    (*1796–1876*)
  advice, 6
LAGUARDIA, Fiorello Henry
    (*1882–1947*)
  making a mistake, 180
LAING, R. D. (*b. 1927*)
  psychiatrists, 271
LAMB, [Lady] Caroline (*1785–1828*)
  Byron, 134
  quotations, 247
LAMB, Charles (*1775–1834*)
  borrowers & lenders, 185
  cards, playing, 99
  familiar faces gone, 8
  time & space, 270
LANCHESTER, Elsa (*b. 1902*)
  butter that wouldn't melt anywhere,
    134
LAND, Edwin Herbert (*b. 1900*)
  bottom line, 142
LANGBRIDGE, Frederick (*1849–1923*)
  looking through bars, 327
LAO-TZÜ (also LAO TZE
    (*c. 604–531 B.C.*)
  action vs competition, 335
  beginning (journey . . . single step), 35
  nature, 191
  simplicity, 281
  victory in war, 330
  the way [Tao] (2 quotes), 187
LA ROCHEFOUCAULD, [Duc de]
    (given name, François A. F.
    Rochefoucauld-Liancourt)
    (*1613–1680*)
  advice, 6
  appearances, 19
  confessing faults, 123
  fortune, 109

LA ROCHEFOUCAULD (*continued*)
  friends, 97
  hypocrisy, 129
  intellect & the heart, 114
  jealousy, 136
  justice, 138
  love (3 quotes), 154
  love & hate, 154
  marriages, 167
  misfortunes of friends, 310
  passions, great, 82
  passions, resisting, 278
  passions & the heart, 112
  self-love, 274
  vanity, (2 quotes), 239
  virtue & vanity, 324
  virtue, 324
  women & love, 154
  youth, 350
LAUDER, Leonard (*b. 1933*)
  money & experience, 39
LAWRENCE D[avid] H[erbert]
    (*1885–1930*)
  American soul, 12
  animals, 194
  sex & beauty, 278
LAWRENCE, James (*1781–1813*)
  don't give up ship, 16
LAZARUS, Emma (*1849–1887*)
  give me your poor (Statue of
    Liberty), 16
LEAR, Edward (*1812–1888*)
  Owl & Pussy Cat, 273
LEC, Stanislaw (*b. 1909*)
  progress, 243
  smashing monuments, 260
LE CORBUSIER
  See CORBUSIER, Le
LEE, Henry "Light-Horse Harry"
    (*1756–1818*)
  G. Washington, 16
LEIBNIZ, [Baron] Gottfried Wilhelm
    von (*1646–1716*)
  doctors, 67
  soul, 288
LENCLOS, Ninon de (*1620–1705*)
  age & women, 8
  love, 154
LENIN, Nikolai (given name,
    V[ladimir] I[lyich] Ulyanov)
    (*1870–1924*)

LENIN *(continued)*
  politics & economics, 69
  press, the, 238
LEO XIII [Pope] *(1810–1903)*
  revolution, 261
LEONARDO DA VINCI
  See VINCI
LEONCAVALLO, Ruggiero
    *(1858–1919)*
  *commedia è finita* (note under
    Rabelais), 60
LEOPOLD, Aldo *(1886–1948)*
  conservation, 75
LESSING, Doris *(b. 1919)*
  intelligence, 178
  small things & small minds, 92
LESSING, Gotthold Ephraim
    *(1729–1781)*
  prayer, 233
LEVIS, [Duc de] *(1764–1830)*
  *noblesse oblige,* 119
LEWIS, C[live] S[taples] *(1898–1963)*
  middle age, 172
LEWIS, Sinclair *(1885–1951)*
  Babbitt & his car, 299
  professionals & literature, 24
LEY, Robert *(1890–1945)*
  strength & joy, 291
LIBERACE *(b. 1919)*
  criticism, 24
LINCOLN, Abraham *(1809–1865)*
  ballot vs bullet, 62
  events, 88
  common-looking people, 19
  conservatism, 225
  country belongs to the people, 12
  fooling the people, 219
  freedom, 94
  genius, 100
  Gettysburg Address (four score & 7
    years ago . . .), 16
  house divided, 16
  losing, the hurt of, 333
  Negro—let him alone, 249
  people's justice, 219
  with malice toward none, 16
LINNAEUS (also called, Carl von
    Linné) *(1707–1778)*
  medicine, 131
LIPPMANN, Walter *(1889–1974)*
  government, 105

LIVY *(59 B.C.–17 A.D.)*
  money, 185
  peace, 217
  truth, 313
LOCKE, John *(1632–1704)*
  error, 85
  experience, 83
  health, 113
  law, 145
  new opinions, 205
  a son's respect, 211
  truth (2 quotes), 314
  virtue, 324
  wealth, 185
LOGAU, Friedrich von *(1604–1655)*
  mills of God, 103
LOMBARDI, Vince[nt T.] *(1913–1970)*
  winning, 333
LONG, Huey Pierce *(1893–1935)*
  everyman a king, 219
LONGFELLOW, Henry Wadsworth
    *(1807–1882)*
  art & time (note under Anonymous),
    21
  boys & youth, 350
  cares . . . like Arabs, 310
  children's hour, 45
  little girl with curl, 45
  mills of God (note under Logau), 103
  music & poetry, 22
  nightfall, 202
  Paul Revere, 117
  rain must fall, 310
  ship of state, 12
  ships in the night, 149
  sorrow, silence, endurance, 220
  speak for yourself, 159
  suffer & be strong, 310
  village smithy, 345
LONGWORTH, Alice Roosevelt
    *(1884–1979)*
  gossip, 53
LORCA, García
  See GARCÍA LORCA
LOUIS XIV *(1638–1715)*
  *l'état ç'est moi,* 119
LOUIS XVIII *(1755–1824)*
  punctuality, 165
LOVELACE, Richard *(1618–1658)*
  love & honor, 324
  prison, 178

LOVELL, Maria *(1803–1877)*
two souls, 154
LOWELL, Amy *(1874–1925)*
patterns, 216
LOWELL, James Russell *(1819–1891)*
day in June, 200
endurance & patience, 220
world born each day, 236
LOWRY, Malcolm *(1909–1957)*
regret, 252
LUCE, Clare Boothe *(b. 1903)*
good deeds (note under Coffin), 323
women & money, 339
LUCIAN *(c. 120–200)*
soul, the, 289
LUCIANO, "Lucky" (given name,
Salvatore Lucania *(1897–1962)*
no crumb, 240
LUCRETIUS *(99–55 B.C.)*
creation, 55
food/poison, 320
generations, 99
life, 149
love, 154
victory, 333
LUTHER, Martin *(1483–1546)*
astrology, 207
God (2 quotes), 103
heart, 114
here I stand, 255
marriage, 167
ox—whose is gored, 275
war, 330
wine, women & song (note under
Anonymous), 114
LYLY, John *(c. 1554–1606)*
love, 154
marriage, 167
night, 202
truth, speaking, 123
LYTTON, BULWER-
See BULWER-LYTTON

MacARTHUR, Douglas *(1880–1964)*
old soldiers, 16–17
I shall return, 16
war & will, 330
MACAULAY, Thomas Babington,
[Lord] *(1800–1859)*
business of everybody (note under
Anonymous), 258

MACAULAY *(continued)*
demagogues, 226
fourth estate, 238
Horatius, 117
money, interest on, 69
politicians, 226
MACHIAVELLI, Niccolò *(1469–1527)*
being feared vs being loved, 291
cruelties, 37
dangers, 59
prince & affection of people, 119
prince & virtue, 119
prophets, armed, 328
war, 330
.world, the, 149
MACLEOD, Fiona (real name, William
Sharp) *(1856–1905)*
heart, a lonely hunter, 114
MACMILLAN, Harold [Earl of
Stockton] *(b. 1894)*
wind of change, 43, 189
MAIMONIDES *(1135–1204)*
poverty, 229
MAINTENON, [Madame] Françoise
de *(1635–1719)*
delicacy & love, 154
MAISTRE, Joseph de *(1753–1821)*
governments, 105
MALCOLM X *(1925–1965)*
patriotism, 215
power, 231
restraint & violence, 321
MALLARMÉ, Stéphane *(1842–1898)*
flesh & books, 63
soul, the, 289
MALLORY, George H. L. *(1886–1924)*
Everest, 290
MALTHUS, Thomas Robert
*(1766–1834)*
population, 98
MANN, Thomas *(1875–1955)*
death, 60
love, 154
mathematics & lust, 269
truths, 314
MAO TSE-TUNG *(1893–1976)*
Communists & the people, 51
100 flowers, 320
people & the army, 174
people & world history, 219
political power, 231

MAO TSE-TUNG (*continued*)
politics & war, 226
reactionaries, 226
revolution, 261
MARCUS AURELIUS ANTONINUS
(*121–180*)
every act as if one's last, 106
distress, 310
happiness, 109
sins of commission & omission, 81
thought & life,, 178
MARE, DE LA
See DE LA MARE, Walter
MARIE-ANTOINETTE [Queen]
*1755–1793)*
eat cake, 91
MARLOWE, Christopher (*1564–1593*)
Faust's last hour, 142
Helen of Troy & 1,000 ships
(2 quotes), 341
hell, 115
live with me & love, 160
love at first sight, 154
MARQUEZ
See GARCÍA MÁRQUEZ
MARQUIS, D[onald R. P.] (*1878–1937*)
civilization, 50
dance, Mehitabel, 8
earth, the, 75
generations & greed, 100
having kittens, 211
hypocrisy, 129
ideas, 130
integrity, 123
mehitabel & *joie de vivre*, 109
middle age, 173
optimists, 209
pessimist & optimists, 209
publishing poetry, 28
rich man, 185
unlucky persons, 162
MARSHALL, Thomas Riley
(*1854–1925*)
5-cent cigar, 305
MARSHALL, John (*1755–1835*)
tax, power to, 297
MARTÍ, José [Julian] (*1853–1895*)
freedom, 95
MARTIAL (*c. 40–c. 104*)
death & glory, 330
health, 113

MARTIAL (*continued*)
the poor & the rich, 112
the present (2 quotes), 236
suicide, 295
writing, 31
MARVELL, Andrew (*1671–1678*)
coyness, 115
time, 303
MARX, Chico (given forename,
Leonard) (*1886–1961*)
chorus girl, whispering to, 83
MARX, Groucho (given forenames,
Julius Henry) (*1895–1977*)
bigamy, 167
club, private, 71
money, 185
posterity, 100
MARX, Karl (*1818–1883*)
class struggle & history, 121
communism—abilities & needs, 51
constant labor, 346
hell, 116
political power, 231
religion, 255
specter of communism, 51
workers unite!, 261
MARY TUDOR (Mary II)
(*1516–1558*)
calais, 252
MASEFIELD, John (*1878–1967*)
seas & ships, 273
MASON, Donald Francis (*b. 1913*)
sighted sub, 176
MASSINGER, Philip (*1583–1640*)
governing others, 274
MATISSE, Henri (*1869–1954*)
art, 27
color, 27
MAUGHAM, W[illiam] Somerset
(*1874–1965*)
adultery, 282
criticism, 6
excess, 82
impropriety & wit, 128
love & aging, 154
misfortune, 311
money, 185
mothers, 211
old age, 8
parents, 211
religion, 255

MAUGHAM *(continued)*
  suffering, 311
  youth, 350
MAUPASSANT, Guy de *(1850–1893)*
  patriotism, 215
McAULIFFE, Anthony C[lement]
    *(1898–1975)*
  nuts!, 17
McCARTHY, Mary *(b. 1912)*
  sex, 278
  violence, 321
McCLELLAN, George B[rinton]
    *(1826–1885)*
  quiet on the Potomac, 17
McLUHAN, Marshall *(1911–1980)*
  ads, 5
  automation, 299
  cars, 299
  electric age & global network, 299
  electronics & global village, 169
  life & art, 250
  medium is message, 169
McCORD, David *(b. 1897)*
  waiter's epitaph, 91
MEAD, Margaret *(1901–1978)*
  men, 343
MEARNS, Hughes *(1875–1965)*
  man who wasn't there, 163
MEIR, Golda *(1898–1978)*
  old age, 8
  time, 303
  women's interests, 339
MELVILLE, Herman *(1819–1891)*
  drunken Christian, 10
  forbidden seas, 308
  Ishmael, 273
MENANDER *(c. 342–292 B.C.)*
  love, 155
  marriage, 167
  whom gods love, 60
  women, 339
MENCIUS *(372–189 B. C.)*
  greatness, 107
  music, 26
MENCKEN, H[enry] L[ouis]
    *(1880–1956)*
  age & wisdom, 8
  American heroes (liars), 12
  American voter & intelligence, 12
  burying the damned, 181
  conscience, 52

MENCKEN *(continued)*
  democracy, 62
  faith, 86
  farming, 346
  God, 103
  governments & morality, 105
  ideas, 130
  philosophy, 221
  piety & fear, 255
  progress, 243
  religion, respecting, 255
  war, 330
  women, (2 quotes), 339
  work, 346
MERRITT, Dixon *(1879–1954)*
  pelican, 194
MIES VAN DER ROHE *(1886–1969)*
  less, 23
MILL, John Stuart *(1806–1873)*
  happiness, 109
  originality, 205
  trade, 39
MILLAY, Edna St. Vincent
    *(1892–1950)*
  candle burns at both ends, 82
  childhood, 45
  life, 149
  Staten Island ferry, 350
MILLER, Arthur *(b. 1915)*
  fighting fair, 55
  justice, 138
  kidders, 128
  not well liked, 85
  suicide, 295
  work a lifetime, 346
MILLER, Henry *(1891–1980)*
  America, 13
  Americans & youth, 350
  democracy, 63
  Greece, 189
  talking to each other, 53
MILLER, [Dr.] Jonathan [Wolfe]
    *(b. 1934)*
  illness, 131
MILLET, Kate *(b. 1934)*
  women & conditioning, 339
MILLIGAN, Spike *(b. 1918)*
  contraceptives, 278
MILTON, John *(1608–1674)*
  Adam & Eve, 343
  care, 311

MILTON (*continued*)
  books, destroying, 42
  Christmas, 47
  evening & morning stars, 198
  Evil be my Good, 81
  force, 321
  hell, way out of, 116
  hell, reigning in, 240
  hell is myself, 116
  hypocrisy, 129
  justice & mercy, 138
  justify the ways of God, 235
  license & liberty, 95
  mind, 178
  morning star, 198
  peace, 217
  Sabrina, 235
  spirit creatures, 207
  they serve who wait, 214
  virtue, 324
  virtue & experience, 324
  war, 330
  wisdom, 335
  woman, creation of, 339
MINOW, Newton N[orman] (*b. 1926*)
  television (2 quotes), 170
MIRÒ, Joan (*1893–1983*)
  colors, 27
MITCHELL, John (*b. 1913*)
  tough going (note under
    Anonymous), 291
MITCHELL, Margaret (*1900–1949*)
  don't give a damn, 134
  tomorrow, 98
MIZNER, Wilson (*1876–1933*)
  be nice to people, 294
  plagiarism vs research, 31
MOLIÈRE (given name, Jean Baptiste
    Poquelin) (*1622–1673*)
  certain pleasures, 282
  deeds vs promises, 68
  getting rich, 185
  hypocrisy, 129
  love & deception, 155
  medicines, 131
  prose, 141
  reason, 335
  tobacco, 305
  value, 319
  vices, fashionable, 282
  virtue (2 quotes), 325

MONDALE, Walter Frederick
    (*b. 1928*)
  World War III, 330
MONTAGUE, [Lady] Mary Wortley
    (*1689–1762*)
  satire, 31
  writing clearly, 29
MONTAIGNE, Michel E. de
    (*1533–1592*)
  cat, playing with, 194
  death & cabbages, 197
  defeats & victories, 333
  dreams, 271
  fear, 89
  life,—a dream, 150
  life, value of, 149
  living well, 107
  lying, 66
  marriage, 167
  maturity, 173
  modesty, 278
  oneself, belonging to, 274
  philosophy (2 quotes), 221
  prayer, 233
  saying & doing, 68
  science, 265
  study, excessive, 70
  what do I know?, 284
  wife's & valet's view, 135
MONTENAEKEN, Léon (*1859–?*)
  life, 150
MONTESQUIEU, Charles, [Baron de]
    (*1689–1755*)
  empire & war, 330
  God, 103
  laws, 145
  liberty (2 quotes), 95
  Parisiens, lunch, & supper, 91
MOORE, Clement C[larke]
    (*1779–1863*)
  night before Christmas, 47
MOORE, George (*1852–1933*)
  beauty, 34
  being Irish, 189
  long visits, 165
  psychology, 271
  verbal felicity, 30
MOORE, Thomas (*1779–1852*)
  last rose of summer, 201
  love, 155
  women rule, 343

MORE, [Sir] Thomas (*1478–1535*)
  lawyers, 145
MOREAU, Jeanne (*b. 1929*)
  success, 294
MOREHEAD, John Motley
    (*1796–1866*)
  between drinks (note under R. L.
  Stevenson), 10
MORLEY, Christopher (*1890–1957*)
  success & life, 294
MORRELL, Thomas (*1713–1784*)
  conquering hero, 117
MORRIS, George Pope (*1802–1864*)
  spare that tree, 197
MORRISON, Toni (*b. 1931*)
  reading & writing, 32
MORSE, Samuel Finley Breese
    (*1791–1872*)
  telegraph, 268
MOTION PICTURE PRODUCERS
    & DISTRIBUTORS OF
    AMERICA, INC.
  censorship code (2 quotes), 42
MUIR, John (*1838–1914*)
  wilderness, 191
MUMFORD, Lewis (*b. 1895*)
  generations, 100
MURDOCH, [Jean] Iris (*b. 1919*)
  fantasy & reality, 250
MUSSET, Alfred de (*1810–1857*)
  artists, 22

NABOKOV, Vladimir (*1899–1977*)
  genius, 100
  life, 150
  solitude, 287
NAPOLEON BONAPARTE
    (*1769–1821*)
  aggressors, 321
  army & its stomach, 174
  bullet that will kill me, 275
  do it yourself, 277
  England, 73
  fear & interest, 318
  generals, 174
  I am the state, 316
  leaders, 119
  pyramids, 176
  religion, 255
  revolution, 261

NAPOLEON (*continued*)
  soldiers & generals, 174
  sublime to ridiculous, 263
  vices & virtues, 282
NASH, Ogden (*1902–1971*)
  canaries, 194
  candy vs liquor, 10
  dogs, 194
  kin & kith, 87
  kittens, 194
  women, 339
NEHRU, Jawaharlal (*1889–1964*)
  capitalism, 40
  change, 43
  communism, 51
  coexistence, 217
  democracy & socialism, 63
  economic equality, 76
  religion, 255
  socialism, 286
NERVAL, Gérard de (given name,
    Gérard Labrunie) (*1808–1855*)
  flowers, 197
NEWMAN, John Henry [Cardinal]
    (*1801–1890*)
  dogma & religion, 255
  gentlemen & kindness, 165
NEWTON, [Sir] Isaac (*1642–1727*)
  action & reaction, 270
  hypotheses, 265
  on the shoulder of giants, 265
  playing on the sea-shore, 265
NICHOLAS I (*1796–1855*)
  Generals January & February, 174
NIEBUHR, Reinhold (*1892–1971*)
  science & happiness, 182
  serenity prayer, 235
NIETZSCHE, Friedrich Wilhelm
    (*1844–1900*)
  evolution, 267
  Germany, 189
  God, 104
  herd morality, 78, 182
  Jesus, 137
  liberal institutions, 226
  love & giving, 155
  monsters & the abyss, 81
  people who punish, 246
  right, 262
  skepticism, 284
  strength, developing, 311

NIETZSCHE (*continued*)
suicide, 295
superman, 126
truth, 314
war, 330
woman & God, 343
wisdom, 336
wit, 128
words, 141
NIGHTINGALE, Florence
(*1820–1910*)
statistics, 269
NIVELLE, Robert Georges
(*1856–1924*)
they shall not pass, 176
NIXON, Richard M[ilhous] (*b. 1913*)
Nixon to kick around, 17
not a crook, 17
pitiful helpless giant, 13
NORTH, Christopher (given name,
John Wilson) (*1785–1854*)
laws, 145
NOYES, Alfred (*1880–1958*)
moon, 198

OCKHAM (or OCCAM), William of
(*c. 1300–c. 1348*)
Ockham's razor, 265
O'NEILL, Eugene (*1888–1953*)
doctors, 67
the past (2 quotes), 213
present—strange interlude, 236
OPPENHEIMER, J. Robert
(*1905–1967*)
I am become Death, 266
OPPENHEIMER, Martin (*b. 1930*)
today's city, 49
ORCZY, Emmuska [Baroness]
(*1865–1947*)
Pimpernel, 117
ORTEGA Y GASSET, José
(*1883–1955*)
violence, 182
ORWELL, George (*1903–1950*)
Big Brother, 316
controlling history, 316
equality (all animals are equal), 76
fat man, thin man, 36
future, 98
political speech & writing, 226
sports, 290

O'SULLIVAN, John L. (*1813–1895*)
government, 106
manifest destiny, 13
OTIS, James (*1725–1783*)
house is castle, 241
taxation without representation, 298
OVID (*43 B.C.–A.D. c. 18*)
gods, 104
guilt, 108
habit, 108
love, 155
love, ambivalent, 343
men & good looks, 20
middle way, 245
present times, 236
pretty women, 279
simplicity, 281
soul, 289
time—best medicine, 303
woman, 339

PAIGE, Satchel (*c. 1906–1982*)
age, 8
looking back, 213
PAINE, Thomas (*1737–1809*)
country & religion, 78
government, 106
religion, 255
revolutions, 261
summer soldier, 17
times that try men's souls, 17
war, 331
PALEY, Barbara Cushing "Babe"
(*1915–1978*)
being skinny & rich, 185
PALEY, William (*1734–1805*)
white lies, 66
PANKHURST, Christabel (*1880–1958*)
evil today, 182
anger & politics, 226
PANKHURST, Emmeline (*1858–1928*)
die fighting, 20
freedom, 95
PARKER, Dorothy (*1893–1967*)
gamut of emotions, 134
girls at Yale prom, 282
girls who wear glasses, 279
highballs, 10
"House Beautiful," 134
love (2 quotes), 155
novel to throw aside, 134

PARKER (*continued*)
  suicide, 295
  under the host, 283
  worms, 60
PARKER, Hubert Lister [Lord of
    Waddington] (*1900–1972*)
  facts of life, 145
PARKER, Ross (*b. 1914*) & HUGHIE
    S. CHARLES (*b. 1907*)
  England, 73
PARKINSON, C[yril] Northcote
    (*b. 1909*)
  Parkinson's law, 346
  politics, 226
PASCAL, Blaise (*1623–1662*)
  beginnings, 35
  Cleopatra's nose, 341
  evil, 81
  God, seeking, 104
  heart, the, 114
  justice & force, 139
  movement vs rest, 68
  nature, 192
  obedience, 207
  passions, 283
  religion, 255, 256
  silence, 280
  space, 198
  truth, 314
  virtue & guilt, 325
  wisdom, 336
  writing concisely, 30
PASTERNAK, Boris (*1890–1960*)
  snow, 201
PATER, Walter (*1839–1894*)
  art, 26
  gem-like flame, 150
PATTON, George S. (*1885–1945*)
  risks, 37
PAVLOV, Ivan Petrovich (*1849–1936*)
  learning & facts, 84
PAZ, Octavio (*b. 1914*)
  reality, 250
PÉGUY, Charles (*1873–1914*)
  tyranny, 36
PEIRCE, C[harles] S[anders]
    (*1839–1914*)
  doubt, 285
PENN, William (*1644–1718*)
  nature, 192
  Christian, being, 256

PERKINS, Frances (*1882–1965*)
  U.S. & public opinion, 13
PERRY, Oliver Hazard (*1785–1819*)
  enemy is ours, 17
PETER, Laurence J. (*b. 1919*)
  Peter Principle, 346
PETRONIUS (*d. c. 66*)
  great majority, 60
  a man's face & walk, 36
PICASSO, Pablo (*1881–1973*)
  miracles, 179
PIERSON, [Dr.] Elaine (*20th cent.*)
  sex, 279
PIGRES (*c. 6th cent. B.C.*)
  fox & hedgehog, 55
PINDAR (*518–c. 438 B.C.*)
  custom, 58
  water, 10
  lawless joys, 283
PINDAR, Peter
  See WOLCOT, John
PINERO, [Sir] Arthur (*1855–1934*)
  middle age, 173
PIRANDELLO, Luigi (*1867–1936*)
  drama, 25
  facts, 84
PITT, William [Earl of Chatham]
    (*1708–1778*)
  America—unconquerable, 13
  law & tyranny, 145
PITT, William (*1759–1806*)
  tyranny, 316
PLANCK, Max (*1858–1947*)
  physical laws, 271
PLATH, Sylvia (*1932–1963*)
  dying, 60
PLATO (*c. 428–348 B.C.*)
  astronomy, 271
  beginnings, 35
  boys, 45
  conversation, 53
  democracy & despotism, 63
  education, 70
  geometry (2 quotes), 269
  health, 113
  honesty, 123
  ideas, haters of, 130
  income tax, 298
  justice, 139
  love, 155
  necessity & invention, 205

PLATO (*continued*)
old age, 8
philosophy & wonder, 222
punishment, 246
rich, the, 185
simplicity, 281
truth, 314
understanding, 306
women & education, 339
PLAUTUS, Titus Maccius
(*254–184 B.C.*)
manners, 165
pleasure, 115
rumor, 264
value, 319
PLINY, THE ELDER (*23–79*)
Africa, 189
suicide, 269
wine (note under Anonymous), 9
wise men, 336
PLUTARCH (*46–120*)
perseverance, 220
silence, 280
POE, Edgar Allan (*1809–1849*)
an animal's love, 195
Annabel Lee, 160
dream within a dream, 251
I have not been as others were, 163
midnight dreary, 208
the Raven, 208
POGO
See Walt Kelly
POINCARÉ, [Jules] Henri (*1854–1912*)
science & facts, 266
POMPADOUR, [Madame de]
(*1721–1764*)
*le déluge*, 261
POPE, Alexander (*1688–1744*)
ambition, 11
criticism, 24
do good by stealth, 325
doctors, disagreeing, 67
education, 70
erring is human, 93
fame, 295
fools, 93
government, 106
happy the man who loves home, 122
honest man, 123
hope springs eternal, 124
husbands & lap dogs, 167

POPT (*continued*)
know thyself, 276
little learning, 70
Lo, the poor Indian, 104
look on her face, 341
merit vs charm, 325
misfortunes of others, 311
nature, art in, 192
new & old, 245
Newton, 266
order, 269
people, voice of the (note under
Alcuin), 218
political parties, 226
proper study of mankind, 276
reason & wisdom, 251
universe & god, 319
virtue in old age, 325
where'er you walk, 197
wit, 30
women, 339
writing, 31
PORTER, William Sydney
See HENRY, O
POTTER, Beatrice
See WEBB, Beatrice Potter
POUND, Ezra (*1885–1972*)
winter is icumen, 201
POUND, Roscoe (*1870–1964*)
law, 145
PRAYERS
See ANONYMOUS (PRAYERS);
BOOK OF COMMON PRAYER
PRESCOT, William (*1726–1795*)
whites of their eyes (note under
Putnam), 17
PRIESTLEY, J[ohn] B[oynton]
(*b. 1894*)
communication, 170
PRIOR, Matthew (*1664–1721*)
ends & means, 78
hope, 124
physicians, 67
tasting & thinking, 93
PRITCHETT, V[ictor] S[awdon]
(*b. 1900*)
clergymen, 256
PROTAGORAS (*c. 485–c. 410 B.C.*)
gods, knowledge of, 285
man, measure of all things, 126

PROUDHON, Pierre-Joseph
  *(1809–1865)*
  law, 145
  property, 41
PROUST, Marcel *(1871–1922)*
  art, 22
  chronology, 303
  habit, 108
  happiness vs grief, 311
  love, 155
  maladies, 131
  neurotics, 131
  passion & writing, 32
  sunsets, 199
  time, perception of, 303
  time & people, 303
  unhappiness & morality, 78
PROVERBS
  See ANONYMOUS (PROVERBS)
PUBLILIUS SYRUS *(1st cent. B.C.)*
  exterior, a good, 88
  giving promptly, 44
  heirs, 186
  honesty, 123
  losers, 333
  necessity, 145
  obedience, 207
  plans, 223
  remedy & disease, 131
  solitude, 287
  speech, 141
  trying things, 68
  variety & pleasure, 320
  vices & excuses, 283
PUTNAM, Israel *(1715–1790)*
  Bunker Hill (don't fire . . .), 17
PYRRHUS [King of Epirus]
  *(c. 318–272 B.C.)*
  victory, costly, 176


QUARLES, Francis *(1592–1644)*
  worldliness, 245
QUESNAY, François de *(1694–1774)*
  *laissez-faire* (note under Argenson),
  40


RABELAIS, François *(c. 1495–1553)*
  following one's will, 115
  last words (pull the curtain . . .), 60

RABELAIS *(continued)*
  nature & vacuums, 271
  night, 203
  other half—how it lives, 112
RACINE, Jean *(1639–1699)*
  crime, 57
  tyranny, 316
RALEIGH, [Sir] Walter *(c. 1552–1618)*
  world, a prison, 150
RALEIGH, [Sir] Walter Alexander
  *(1861–1922)*
  exams, 70
  human race, 180
RAND, Ayn *(1905–1982)*
  great men, 107
  civilization & privacy, 50
RANDS, William Brightly *(1823–1882)*
  procrastination, 242
RAYBURN, Sam [Taliaferro]
  *(1882–1961)*
  getting along, 245
REAGAN, Ronald *(b. 1911)*
  being shot at (note under Churchill),
  58
REED, Ishmael *(b. 1938)*
  universe, 319
RENAN, [Joseph] Ernest *(1823–1892)*
  science education, 266
RESTON, James [Barrett] *(b. 1909)*
  politics, 226
REUTHER, Walter *(1907–1970)*
  looking like a duck, 79
REXFORD, Eben Eugene *(1848–1916)*
  growing old—silver hairs, 8
RHODES, Cecil [John] *(1853–1902)*
  so much to do (last words), 60
RICE, Grantland *(1880–1954)*
  playing the game, 334
RICHELIEU, [Cardinal] Armand Jean
  du Plessis, [Duc de] *(1585–1642)*
  reason, 251
RICHLER, Mordecai *(b. 1931)*
  capitalism vs revolution, 41
RICKEY, Branch [Wesley]
  *(1881–1965)*
  luck, 162
RIESMAN, David *(b. 1909)*
  etiquette, 165
RILEY, James Whitcomb *(1849–1916)*
  frost on punkin, 201
  ripest peach, 11

RILKE, Rainer Maria *(1875–1926)*
    marriage, 167
    heroes, 118
    religion, 256
RIMBAUD, J.-A. *(1854–1891)*
    hell, 116
ROCHEFOUCAULD, LA
    See LA ROCHEFOUCAULD
ROCHESTER, John Wilmot [Earl of]
    *(1647–1680)*
    Charles II (never said a foolish
        thing . . .), 134
ROCKEFELLER, John D. *(1874–1960)*
    money, 186
    rights & responsibilities, 258
ROCKNE, Knute *(1888–1931)*
    losers, 334
    win for the Gipper, 290
ROGERS, Samuel *(1763–1855)*
    marriage, 167
ROGERS, Will *(1879–1935)*
    humor, 128
    newspapers, 238
    politicians & public opinion, 226
    politics, 226
    progress & civilization, 50
    rumor, 264
    seeing ahead, 328
    taxes, 298
ROHE
    See MIES VAN DER ROHE
ROLAND, [Mme] *(1754–1793)*
    liberty, 95
ROMAINS, Jules *(1885–1972)*
    health & sickness, 113
ROOSEVELT, [Anna] Eleanor
    *(1884–1962)*
    Communism, 51
    nature, 192
    peace, 217
    war, 331
    work, 346
ROOSEVELT, Franklin Delano
    *(1882–1945)*
    arsenal of democracy, 13
    date will live in infamy (Pearl
        Harbor), 18
    fear, 17
    four freedoms, 95
    minorities' rights, 249
    national toughness, 291

ROOSEVELT *(continued)*
    new deal, 17
    peace, 217
    radicals, conservatives, reactionaries,
        227
    rendezvous with destiny, 18
    rich complain more than poor, 186
    soil, 75
    son of a bitch, ours, 318
    spiritual force, 291
    taxes, 298
ROOSEVELT, Theodore *(1858–1919)*
    Americanism, 100%, 13
    big stick, 292
    evil & expediency, 81
    law, 145
    square deal, 18
    wisdom, 336
    work, 346
ROSSETTI, Christina Georgina
    *(1830–1894)*
    no sad songs, 60
    the wind, 203
ROSTAND, Jean *(b. 1894)*
    adulthood & solitude, 288
ROSTEN, Leo C[alvin] *(b. 1908)*
    dogs & babies, 180
ROUSSEAU, Jean Jacques *(1712–1778)*
    cities, 49
    everything degenerates in man's
        hands, 126
    God & justice, 139
    innocence, 132
    law, 146
    man is in chains, 316
    poverty, 229
    punishment, 246
    silence, 280
    strength, 292
    truth, 314
ROWAN, Carl *(b. 1925)*
    questions, 238
ROWLAND, Helen *(1875–1950)*
    love & marriage, 168
ROWSE, A. L. *(b. 1903)*
    architecture, 23
RUBINSTEIN, Arthur *(b. 1887)*
    seasons & symphonies, 201
RUDOFSKY, Bernard *(b. 1905)*
    Japanese, 189

RUNYON, [Alfred ] Damon
  *(1884–1946)*
  betting strategy, 290
RUSKIN, John *(1819–1900)*
  beauty, 34
  build forever, 23
  flowers, 197
  life, 150
  pathetic fallacy, 23
  possessions, 301
  science, 266
  weather, 204
  work, 346
RUSSELL, Bertrand [Lord]
  *(1872–1970)*
  atheist's credo, 33
  controversies, 79
  ethical metaphysics, 78
  fear, 89
  government & law, 106
  happiness, 109
  hope, 124
  life, 126
  machines, 299
  marriage, 168
  mathematics, 269
  mysticism, 187
  philosophy (2 quotes), 222
  progress, 243
  punishment, 246
  science, 266
  sex and love, 279
  time, 303
  work, 346
RUSSELL, Bill *(b. 1934)*
  identity, 249
RUTHERFORD, [Lord] Ernest
  *(1871–1937)*
  Universe, 319
RYLE, Gilbert *(1900–1976)*
  Ghost in the Machine, 178


SABATINI, Rafael *(1875–1950)*
  Scaramouche: born with a gift of
    laughter, 118
SACKVILLE-WEST, Vita
  *(1892–1962)*
  ambition, 11
  summer, 201
  travel, 308

SAINT-EXUPÉRY, Antoine de
  *(1900–1944)*
  logic, 251
  machines, 299
  night, 203
  responsibility, 258
  travel light, 308
  war, 331
SANDBURG, Carl *(1878–1967)*
  Chicago, 49
  fog, 204
  hell, 116
  machines, 299
  past, the, 213
  people, the, 219
  slang, 141
  war, 331
SANGER, Margaret *(1883–1966)*
  mothers, 339
SANTAYANA, George *(1863–1952)*
  atheism, 33
  Bible, 256
  domesticity, 168
  fame, 295
  fanaticism, 74
  happiness, 109
  miracles, 179
  oneself, understanding, 274
  past, remembering, 213
  religion, 256
  understanding, 178
  wisdom, 336
  wit, 128
  words, 141
SAPPHO *(fl. c. 620 B.C.)*
  death, 60
SARTRE, Jean-Paul *(1905–1980)*
  freedom, 95
  hell, 116
  victory & defeat, 334
  violence, 321
  war & the rich, 331
SASSOON, Siegfried *(1886–1967)*
  singing, 110
SAYERS, Dorothy *(1893–1957)*
  age & curiosity, 279
SCHELLING, Friedrich von
  *(1775–1854)*
  architecture (note under Goethe), 23
SCHIAPARELLI, Elsa *(1890?–1973)*
  a good cook, 91

SCHILLER, Johann C. Friedrich von
　*(1759–1805)*
　children & the state, 46
　heart, 114
　history, 121
　soul, beautiful, 289
　stupidity, 93
SCHLEGEL, Friedrich von
　*(1772–1829)*
　historians, 121
SCHOPENHAUER, Arthur
　*(1788–1860)*
　every day, every morning, 203
　marriage, 168
　rudeness, 165
　suicide, 296
　truth, 314
SCHUMACHER, E[rnst] F[riedrich]
　*(1911–1977)*
　smallness, 65
SCHURZ, Carl *(1829–1906)*
　country right or wrong (note under
　　Decatur), 215
SCOTT, [Sir] Walter *(1771–1832)*
　Christmas, 47
　gude time coming, 98
　Hail to the chief, 118
　Lochinvar, 118
　native land, 215
　November, 201
　tangled web, 66
SEATTLE *(1786–1866)*
　red man & white man, 249
　death, 60
　regret & mourning, 252
SECOMBE, Harry [Donald] *(b. 1921)*
　head waiter,
SEEGER, Alan *(1888–1916)*
　rendezvous with death, 60
SEGAL, Erich *(b. 1937)*
　love, 155
SELDEN, John *(1584–1654)*
　ignorance of the law, 146
　marriage, 168
　silence in dangerous times, 280
SELFRIDGE, H[arry] Gordon
　*(1864?–1947)*
　customer is right, 39
SENDAK, Maurice [Bernard] *(b. 1928)*
　life, 150

SENECA, Lucius Annaeus
　*(c. 4 B.C.–65 A.D.)*
　adversity, 311
　art & nature, 22
　crime, 57
　fear, 89
　fools—mortals (note under
　　Shakespeare), 93
　fortune, 162
　genius, 100
　God, 256
　guilt, 108
　love of one's country, 216
　luck, 162
　mind, a good, 178
　nature & God, 192
　soul, 289
　time, 303
　vices, 283
　violence, 321
　virtue, 325
　war, 331
SERVICE, Robert W[illiam]
　*(1874–1958)*
　later than you think, 303
SÉVIGNÉ, [Mme. de] *(1626–1696)*
　dogs vs men, 180
SHAKESPEARE, William *(1564–1616)*
　acting, art of (3 quotes), 23
　adversity—sweet uses of, 311
　adversity & philosophy, 222
　age & youth, 87
　age cannot wither, nor custom
　　stale . . ., 341
　all must die, 61
　ambition, 11
　angels defend us, 235
　apparel, 88
　bawdy planet, 283
　be what you seem, 123
　bed, 2nd best for wife, 168
　beef, eating, 92
　better days, 311
　Birnam Wood, 179
　blood—old man had so much, 57
　blood & perfumes of Arabia, 108
　borrowing & lending, 186
　brave new world, 127
　breach, once more into, 73
　brevity & wit, 30
　Caesar (bestrides the world), 317

SHAKESPEARE (*continued*)
Cassius—lean & hungry, 59
charmed life, 275
child, thankless, 211
city is its people, 49
Cleopatra, 341
compare thee to a summer's day?, 160
comparisons (note under Fortescue), 52
courage—screw to sticking place, 54
cowards die many times, 54
crime, smiling at, 57
crown (uneasy lies the head), 119
cry havoc, 331
custom honored in the breach, 58
customs & kings, 119
cut him out in little stars, 160
dagger I see before me?, 163
damned spot, 163
dancing eyes are past, 8
darling buds of May, 201
death (all must die), 61
death (all must endure going hence), 61
death & being merry, 61
death (nothing became him more), 61
death (man can die but once), 61
delays, 242
desire outlives performance, 279
desperate situations, 261
devil—a gentleman, 65
devil can cite Scripture, 256
devil—sugared over, 129
discretion & valor, 245
double, double, toil & trouble, 208
doubt, 285
dyer's hand, 346
eaten me out of house & home, 91
England (never shall be conquered), 73
England (royal throne of kings, sceptered isle), 74
Et tu, 35
evil that men do, 81
excusing a fault, 83
eye of newt, 208
Exit pursued by bear, 25
father, wise, 211
fault, not in the stars, 258
flattery, 89
flesh, too too solid, 36

SHAKESPEARE (*continued*)
flesh & frailty, 36
follow others—he will not, 240
fools, these mortals be, 93
forgetfulness, 85
Fortune's fool, 88
foul & fair day, 315
frailty is woman, 340
friend, you never can be old, 97
friends, grapple them to you, 97
friends, Romans, countrymen, 55
God for Harry, England & Saint George, 73
gods kill us for sport, 104
gold (all that glisters), 20
good deed, 325
good deeds, regetted, 81
goodnight sweet prince, 235
great men soon forgotten, 295
greatness, 107
hands, washing (Lady Macbeth), 163
hanging & wiving, 168
he was a man, 118
he will never follow others, 240
head that wears a crown, 119
a hit, 290
home vs travel, 308
honest tale, plainly told, 32
honesty—not safe, 123
honesty—a fault, 123
honor, 325
hope, 124
horse, my kingdom for, 195
horse with wings, 76
ides of March, 59
if it 'twere done . . . 'twere well done quickly, 37
I'll break my staff, 208
an ill-favoured thing, 301
jealousy, 136
Jews—do we not bleed?, 249
Juliet is the sun, 160
kings, great, & customs, 119
kings & ceremony, 119
kiss me, Kate, 160
lady doth protest too much, 108
lawyers, let's kill, 146
lay on Macduff, 321
lechery & wars, 315
life—a tale by an idiot, 151
life—a twice-told tale, 150

SHAKESPEARE (*continued*)
life—a stage of fools, 150
living in torment, 296
love, course of, 156
love, men do not die of, 155
love, showing, 156
love comforteth, 156
love is a devil, 155
love is blind, 156
love is not love which alters, 156
love—speak low of, 156
loved not wisely but too well, 156
madness in great ones, 163
man, this was, 118
man, what a piece of work is, 171
man delights not me, 180
man is noble, 171
marriage, 168
masters, 231
May, darling buds of, 201
men—deceivers ever, 172
men must endure going hence, 61
men sometimes forget, 85
mercy, 94
mercy & nobility, 94
midsummer madness, 201
mind diseased, 272
miracles are past, 179
mirror up to nature, 25
misery & bedfellows, 311
more sinned against than sinning, 83
mortals are fools, 93
mount, my soul!, 235
murder most foul, 57
Muse of fire, 22
music, food of love, 26
music, sweet & sadness, 26
name, what's in a natural touch, 134
nature, touch of, 192
noblest Roman, 118
nothing became him in his life like
    leaving it, 61
nothing comes of nothing, 346
O Romeo, 160
obeying, 207
old, you can never be, 97
once more into the breach, 73
out damned spot, 163
past is prologue, 213
past & gone, 253
parting, such sweet sorrow, 160

SHAKESPEARE (*continued*)
patience, 214
pay & satisfaction, 69
peace, 217
people are the city, 49
perfumes of Arabia, 108
philosophers & toothache, 132
philosophy, Horatio's, 222
pity, 94
play's the thing, 25
politician, 227
prayer—a fault, 233
praying with words not thoughts, 233
pride, 240
prince of darkness, 65
queen, I would not be, 119
remedies are in ourselves, 274
respect, 165
robbed that smiles, 57
rogue & peasant slave, 63
Romeo, Romeo, 160
rosemary & rue, 197
rosemary for remembrance, 197
rotten apples, 311
ruling vs obeying, 207
sad tale & winter, 201
scripture & the devil, 256
self—be true to, 274
setting sun, 263
shall I compare thee to a summer's
    day?, 160
sharper than a serpent's tooth, 211
she leans her cheek upon her hand,
    160
she who is fair is not foolish, 341
silence of pure innocence, 280
sins, old—ways, new, 283
sleep & Macbeth, 286
smiling at a thief, 57
sorrows, 311
spirits, calling from the deep, 208
spot, damned, 163
staff—breaking, 208
stage of fools, 150
strength & tyranny, 292
suicide, 296
summer's flower, 197
tale plainly told, 32
tale told by idiot, 151
tempt not desperate man, 300

SHAKESPEARE (*continued*)
  things present, 236
  thinking makes things good or bad,
    178
  this was a man, 118
  tide in affairs of men, 37
  time, 303
  time, wasted, 303
  time is out of joint, 315
  to be or not to be, 296
  to thine own self be true, 274
  tomorrow & tomorrow, 64
  too much of a good thing?, 82
  toothache, 132
  trick, 55
  'twere well done quickly, 37
  uneasy lies the head, 119
  unkindest cut of all, 35
  valor & discretion, 245
  violent delights, 82
  virtue, assume a, 325
  virtue, dying for, 325
  virtue & goodness, 325
  voice, woman's, 340
  war, 331
  washing hands, 163
  we happy few, 71
  we are such stuff as dreams are made
    on, 127
  we do sugar devil himself, 129
  well satisfied—well paid, 69
  what's done, 252
  what's mine is yours, 160
  what we may become, 276
  wheel come full circle, 216
  when he shall die, cut him in stars,
    160
  wife, light, 168
  winter of discontent, 119
  wisely & slowly, 111
  wish, father to that thought, 178
  wit & brevity, 30
  witching time, 203
  woman may be won, 279
  women, kindness in, 343
  wonderful, wonderful, 110
  words & debts, 141
  world's a stage, 150
  the worst, 311
  worst, fearing, 209

SHAKESPEARE (*continued*)
  yesterday, calling back, 253
  Yorick, 61
  you blocks, you stones, 134
SHARP, William
  See MACLEOD
SHAW, George Bernard (*1856–1950*)
  artist, true, 22
  British military, 174
  Cain, brand of, 57
  censorship & assassination, 42
  common man, 229
  democracy, 63
  doing vs teaching, 70
  Englishmen & morality, 74
  Golden Rule, 165
  happiness, consumption of, 109
  happiness, lifetime of, 110
  hate, 112
  health, 113
  heart's desire, 295
  home & women, 122
  joking & truth, 128
  journalism, 135
  marriage, why popular, 168
  marriage, woman's business, 168
  married life (2 quotes), 168
  mistakes, 181
  money, lack of, 186
  money, regard for, 186
  morals & poverty, 229
  men over 40, 172
  musical amateurs, 26
  parents bore children, 212
  politics, 227
  poverty, 229
  prisons, 246
  progress, 243
  property, 41
  religion, 256
  roulette, 99
  revolutions, 261
  science, 266
  soldiers, 174
  teaching, 70
  tobacco, 305
  unreasonable man, the, 251
SHEEN, [Bishop] Fulton J[ohn]
    (*1895–1979*)
  atheists, 33

SHEFFIELD, John [Duke of
    Buckingham & Normandy]
    *(1648–1721)*
  writing, 32
SHELDON, A. F. *(1868–1935)*
  (International Rotary motto)
    service, 325
SHELLEY, Percy Bysshe *(1792–1822)*
  death, 61
  Devil (note under Shakespeare), 65
  earth & ocean, 192
  evil, 81
  familiar acts & love, 156
  Hell—a city like London, 49
  love, 156
  mingling & love, 156
  Ozymandias, 120
  past, 213
  poetry, 28
  poets, 28
  power, 231
  rulers, 120
  skylark (Hail to thee, blithe spirit),
    195
  soul, an enchanted boat, 26
  soul & the world, 289
  speech & thought, 178
  sweet songs, sad thoughts, 26
  teas & small talk, 53
  waking at night, 203
  waste & solitary places, 288
  West Wind, 204
  Wild Spirit, 235
  winter & spring, 201
  wisdom & love, 336
SHERIDAN, Richard Brinsley
    *(1751–1816)*
  unnatural acts, 283
SHERMAN, William Tecumseh
    *(1820–1891)*
  hold the fort, 18
  voice of the people (note under
    Alcuin), 218
  will not accept if nominated, 18
  war (3 quotes), 331
SHOIN, Yoshida
  See YOSHIDA SHOIN
SIMONIDES *(c. 556–468 B.C.)*
  epitaph at Thermopylae, 176
SKINNER, B[urrhus] F[rederic]
    *(b. 1904)*

SKINNER *(continued)*
  education, 70
  reading, 38
  thinking, 299
SMILES, Samuel *(1812–1904)*
  place for everything, 301
SMITH, Adam *(1723–1790)*
  invisible hand, 41
  price fixing, 57
  science, 266
  self-interest, 41
SMITH, Al[fred Emanuel] *(1873–1944)*
  baloney, 135
SMITH, Bessie *(1898–1937)*
  youth, 350
SMITH, Edgar *(1857–1938)*
  the Working Girl, 347
SMITH, Logan Pearsall *(1865–1946)*
  enjoying success, 110
  poverty, 229
  reading, 38
  sunshine, 204
SMITH, "Red" Walter *(b. 1905)*
  writing, 32
SMITH, Stevie *(1902–1971)*
  drowning, 64
SMITH, [Reverend] Sydney
    *(1771–1845)*
  the country, 54
  digestion, 92
  praying for an acquaintance, 135
SNOW, C[harles] P[ercy] *(1905–1980)*
  foreigners, 308
SOCRATES *(469–399 B. C.)*
  a good man, 325
  citizen of the world, 222
  things not needed, 301
  unexamined life, 222
  youth, 350
SOLON *(c. 638–c. 559 B.C.)*
  excess, 82
  happiness, 110
  law, 146
  obedience, 207
  poets, 28
SOLZHENITSYN, Alexander
    Isayevich *(b. 1918)*
  literature, 38
  writers, 32
SONTAG, Susan *(b. 1933)*
  critical interpretation, 24

SOPHOCLES *(c. 495–406 B.C.)*
 age & love of life, 8
 bringing bad news, 238
 grief & minds, 312
 griefs, self-caused, 312
 happiness, 110
 justice (2 quotes), 139
 learn by doing, 68
 love, 156
 money, 186
 reason, 178
 stranger & strange country (note
  under Bible), 10
 time, 314
 truth, 314
 wisdom, 336
 women, 340
 wonders & man, 127
SOULE, John Babsone Lane
  *(1815–1891)*
 Go West, 18
SOUTHEY, Robert *(1774–1843)*
 Father William (note under Carroll),
  7
SPARK, Muriel *(b. 1918)*
 old age, 9
 one's prime, 173
SPENCER, Herbert *(1820–1903)*
 billiards (note under Anonymous), 98
 education & character, 70
 freedom, morality, & happiness, 78
 progress, 243
 socialism, 286
 survival of fittest, 267
 time (note under Boucicault), 302
SPENSER, Edmund *(1552?–1599)*
 mind & happiness, 178
SPINOZA, Baruch *(1632–1677)*
 man—eternal, 127
 man—a social animal, 127
 nature vacuum (note under Rabelais),
  271
 pride & flattery, 89
 virtue, 325
SPOCK, Benjamin *(b. 1903)*
 parents' knowledge, 212
STAËL, Mme de *(1766–1817)*
 countries, other & one's own (note
  under Belloy), 214
 intellect, 178
 understanding & pardoning, 306

STALIN, Joseph *(1879–1953)*
 a million deaths, 61
 Pope's divisions, 256
STANLEY, [Sir] Henry Morton
  *(1841–1904)*
 Dr. Livingston, 268
STANTON, Elizabeth Cady
  *(1815–1902)*
 kings & queens, 343
 men, women, & equality, 343
 truth, 314
STEELE, [Sir] Richard *(1672–1729)*
 growing old, 9
 reading, 38
STEFFINS, Lincoln *(1866–1936)*
 future, 98
STEIN, Gertrude *(1874–1946)*
 rose, 197
STEINEM, Gloria *(b. 1935)*
 American children & parents, 212
STENDHAL (given name, Marie
  Henri Beyle) *(1783–1842)*
 women, 340
STENGEL, ("Casey") Charles Dillon
  *(1890–1975)*
 curfews, breaking, 283
STERNE, Laurence *(1713–1768)*
 country, one's own, 308
 woman's pulse, 279
 writing, 32
STEVENS, Wallace *(1879–1955)*
 emperor of ice cream, 120
 poets, 28
STEVENSON, Adlai E[wing]
  *(1900–1965)*
 Americans—suckers for good news,
  13
 communism, 51
 freedom & security, 95
 gains & pains, 5
 hunger, 229
 lying, 66
 E. Roosevelt (lighting candles against
  darkness), 326
STEVENSON, Robert Louis
  *(1850–1894)*
 books vs life, 38
 children & manners, 46
 expressing dislike, 135
 home is the sailor & hunter, 61
 life—a last cruise, 151

STEVENSON (*continued*)
life vs books, 38
long time between drinks, 10
marriage, 168
mortality, 151
politics, 227
travel, 308
travelling vs arriving, 347
winter & summer, 202
world & happiness, 110
STOCKHOLM CONFERENCE,
THE
earth, the, 75
STOWE, Harriet Beecher (*1811–1896*)
foxes, little (note under Bible, *Song
of Solomon*), 309
Topsy ("growed"), 249
STRAVINSKY, Igor [Fyodorovich]
(*1882–1971*)
music, 26
STRUNK, William, Jr. (*1869–1946*)
vigorous writing, 30
SUETONIUS (*c. 70–c. 140*)
Nero & philosophy, 222
SULLIVAN, John L. (*1858–1918*)
hard falls (note under Fitzsimmons),
290
SULLIVAN, Louis Henri (*1856–1924*)
form & function, 23
SULLIVAN, Timothy "Big Tim" D.
(*1853–1913*)
publicity, 238
SULLY, [Duc de] (given name,
Maximilien de Béthune)
(*1559–1641*)
the English & pleasure, 74
SUN TZE (*fl. early 4th cent. B.C.*)
art of conquest, 174
SUNYIN, Han
See HAN SUNYIN
SUTZKEVER, Abraham (*b. 1913*)
childhood, retaining, 133
SWIFT, Jonathan (*1667–1745*)
clergy, 256
flattery, 90
fleas & smaller fleas, 195
nice man, nasty ideas, 130
old age, 9
prayer, 233
religion, 256

SWIFT (*continued*)
style (proper words), 30
vision, 328
SWINBURNE, Algernon Charles
(*1837–1909*)
pale Galilean, 137
leaving, 76
SYNGE, J[ohn] M[illington]
(*1871–1909*)
fear & the sea, 273
SZASZ, Thomas Stephen (*b. 1920*)
God, talking to, 272
happiness, 110
two wrongs, 83
SZILARD, Leo (*1898–1964*)
lies, 66

TACITUS, Cornelius (*c. 55–c. 117*)
hate, 112
peace, 217
rumor, 264
strength & the gods, 292
TAGORE, Rabindranath (*1861–1941*)
butterfly & time, 304
logic, 251
mistakes & truth, 181
morning, 236
power, 231
TALLEYRAND, Charles-Maurice de
(*1754–1838*)
invasion of Russia, 176
war, 331
zeal, 74
TALMUD, THE
eating, 92
fear, sin & travel, 308
stranger in the night, 203
TEALE, Edwin Way (*1899–1980*)
time & space in the future, 98
nature, 192
TEILHARD DE CHARDIN, Pierre
(*1881–1955*)
faith, 86
TENNYSON, Alfred [Lord]
(*1809–1892*)
bar, crossing the, 61
brook goes on forever, 192
Christmas, 47
death (day less or more . . . we die),
61

TENNYSON (*continued*)
  death (after many a summer dies the swan), 61
  death & noble work, 5
  deaths & births, 100
  eagle, the, 195
  flower in wall, 197
  friends & foes, 72
  kind hearts & coronets, 326
  knowledge & wisdom, 336
  life & labor, 347
  Light Brigade (4 quotes), 174, 176
  love (better to have loved & lost), 156
  love (in spring), 202
  love is long, 157
  man is master of his fate, 88
  man dies, man is born, 100
  mother, 212
  nature, 192
  old order changeth, 43
  past, the dreadful, 213
  prayer, 233
  purpose in the universe, 243
  ring out the old, 206
  sleep my little one, 286
  so near & yet so far, 61
  spring & love, 202
  strength & a pure heart, 326
  things seen, 79
  we shall live to fight again, 297
  wind—sweet & low, 204
  woman's cause & man's, 343
  women hard on women, 340
  women's & men's roles, 343
  work of noble note, 5
  world, 319
  worst is to come, 312
TERENCE (*c. 190–159 B.C.*)
  extreme law, 146
  fortune, 162
  I am a man, 127
  life & hope, 151
  moderation, 245
  nothing new to be said, 205
  oneself, 274
TERESA, [Mother] (*b. 1910?*)
  forgiveness, 94
  silence, 280
TERTULLIAN (*c. 160–240*)
  faith & impossibility, 86
  God, 104

TERTULLIAN (*continued*)
  politics, 227
  work, 347
THACKERAY, William Makepeace (*1811–1863*)
  women & bad men, 343
THALES OF MILETUS (*c. 640–c. 546 B.C.*)
  water, 271
THATCHER, Margaret (*b. 1925*)
  politics, men & women, 227
THAYER, Ernest L[awrence] (*1863–1940*)
  Casey, 291
THEOGNIS (*fl. c. 545 B.C.*)
  haste, 111
  youth, 351
THEROUX, Paul (*b. 1941*)
  the Japanese, 189
THOMAS, Dylan (*1914–1953*)
  death (do not go gentle), 62
  youth & time, 304
THOMAS AQUINAS
  See AQUINAS
THOMPSON, Francis (*1859–1907*)
  hound of heaven, 104
  a flower & a star, 319
THOMSON, James (*1834–1882*)
  cities, 49
THOREAU, Henry David (*1817–1862*)
  books (2 quotes), 38
  circumstantial evidence, 79
  conforming outwardly, 130
  lives of quiet desperation, 151
  enterprises requiring new clothes, 88
  facts, 84
  man & tools, 300
  pleasures, cost of, 186
  reading, 38
  regret, 253
  simplify life, 65
  solitude, 288
  time, 304
  truth, 314
  wildness, 75
  wisdom, 336
THUCYDIDES (*471?–401 B.C.*)
  armies & obedience, 174
  Greeks, 189
  war, 331

THURBER, James *(1894–1961)*
  Burgundy, Naive, 92
  hesitation, 242
  humor, 128
THURLOW, Edward [First Baron]
    *(1731–1806)*
  corporations, 40
TIBERIUS (given name, Claudius
    Nero) *(42 B.C.–37 A.D.)*
  responsible shepherd, 258
TOCQUEVILLE, [Count] Alexis de
    *(1805–1859)*
  Americans, 13
  Americans & money, 13
  justice & law, 139
  women, American, 337
TOLSTOY, Leo Nikolaevich
    *(1828–1910)*
  beauty, 34
  happy & unhappy families, 87
  military service love, 157
  power, 231
  sorrow & joy, 312
  understanding & love, 157
  wisdom & science, 336
TOLSTOY, Sophie *(1844–1919)*
  love, 161
TREVELYAN, G[eorge] M[acaulay]
    *(1876–1962)*
  education, 70
TRILLING, Lionel *(1905–1975)*
  American reality, 251
TROLLOPE, Anthony *(1815–1882)*
  chatter, 53
  daily work, 347
  pride, 240
  writing, 32
TROTSKY, Leon *(1870–1940)*
  force, 322
  old age, 9
TROUBRIDGE, St. Vincent *(b. 1895)*
  iron curtain (note under Churchill), 9
TRUMAN, Harry S. *(1884–1972)*
  advising children, 212
  buck stops here, 258
  heat, standing, 292
  hell, giving, 18
  hell is the truth, 314
  recession & depression (note under
    Anonymous), 69

TRUMAN *(continued)*
  statesman, 227
  truth, 314
TRUTH, Sojourner *(c. 1797–1883)*
  women (2 quotes), 340
  rich & poor, 57
TUBMAN, Harriet *(1815?–1913)*
  liberty & death, 95
TUCHMAN, Barbara *(b. 1912)*
  war, 331
TUCKER, Sophie *(1884–1966)*
  breathing, 113
TUPPER, Martin *(1810–1889)*
  good books, 38
TURENNE [Vicomte de] *1611–1675)*
  God & big battalions, 175
TURGENEV, Ivan Sergeyevich
    *(1818–1883)*
  prayer, 233
TWAIN, Mark (given name, Samuel
    Langhorne Clemens) *(1835–1910)*
  adjectives, 30
  America, finding, 268
  anger, 19
  babies, 46
  black people & white people, 250
  buttons etc., 301
  censorship, self-, 42
  Congress, 277
  courage, 54
  death, his own reported, 238
  differences of opinion, 320
  dog vs man, 127
  eggs in one basket, 245
  facts, 84
  familiarity, 135
  fools & the rest of us, 93
  forbidden things, 283
  friendship & money, 97
  good breeding, 165
  good examples, 326
  humor, 128
  kings, 120
  madness, 163
  modern inconveniences, 182
  petrified opinion, 130
  right, doing, 326
  soap & education, 71
  success, 295
  training, 71
  truth, 314

TWAIN (*continued*)
  weather, 204
  women, 324
  word, the right, 30


UDALL, Stewart L[ee] (*b. 1920*)
  power vs greatness, 231
ULUGH-BEG, Mirza Mahommed Ben
    Shah Rok (*1394–1449*)
  science, works of, 266
UNAMUNO, Miguel de (*1864–1936*)
  belief in God, 86
  doubt & faith, 285
  habit, 108
  ideas & languages, 141
  science, 266
UPDIKE, John (*b. 1932*)
  education, 71
  writing, great, 32


VALÉRY, Paul (*1871–1945*)
  ideas & humor, 130
  memories, 171
  oneself, knowing (2 quotes), 276
  politics, 227
  truth, 314
  vanity, 240
VANDERBILT, William H.
    (*1821–1885*)
  public be damned, 40
VAN DER ROHE
  See MIES VAN DER ROHE
VARÈSE, Edgard (given name, Edgar)
    *1883–1965*)
  genius, 100
VAUVENARGUES, [Marquis de]
    (*1715–1747*)
  great enterprises, 107
  great thoughts, 114
  hope, 124
  lazy people, 146
VEBLEN, Thorstein [Bunde]
    *1857–1929*)
  beautiful products, 34
  conspicuous consumption, 41
  wealth & community standards, 186
VEGA, Lope de (*1562–1635*)
  love & jealousy, 136
VERLAINE, Paul (*1844–1896*)
  eloquence, 30

VICTORIA, [Queen] (*1819–1901*)
  not amused, 128
VIDAL, Gore (*b. 1925*)
  the birch, 246
VIGNY, Alfred de (*1797–1863*)
  the army, 175
  calm despair, 257
  God & ideas, 130
  silence, 280
VILLARD, Oswald Garrison
    (*1857–1949*)
  military intelligence, 175
VILLARS, Claude L. H. [Duc de]
    (*1653–1734*)
  friends & enemies, 97
VILLON, François (*1431–1465?*)
  snows of yesteryear, 213
VINCI, Leonardo Da (*1452–1519*)
  the cock is cheerful, 195
  inaction, 147
  intellectual passions, 178
  labor, 347
  painting, 27
VIRGIL (*70–19 B.C.*)
  anger & arms, 19
  arms & the man, 118
  causes of things, 266
  endurances, 297
  Fortune & daring, 37
  Greeks, 189
  hell, 116
  love, 157
  self, belief in, 275
  snake in grass, 59
  time, 304
VOLTAIRE (given name, François
    Marie Arouet) (*1694–1778*)
  best of all possible worlds, 209
  the best vs the good, 107
  common sense, 245
  écrasez l'infâme, 256
  error, pardoning, 94
  friends & enemies (note under
    Villars), 97
  God, inventing (2 quotes), 104
  God & battalions (note under
    Turenne), 175
  guilty & innocent on trial, 146
  history, (2 quotes), 121
  Holy Roman Empire, 189
  love, 157

VOLTAIRE (*continued*)
orange, squeezed, 317
right to speak, 96
shooting an admiral, 175
solitude & happiness, 288
suicide, 296
virtue, study, & gaiety, 326
wisdom & sadness, 336
work, 347

WALLACE, W[illiam] R[oss]
(*1819–1881*)
hand that rocks cradle, 340
WALLACE, Henry A[gard]
(*1888–1965*)
century of common man, 182
WALLER, Thomas "Fats" (*1904–1943*)
one never knows, 285
rhythm, 27
WALPOLE, Horace (*1717–1797*)
America, 13
world, 151
WALPOLE, [Sir] Robert (*1676–1745*)
men have their price, 186
WALTON, Izaak (*1593–1683*)
everybody's business (note under
Anonymous), 258
rivers & fishing, 291
WANAMAKER, John (*1838–1922*)
advertising, 6
WARBURTON, William (*1698–1779*)
orthodoxy, 257
WARHOL, Andy (*b. 1927*)
future & fame, 295
WARNER, Charles Dudley
(*1829–1900*)
politics, 227
weather (note under Twain), 204
WASHINGTON, Booker T[aliaferro]
(*1856–1915*)
farming, 347
slavery, 250
WASHINGTON, George (*1732–1799*)
discipline & an army, 175
foreign policy (no permanent
alliance), 18
honesty is best policy, 123
WATTS, Isaac (*1674–1748*)
birds in nest, 87
busy bee, 347
idle hands, 147

WEBB, Beatrice Potter (*1858–1943*)
religion, 257
WEBSTER, Daniel (*1782–1852*)
room at the top, 295
WEBSTER, John (*c. 1580–c. 1625*)
fortune, 162
old is best, 208
WELLES, Orson (*1915–1985*)
Swiss & other nations, 190
WELLINGTON, Arthur Wellesley,
[Duke of] (*1769–1852*)
anything impossible?, 238
battle lost, 176
battles, 176
fear, 89
publish & be damned, 239
Waterloo & Eton, 177
WELLS, H[erbert] G[eorge]
(*1866–1946*)
history—a race, 121
past & future, 213
WESLEY, John (*1703–1791*)
cleanliness, 50
passion & prejudice, 252
WESLEY, Samuel (*1662–1735*)
style, 30
WEST, Mae (*1892–1980*)
come up sometime, 125
evils, two, 81
good & bad, being, 283
a good thing, too much of, 82
goodness, 283
humor, 128
man in the house, 172
Snow White, 133
temptation, 300
WEST, Nathanael (*1902–1940*)
numbers, 269
WHARTON, Edith (*1862–1937*)
Culture, pursuing, 22
WHICHCOTE, Benjamin (*1609–1683*)
Jesus, 137
mystery & mysticism, 187
politicians & religion, 228
WHITE, E[lwyn] B[rooks]
(*1899–1985*)
car trips, 300
friend & writer, 97
luck, 162
never hurry or worry, 111
profit system, 41

WHITE (*continued*)
 spinach, 92
 television, 170
WHITE, William Allen (*1868–1944*)
 all dressed up, 88
WHITEHEAD, Alfred North
  (*1861–1947*)
 civilization, 50
 dogs vs cats, 195
 familiar things, 267
 life, 151
 literal adherence to Gospels, 257
 mathematics, 269
 philosophy, European, 222
 philosophy & wonder, 222
 technology & speed, 300
WHITMAN, Walt (*1819–1892*)
 animals, 195
 celebrate myself, 274
 contradict myself, 52
 human body, 36
 O amazement of things, 319
 O Captain, 273
 poets & audiences, 29
 simplicity, 281
WHITTIER, John Greenleaf
  (*1807–1892*)
 justice, 139
 peace, 217
 sad words—"It might have been," 253
 shoot if you must, 216
WHITTON, Charlotte (*1896–1975*)
 women vs men, 340
WIENER, Norbert (*1894–1964*)
 progress, 243
WILBUR, Richard (*b. 1921*)
 soul, 289
WILCOX, Ella Wheeler (*1855–1919*)
 laughter, 143
WILDE, Oscar (*1854–1900*)
 appearances, 20
 art, 22
 books, 38
 charming people, 44
 country, being good in the, 54
 diaries & travel, 308
 a dreamer, 328
 Englishman foxhunting, 291
 enemies, 72

WILDE (*continued*)
 experience, 83
 excess, 82
 fiction, 139
 genius to declare, 240
 ideas, 130
 life & art, 151
 lower orders, 112
 man kills the thing he loves, 57
 married life (2 quotes), 168
 loving oneself, 274
 married women, 283
 mothers, 212
 old age, 9
 parents & children, 212
 pianist, do not shoot, 27
 pleasure, 115
 press, 239
 price vs value, 319
 prison, 246
 sincerity, 123
 stupidity, 93
 style, 292
 temptation, 300
 truth, 315
WILDER, Billy (*b. 1906*)
 dry martini (note under Benchley), 9
WILDER, Thornton (*1897–1975*)
 animals, 195
 money, 186
 woman's work, 340
WILLIAM HENRY [Duke of
  Gloucester]
 See GLOUCESTER
WILLIAMS, Tennessee (*1914–1983*)
 caged birds, 95
 memory, 171
 memory & the present, 237
WILLKIE, Wendell [Lewis]
  (*1890–1944*)
 equality, 14
 socialism, 287
WILSON, Charles E. (*1890–1961*)
 General Motors, 40
WILSON, John
 See NORTH, Christopher
WILSON, Woodrow (*1856–1924*)
 corporations, 40
 democracy, world safe for, 18

WILSON (*continued*)
 economic system, 69
 hunger, 229
 peace, 217
 peace & self-respect, 20
 politics & prosperity, 228
WINDSOR, [Duke of]
 See EDWARD VIII
WINTHROP, John (*1588–1649*)
 city upon a hill, 14
WITTGENSTEIN, Ludwig [Josef
  Johann] (*1889–1951*)
 death, 62
 philosophy (2 quotes), 222
 a picture, 27
 silence, 280
 world (note under Wittgenstein), 222
WOLCOT, John (pseudonymn, Peter
  Pindar) (*1738–1819*)
 fame, 294
WOLFE, Thomas (*1900–1938*)
 home, 122
WOOLF, Virginia (*1882–1941*)
 beauty, 34
 dining well, 92
 habit, 108
 recording events, 121
 stately home of England, 74
 telling the truth, 123
 women & men, 342, 343
WOOLLCOTT, Alexander
  (*1877–1943*)
 things I like to do, 284
 wet clothes, dry martinis (note under
  Benchley), 9
WORDSWORTH, William
  (*1770–1850*)
 acts of kindness & love, 326
 birth & the soul, 46
 child, father of the man, 46
 daffodils, 198
 the good die first, 62
 love, dying for, 157
 madness, 163
 maid whom there were none to
  praise, 288
 nature & humanity, 192
 nature & heart that loves her, 192
 piety, 257

WORDSWORTH (*continued*)
 plain living & high thinking, 182
 poetry & recollection, 29
 poets, 29
 primrose, 198
 rainbow, 199
 suffering, 312
 vernal wood, learning from, 79
 wandered lonely as a cloud, 198
 warrior, happy, 175
 wisdom, 336
 world too much with us, 151
 youth, 351
WORK, Henry Clay (*1832–1884*)
 Father, dear father, 10
WOTTON, [Sir] Henry (*1568–1639*)
 ambassadors, 66
WRIGHT, Frank Lloyd (*1869–1959*)
 luxuries, 115
 TV (note under Brown), 169
WRIGHT, Richard (*1908–1960*)
 self-realization, 275
WYLIE, Elinor (*1885–1928*)
 avoid the herd, 288

XENOPHON (*c. 430–c. 355 B.C.*)
 despots, 317

YANKVICH, Léon R[ené] (*b. 1888*)
 children, 212
YEATS, William Butler (*1865–1939*)
 anarchy of modern times, 182
 beast slouches toward Bethlehem, 348
 best lack all conviction, 182
 change & a terrible beauty, 261
 heart, lonely of, 288
 heart, rag & bone shop of, 114
 Innisfree, 77
 Ireland, 190
 love & pity, 157
 love, enduring into old age, 161
 moon & sun, 199
 sacrifice, 312
 stars, death of, 348
 years like black oxen, 304
YEVTUSHENKO, Yevgeny (*b. 1933*)
 strength, 292

YOSHIDA SHOIN *(1830–1859)*
  ordinary men & oneself, 71
YOUNG, Edward *(1683–1765)*
  lips that touch liquor, 10
  procrastination, 242
  quotations, 247
  wisdom, 336

ZANGWILL, Israel *(1864–1926)*
  melting pot, 14
ZENOBIUS *(fl. early 2nd cent. A.D.)*
  Jupiter, 106
ZOLA, Emile *(1840–1902)*
  j'accuse, 250
  truth, 315